BIRDS OF
WESTERN ECUADOR

BIRDS OF WESTERN ECUADOR

A PHOTOGRAPHIC GUIDE

NICK ATHANAS AND
PAUL J. GREENFIELD

WITH SPECIAL CONTRIBUTIONS BY **IAIN CAMPBELL, PABLO CERVANTES DAZA, SAM WOODS,** AND **ANDREW SPENCER**

PRINCETON UNIVERSITY PRESS

PRINCETON AND OXFORD

Copyright © 2016 by Princeton University Press

Published by Princeton University Press, 41 William Street,
Princeton, New Jersey 08540

In the United Kingdom: Princeton University Press, 6 Oxford
Street, Woodstock, Oxfordshire OX20 1TW

press.princeton.edu

Photographs: Front cover © Nick Athanas. Back cover © Pablo
Cervantes Daza

ISBN 978-0-691-15780-1

Library of Congress Control Number: 2016930081

British Library Cataloging-in-Publication Data is available

This book has been composed in Perpetua (main text) and Avenir
(headings and captions)

Printed on acid-free paper. ∞

Images previous page: Toucan Barbet (*Semnornis ramphastinus*),
top left; Scarlet-and-White Tanager (*Chrysothlypis salmoni*), top
right; Yellow-breasted Antpitta (*Grallaria flavotincta*), bottom left;
Ocellated Tapaculo (*Acropternis orthonyx*), bottom right.

Designed by D & N Publishing, Baydon, Wiltshire, UK

Printed in China

10 9 8 7 6 5 4 3 2 1

CONTENTS

■ INTRODUCTION

Western Ecuador is a remarkably diverse area and home to some of the most colorful and spectacular birds on earth, hosting more than 1,000 bird species in an area roughly comparable to the US state of New York. That is more than have ever been recorded within the continental United States and Canada combined, an area 140 times larger. This remarkable diversity exists primarily because of the influence of the Andes, the spectacular mountain range that dominates the region, reaching a height of 6,268m (20,564ft) at the summit of the Chimborazo volcano. This mountain range is very steep, giving rise to a set of distinct elevational life zones with different climatic conditions, each one with different vegetation and birds, ranging from tall, wet rain forest in the lowlands and lower elevations, to lush, epiphyte-laden cloud forest at middle elevations, stunted elfin forest near tree line, and the vast *páramo* grassland and *Polylepis* woodland at the highest elevations. Ocean currents also contribute to this diversity; Ecuador lies at the boundary between the warm equatorial current to the north, and the cool Humboldt Current to the south. The equatorial current helps make northwestern Ecuador one of the wettest regions on earth, which gives rise to the lush rain forests. These forests extend northward through western Colombia to eastern Panama, an area often referred to as the Chocó bioregion; this is one of earth's most biodiverse areas, possessing more than 60 endemic bird species. In contrast, the cool Humboldt Current holds little moisture, and its influence has led to the formation of deserts,

Black-chinned Mountain-Tanager is one of many colorful birds endemic to the Chocó bioregion

White-tailed Jay, one of the most striking birds endemic to the Tumbesian bioregion

dry forests, and arid scrub on the mountain slopes and lowlands of southwestern Ecuador. This area is part of the Tumbesian bioregion, which extends southward into western Peru. While diversity is distinctly lower there than in the Chocó bioregion, endemism is very high, and the region as a whole has nearly as many endemic birds as the Chocó.

In this guide we provide species accounts and photographs covering the vast majority of birds found in western Ecuador, including all that a casual observer is likely to encounter on a short trip.

The photographs are, except for a very few exceptions, of wild, unrestrained birds in their natural habitats. Where possible, we have chosen photos that illustrate the key field marks of each species in a way that the field observer can expect to see them; as such these photos are not always of the "best" quality from a technical or artistic standpoint. We avoided using flash in most photos, since this can change or artificially enhance plumage colors and features.

This book would have been impossible even just a few years ago. Rapid technological advances in digital cameras and lenses have allowed photographers to capture images in low light conditions that were simply impossible before. These advances have in turn led to an explosion of interest in photography in the birding community, resulting in wide availability of superb images. Despite our best efforts, in a few cases no suitable photos were available. For several birds, we digitally modified a photo of a similar species; this is always mentioned in the text.

We chose to begin with western Ecuador because it has a more manageable number of species than the east, and excellent images are available for all but a few of them. We hope in the future to produce a sister volume that covers the eastern half of Ecuador, or even the entire country. At the moment, eastern Ecuador is not as well covered photographically, but this situation is rapidly changing.

REGION COVERED

The continental divide almost exactly divides the country in half by area. It served as a convenient and biogeographically sensible dividing line as we determined which species to include in this guide. We do not include the Galapagos Islands, since the avifauna is so completely different that it deserves, in all fairness, its own book.

In the interest of space, we have chosen to exclude certain species, such as extreme rarities and vagrants, species that are primarily pelagic and thus unlikely to be seen from shore, and certain birds that range primarily in the East but spill over very locally west of the divide. These species are detailed in Appendix I.

RANGE MAPS

The map provided for each species indicates its approximate known distributional range within Ecuador. Ranges, along with the elevation and habitat descriptions given in the text, can be very useful identification aids.

The ranges of many species in western Ecuador have contracted due to deforestation, and we have endeavored to map these species' modern ranges rather than historical distributions.

Please bear in mind that these maps are only a general guide. The ranges of many species are still imperfectly known, and some birds are highly prone to wandering. Seeing a resident species slightly outside its mapped range is probably not very remarkable, as long as the habitat is appropriate. However, if a resident species is recorded well outside its mapped range, it should be identified with care and documented with field notes, photographs, and/or sound recordings. Records of unusual sightings can be submitted to the Ecuadorian Ornithological Records Committee at cero.ecuador@gmail.com, and entered into online databases such as eBird.

Ecuador's three largest cities, Guayaquil, Quito, and Cuenca, are marked with black stars on the range maps. Smaller cities are marked with black dots. The topography map shows the cities as well as many of western Ecuador's most visited birding sites. In the range maps, resident (breeding) species are mapped in green. They are present year-round, and while some species may move short distances seasonally, they do not undertake long-distance migrations.

Major cities in and near western Ecuador

Long-distance migrants from North America (boreal migrants) are mapped in blue. These species do not breed in Ecuador, and may spend only the boreal winter in the country or may merely pass through briefly as transients. The accompanying text indicates which months these birds typically occur in our region. In some species, small numbers can be seen even during the boreal summer months. Boreal migrants are occasionally seen well outside their mapped ranges, especially during northward and southward passage.

Migrants from the south (austral migrants) are mapped in red. Only a few of these occur in western Ecuador, and the months in which they are typically encountered are mentioned in the text.

Single dots represent isolated populations or, in the case of migratory species, isolated records. For very rare vagrants, only the locations of known, documented sightings are marked.

Map of western Ecuador showing cities or towns (red dots) and birding sites (blue dots)

A question mark on the map indicates either (1) the species may occur in the indicated area, based on habitat requirements and existing records, but there are no documented sightings known to us; or (2) the species formerly occurred in that location, but there are no recent records, and it may no longer persist there due to habitat alteration.

FORMAT OF THE SPECIES ACCOUNTS

The heading for each species account gives the English common name, the scientific name, and the body length (from bill to tip of tail) in centimeters (cm) and inches (in). Sometimes a range of sizes is given; in sexually dimorphic species, it can be assumed that the male is larger than the female, unless otherwise stated (e.g., most birds of prey). The text begins with the range of elevations, in meters (m), in which the species is typically found in western Ecuador (which is not necessarily the same elsewhere in its range). As with geographical ranges, this is only a guide. It is not unusual to find a species at a slightly higher or lower elevation, but it is generally very unusual to find a resident species more than several hundred meters outside the ranges given here.

The text following the elevation indicates the likelihood that the species will be encountered in the correct range and habitat. An experienced observer, such as a birding tour guide, will be able to find many of the scarcer species much more reliably than a casual observer. The descriptive terms used are subjective and should be taken only as rough estimates. *Abundant*: encountered every day in very large numbers; *common*: usually encountered daily and often in large numbers; *fairly common*: encountered on most days but sometimes missed; *uncommon*: not encountered on most days; *rare*: unlikely to be encountered, even over the course of a long trip; *very rare*: never expected—these species should be carefully observed and documented if possible. Species are sometimes said to be "local," which indicates that they are known only from scattered locations, or are much more likely to be found in certain locations; this is often the status of rare species that have been staked out at a particular lodge, reserve, or other such location.

We then detail the bird's habitat preferences; habitat is often a very useful feature when the observer is dealing with difficult groups such as flycatchers or furnariids. As an extreme example, if the stated habitat is "inside humid lowland rain forest," the species would never be expected in a cow pasture or in a park in Quito. See p. 13 for more details on habitats in our region. A physical description of the bird follows; this often includes comparisons to similar species. For striking species that are virtually unmistakable, this section may be only a sentence, whereas for confusing species it will be quite lengthy. A large number of species are sexually dimorphic, which means the male and female differ in plumage, size, and/or other features. If significant differences exist, they are noted in the text. If male and female are not separately mentioned or described, the sexes are identical in appearance, or their differences are so minor as to be unnoticeable in the field.

We then provide some commentary on the behavior of the species, and often some additional information, such as specific locations where it is most likely to be found. Finally, for most birds, when it is deemed to be helpful, we include a voice description; transcribing bird songs and calls is not an easy task, but we hope that these might be useful in some instances.

Individual photos are labeled numerically, and where appropriate, with an additional label indicating a specific plumage type or subspecies mentioned in the species account: male ($\male$). female ($\female$), adult (ad.), juvenile (juv.), immature (imm.), alternate (alt.), basic (bas.) If no additional label is given, it can be assumed that the photo refers to adult plumage and that the species is not significantly sexually dimorphic.

TAXONOMY

The taxonomy used in this book generally follows the standard set by the International Ornithological Committee (IOC), though we have occasionally diverted from it in the

Despite their dramatic plumage differences, Piura Hemispingus (left) and Western Hemipingus (right) are sometimes considered the same species, Black-eared Hemispingus

interest of making the book more user-friendly. We expect many birders to use this book in conjunction with the existing *Birds of Ecuador* (2001) by Robert S. Ridgely and Paul J. Greenfield, and therefore we have tried, where possible, to use the same names or to mention them in the text. Due to the ever-changing interpretation of bird taxonomy, several English names may exist for the same species, and we list alternative names where appropriate. The taxonomic sequencial order used here was also based on the IOC list, but we modified it occasionally in order to keep similar-looking species close together. While we were preparing this guide, the IOC redesignated the affiliations of numerous species, tranferring many from one family to another, and more changes are sure to come in the future. This has resulted in some mixing of families in this guide, especially with the tanagers and finches. Since knowing the family of a given species is not normally necessary to identify it, we generally do not mention scientific family names, unless they are needed in descriptions of features or behaviors common to an entire family or in discussions of taxonomy.

CONSERVATION

Ecuador's exceptional wealth of biodiversity is constantly under threat by human activities, as is true in so many parts of the world. Human population growth and expansion into natural areas, along with the often indiscriminate and unsustainable exploitation of natural resources, have plagued the country for decades. Deforestation levels, especially throughout the 1980s and 1990s, left Ecuador with a 90–97 percent deforestation rate in the Andes and the Pacific coastal lowlands; several private-sector and government-driven "mega-projects" added to the negative impacts on the land. Surprisingly, this trend has slowed to some degree, in no small part due to the realization that Ecuador's natural beauty and biodiversity possess a value that could benefit the country and its people if managed more sustainably. The National System of Protected Areas covers nearly 20 percent of the country, but many of these parks and reserves essentially exist on paper only and are not effectively protected; they are not nearly enough on their own to adequately protect Ecuador's threatened species. Several

Nongovernmental organizations, such as Mindo Cloudforest Foundation, are very important for conserving habitat in Ecuador

nongovernmental organizations, private landowners, and forward-thinking communities have taken it upon themselves to create their own reserves and, at the same time, begin encouraging sustainable ecotourism and "avitourism" throughout the country. This approach has been impressively effective; today, nearly all of the country's rare and endangered species receive some level of protection. However, conservation is a never-ending battle. In some areas, unsustainable exploitation of natural resources continues, either by private companies or by the Ecuadorian government. More work is needed to develop more sustainable land-development practices and to continue to promote sustainable ecotourism.

HABITATS

We describe the habitats and elevational zones that are most frequently mentioned in the species accounts. When referring to forest types in the species accounts, we often also use modifiers such as "forest edge" or "inside forest." Edge species can, for example, be seen along roadsides and in forest clearings, but birds listed as being "inside forest" are likely to be seen only along forest trails. "Primary forest" refers to old-growth forest that has never been logged; little now remains in western Ecuador. "Secondary forest" was partially or completely logged but is currently in a state of regrowth. Secondary forest that has been only partially logged or that has had significant time to recover may be almost indistinguishable from primary forest to the untrained eye. Where forest was totally removed and only dense scrub has regrown, this is often referred to as "secondary growth."

Humid forest—Humid forest, often called rain forest, receives high levels of rainfall, and its trees retain their leaves throughout the year. In hilly and mountainous areas that are frequently enshrouded in mist or fog, rain forest is referred to as cloud forest. Cloud forest is a rather vague term, since such misty conditions can occur over a vast elevational range. When referring to humid forest, we typically also mention the elevational zone in order to further define the habitat; elevational zones are described in more detail on p. 19.

Humid lowland forest at Playa de Oro

Primary humid lowland forest has impressively large trees, up to 40m (130ft) tall, and a relatively open understory. At slightly higher elevations in the foothills, trees are not quite as tall, and they are often blanketed with epiphytes such as orchids and bromeliads. Very little primary forest now remains in the humid lowlands and foothills, and most of it is in the lower reaches of the Cotachi-Cayapas Ecological Reserve. Most humid lowland and foothill sites visited by birders, such as the Río Silanche and Milpe Bird Sanctuaries, Río Palenque Science Center, Tinalandia Nature Reserve, and Buenaventura Reserve, were in the past selectively logged, and nearly all the larger trees have been removed.

Humid subtropical forest occurs higher in the Andes and is what many people think of when they hear the term "cloud forest." Slopes are usually very steep, and the larger trees can be covered with mosses and epiphytes. While trees in primary forest can reach 20m (66ft) or higher, the canopy can be shorter on steep, mountain slopes where soil is not as rich and landslides are frequent. A significant amount of primary (or nearly so) humid subtropical forest still remains in many areas of northwestern Ecuador. Some well-known examples of this habitat include much of the Paseo del Quinde (Nono-Mindo) Ecoroute (including the Tandayapa Valley), the Paz de las Aves Refuge (between Tandayapa and Mindo), and the slopes above Mindo.

*Humid sub-
tropical forest
near Tandayapa*

Humid temperate forest just west of the continental divide near Cerro Toledo

Above the subtropical forest, the climate is distinctly cooler and the forest is more stunted; this is often referred to as humid temperate forest. Close to tree line, the canopy may be only about 5–10m (16–33ft) tall, and this dense, gnarly vegetation is often called "elfin forest." While primary temperate forest does remain in a number of areas, much of it is inaccessible without a major expedition. The Yanacocha Reserve near Quito is arguably the best and most easily accessible expanse of primary temperate forest on the western slope. Other examples in our region include the upper parts of Pululahua Geobotanical Reserve, Utuana Reserve, and Pasochoa Reserve.

Deciduous forest—Much of western and southwestern Ecuador has a dry climate, and nearly all rain falls between January and April. Outside of this "wet season," most trees lose their leaves, and the forest can appear dry and dead, though this is certainly not the case. All but a few bird species remain in this area year-round; while they may sing less, some are actually easier to see in the dry season, since there are few leaves to hide behind. Pristine deciduous forest can be quite tall, reaching 25m (82ft), and in some areas is dominated by enormous *Ceiba* trees, with their characteristic smooth green bark and bulbous trunks. Deciduous forest is found mainly in the lowlands and foothills; most higher-elevation areas receive enough rain that at least some of the trees retain their leaves year-round. Primary deciduous forest can still be found in many areas; some of the most well-known sites include the Jorupe Reserve, Machalilla National Park, and Cerro Blanco Protected Forest.

Semi-humid forest—We use the term "semi-humid" to describe forest intermediate between humid and deciduous forest. In most years, it receives enough rainfall for the taller trees to remain green all year, though smaller trees will lose their leaves in the dry season. Examples include the forest of the Río Ayampe Reserve, much of that in Manglares-Churute Ecological Reserve, and subtropical forest around the town of Sozoranga.

During the short rainy season, deserts on the Santa Elena Peninsula briefly become green and lush

Mangrove forest—Mangroves are distinctive trees with stilt-like roots that grow in saline coastal areas. In Ecuador, unlike some areas of the world, only a few bird species are restricted to mangroves. The extent of mangrove forests in Ecuador has been greatly reduced, primarily by shrimp-farming activities. Extensive mangroves can still be found in a few areas such as Manglares-Churute Ecological Reserve, the Muisne area, and near the town of San Lorenzo along the Colombian border.

Desert—Arid areas dominated by low scrub with only scattered trees. During the very brief rainy season (usually around February to March), deserts can briefly become some of the most verdant areas in Ecuador, with tall, lush grasses and abundant flowers; birds then go into a breeding frenzy and their songs ring through the desert. Rainfall varies seasonally, and in some years there is almost none. Ecuador's most extensive deserts are found in the coastal lowlands west of Guayaquil, especially on the Santa Elena Peninsula, as well as in the far southwest along the Peruvian border.

Páramo at the continental divide, with the Antisana Volcano in the background

Páramo—Páramo is found at very high elevations above tree line. In its pristine form, it consists of tall, wet grassland intermixed with small shrubs, though in many areas it has been converted to pastureland. Most of Ecuador's páramo is in the east. The most pristine examples frequently visited by birding tourists are at Papallacta Pass, Antisana Ecological Reserve, and El Cajas National Park. The continental divide bisects all three of these areas, so at least some parts of them are on the western slope.

Inter-Andean valleys—Also known as intermontane valleys, these do not really constitute a habitat, but more of a microclimate. Some valleys in the Andean highlands experience a rain-shadow effect, as the air loses its moisture when it is forced up the outside slopes of the Andes. Inter-Andean valleys typically have dense arid scrub on their slopes and taller woodland near watercourses at their bases. Several bird species are mostly or entirely restricted to these valleys. Some examples of inter-Andean birding sites include the pass and the abandoned racetrack near Calacalí and the Jerusalem Recreational Park (both north of Quito), and the upper Río Mira Valley north of Ibarra.

Wetlands—Numerous wetland habitats occur in western Ecuador. The largest wetlands are in the coastal plain, but there are also a number of highland lakes that are key

habitats for a variety of bird species. Lowland wetlands include not only natural marshes and swamplands, but also man-made rice paddies, salt evaporation ponds, and shrimp cultivation ponds. Even the man-made habitats can be extremely important for resident species, as well as for long-distance migrants. Some of the most renowned wetland birding sites in the lowlands include the La Segua marshes (sometimes called Chone Lakes), the Ecuasal salt lagoons on the Santa Elena Peninsula, the Manglares-Churute Ecological Reserve, and the shrimp ponds near Santa Rosa. Highland lakes provide critical habitat for both resident and migrant waterfowl, coots, grebes, rails, and shorebirds. Lago San Pablo near Otavalo and Laguna Yahuarcocha near Ibarra are two well-known natural lakes in the west. Man-made reservoirs such as the ones in Cumbayá (a Quito suburb) and adjacent to the Quito airport attract many species; these are frequently checked by dedicated birders, who have discovered a number of extreme rarities in recent years.

ELEVATIONAL ZONES

We use only meters to delimit elevations in the species accounts. Feet are not used (or even understood) as a unit of measure anywhere in Ecuador, so we believe it is not helpful to include them. The elevation ranges given below are approximate.

Lowlands—0–400m. The relatively flat (at best slightly hilly) areas between the Andes and the Pacific coast.

Foothills—400–1300m. The lower slopes of the Andes and the upper elevations of the coastal range.

Subtropics (or subtropical zone)—1300–2500m. The mid-elevation slopes of the Andes.

Temperate zone—2500m to tree line. Tree line varies from location to location based on sun exposure, prevailing winds, and other climatic factors. It can be anywhere from 2800m to as high as 3800m on the western slopes of the Pichincha volcano (west of Quito).

BIRD TOPOGRAPHY

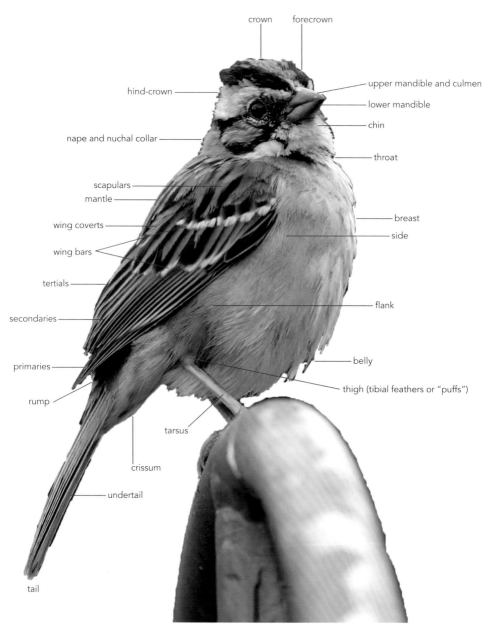

crown

forecrown

hind-crown

upper mandible and culmen

lower mandible

chin

nape and nuchal collar

throat

scapulars

mantle

breast

side

wing coverts

wing bars

tertials

flank

secondaries

primaries

belly

thigh (tibial feathers or "puffs")

rump

tarsus

crissum

undertail

tail

crown stripe

supraloral

superciliary

eye-ring and periocular area

postocular line

auriculars

malar

lores

cere

leading edge

wing lining

primaries

trailing edge

tarsus

secondaries

terminal band

subterminal band

Species Accounts

FOREST TINAMOUS

Tinamous are a primitive family of plump, terrestrial quail-like birds. They appear almost tailless, with thin necks, narrow bills, and cryptic plumage in mostly earthen tones. Most Ecuadorian tinamous, and all the species on this page, are found inside forest. They are usually very difficult to see, as they stroll quietly about on the forest floor and quickly move away from any perceived threat. Their vocalizations are often haunting and resonant, frequently the only clue to their presence and abundance. If startled, one may offer the observer a fleeting glimpse as it bursts up explosively in brief, frantic flight. In W Ecuador, tinamous are found at both lower and higher elevations, though largely absent from the subtropical zone.

1 GREAT TINAMOU · *Tinamus major* 38–46cm/15–18in

0–700m. This very large, brown tinamou was formerly widespread inside primary forest in the humid lowlands. It is now quite rare and local in W Ecuador, its numbers impacted by deforestation and hunting, and is likely to be encountered only in remote, forested areas in the far NW such as Playa de Oro or the Río Canandé Reserve. Its large size and white neck speckling set it apart from any other lowland tinamou, as does its song, a deep, quavering series of ringing *whoo* notes, distinctly lower pitched than those given by the more common and widespread Little Tinamou.

2 TAWNY-BREASTED TINAMOU · *Nothocercus julius* 35–38cm/14–15in

2300–3500m. Uncommon and especially difficult to see, found in humid subtropical and temperate forest; the only high-elevation forest tinamou in W. Note its large size, rich tawny-rufous head and underparts, and white throat. Seldom encountered, though the odd individual may occasionally venture out into clearings adjacent to its accustomed dense forest home. Song consists of a long series of evenly spaced, dry, churred notes, sometimes with a faster-paced finale.

3 BERLEPSCH'S TINAMOU · *Crypturellus berlepschi* 28cm/11in

0–900m. Uncommon inside mature humid lowland and foothill forest; found only in areas where forest cover remains extensive. Good photos do not yet exist for this species, so it is not shown. Very dark gray plumage, often appearing black in low light, is diagnostic, but also note white irides and orange lower mandible. Little Tinamou is smaller, notably paler, and rufous brown. Berlepsch's song is a piercing, high-pitched and slightly down-slurred whistle repeated every 10–15 sec.

4 LITTLE TINAMOU · *Crypturellus soui* 21–23cm/8.5–9in

0–1600m. Fairly common in secondary forest, woodland, plantations, and overgrown fields in lowlands and foothills (occasionally higher). Plumage varies from rufous brown to gray; crown is often darker; irides brown. Never as dark as Berlepsch's Tinamou, which has white irides. Little Tinamou is significantly smaller than Great Tinamou, and lacks white speckling on neck. Despite being rather common and very vocal, Little Tinamou is a tough species to see, tending to remain within dense cover. It is perhaps more often seen when scampering across a trail or country road. Its song, most often heard at dawn or dusk, consists of a series of ringing querulous notes, each rising slightly in pitch.

5 PALE-BROWED TINAMOU · *Crypturellus transfasciatus* 25cm/10in

0–1600m. Fairly common inside deciduous forest in W and SW. The only tinamou in much of its range, though may come close to overlapping with Little Tinamou in semi-humid zones. No other tinamou in range has prominent whitish superciliary and extensive black and buff barring on upperparts. Only the female is shown; male is similar but browner. Its song, heard primarily in the January to April rainy season, is a short, ringing *oooEEEEE!*, often the only clue to the species' presence. Despite being frustratingly quiet in the dry season, Pale-browed can sometimes be easier to find then in the leafless understory, and foraging birds can be heard crunching about in dry leaf litter. Occasionally visits feeders at Jorupe Reserve.

Ecuador's two *Nothoprocta* tinamous range in more open habitats at higher elevations in the Andes than the forest tinamou on the preceding pages. *Penelope* guans are large, arboreal, turkey-like birds of humid forest; plumage is similar among the species, and all have red, often conspicuous dewlaps. Guans are hunted extensively and can be quite scarce except in parks, reserves, and other protected areas. Guans occasionally produce a surprisingly loud, mechanical wing rattle in flight.

1 ANDEAN TINAMOU *Nothoprocta pentlandii* 28cm/11in

1000–2300m. Uncommon and rather local in montane scrub, grassland, and overgrown fields in S highlands. The only tinamou in its range and habitat, but note yellow, decurved bill, buffy underparts, and grayish breast with pale buff spotting. Similar Curve-billed Tinamou, found at higher elevations, has a richer tawny-rufous coloration. Song is a rather thin, sharp, and high-pitched *weeoowhEE!* or *weooWEET!*

2 CURVE-BILLED TINAMOU *Nothoprocta curvirostris* 28cm/11in

3000–3900m. Uncommon in páramo, grassland, pastures, and shrubby fields at very high elevations in N. It becomes rare and local farther S, where it occurs above the elevation of the similar Andean Tinamou. No other high-elevation tinamou occurs in nonforest habitats. Similar to Andean Tinamou, but with a darker bill and underparts more rufous, lacking any gray. Wings show rufous barring in flight. Nearly silent, but occasionally gives a *WHEET!-wit-wit-wit, wit* when flushed. Birds can occasionally be seen along the entrance road to the Yanacocha Reserve early in the morning.

3 BEARDED GUAN *Penelope barbata* 55–60cm/21.5–23.5in

1900–2700m. This threatened and range-restricted guan is uncommon in montane forest near the continental divide in the S Andes. It is the only guan in its small range; replaced to the N by the similar Andean Guan. Note Bearded Guan's frosted facial plumage and rufous tail tip; its dewlap is rather inconspicuous. Usually encountered foraging in pairs or occasionally in small groups and can be quite tame in protected areas where not hunted. Often seen in the Cajanuma sector of Podocarpus National Park, which straddles the continental divide. Typical call is a fairly fast series of soft grunts.

4 BAUDÓ GUAN *Penelope ortoni* 57–62cm/22.5–24.5in

100–1000m. Now rare and local in more extensive humid lowland and foothill forest in the NW, where it has recently been recorded as far S as Milpe Bird Sanctuary, and may still occur slightly farther S. Very similar to the larger Crested Guan; the two species can occur together and can be very difficult to tell apart if size cannot be judged. Baudó lacks the chestnut tones found on the belly and tail of Crested Guan, and usually appears less crested, with a smaller dewlap. Baudó Guan is usually seen in small groups and can be rather tame when finally located. Calls include soft grunts and a harsh *grauw*.

5 ANDEAN GUAN *Penelope montagnii* 53–59cm/21–23in

2500–3600m. Locally fairly common in temperate forest, edge, and wooded clearings. Replaced in far S by the similar Bearded Guan (no known overlap). No similar guan occurs with it; Sickle-winged and Wattled Guans (p. 28) have uniform, unmarked plumage. Andean's dewlap is rather inconspicuous. Singles, pairs, and occasionally small groups forage at varying heights inside montane forest and edge; can be quite tame where not disturbed. Most common call is a quick series of soft clucks.

6 CRESTED GUAN *Penelope purpurascens* 84–91cm/33–36in

0–1500m. This large and robust guan is uncommon and local inside more extensive humid forest in the lowlands, foothills, and subtropics; now found only in areas where hunting is absent or minimal. Note large size, bushy crest, conspicuous red dewlap, white markings on neck and breast, and chestnut belly and upper tail. It could be confused with the much smaller Baudó Guan, which lacks the chestnut. Singles, pairs, and small groups forage at varying heights inside forest, occasionally coming to edge to feed in fruiting trees. Can be quite noisy, emitting loud yelps, whistles, and honks.

The two guans presented here have dark, unpatterned plumage and distinctive blue facial or bill coloration; as with other guans, they occasionally produce an explosive wing rattle in flight. Chachalacas are small, gregarious guans. W Ecuador's one species of curassow is nearly extirpated due to hunting, and occurs only in remote areas of extensive humid forest. Horned Screamer is a peculiar, robust wetland species, closely allied to ducks and geese.

1 WATTLED GUAN *Aburria aburri* 74–81cm/29–32in

1200–2200m. This large, all-black arboreal guan is uncommon in humid foothill and subtropical forest and edge. Best identified by its black plumage and blue base to bill; also note its bright yellow dewlap and legs. The more common Sickle-winged Guan is smaller and has a rufous belly, blue facial skin (not just base of bill), and reddish legs. Wattled is seldom seen, though often sings from an exposed perch, and very occasionally can be encountered foraging quietly in a fruiting tree. Its bizarre song is frequently heard at dawn, dusk, and occasionally in the middle of the night. It is a long, far-carrying, grating, and mechanical-sounding *grrRRREEEEEEEOOoooooow*, rising in pitch and then dropping as it tapers off.

2 SICKLE-WINGED GUAN *Chamaepetes goudotii* 51–55cm/20–21.5in

900–2600m. Fairly common in humid forest, edge, and adjacent wooded clearings from the foothills to the temperate zone. No other guan is primarily gray with a rufous belly. Facial skin is usually blue but can appear dark in young birds. Wattled Guan is larger and all black, with a blue bill rather than facial skin. The larger *Penelope* guans (p. 26) show large red dewlaps and extensive white forepart markings. The similar-size Rufous-headed Chachalaca is easily distinguished by its conspicuous rufous head and neck. Sickle-winged Guan is usually found singly or in pairs, foraging in fruiting trees at mid to upper strata of the forest, occasionally coming lower at edge. Typical call is a wheezy *whee-YIT*, often repeated over and over.

3 RUFOUS-HEADED CHACHALACA *Ortalis erythroptera* 56–61cm/22–24in

0–1000m; up to 1800m in SW. The only chachalaca in W, where it is found in both dry and humid forest and woodland. It is locally fairly common in W and SW; in NW it can be fairly common near the coast, but is rare and perhaps seasonal farther inland. Readily found at several locations, including the Buenaventura, Jorupe, and Río Ayampe Reserves. Its rufous head, neck, and flight feathers are diagnostic. Generally encountered foraging in small groups of up to six individuals, though the species' presence is most often made evident by its incredibly loud and raucous call, *AHHH-AHH-AHH, ahh-ahh-ahh, AHH-AHH-AHH, ahhh-ahh-ahh*, given by several birds together.

4 GREAT CURASSOW *Crax rubra* 89–94cm/35–37in

100–800m. Now very rare due to intense hunting pressure. A few birds persist in the last remnants of extensive humid forest in the extreme NW, with one recent report from Bola de Oro in the coastal range near Machalilla National Park. This very large, sexually dimorphic bird will not be mistaken if seen well. Pairs strut about the forest floor, mainly foraging on fallen fruit; may flush up to an exposed perch when disturbed. Male's song is an incredibly low-pitched and very soft *woo-oo-oooo, oh*; call is a sharp *whick!*

5 HORNED SCREAMER *Anhima cornuta* 84–92cm/33–36in

0–100m. Rare in lowland wetlands, except for a healthy population found at the Manglares-Churute Ecological Reserve SW of Guayaquil; inhabits marshland, ponds, river edge, and adjacent flooded fields. This huge and ungainly bird is unique in Ecuador; the whitish plume ("horn") protruding from its forehead is hard to see at a distance, and can be broken or missing. Usually found in pairs or small flocks, it forages on the ground but spends quite a bit of time perched conspicuously atop trees and bushes. Screamers take flight with difficulty, but once airborne they are good fliers, and can at times be spotted soaring at great heights. The bizarre, honking song can be heard at great distances.

Quails are compact, short-tailed terrestrial birds with short, stout bills. In our region, they inhabit humid forest, where they move warily about the forest floor in pairs or small coveys, and are very difficult to see. Whistling-ducks are lanky, long-legged waterfowl of the lowlands that can be found in a variety of wetland habitats. They sometimes occur in large flocks and can even be active during the night.

1 RUFOUS-FRONTED WOOD-QUAIL *Odontophorus erythrops* 23–26cm/9–10in

100–1200m; up to 1600m in SW. Fairly common inside humid lowland and (especially) foothill forest; locally higher in SW. A distinctive species whose bold, white foreneck crescent separates it from other similar ground-dwelling species. Pairs and small coveys wander the forest floor, feeding on fallen seeds and fruit. Very shy and difficult to actually see unless accidentally flushed, at which time a blurred shape will rocket up in startling, explosive flight. On rare occasions, one or more can be seen crossing a quiet forest trail. Song is a sharp, rapid, far-carrying antiphonal duet, *do-do-WHAT-do-do-WHAT-do-do-WHAT*... repeated for up to 15 sec. Single birds give a simpler *do-WHAT, do-WHAT*....

2 DARK-BACKED WOOD-QUAIL *Odontophorus melanonotus* 23–26cm/9–10in

1100–2000m. Fairly common inside humid subtropical forest; also found locally down into the foothills. It occurs mostly at higher elevations than Rufous-fronted Wood-Quail (though overlap is possible). Rather plain, but no other ground-dwelling species in its range is mostly brown with an orange throat and breast. Shy and seldom seen, it is most often encountered in the Tandayapa-Mindo area and is seen regularly at the Paz de las Aves Refuge, where birds sometimes come in to a feeder. Behavior and voice are similar to those of Rufous-fronted Wood-Quail, but song tends to be faster, with phrases more slurred together, e.g., *who-woo-choh-who-woo-choh-who-woo-choh*....

3 TAWNY-FACED QUAIL *Rynchortyx cinctus* 19cm/7.5in

100–700m. This small, sexually dimorphic quail is rare inside humid lowland and foothill forest in the far NW. Distinctive if seen well, which can be a challenge. Only female is shown; male differs mainly by having gray breast, fainter barring on lower underparts, and a dark rather than white superciliary. The only other quail in its range is the very different Rufous-fronted Wood-Quail, which has a white foreneck crescent. Behavior is similar to that of wood-quails, and it is just as difficult to see. Song is variable, consisting of a series of mournful whistles that may change pitch slightly and is sometimes followed by some slightly higher notes, e.g., *you, you, you-wah?-wah?* or *you, weh-weh-wah?-wah?* Also gives a long series of rather random soft notes and squeaks.

4 FULVOUS WHISTLING-DUCK *Dendrocygna bicolor* 48–53cm/19–21in

0–100m. Uncommon to locally common in marshland, lakes, ponds, and rice fields in W lowlands. Note white flank plumes, crissum, and rump band, as well as the dark bill and lanky shape; usually distinctive, but see immature Black-bellied Whistling-Duck. In flight, Fulvous Whistling-Duck differs from all other brown ducks by plain wings that lack any trace of a speculum or patch. Encountered in groups ranging from just a few birds to impressively large flocks of several hundred; unlike Black-bellied, it rarely or never perches in trees. Calls are similar to those of Black-bellied, but buzzier and less varied.

5 BLACK-BELLIED WHISTLING-DUCK *Dendrocygna autumnalis* 46–51cm/18–20in

0–200m; occasionally wandering to 2800m. Fairly common in marshland, rice fields, mangroves, coastal ponds, and lagoons in W lowlands; wanderers may turn up elsewhere. Adults are easy to ID by coral red bill, black belly, and bold white wing stripe. Immature has black bill and reduced black on underparts, and might be confused with Fulvous Whistling-Duck; Fulvous never shows any black on underparts and has black and rusty bands on the back. Black-bellied Whistling-Duck is usually found in small to medium-size flocks, perching on the ground or conspicuously in leafless, open treetops. Flight is characterized by hunched posture, with head and neck dangling slightly downward, and conspicuous white wing patches flashing. Birds taking flight give a series of high-pitched, squealing whistles.

ad. (left), imm. (right) 5

Presented here are five sexually dimorphic but otherwise very different ducks from all over the region. Comb and Muscovy are the largest ducks in Ecuador.

1 COMB DUCK *Sarkidiornis melanotos* 53–71cm/21–28in

0–500m. This distinctive duck is uncommon and very local in rivers, ponds, and flooded rice fields in lowlands and foothills. It is most easily seen in the far SW in the Zapotillo-Macará region. Black-and-white plumage is unique in its range. Female (not shown) is similar to male, but smaller and lacks "comb" on bill. Usually encountered in pairs or small groups; may occasionally perch on bare tree branches, and can be active at night. Also called **Knob-billed Duck**.

2 MUSCOVY DUCK *Cairina moschata* 71–84cm/28–33in

0–100m. Wild Muscovies, now rare and local due to hunting, are found on rivers, ponds, and swamps in W lowlands; perhaps most reliably seen in the Manglares-Churute Ecological Reserve. Wild birds are basically black, with a glossy green back, bare red face, and distinctive white wing patches (best seen in flight). Male is markedly larger than female and has red warts on face and bold white in the wings. Dull, sooty immature (not shown) shows little or no white in wing. Domesticated Muscovies are commonly found around human dwellings throughout Ecuador, though they may wander; these birds typically show large white blotches in plumage, and large, ugly, bulging patches of bare facial skin. This species is most often encountered alone or in pairs; it is quite wary, readily perches in trees, and tends not to associate with other waterfowl; flight is strong.

3 LESSER SCAUP *Aythia affinis* 38–43cm/15–17in

0–4100m. A locally uncommon boreal migrant to wetlands in the W lowlands, especially La Segua marshes; also a rare vagrant to highland lakes. Found in Ecuador mainly from November to March. Formerly very rare, but flocks of up to 100 birds have been seen in recent years. Male is distinctive; female duller, but no other duck in Ecuador is all brown with white only on foreface and with an all-black bill. In flight, note white wing stripe along secondaries in both male and female.

4 ANDEAN DUCK *Oxyura ferruginea* 41–43cm/16–17in

2100–4000m. Locally common on highland lakes and ponds. Thickly built, with short, broad neck; male is distinctive in range and habitat (but see Masked Duck, known from a few old highland records). Female is uniformly brown, darker and plainer than other highland ducks; perhaps best identified by body and bill shape, behavior, and by its accompanying male. Andean Duck is generally found in scattered groups out on open water, appearing to float low on the surface. It feeds by diving, often disappearing for surprisingly long periods beneath the water's surface in a rather grebe-like fashion, only to resurface a few minutes later, seemingly out of nowhere. Also called **Andean Ruddy-Duck**, and sometimes lumped with **Ruddy Duck** (*O. jamaicensis*).

5 MASKED DUCK *Nomonyx dominicus* 33–35cm/13–14in

0–300m. Rare, local, and easily overlooked in W lowlands; prefers densely overgrown freshwater ponds, marshes, and even ephemeral pools; there are also old records from highland lakes. Male distinctive in lowland range; in highlands it is distinguished from Andean Duck by bold black markings on back. Female is duller, but no other duck in Ecuador shows such conspicuous facial stripes. Singles, pairs, or small family groups swim inconspicuously through dense aquatic vegetation, maintaining body low in the water; tail only sometimes held erect.

♂ (lower), ♀ (upper)   **5**

Teals and pintails, familiarly known as dabbling ducks, characteristically feed on submerged vegetation by tipping, head-down, into water, and taking flight by uplifting straight off the water's surface. All species show a colorful speculum, and several species are sexually dimorphic. Males of the first two teals featured here go through an eclipse phase, at which time they resemble their respective females. Southern Pochard is a rare, sexually dimorphic species found locally in the W lowlands.

1 BLUE-WINGED TEAL   *Anas discors*   35–41cm/14–16in

0–4000m. This boreal migrant can be locally common on lakes, ponds, salt lagoons, shrimp ponds, and marshland throughout W Ecuador, mainly in the lowlands but also in inter-Andean valleys and páramo. Occurs mainly from September to April; occasionally during other months. Both sexes show a conspicuous pale blue speculum, obvious in flight. Alternate plumage male easily distinguished by white facial crescent. Female and eclipse male are mostly mottled brown and best identified by faint white facial spot, throat, and broken eye-ring; they are often indistinguishable from female Cinnamon Teal. Blue-winged Teal can be found in enormous flocks in lowland marshes such as La Segua, but in the highlands it is usually found in small numbers.

2 CINNAMON TEAL   *Anas cyanoptera*   35–41cm/14–16in

0–100m; formerly 2500–2800m. Uncommon and local (possibly increasing) in coastal lagoons and shrimp ponds; formerly also occurred on lakes in the N highlands but now extirpated. Both sexes show a conspicuous pale blue speculum, obvious in flight. Alternate plumage male is rich chestnut, with a red eye; no really similar bird occurs with it. Female and eclipse male are almost identical to the much more common Blue-winged Teal and often not safely separable; Cinnamon Teal may show fainter white facial markings. Behavior much like that of Blue-winged.

3 WHITE-CHEEKED PINTAIL   *Anas bahamensis*   44–47cm/17.5–18.5in

0–200m; rarely to 4000m. Locally common on lakes, shrimp and salt ponds, and marshes fairly near the coast; occasionally wanders to highland lakes. Sexes similar; white cheeks and red bill patch are diagnostic. In flight, wings show green and cinnamon speculum. Usually encountered in flocks ranging from a few birds to a thousand or more.

4 ANDEAN TEAL   *Anas andium*   41–43cm/16–17in

3000–4000m. Fairly common on highland lakes and marshes, especially in the páramo. A dull, brown duck, best identified by its contrasting dark head, black bill, strongly spotted and scaled breast, and plain flanks. Female and eclipse Blue-winged Teals have paler heads, white facial markings, and blue wing patches. Yellow-billed Pintail has a bright yellow bill and strongly marked flanks. Andean Teal ranges in pairs and small groups, often seen swimming close to shore or snoozing on grassy banks; regularly encountered hunkered down beside even very tiny pools.

5 YELLOW-BILLED PINTAIL   *Anas georgica*   48–56cm/19–22in

2200–4000m. Locally common on highland lakes and ponds. The yellow bill is diagnostic within its Ecuadorian range, but also note its graceful shape, long, pointed tail, and strongly scaled underparts. Usually encountered in pairs or small flocks, occasionally in larger flocks of up to 100 or so birds; tends to favor grassy shorelines.

6 SOUTHERN POCHARD   *Netta erythrophthalma*   46–48cm/18–19in

0–100m; old records from lakes in N highlands. Very rare and local in freshwater lakes and marshland in lowlands; nearly all recent records come from the La Segua marshes. Both sexes show distinctive white wing stripe, most obvious in flight; otherwise, sexes are very dissimilar. Male is mostly glossy black with a chestnut tinge to back and neck and irides red; no really similar species in range. Female is dark brown with a variable white facial pattern that usually consists of a white postocular line, neck patch, and spot next to bill. Female Lesser Scaup (p. 32) shows white only on foreface; also compare female Blue-winged and Cinnamon Teals. In Ecuador, Southern Pochard is seen mainly in pairs or very small groups, though it occurs in larger flocks elsewhere in its range.

Torrent Duck is an attractive and intrepid inhabitant of rocky, rapid-flowing Andean rivers and streams. Grebes are truly aquatic diving birds, unable to walk on land. They appear tailless and rarely fly, and adults often carry young on their backs. Wood Stork is a tall, long-legged bird with a bulky, decurved bill, which primarily inhabits wetland habitats.

1 TORRENT DUCK *Merganetta armata* 38–42cm/15–16.5in

700–4000m. An entertaining denizen of rapid, boulder-ridden rivers and streams in the Andes; fairly common in the subtropical and temperate zones but also occurs in smaller numbers down into the foothills. Both sexes are striking and easy to ID, especially given their specialized habitat. Singles, pairs, and occasionally family groups swim easily in rapids, even against the strong current, diving to feed on aquatic invertebrates. While resting, they often perch up on prominent boulders amid the rapids. When alarmed, pairs jerk their heads and bob up and down; they tend to swim away rather than fly, but when they fly, their flight is low over the water's surface.

2 PIED-BILLED GREBE *Podilymbus podiceps* 28–33cm/11–13in

0–200m and 2100–3500m. Ecuador's most widespread grebe, locally fairly common on lakes, ponds, coastal marshes, and slow-flowing rivers in both the W lowlands and central highlands. Dark irides, stout bill, and white crissum help separate this species from Least Grebe in any plumage. Adults in alternate plumage have a white bill, its tip slashed with black, white eye-ring, and black throat. Basic adult and immature (not shown) are more rufous and have plainer bills. Behavior similar to that of Least Grebe, but Pied-billed is usually found in deeper water.

3 LEAST GREBE *Tachybaptus dominicus* 21–23cm/8.5–9in

0–200m. Uncommon to locally fairly common on relatively shallow freshwater lakes, ponds, and flooded rice fields in the W lowlands. Adult male is shown; other plumages are browner. In any plumage, distinguished from Pied-billed Grebe by small size, thin bill, and yellow irides. Generally encountered swimming in pairs or in small, loose groups that dive beneath the surface to feed on small fish and aquatic insects.

4 SILVERY GREBE *Podiceps occipitalis* 29–31cm/11.5–12in

2200–4100m. Locally fairly common on highland lakes, mainly E of the continental divide, though a few persist on lakes in the NW. Formerly occurred on the lakes near Otavalo and Ibarra (Lago San Pablo and Laguna Yahuarcocha), but there are no recent records. A plump little gray and white grebe with red irides; no similar species occur with it. Behavior similar to that of other grebes, but Silvery seems to dive less often.

5 GREAT GREBE *Podiceps major* 70–78cm/27.5–30.5in

0–100m. This large grebe is a newcomer to Ecuador; recent records in and around the Santa Elena Peninsula, and in the La Segua marshes. Large size, long neck with rufous foreneck, and daggerlike bill are diagnostic. Basic plumage is shown; alternate plumage is very similar but brighter. Encountered alone in Ecuador. Swims calmly, occasionally plunging headfirst to feed.

6 WOOD STORK *Mycteria americana* 89–101cm/35–40in

0–100m; rarely wanders to highlands. W Ecuador's only stork, locally fairly common in marshes, rice fields, shrimp ponds, and mangroves in the lowlands; tends to wander and occasionally can be seen flying high over the Andes. Distinctive within its range; no other large, white wading bird has a dark, unfeathered head and neck. Flight feathers are black, best appreciated as it flies, with neck outstretched and long legs trailing behind. It sometimes soars at great heights, where it could even be confused with King Vulture (p. 56). Wood Stork is somewhat sluggish, usually seen in small groups foraging with other waders; readily perches in trees.

alt. 2

bas. 2

ad. ♂ 3

4

bas. 5

6

6

These are seafaring birds; most will not be seen from land unless one spends significant time with a scope at sea-watching hot spots such as La Chocolatera on the Santa Elena Peninsula. Only the six species most likely to be seen in coastal waters are treated here, though numerous other species also occur, mostly well offshore (see p. 426).

1 WAVED ALBATROSS *Phoebastria irrorata* 86–92cm/34–36in

Found mostly well offshore, but a small nesting colony exists on Isla de la Plata from late March to December, during which time sightings from the coast are much more likely. The only regularly occurring albatross in Ecuadorian waters, this large, long-winged seabird should not be mistaken if seen well. Note adult's white head and bright yellow bill; juvenile is mostly brown with a dull yellow bill. Flies with slow, shallow wingbeats or long glides on stiff, narrow, down-bowed wings. Single birds, occasionally small groups, are encountered either in characteristic flight or floating on open water, often with bright head held erect.

2 BLACK PETREL *Procellaria parkinsoni* 46cm/18in

Fairly common well offshore, though only rarely seen from land; most sightings are off the Santa Elena Peninsula and around Isla de la Plata. This stocky petrel is all dark, with a fairly stout, pale, black-tipped bill. Sooty-black overall, appears round-headed; in flight, underside of primaries can appear silvery in good light, and feet may protrude beyond its somewhat wedge-shaped tail. Sooty Shearwater is distinctly grayer, thinner-bodied and -billed, different in shape, and has a prominent white underwing stripe. Pink-footed Shearwater has white underparts, and usually shows conspicuous white on the underwing. Single Black Petrels are typically encountered flying low over the ocean's surface; flight is rather heavy: birds glide and wheel with interspersed bouts of flapping on somewhat stiff, slightly bowed wings. In stronger winds, birds arc higher over the water. Also called **Parkinson's Petrel**.

3 SOOTY SHEARWATER *Puffinus griseus* 43–46cm/17–18in

The most numerous pelagic species in Ecuadorian waters, and the one most likely to be seen from shore. Note overall dusky coloration, rather sleek look, with thin black bill and swept-back long and narrow wings that show variable silvery-white underwing stripes. With experience, the distinctive silhouette alone is enough to ID it; silvery underwing flash is helpful if seen. Black Petrel is larger, bulkier, and blacker, with a thicker bill. Pink-footed Shearwater is larger and broader-winged and has whitish underparts and a pink bill. Sooty is encountered in variable numbers, sometimes in large loose flocks or rafts. Flies strongly, usually low over water, with stiff, rapid wingbeats alternating with long glides. Under windy conditions, their glides arc higher over the water. Feeds on the surface or by surface or plunge diving, remaining submerged only briefly.

4 PINK-FOOTED SHEARWATER *Puffinus creatopus* 46–48cm/18–19in

An uncommon, large, two-tone shearwater recorded year-round in offshore waters. Uniformly dull brown above, blending into white below; legs pink; bill pink with a dark tip. Most birds, like the one shown, have a distinct white bar on the underwing; some have a mostly dark underwing. No other regularly occurring petrel or shearwater shows a similar two-tone plumage or pink feet and bill. Flight is characteristically sluggish, with slow-paced wingbeats interspersed with extended glides, usually low over the water. Under very windy conditions, glides are longer, with broad banking in high arcs. Single birds are usually encountered in Ecuadorian waters, though elsewhere the species can be gregarious.

5 WHITE-VENTED STORM-PETREL *Oceanites gracilis* 15–16cm/6–6.5in

A fairly common visitor to offshore waters throughout the year, though numbers fluctuate; perhaps more numerous during austral winter and El Niño events; can occasionally be seen from shore, especially from La Chocolatera on the Santa Elena Peninsula. A small, compact seabird with broad-based rounded wings, and feet extending beyond tail in fight; note narrow white rump band and white on belly (not easy to see on distant birds). Wedge-rumped Storm-Petrel looks blacker, with more ample white rump and pointed wings; feet do not project beyond tail. White-vented flies low over water, with rather fluttery, shallow wingbeats; sometimes glides and circles back. When foraging, regularly "tap-dances" on water's surface with wings held up in a V. Also called **Elliot's Storm-Petrel**.

6 WEDGE-RUMPED STORM-PETREL *Oceanodroma tethys* 15–17cm/6–6.5in

A common visitor to offshore waters throughout the year, in quite large numbers; perhaps more numerous during austral winter and El Niño events; can occasionally be seen from the shore or on trips out to Isla de la Plata. This small seabird appears quite blackish and sometimes even tailless (or white-tailed) at sea; note ample triangular white rump, the largest white rump of all similar species. Flight is direct and rapid, usually not very low over the water, with deep, steady wingbeats interspersed sporadically with brief glides, often banking back and forth; when foraging, birds bound and skip, touching the water's surface with their feet.

ad. 1

ad. 1

juv. 1

2

3

4

5

6

Here is a rather eclectic mix of seabirds and coastal waders.

1 RED-BILLED TROPICBIRD *Phaethon aethereus* 90–105cm/35.5–41.5in

Sea level. Uncommon along the entire coast and rarely seen from shore; there is a small nesting colony on Isla de la Plata. Ethereal and elegant adult will not be mistaken if seen well. Immature (not shown) lacks long tail streamers, and bill is mostly yellow. Generally seen alone, except near nesting colonies; flight is rapid and direct, with shallow and stiff wingbeats; when resting on the ocean surface, tail is held cocked in a graceful arc. If a nest is disturbed, the irate parents emit an almost shockingly shrill screech as they circle about repeatedly before alighting.

2 CHILEAN FLAMINGO *Phoenicopterus chilensis* 99–109cm/39–43in

0–100m. Mainland Ecuador's only flamingo, found locally in coastal lagoons and mangroves. Numbers fluctuate greatly, but at least some are usually present on the Ecuasal salt lagoons on the Santa Elena Peninsula. Immature (not shown) is mostly grayish white, with greatly reduced pink coloration. Flight is strong and direct, with long neck and legs held outstretched. Roseate Spoonbill is also pink, but it is much smaller, and bill shape is different. Chilean Flamingo is generally encountered in flocks, wading up to chest deep in water, often foraging with head and neck fully submerged. Takes flight only after an awkward take-off run.

3 WHITE IBIS *Eudocimus albus* 56–61cm/22–24in

0–100m. Fairly common in mudflats, mangroves, shrimp ponds, flooded rice fields, and marshes; the largest numbers occur in coastal areas surrounding the Gulf of Guayaquil. Adults are easily identified; in flight they show broadly black-tipped primaries. Immature is duller and mostly brown above, but underparts are always much paler than those of Glossy Ibis. White Ibis is most often encountered in flocks, wading in shallow water or foraging on mudflats, probing the ground with its bill.

4 GLOSSY IBIS *Plegadis falcinellus* 56–61cm/22–24in

0–100m. Found mainly in freshwater marshes and rice fields in lowlands, especially in and around the La Segua marshes, where they can be fairly common. The only all-dark ibis found in W, though the very similar **White-faced Ibis** (*Plegadis chihi*; not yet recorded from Ecuador) could possibly occur as a vagrant. Immature White Ibis has mostly brown upperparts but always shows ample white on underparts. Behavior is similar to that of White Ibis, though Glossy is more likely to venture out into deeper water.

5 ROSEATE SPOONBILL *Ajaia ajaja* 71–79cm/28–31in

0–100m. Large and distinctive, this unique pink, spatulate-billed wading bird is locally fairly common in mangroves, shrimp ponds, mudflats, and marshland. Pink plumage and unusual bill shape make it easy to ID. Immature (not shown) is similar but has reduced pink and a fully feathered head. Pink plumage may suggest a flamingo, but size, overall shape, and bill are very different. Spoonbills are usually encountered in small groups, foraging in shallow water with bill submerged, swinging head from side to side. Flight is direct, with neck and feet extended, combining bursts of stiff wingbeats with short glides.

Ecuador's two tiger-herons are robust and broad-necked, with thick bills and relatively short legs; they have almost identical immature plumages. W Ecuador's two very different looking bitterns inhabit marshy areas, where they are exceedingly inconspicuous, usually hiding among tall grasses and aquatic vegetation. Tricolored Heron is actually an aberrant egret, most commonly found in coastal wetlands.

1 RUFESCENT TIGER-HERON *Tigrisoma lineatum* 66–76cm/26–30in

0–250m. Rare in the lowlands of W Ecuador; much more common in E. Inhabits swampy woodland and forest around lakes and streams; found occasionally in adjacent marshland. Adult is distinctive, with chestnut head and neck. Immature is boldly banded black and buff, almost identical to immature Fasciated Tiger-Heron, which is found only along fast-moving streams and rivers (no overlap). Immature is also similar to adult Pinnated Bittern, which has fine brown and white barring on hindneck, and bold streaks on foreneck; note habitat differences. Rufescent Tiger-Heron perches motionless in hunched-over posture, often on thick branches at edge of forest-lined streams; may allow close approach or flush off with heavy but quiet flight.

2 FASCIATED TIGER-HERON *Tigrisoma fasciatum* 61–66cm/24–26in

100–2200m. Uncommon along fast-flowing rivers and streams, mostly at higher elevations than Rufescent Tiger-Heron. May be encountered perched on boulders in rapids, especially at dawn or dusk. Adult is dark gray with fine cinnamon vermiculations on upperparts and a white stripe down the foreneck. Immature is almost identical to immature Rufescent Tiger-Heron, but Rufescent is found only at low elevations and near standing water or sluggish rivers, never along the rapid, rocky rivers that Fasciated requires. Fasciated is usually encountered alone, rarely in pairs; if approached or surprised, will often fly up to a thick branch within the forest.

3 PINNATED BITTERN *Botaurus pinnatus* 63–76cm/25–30in

0–100m. A rare to locally uncommon (e.g., La Segua marshes) bird of marshland and wet, grassy pastures; easily overlooked, due to its intricately patterned, camouflaging plumage. Superficially similar to immature tiger-herons, but note fine brown and white barring on hindneck and bold streaks on foreneck; general shape, behavior, and heavy bill are also good clues. It is often difficult to see, standing motionless in tall grass, often with just its head and beak exposed. Perhaps the best chance of seeing it is in early morning, when a single bird may forage in the open or fly briefly low over the vegetation. Rarely heard song is an amazingly low-pitched boom.

4 LEAST BITTERN *Ixobrychus exilis* 28–31cm/11–12in

0–100m; a few records from highlands. A small, furtive, and attractively patterned inhabitant of freshwater marshes and swamps. Very rarely seen; status and distribution in the region are poorly understood. Buff, tawny, and rufous, with basically black upperparts, two white back stripes, and conspicuous buff and rufous wing patches. Striated Heron (p. 44) is similar in size and shape, but is mostly gray. Least Bittern is usually seen alone in reeds or tall grasses; often freezes when disturbed, holding neck outstretched and bill pointing skyward. Flies low over vegetation. Calls include a harsh *grauw* and an owl-like hoot.

5 TRICOLORED HERON

Egretta tricolor 58–69cm/23–27in

0–100m. Locally fairly common on coastal mudflats, estuaries, and in mangroves. No other Ecuadorian heron has a white neck stripe and white lower underparts; note white occipital plumes in alternate plumage. Immature (not shown) is similarly patterned but has rufous on head, neck, and wings. Tricolored is generally encountered alone or in loose groups; forages actively, at times running about in shallow water or wading up to belly deep, stealthily stalking, then spearing its prey.

ad. 1

imm. 1

ad. 2

imm. 2

3

4

The two night-herons are mainly nocturnal feeders; adults are boldly patterned but their respective immatures are quite similar, with mainly brown and speckled plumages. *Butorides* are the smallest herons in W Ecuador, one species is common and widespread, while the other is an exceedingly rare boreal migrant.

1 BLACK-CROWNED NIGHT-HERON *Nycticorax nycticorax* 56–61cm/22–24in

0–200; 2200–3300m. Locally fairly common along the coast in mangroves, swampy woodland, and other wetland habitats; also occurs locally around highland lakes (e.g., Laguna Yahuarcocha near Ibarra). Adult might be confused with a very gray Striated Heron, but lacks streaking on breast, scaling on back, and the yellow lores. Immature easily confused with Yellow-crowned Night-Heron immature; Black-crowned immature distinguished by mostly yellow (not black) bill; in flight, feet do not completely extend beyond tail. Black-crowned Night-Heron is mainly nocturnal, generally encountered singly or in pairs, often perched in trees; feeds on fish and a wide variety of other aquatic prey, usually ambushing it at the water's edge.

2 YELLOW-CROWNED NIGHT-HERON *Nyctanassa violacea* 56–61cm/22–24in

0–200m. Locally fairly common along the coast, mainly in mangroves, tidal flats, and remote, undisturbed beaches; very rare inland. Adult's white cheek patches are diagnostic. Immature is very similar to Black-crowned immature but has all-black (not yellowish) bill, and in flight, feet extend entirely beyond tail. Yellow-crowned is found alone or in loose groups, foraging on mudflats and beaches for crabs and other prey; largest numbers are seen during low tide, when birds come out to feed as the waters recede. More active during daylight hours than Black-crowned; roosts mainly in mangroves.

3 STRIATED HERON *Butorides striata* 38–43cm/15–17in

0–3300m. Fairly common and widespread throughout the lowlands and lower Andean slopes in virtually any wetland habitat; also very local around highland lakes. Adults can be distinguished from Black-crowned Night-Heron by their streaked underparts, scalloped upperparts, and yellow lores. Striated Heron is also similar to the very rare Green Heron; see that species for details. Striated is usually encountered alone, locked in a frozen, crouched stance at water's edge, or perched on a low, overhanging branch as it stalks small fish and other aquatic prey. When disturbed, may flex its expressive crest and cock its tail or flush off with a sharp *cheeouk!* call.

4 GREEN HERON *Butorides virescens* 38–43cm/15–17in

0–400m(?). Status and even actual presence in W Ecuador is under review; probably a very rare boreal migrant, though there is some evidence that most or all previous records refer to the more common and widespread Striated Heron. Adult is much like Striated Heron but has a rufous neck and more extensive white on throat. Striated Heron may show some faint rufous on the neck, but never as bright as on fully adult Green Heron. Immature bird (not shown) cannot be safely distinguished from Striated Heron in the field. Habitat preference, behavior, and voice much like those of Striated Heron.

Ardea herons are tall and statuesque, long-necked, long-legged wading birds with extended, daggerlike bills, found mainly in the lowlands. *Egretta* species are smaller (Tricolored Heron, p. 42, is also an *Egretta*). All species shown here fly with neck retracted, doubled-back in an S shape, and with legs protruding beyond tail. Cattle Egret (*Bubulcus*) is small and often encountered in open pastureland around livestock.

1 COCOI HERON *Ardea cocoi* 104–127cm/41–50in

0–400m. Uncommon to fairly common in the lowlands, found in a wide variety of both saltwater and freshwater habitats. Handsome and distinctive. Immature (not shown) is similar to adult but duller and has a gray neck. Confusion is possible only with the rare Great Blue Heron; in all plumages, Cocoi is distinguished by its white (not chestnut) thighs and its entirely black crown, lacking a white crown stripe. Single birds, or occasionally loose groups, are encountered standing or wading stoically in shallow water, with neck retracted or extended. Cocoi Heron stalks its prey slowly and methodically; occasionally perches in trees. Flight is slow and steady, with heavy wingbeats.

2 GREAT BLUE HERON *Ardea herodias* 104–127cm/41–50in

0–500m; highland records to 3000m. A rare boreal migrant recorded at scattered locations along the coast; very rare on lakes in N highlands; most records are from October through March. Quite similar to the lowland, year-round resident Cocoi Heron but darker blue-gray, with chestnut thighs and a white crown stripe. Behavior similar to that of Cocoi.

3 LITTLE BLUE HERON *Egretta caerulea* 56–66cm/22–26in

0–500m; 2200–3300m. Uncommon to fairly common in a variety of wetland habitats; common along the coast, smaller numbers elsewhere in the lowlands and on highland lakes. Adult is the only small, uniformly dark heron in Ecuador. Immature is very different; all white; two-tone bill (grayish with black tip) sets it apart from all similar egrets; also note yellowish legs and feet. Immatures that are transitioning to adult plumage show varying amounts of dark blotching in their plumage. Encountered singly or in loose groups, feeds slowly, stalking prey with head and neck held low. Flight is similar to that of other herons; neck is often held outstretched, less doubled back.

4 SNOWY EGRET *Egretta thula* 53–64cm/21–25in

0–3300m. A widespread, delicate, and graceful egret, fairly common in both saltwater and freshwater habitats throughout the lowlands; also found locally around mountain streams and highland lakes. The only small, white egret with a black bill, yellow lores, and yellow feet that contrast strongly with black legs. Snowy Egret is often numerous, though away from coast normally encountered in smaller numbers. Forages actively in shallow water; may hold still to gaze intently for prey; regularly perches in trees.

5 CATTLE EGRET *Bubulcus ibis* 47–52cm/18.5–20.5in

0–3300m. Common to locally abundant in pastureland in all but the highest elevations; not as strongly tied to water as many other egrets. Like a small, chunky version of Great Egret; size, shape, and habitat preference is usually enough to tell the two apart; distant, flying birds can be difficult, but Cattle Egret shows a shorter, thicker neck and has faster wingbeats. Most often encountered feeding around grazing cattle, though can also be found in virtually any open habitat or in wetlands; roosts communally in trees, often in huge concentrations, and large morning and afternoon flights can be seen as birds commute between roosts and feeding grounds.

6 GREAT EGRET *Ardea alba* 91–99cm/36–39in

0–3300m. Common and widespread in a variety of wetland habitats throughout the lowlands, with smaller numbers occurring well up into the highlands. Large size, all-white plumage, yellow bill, and all black legs and feet are diagnostic. At great distances, where size cannot be judged, it is easy to confuse with the smaller, more compact Cattle Egret. Great Egret can be encountered alone or in very scattered flocks, often standing tall with neck extended; regularly perches in trees, and nests colonially. Flight is slow and steady, with somewhat heavy wingbeats; often flies with neck extended.

Magnificent Frigatebird is the only member of its family regularly seen in mainland Ecuador. It plucks food items from the water's surface or steals prey from other seabirds. Pelicans are robust coastal seabirds known for their characteristic long, hooked bill with ample gular pouch, used for collecting fish. Both Ecuadorian species plunge dive headfirst to capture their prey. The two species are very similar, brown overall and best distinguished by size; they show a variety of potentially confusing plumage types.

1 MAGNIFICENT FRIGATEBIRD *Fregata magnificens* 96–107cm/38–42in

0–100m; wanderers to 2000m. The elegant silhouette of this skillfully aerial seabird is very familiar along Ecuador's entire Pacific coastline, often seen soaring effortlessly at great heights. Breeds on several offshore islands, including Isla de la Plata. Prone to wandering, and the occasional bird can be seen well inland, sometimes even quite high up in the Andes. There is no significant difference in size between the sexes. General shape and behavior should make ID straightforward (but see note); other large soaring birds have broader, rounder wings. Generally seen in high, lazy, soaring flight, but drops abruptly close to the water's surface to feed by picking up floating morsels or by harassing other seabirds until they drop their hard-earned catch. *Note*: **Great Frigatebird** (*F. minor*; not shown) is a strictly pelagic species with only one record from the Ecuadorian coast. It could be overlooked, since it is very hard to ID except at close range. Female has a pale gray throat and looks less hooded than female Magnificent, while immatures may show a distinctive cinnamon head and throat.

2 BROWN PELICAN *Pelicanus occidentalis* 117–132cm/46–52in

0–100m. A common and familiar year-round resident along the entire Pacific coast and in the Gulf of Guayaquil; occurs along beaches, in mangroves and estuaries, and on salt lagoons. Very large and heavy-bodied; plumage is mostly brown and gray, and very variable; in all plumages very much like the larger Peruvian Pelican; see that species for details for separating them and also note range. Large flocks are often seen flying in formation low over water's surface, with a characteristic series of flaps and glides on broad, long wings. Neck is held doubled back in typical flight posture, and often even when perched.

3 PERUVIAN PELICAN *Pelicanus thagus* 127–152cm/50–60in

0–100m. A huge and heavy-bodied pelican found in W and SW coastal waters, mostly along beaches and on salt lagoons; in greatest numbers around the Santa Elena Peninsula. Population fluctuates seasonally; more common during the austral winter. In all plumages it is very much like Brown Pelican, and many birds cannot be safely identified in the field. Peruvian's best ID feature is the distinct, well-defined white patch on the upper wing; this feature is most obvious in alternate plumage, but younger birds often show it as well. Some Brown Pelicans are distinctly white on the upperwing, but the white tends to merge more seamlessly with the white on the back, creating a distinctly less patchy appearance. The two species frequently occur together, especially on the Santa Elena Peninsula, where the obvious size difference can also be used to separate them. Behavior of Peruvian Pelican is much like that of Brown.

2 (below), **3** (above)

A family of large, long-winged seabirds with graduated tails and broad-based bills that taper toward the tip; two species have bright-colored legs. Four species are treated on this spread and the next; an additional two species have been recorded only as vagrants well offshore. Boobies have a decidedly steady, somewhat undulating flight, with alternating wing flaps and glides. They feed on prey obtained beneath the water's surface by undertaking spectacular plunge dives, often from considerable heights.

1 BLUE-FOOTED BOOBY *Sula nebouxii* 76–84cm/30–33in

This is the common booby along Ecuador's coastline, regularly seen from shore, even from popular beach resorts; breeds on offshore islands (e.g., Isla de la Plata). Adults are easy to ID at close range; from a distance, note diagnostic white patches on upper mantle, rump, and base of tail. Immature is distinctly hooded and similar to immature Nazca Booby (p. 52); Nazca lacks the white rump and tail base, and white on neck is contiguous with underparts, not a discrete patch. Juvenile Blue-footed Booby is browner than immature, imparting a less hooded appearance. Generally observed in flight away from nesting grounds; single birds, or orderly formations of several individuals advancing in single-file, fly fairly low over the water's surface. Swimming birds also can be seen close to shore; may congregate in fairly large flocks near dense concentrations of fish. *Note:* **Brown Booby** (*S. leucogaster*; not shown) is a rare pelagic in our area, but is seen occasionally from La Chocolatera on the Santa Elena Peninsula; adult could be confused with immature Blue-footed Booby, but brown hood is much larger, reaching breast and mantle and merging with wings. Immature Brown Booby is almost uniformly brown.

2 PERUVIAN BOOBY *Sula variegata* 71–76cm/28–30in

Uncommon but possibly increasing in offshore waters; now regularly observed from the Santa Elena Peninsula, especially at La Chocolatera. Numbers rise substantially during El Niño events. Adult appears boldly black and white in the field, even at a distance, lacking the gray streaking of adult Blue-footed Booby. Adult Nazca Booby (p. 52) has unmarked black-and-white wings and orange bill. Immature Peruvian Booby (not shown) is uniformly gray-brown, lacking the hooded appearance of immature Blue-footed and Nazca Boobies; immature Peruvian is darker and browner than immature Red-footed Booby (p. 52). Behavior of Peruvian Booby is similar to that of the more common Blue-footed.

ad. 1

ad. 1

juv. 1

imm. 1

BOOBIES

1 NAZCA BOOBY *Sula granti* 79–86cm/31–34in

A predominantly pelagic species; unlikely to be seen from the mainland, though it maintains a significant nesting colony on Isla de la Plata. Large and striking; white with contrasting black flight feathers, narrow mask and tail; bill orange. Bold black-and-white wing pattern separates adult from Peruvian Booby (p. 50). Pale morph Red-footed Booby (unlikely to be seen in our region) can appear similar at a distance, but has a mostly white tail. Immature Nazca Booby is distinctly hooded, and might be confused with immature Blue-footed Booby (p. 50), but lacks white on rump and base of tail, and white collar is contiguous with underparts, not a discrete white patch. Nazca Booby is rarely observed from land except at Isla de la Plata. Generally more solitary than Blue-footed; single birds can be seen flying steadily, at low to mid heights over the water. When swimming, the gleaming white plumage can be spotted at great distances. Nazca feeds predominantly on flying fish. Nests are placed on the ground. *Note*: **Masked Booby** (*S. dactylatra*; not shown) might occur in our region as a rare vagrant; it is nearly identical to Nazca Booby but has a yellow rather than orange bill.

2 RED-FOOTED BOOBY *Sula sula* 66–73cm/26–28.5in

A small, pelagic booby that maintains a small nesting colony on Isla de la Plata; very rarely seen from the mainland. Red legs and feet, along with colorful azure and red bill, are distinctive at close range. Dark morph is shown; light morph (not shown; rare in Ecuadorian waters away from the Galapagos) is similar to Nazca Booby but has mostly white, rather than black, tail. Immature is rather featureless; a dull, uniform brown, a bit paler on the belly. From a distance, immature and even dark morph adult can be confused with immatures of other boobies, but the lack of any white dorsal patch or nuchal collar should aid in ID. Red-footed Booby nests above the ground in shrubs, but its behavior is otherwise similar to that of other boobies.

ad. dark morph **2**

ad. 1

ad. 1

imm. 1

ad. dark morph 2

imm. 2

ANHINGA AND CORMORANTS

Cormorants are found in freshwater and saltwater habitats throughout the world. Two species are recorded from mainland Ecuador, one is common and widespread, and the other is rare and erratic along the coast. They share characteristic thin necks, hook-tipped bills, fairly long, stiff tails, and relatively short, rounded wings; they capture aquatic prey in swift underwater pursuit and can swim to great depths. Anhinga is a freshwater species, reminiscent of cormorants, with long, thin neck; long, fan-shaped tail; and slender, daggerlike bill used to spear fish during underwater pursuit.

1 ANHINGA *Anhinga anhinga* 82–89cm/32.5–35in

0–400m. Uncommon and local along sluggish freshwater rivers, streams, lakes, and wooded swamps in the lowlands. Somewhat cormorant-like, but larger and lankier, with long spear-like bill, snaky neck, and prominent white wing markings. Male head and neck black like rest of body plumage; female has contrasting tan head and neck; there is no significant size difference between sexes. Neotropic Cormorant shows no white in wings or tail, bill is shorter and hooked. Anhinga is normally encountered alone or in pairs, often seen perched over water in a shrub or tree with wings extended; swims low in the water, at times only exposing its long neck and head. Flight is somewhat labored on long, relatively thin wings, with long neck and fanned tail extended, giving a cross-shaped appearance; readily soars effortlessly at great heights.

2 NEOTROPIC CORMORANT *Phalacrocorax brasilianus* 63–69cm/25–27in

0–4000m. Common throughout the lowlands in marshes, lakes, rivers, and mangroves; uncommon and local at higher elevations. Adult is all blackish; in alternate plumage note white-bordered orange throat pouch, less prominent in basic plumage. Immature is browner and shows some white on throat and neck. Hooked bill and lack of white in wing separate all plumages from Anhinga. Neotropic Cormorant is usually found in loose swimming groups, occasionally diving for fish; regularly perches with wings spread to dry off. Roosts in trees, sometimes in very large numbers. Flight is direct, often high, with neck outstretched, head held slightly higher.

3 GUANAY CORMORANT *Phalacrocorax bougainvillii* 68–74cm/27–29in

An erratic visitor to coastal waters; usually very rare but perhaps more numerous during El Niño events, when birds have been recorded up the Río Guayas to around Guayaquil. Adult, with its striking black-and-white plumage and red periocular skin, is unlike any other coastal bird in Ecuador. Immature (not shown) has the same pattern, but is browner and has pink or orange periocular skin. In Ecuador, usually found alone or in very small numbers, swimming and diving close to shore or resting quietly on rocks or quiet beaches.

NEW WORLD VULTURES

Vultures are large to very large, broad-winged, eagle-like birds with unfeathered heads and necks, and hooked bills adapted for feeding on carrion; all take advantage of thermal air currents to soar effortlessly, even to great heights; in flight wing tips show prominent "fingers." Two species are common and widespread; the others are uncommon and local.

1 ANDEAN CONDOR *Vultur gryphus* 102–127cm/40–50in

2000–4200m. This colossal vulture (3m/10ft wingspan) used to be widespread over most of the high Andes; it is now rare in most of its Ecuadorian range, regularly seen only in the Antisana Ecological Reserve. Adult has conspicuous white neck ruff and upperwing coverts; male has conspicuous forehead comb, lacking in female. Immature is sandy brown, lacking any trace of white, but uniformly brown plumage and sheer size separate it from other vultures. Flight is "solid" and steady, with slow banking and turning. Singles, pairs, or family threesomes are usually encountered, but larger groups will gather at a carcass. Andean Condor roosts and nests on cliffs.

2 TURKEY VULTURE *Cathartes aura* 66–76cm/26–30in

0–3000m. Common and widespread over a wide range of habitats almost throughout Ecuador; absent only from the highest elevations. At close range, the naked red head (whitish nape in much of Ecuador) is diagnostic. In flight, look for two-tone wings with dark wing lining contrasting with silvery flight feathers. Flight is distinctive: wings are long and held in a distinct dihedral; tail is fairly long and often fanned; soaring birds rock and tip, looking quite unstable. Black Vulture is smaller, more compact, with shorter wings showing white in primaries; head is black. The scarce Zone-tailed Hawk (p. 78) convincingly mimics Turkey Vulture; its shape and flight style can easily fool even an experienced observer, especially at a distance; note its fully feathered head and banded tail. Turkey Vulture can be quite gregarious, and often soars quite high, regularly with other vultures as well as hawks and other raptors; locates carrion through its uncanny sense of smell.

3 BLACK VULTURE *Coragyps atratus* 56–64cm/22–25in

0–3000m. Common and widespread in a wide range of habitats throughout Ecuador, mostly absent from extensive forest, but found regularly around towns and cities, especially near municipal garbage dumps, where it can be abundant; often fearless of human presence. Black plumage and unfeathered black head are easily recognized at close range; in flight note the diagnostic white patches in primaries. At take-off or in calm conditions, often flaps vigorously, but is also capable of soaring effortlessly at great heights, often with other vultures or raptors. Black Vulture is quite agile on the ground, squabbling around garbage dumps or daringly attending roadkills, even amid traffic. Regularly loafs around on the ground or perches in a tree with wings outstretched.

4 KING VULTURE *Sarcoramphus papa* 71–81cm/28–32in

0–500m. This massive and striking vulture is now uncommon and very local in W Ecuador, restricted to areas of extensive and relatively undisturbed forest (both humid and deciduous); seen perhaps most regularly at Cerro Blanco Protected Forest and the Jorupe Reserve. Spectacular adult will not be mistaken; no other Ecuadorian raptor shows a similar black-and-white-pattern, which can be discerned even at tremendous distances. Wood Stork (p. 36) shows a similar plumage pattern in flight, but long neck and bill should be obvious. Immature King Vulture (not shown) appears mostly dark but may have an orange tinge on head and bill; in flight, some white is usually visible on wing lining and lower underparts; large size and short tail can be the best clue; Black Vulture is smaller and has white primary patches. Single King Vultures are usually seen soaring lazily at great heights with other vultures; it is a rare treat to see one perched. King Vulture often depends on Turkey Vulture's sense of smell to locate carrion, but once at a carcass, this species is, unsurprisingly, dominant.

ad. ♂ **1**

ad. ♂ (above), ♀ (below) **1**

imm. **1**

2

2

3

3

OSPREY AND KITES

Three very different raptors from primarily lower elevations, though Ospreys also reach highland lakes. Females are larger than males.

1 OSPREY *Pandion haliaetus* 54–59cm/21.5–23in

0–3000m. A large, bicolor, fish-eating eagle encountered locally around lakes, bays, salt ponds, and rivers throughout W Ecuador from the coastal lowlands to the Andean highlands. Ospreys are boreal migrants and do not breed in Ecuador, but immature birds may remain year-round for two to three years before migrating to breeding grounds in North America. Broad brown facial stripe is diagnostic; also note brown and white pattern, large size, and lanky wings. Usually encountered singly, either in flight or perched on an exposed bare branch near water. When hunting may hover, then drop rapidly with legs extended and powerful talons held open to pick up its prey. Quite vocal, especially in flight, emitting a ringing *tweep-tweep-tweep*.

2 SNAIL KITE *Rostrhamus sociabilis* 41–45cm/16–17.5in

0–200m. A gregarious species of open marshes, swamps, river edge, and flooded rice fields. Numbers can vary seasonally in any given place; it can be locally abundant during the rainy season. Sexually dimorphic, but both sexes can be recognized by very slender, hooked bill and broad white base to tail. Snail Kite takes four years to reach adult plumage; immature female and younger male resemble adult female; older immature male gradually acquires adult plumage. Flight shape is distinctive, with obviously bowed wings, and birds often tilt and turn as they search for food. Harris's Hawk (p. 70) also has a white tail base but always shows rufous wing coverts and has a different bill shape and general appearance. Immatures of various other hawks that have buff superciliary and some streaking below look superficially like female and immature Snail Kites, but other species lack white tail base and often show tail barring. Snail Kite can congregate in large numbers, perching lazily about on bare branches, posts, and electric wires. It preys mainly on large snails and crabs, adeptly removing them from their shells with its perfectly adapted bill.

3 DOUBLE-TOOTHED KITE *Harpagus bidentatus* 32–36cm/12.5–14in

0–1800m. Uncommon in humid forest and adjacent clearings from lowlands to subtropics. White throat with black mesial stripe is diagnostic within our range in all plumages; note smallish rounded-looking bill. Adults show gray head and upperparts; male has breast barred rufous, gray, and white; female has mostly rufous underparts. Immature is mostly brown and buff, with variably streaked underparts; dark mesial stripe is usually even more conspicuous than in adults. Flight shape is quite *Accipiter*-like, with rounded wings and long, narrow, banded tail; puffy white crissum may be especially visible in flight. Some morphs of Plain-breasted Hawk (p. 64) can look very similar to Double-toothed Kite but lack the mesial stripe and tend to be paler rufous underneath. Double-toothed Kite is usually encountered singly or in pairs, perched quietly in mid-story or lower canopy, or soaring high with other raptors and vultures. May follow troops of monkeys to snatch up insect prey that are flushed up.

♀ 3

These three very different raptors are found mainly at lower elevations. Females are larger than males.

1 PEARL KITE *Gampsonyx swainsonii* 23–26cm/9–10in

0–300m. A beautiful and delicate falcon-like kite of open habitats, especially in arid areas. Small size, mostly dark gray and white plumage, ochre or yellow face and forehead, and rufous flanks set this raptor apart from all others. No falcons are all white below; White-tailed Kite (p. 62) has dark plumage restricted to ocular area and conspicuous shoulder patches. Pearl Kite singles or pairs often sit conspicuously on exposed branches and wires, dropping to the ground to seize lizards; they take insects and small birds as well.

2 HOOK-BILLED KITE *Chondrohierax uncinatus* 38–43cm/15–17in

0–2400m. Uncommon and local in humid and deciduous forest and woodland from the lowlands up into the subtropics. If seen close up, the heavy, deeply hooked bill and yellowish loral patch are diagnostic in all plumages. Flight shape is also distinctive: broad, rounded wings are pinched in at the base and angled forward. Dark morph (sexes and ages similar) is easily mistaken for Black Hawk-Eagle (p. 80) in flight, but is smaller, with a shorter tail, and wings appear less swept forward. Immature looks similar to immature Gray-headed Kite in flight, but usually shows at least some barring on body, and often a faint buffy tinge. Hook-billed Kite is usually encountered singly, most often seen in soaring flight. It can be quite sedentary, perching for long periods mainly in the canopy; feeds primarily on land snails. Occasionally gives a shrill, cackling call.

3 GRAY-HEADED KITE *Leptodon cayanensis* 46–53cm/18–21in

0–1800m. Uncommon in humid forest from the lowlands to the subtropics. Adult's combination of gray head, white body, and bold black-and-white wing and tail pattern is distinctive. Immatures have two morphs: Light morph can be confused with the rare Black-and-white Hawk-Eagle (p. 80), especially in flight, but lacks that species' black lores, orange cere, and white-feathered tarsi; also see immature Hook-billed Kite, which usually shows some faint barring on body. Dark morph immature Gray-headed (not shown) is very different, with upperparts, head, and sometimes breast dark brown, and remainder of underparts heavily streaked brown; it is generally much darker overall than immatures of other raptors, with crisper, more contrasting underpart streaking. Single birds are most readily seen in high soaring flight; only rarely seen perched since it tends to stay inside dense canopy. Distinctive flight display includes a sharp ascent and a bout of rapid wingbeats followed by a quick descending glide with wings held upward. Occasionally emits a loud *yeeeeeOW* or a long, rising series of *koAAH* notes.

ad. **3**

ad. **3**

light morph imm. **3**

ad. ♂ **2**

ad. ♀ **2**

dark morph ad. **2**

imm. **2**

KITES

The three species here have narrow, pointed, somewhat falcon-like wings, small hooked bills, and short legs; all soar gracefully. Females are larger than males.

1 SWALLOW-TAILED KITE *Elanoides forficatus* 56–61cm/22–24in

0–2000m; wanders to 3500m. A stunning and elegant raptor encountered widely from the lowlands to the subtropics, though occasionally wanders to the highlands. Black-and-white plumage; graceful shape; long, pointed wings; and long, forked tail are diagnostic. Immature (not shown) has shorter, less forked tail. White-tailed Kite is similarly white but is smaller, has black shoulders and carpal spots, and lacks forked tail. Swallow-tailed Kite is almost always seen in flight, sometimes in large flocks, and can soar at great heights. Rarely encountered perched, but very occasionally large concentrations can be found resting in forest canopy. Foraging birds swoop down one by one to pick off prey from treetops, ascending again with slow, deep wing flaps before devouring their catch on the wing.

2 WHITE-TAILED KITE *Elanus leucurus* 38–41cm/15–16in

0–1200m; rarely to 2800m. Uncommon over pastureland, fields, and scrub in the lowlands and foothills; occasional sightings in the highlands. A small, gleaming-white raptor with black shoulders; in flight, also note black carpal spots. Immature (not shown) is very similar, but shows faint, brownish streaking on head and breast. Swallow-tailed Kite is much larger and longer-winged, with obvious forked tail and different black-and-white wing pattern. Pearl Kite (p. 60) has mostly dark upperparts, lacks the contrastingly black shoulder patches; when seen from below in flight, it also lacks the black carpal spots. White-tailed Kite is usually encountered alone, often hovering in place with deep wing strokes or gliding buoyantly near the ground. Readily perches in the open on fences, wires, and the like.

3 PLUMBEOUS KITE *Ictinia plumbea* 34–37cm/13.5–14.5in

0–1000m. Uncommon to locally fairly common in humid lowland and foothill forest. Adults are best identified by combination of gray coloration, rufous primaries, and very long, pointed wings that extend well beyond the tail when perched. Roadside Hawk (p. 74) also shows rufous in primaries, but shape and plumage are otherwise totally different. Plumbeous immature is heavily streaked below, but shape alone separates it from other immature raptors. Plumbeous Kite soars easily over forest in small groups, often reaching great heights; wingbeats are slow and deep when becoming airborne; feeds primarily on insects taken in the air or snatched from treetops; also perches for protracted periods on high, exposed snags. *Note:* **Mississippi Kite** (*I. mississippiensis*; not shown), which is not yet recorded in W Ecuador but could occur as a vagrant, is extremely similar to Plumbeous Kite. Adult lacks tail bands and may show pale patch on secondaries; immature's streaking tends to be brighter rufous.

imm. 3

Accipiters are small to medium-size hawks that specialize in hunting birds. They appear somewhat small-headed, and all have relatively short, broad, and rounded wings as well as long tails and long legs. Their shape is adapted for maneuvering through vegetation in rapid and skillful flight to ambush their prey. Females are larger than males.

1 BICOLORED HAWK *Accipiter bicolor* 36–46cm/14–18in

0–2500m. Rare in humid and deciduous forest and adjacent semi-open areas from lowlands to subtropics. The largest accipiter in our region. Adult is identified by its gray plumage, black cap, and typical accipiter shape; rufous thighs are often hidden by underpart feathers. Immature is extremely variable (two examples are shown); its underparts and partial nuchal collar vary from white to buff and can even be tawny; some individuals (unlike the ones shown) show streaking on underparts and/or a faint white superciliary. Immature Barred Forest-Falcon (p. 88) shows sparsely barred white or buff underparts and lacks rufous thighs. Smaller Plain-breasted Hawk does not have a partial nuchal collar. Bicolored Hawk is encountered rarely, most often in soaring flight; occasionally seen perching conspicuously on an exposed branch.

2 PLAIN-BREASTED HAWK *Accipiter ventralis* 27–34cm/10.5–13.5in

500–4000m. An extremely variable accipiter found in a wide range of elevations in forest and adjacent semi-open areas; the most common accipiter, but still rather scarce. Adult plumages vary markedly, especially underpart coloration; three examples are shown, but intermediate plumages are also possible. Immature (not shown) shows varying amounts of streaking below. All plumages have rufous thighs, but these are frequently hidden. Semicollared and Tiny Hawks show more distinct, clearly defined barring. Double-toothed Kite (p. 58), mostly found at lower elevations, has a mesial stripe and more rufous below (especially female). Immature Bicolored Hawk in some morphs can be similar but is larger and always shows a nuchal collar. Plain-breasted Hawk soars regularly and often perches on exposed branches, intently eyeing its surroundings for unsuspecting avian prey, which it adeptly ambushes in rapid surprise attacks. Sometimes lumped with **Sharp-shinned Hawk** (*A. striatus*).

3 TINY HAWK *Accipiter superciliosus* 22–29cm/8.5–11.5in

0–1200m. Rare in humid lowland and foothill forest and edge. Small size and dense underpart barring are distinctive in its lowland range. Adult male is dark gray above, with gray and white barring below; female (not shown) is similar but browner above. Immatures are variable; some closely resemble the female, while others, such as the bird shown, have rufous upperparts and underpart barring. Semicollared Hawk occurs at higher elevations than Tiny Hawk (no known overlap); Semicollared is stockier and has coarser barring on underparts and a more prominent nuchal collar. Tiny Hawk is not often encountered; most observations are of a single bird perched quietly from the mid-story to subcanopy, occasionally high in the canopy; rarely or never soars.

4 SEMICOLLARED HAWK *Accipiter collaris* 23–30cm/9–12in

1500–2400m. Rare in humid subtropical forest and edge, at higher elevations than Tiny Hawk. Plumages are similar to those of Tiny Hawk, from which it differs by stockier shape, presence of a more prominent nuchal collar, and coarser, more widely spaced underpart barring. Semicollared Hawk is rarely encountered, usually seen perched conspicuously at varying heights; soars occasionally.

ad. 1   imm. 1   imm. 1

light morph 2   medium morph 2   dark morph 2

ad. ♂ 3   imm. 3

BROAD-WINGED FOREST HAWKS

These medium to large, broad-winged and short-tailed forest raptors are all relatively scarce. Females are larger than males.

1 PLUMBEOUS HAWK *Cryptoleucopteryx plumbea* 35–38cm/14–15in

0–1700m. Uncommon inside humid lowland and foothill forest in NW; rarely ranges to the subtropics. Adult is slate gray, with orange cere and legs and a single white tail band (occasionally a narrow second band is present). Immature (not shown) has narrow white barring on flanks and thighs. Crane Hawk (p. 70) is similar but has a gray (not orange) cere and white wing crescents visible in flight; Crane also favors open habitats. Plumbeous Hawk is usually encountered alone, perched inside the forest from mid heights to the subcanopy. Soars very rarely. Most common call is a 1 sec. rising and then falling scream.

2 BARRED HAWK *Morphnarchus princeps* 51–57cm/20–22.5in

300–2200m. Fairly common in humid foothill and subtropical forest. No other hawk shows a dark hood and barred underparts, though the barring may not be visible at a distance. Even so, there are no other hawks in range that show sharp contrast between dark hood and paler lower underparts; also note single white tail band. Black-chested Buzzard-Eagle (p. 72) is a higher-elevation species, and the two do not occur together. Rarely seen perched, Barred Hawk is usually encountered in soaring flight, often very high. Pairs engage in displays that include sweeping dives and even locking of talons as the couple swirls briefly earthward. This species is quite vocal in flight, emitting a loud *WEEEoh!*, often in a rapid series.

3 SEMIPLUMBEOUS HAWK *Leucopternis semiplumbeus* 31–36cm/12–14in

0–1100m. Rare and inconspicuous inside humid lowland and foothill forest in the NW. Combination of slate-gray upperparts, white underparts, and orange cere and legs is diagnostic. Immature (not shown) is similar but has faint streaking on head, neck, and underparts. An attractive but unobtrusive hawk, occasionally encountered perched in subcanopy or at forest edge; does not soar and thus is often overlooked. Rather quiet but sometimes gives a shrill, very slightly down-slurred *Feeeeeeeee* or a series of hesitant whistles.

4 GRAY-BACKED HAWK *Pseudastur occidentalis* 46–52cm/18–20.5in

0–1300m. Locally fairly common in both humid and deciduous forest in W and SW; rare and sporadic in NW. The only hawk in our range to show dark gray back and wings, grayish streaked crown, and entirely white underparts. Tail is white with a single broad, black subterminal band. Light morph of Variable Hawk (p. 72), which is normally not sympatric in range or habitat, is quite similar, especially in flight; in Variable note gray on sides of face (lacks crown and nape streaking), more slender shape with somewhat thinner wings, and narrower black subterminal tail band. Gray-backed Hawk is usually encountered singly or in pairs, often perched confidingly on an exposed branch or soaring over the forest. Typical call is a harsh, grating *Zheeow*, often repeated.

Superficially similar, these dark raptors have a short tail with a single white tail band. Females are larger than males.

1 COMMON BLACK HAWK *Buteogallus anthracinus* 42–47cm/16.5–18.5in

0–100m. Uncommon and local; found only in and near coastal mangroves. A small version of Great Black Hawk; see that species for details on separating the two. No known overlap with the much larger Solitary Eagle of Andean slopes. Immature is similar to immatures of several other species: Savanna and Harris's Hawks (p. 70) show rusty wing coverts; Gray-lined Hawk (p. 74) has much wider tail bands. Common Black Hawk is a sluggish raptor that feeds primarily on crabs, perching inconspicuously in mangroves, often low over water, dropping to exposed muddy banks and roots during low tide to feed; soars regularly. The form in our region was formerly considered a separate species, **Mangrove Black Hawk** (*B. subtilus*).

2 GREAT BLACK HAWK *Buteogallus urubitinga* 53–61cm/21–24in

0–1400m. Uncommon and local in humid and deciduous forest, edge, and adjacent semi-open areas from lowlands to subtropics. Extremely similar to Solitary Eagle; see that species for ID details. Common Black Hawk is restricted to coastal mangroves, but the two species could potentially occur together. Adult Great Black Hawk has a broad white tail base rather than a distinct white median tail band. Immatures of both species are highly variable, with overlapping plumage characteristics; they are best separated by habitat. Immature Savanna Hawk (p. 70) shows conspicuous rufous on wing coverts. Great Black Hawk is encountered mostly in high soaring flight over a wide variety of habitats; feeds on a broad selection of prey, including but not limited to mammals, birds, fish, and crustaceans.

3 SOLITARY EAGLE *Buteogallus solitarius* 68–74cm/27–29in

900–1800m. Very rare in humid and deciduous foothills and subtropical forest in SW. In all plumages it is very similar to Great Black Hawk, but much larger and bulkier, with broader wings and very short tail, which at best extends only a little past wings on perched birds; tail of Great Black Hawk always extends well past wings. Adult Solitary Eagle shows a thin white median tail band, and sometimes shows a fainter band at base, but never shows the broad, white tail base of Great Black Hawk. Immatures of the two species are even more similar; shape is often the best clue, but immature Solitary Eagle has very sparse barring on tail that often makes it look contrastingly white, and has dark thighs. Common Black Hawk is restricted to coastal mangroves in our region and is not known to overlap with Solitary Eagle. Singles or pairs of Solitary Eagles are encountered mostly in slow soaring flight, often quite high over mountainous terrain; on rare occasions spotted resting atop a bare snag, looking rather tailless. Also called **Montane Solitary Eagle**.

ad. 3

ad. 1

ad. 1

imm. 1

ad. 2

ad. 2

imm. 2

sub ad. 3

imm. 3

ASSORTED HAWKS

Both Savanna and Harris's Hawks are found in open habitats, while Crane Hawk is a forest bird. Females are larger than males.

1 SAVANNA HAWK *Buteogallus meridionalis* 53–61cm/21–24in

0–1000m. Fairly common and conspicuous in open habitats, including agricultural areas, in the lowlands and foothills. Adult's combination of rufous plumage, black barring on wings and body, and bold black-and-white tail bands is diagnostic. Immature is variable but can be distinguished from other *Buteogallus* species (p. 68) by rufous wing coverts, black-and-white tail barring, and habitat preference. This long-legged hawk is usually encountered singly or in pairs, standing or hunting on ground; regularly seen atop an elevated mound or low shrub, or even perched on electric wires along major highways; soars regularly, often low to the ground.

2 CRANE HAWK *Geranospiza caerulescens* 46–51cm/18–20in

0–700m. A distinctly long-legged raptor; uncommon in humid and deciduous lowland forest and edge. Perched adults are easily identified by entirely gray face and cere, orange legs, and black tail crossed by two white tail bands; belly is faintly banded (not visible in these photos). In flight, look for narrow white crescents near wing tips, a feature not shown by any other raptor in our range. Immature (not shown) is similar to adult but lightly streaked on head and underparts. Crane Hawk is usually encountered alone; often spotted while gliding briefly over forest or clearings; quite entertaining when foraging, often flapping clumsily to maintain balance while probing crevices, knotholes, and bromeliads with its long legs; feeds on a variety of prey.

3 HARRIS'S HAWK *Parabuteo unicinctus* 48–53cm/19–21in

0–3000m. Uncommon to locally fairly common in deciduous forest and desert scrub in lowlands and foothills; uncommon in dry, inter-Andean valleys in N highlands. Adult is readily identified by its black and rufous plumage and often conspicuous white rump and base of tail. Dark morph Variable Hawk (p. 72) has a narrow black subterminal tail band. Immature Harris's Hawk is heavily blotched below and superficially similar to several other immature hawks, but rusty wing coverts, white rump and crissum, and (in flight) white wing panels help distinguish it; immature and female Snail Kite (p. 58) can also look similar if bill shape cannot be seen. Singles, pairs, and occasionally small groups of Harris's Hawk are encountered soaring or perched on trees, posts, wires, and even on the ground; the species feeds on a variety of prey including small mammals, birds, and reptiles.

ad. 3

ad. 3

imm. 3

These two raptors are found primarily in the high Andes; Variable Hawk also occurs locally in coastal lowlands. Females are larger than males.

1 VARIABLE HAWK   *Geranoaetus polyosoma* 46–61cm/18–24in

0–100m; 700–4400m. A truly polymorphic hawk found at a wide range of elevations and habitats. Fairly common in high-elevation páramo and adjacent temperate forest, but uncommon at lower elevations along the Andean slopes. There is an isolated population in arid areas along the Pacific coast. Plumage varies greatly, but adults of every morph can be identified by white tail with distinct black subterminal band. Light morph female shows faint underpart barring and varying amounts of rufous on the upperparts. Dark morph adult is not easily identified to sex. Gray-backed Hawk (limited overlap, p. 66) shares adult's tail pattern, but its head is streaked gray and white, underparts are pure white, and back is never rufous. Variable Hawk immatures are confusing: most show dark malar area contrasting with paler superciliary and cheeks; buffy-white underparts, variably streaked and chevroned with dusky; pale gray and narrowly barred tail. Immatures are usually much paler below than Black-chested Buzzard-Eagle, and base of wing is much narrower. Variable Hawk was once considered two separate species, **Puna Hawk** (or **Gurney's Hawk**) and **Red-backed Hawk**. Due to significant overlap in the plumage features and size measurements that were used to separate them, most authorities now recognize only one species.

2 BLACK-CHESTED BUZZARD-EAGLE   *Geranaoetus melanoleucus* 61–69cm/24–27in

2000–4000m. A bulky and distinctly short-tailed eagle; fairly common over open areas in Andean highlands and in páramo. Adult easily recognized by dark hood, short tail, broad-based wings, and overall shape; no overlap with Barred Hawk (p. 66). Immature birds are highly variable, but usually quite dark, with underparts variably streaked and mottled with buff and brown; tail is longer and less of a field mark than in adult, and gives immature a less bulky shape, leading to possible confusion with immature Variable Hawk; that species is usually not as dark below, and wings are not as broad at base. Immature Andean Condor (p. 56) is much larger, with protruding primary "fingers." Black-chested Buzzard-Eagle is most often seen alone or in pairs, soaring at low to moderate heights; perches on rocky ledges or even on the ground.

ad. **2**   imm. **2**
ad. **2**   imm. **2**

light morph ad. ♂ 1

dark morph ad. 1

dark morph ad. ♀

imm. 1

light morph ad. ♀ 1

imm. 1

Buteo is a large genus of broad-winged, rounded-winged, and fairly broad-tailed hawks. They inhabit more open terrain, forest edge, and light woodland, and avoid forest interior; all soar regularly. Roadside Hawk, included here, was until recently considered a *Buteo*. Females are larger than males.

1 ROADSIDE HAWK *Rupornis magnirostris* 33–38cm/13–15in

0–2700m. The most widespread Ecuadorian hawk; fairly common throughout the more humid lowlands and foothills; uncommon in arid areas and at higher elevations. Favors forest edge and clearings, and is regularly found along roads and rivers. Perched adult is distinguished from other small raptors by solid grayish-brown head and breast that contrast with rufous underpart barring. Immature is streaked rather than solid on breast, but typically shows an abrupt separation between the streaked breast and barred underparts. Distinctive in flight at any age, with conspicuous rufous primaries, compact shape, and broadly banded tail. Boreal migrant Broad-winged Hawk is similar, but note adult's rufous-brown (not gray) breast; immature Broad-winged has a blackish malar stripe and streaked underparts with less obvious barring. Plumbeous Kite (p. 62) also has rufous primaries, but general shape is very different, with long, pointed wings. Roadside Hawk is a rather sedentary raptor, relatively easy to see, and does not usually soar very high. Perched bird emits a sharp *eeyoouu*; in flight gives a series of *weh* notes.

2 BROAD-WINGED HAWK *Buteo platypterus* 38–43cm/15–17in

0–3000m. A boreal migrant to forest edge and wooded clearings; uncommon in the subtropics and rare at other elevations; recorded from September to April. Perched adult is distinguished from Roadside Hawk by rufous-brown (not gray) breast that is usually scalloped or streaked rather than solid. In flight, adults show bold black tips to all flight feathers (black trailing edge) and broadly banded black-and-white tail. White-throated Hawk (p. 76) lacks bold tail banding. Immature Broad-winged Hawk has fainter underpart barring than Roadside Hawk, and usually lacks the pale face of Gray-lined Hawk, often showing a bold, dark malar. Immature's wing pattern in flight is not as bold as adult's, but trailing edge of wing is more uniformly dark than that of Gray-lined, and it lacks the rufous primary patches of Roadside Hawk. Broad-winged Hawk, similar in behavior to Roadside, is often encountered perched for long periods; soars regularly, sometimes high. Call is a shrill, quavering *yeeeeee?*

3 GRAY-LINED HAWK *Buteo nitidus* 41–45cm/16–17.5in

0–1000m. Uncommon in humid and deciduous forest edge and clearings in the lowlands and foothills. Perched adult rather distinctive: the only small, pale raptor with barring from throat to belly; also note dark irides. In flight, note broad black tips to outer primaries, bold black-and-white tail bands, and lack of rufous in wings. Immature usually has paler face and throat than immature Broad-winged Hawk, and lacks the underpart barring of Roadside Hawk. In flight, Gray-lined's secondaries are less distinctly dark-tipped than those of Broad-winged and lack the rufous patches of Roadside. Gray-lined Hawk is usually encountered on a mid to high perch or soaring at medium heights. Typical call is a short *PEEyer*. Formerly called **Gray Hawk**.

ad. **3**　　ad. **3**　　imm. **3**

BUTEO AND RELATED HAWKS

These species all soar regularly and are rarely encountered perched. Females are larger than males.

1 WHITE-THROATED HAWK *Buteo albigula* 39–43cm/15.5–17in

2000–3600m. Rare to uncommon in subtropical and temperate forest and lightly wooded areas. Poorly known in Ecuador; possibly an austral migrant, as the vast majority of records are from April to September. Dark sides and flanks (appearing in flight as dark "wingpits") separate this species from Short-tailed Hawk. White-throated could also be confused with Broad-winged Hawk (p. 74), but tail is finely barred, often appearing plain at a distance, and sides of breast and flanks are always dark; also note its hooded appearance. White-throated Hawk is generally encountered alone, soaring above forest; only rarely seen perched, where it tends to favor canopy. Call is a short, rising and falling *where!*

2 SHORT-TAILED HAWK *Buteo brachyurus* 39–43cm/15.5–17in

0–2200m. Uncommon in humid forest, edge, and adjacent clearings from lowlands to subtropics. Light morph adult has conspicuous dark sides to head and a narrowly banded tail that may appear plain at a distance; distinguished from similar White-throated Hawk by lack of brown on sides and flanks. Variable Hawk (p. 72) has an obvious subterminal tail band. Rare dark morph Short-tailed Hawk is similar to larger Zone-tailed Hawk (p. 78), but that species has fewer, broader, and more conspicuous tail bands, and tends to fly with wings in an obvious dihedral, reminiscent of a Turkey Vulture. Immature Short-tailed morphs are similar to respective adults: Immature light morph has varying degree of head and breast streaking but usually still shows distinctly dark sides to head; immature dark morph (not shown) is streaked below but still very dark. Short-tailed Hawk is almost always encountered soaring, often with vultures and other hawks. Perched bird rarely seen, as it favors dense, shaded canopy. Typical call is a drawn-out, descending *WEeeeyar*.

3 WHITE-RUMPED HAWK *Parabuteo leucorrhous* 33–38cm/13–15in

2000–3200m. Rare to uncommon in humid forest and lightly wooded areas in the subtropical and temperate zones. Adult is the only small, dark highland raptor with obvious white rump and crissum; also note intense yellow eyes and black tail with two inconspicuous narrow white bands. In flight from below, pale wing lining contrasts strongly with black body. Immature has solid black of adult replaced by rufous brown, appearing much more uniform than immatures of other small raptors; white rump, crissum, and tail band less conspicuous than in adult. White-rumped Hawk is usually encountered in relatively low soaring flight, but sometimes perches on an open branch or snag. Typical call is a piercing, high-pitched *SEEooh*; occasionally gives a longer, more quavering version.

ad. 3

ad. 3

imm. 3

1

1

1

ad. light morph 2

ad. dark morph 2

imm. light morph 2

Zone-tailed Hawk is a somewhat lanky *Buteo* encountered mainly in flight over open terrain. Black-and-chestnut Eagle is a powerful raptor of forested Andean slopes. Cinereous Harrier is a scarce raptor with long wings and tail found in more open terrain in the high Andes. Females are larger than males.

1 ZONE-TAILED HAWK *Buteo albonotatus* 47–56cm/18.5–22in

0–1500m. An uncommon and often overlooked raptor of forest edge and more open country in the lowlands, with a few records up into the subtropics in the W and SW. Encountered mostly in soaring flight, where amazingly reminiscent of Turkey Vulture (p. 56), with which it is often found; look for Zone-tailed Hawk's tail bands and fully feathered head. Adult is also similar to dark morph Short-tailed Hawk (p. 76), but has fewer, broader tail bands and flies with wings in a distinct dihedral. Immature Zone-tailed (not shown) is similar to adult but often spattered with whitish spots; tail has narrower bands. Rarely seen perched; in flight often overlooked as "just another Turkey Vulture" (be alert!). Rarely calls, but has been heard emitting a wheezy *wuh, whee, whee.*

2 BLACK-AND-CHESTNUT EAGLE *Spizaetus isidori* 66–74cm/26–29in

1400–3100m. A large, dark eagle that is rare to locally uncommon in areas of extensive humid subtropical and temperate forest. Adult will not be mistaken if seen well; also easy to ID in flight by obvious pale wing panels and tail base. Immature has distinctly different plumage but is unlikely to be mistaken within its elevation range; see Black-and-white Hawk-Eagle (p. 80) of lower elevations, as well as the note below. Black-and-chestnut Eagle is mostly encountered soaring lethargically over mountain forest, often closely hugging the slopes in search of unsuspecting prey. Perched bird is not seen often as it sits quite stolidly in upper canopy, only occasionally on open branches. Vocalizations include a mournful *where!* and a series of shrill shrieks. *Note:* **Crested Eagle** (*Morphnus guianensis*; not shown) has been occasionally reported from the Tandayapa-Mindo area. It strongly resembles immature Black-and-chestnut Eagle; adult Crested has barring on underparts and much wider black wing and tail bands; immature is even more similar but lacks brown blotching on underparts and wing linings. Any sightings of Crested Eagle in W should be carefully documented and, if possible, photographed.

3 CINEREOUS HARRIER *Circus cinereus* 43–50cm/17–19.5in

3000–4200m. Rare to locally uncommon in open, grassy terrain and páramo at very high elevations. Sexually dimorphic, but both sexes are unique in the species' very restricted range and habitat. Cinereous Harrier can be identified by its distinctive flight, flapping and gliding low to the ground with tilting action, with exposed white rump; wings often held in a distinct dihedral. Perched bird is slender, has an owl-like facial disk and small-headed appearance. Immature (not shown) resembles adult female, but underparts are often densely streaked with brown. At a great distance, female might be confused with Short-eared Owl (p. 144), which also flies low over similar habitats but lacks white rump. Cinereous Harrier is usually encountered alone in low coursing and tilting flight, peering downward in search of prey (primarily rodents and small birds). Occasionally seen perched on a low stump, post, or mound. Quiet; vocalizations in Ecuador have not been recorded.

♂ 3   ♀ 3

Hawk-eagles are large, impressive forest eagles with broad wings, long tails, and feathered tarsi. Females are larger than males.

1 BLACK HAWK-EAGLE *Spizaetus tyrannus* 58–66cm/23–26in

0–1700m. Rare to locally uncommon in humid and deciduous forest from lowlands to subtropics. Fierce-looking, black, and bushy-crested, adult is not likely to be mistaken, even in flight: no other dark raptor shows such conspicuous white wing and tail banding or such wide, forward-swept wings; compare with dark morph of Hook-billed Kite (p. 60). Immature Black Hawk-Eagle is very different but can be recognized by combination of dark ear coverts, rusty sides of neck, and feathered tarsi. This predator hunts mainly from the forest canopy, taking medium to large birds and mammals. Rarely encountered perched; it is most conspicuous in high, soaring flight when it regularly emits a far-carrying *wip, wip, wip-wih-wi-WEEEoh*.

2 ORNATE HAWK-EAGLE *Spizaetus ornatus* 58–68cm/23–27in

200–1200m. Rare and local in semi-humid and humid lowland and foothill forest. Handsome adult is unique within its W range; note its long, pointed crest; bright rufous face, neck, and breast; and barred underparts, thighs, and feathered tarsi. Juvenile and immature have head, neck, and most of underparts white, and lower underparts, sides, and flanks densely barred with black; they can be confused with Black-and-white Hawk-Eagle and immature Gray-headed Kite (p. 60), but note size and barred flanks. Closely tied to forest, Ornate Hawk-Eagle favors canopy, where it ambushes its unsuspecting prey; tends to soar at low to medium heights above the forest. Typical flight call is *whip-WHIP-wih-wi-wer*, often given in a continuous series.

3 BLACK-AND-WHITE HAWK-EAGLE *Spizaetus melanoleucus* 53–61cm/21–24in

200–1400m. Very rare in humid lowland and foothill forest and adjacent wooded clearings. Adults and immatures (not shown) are quite similar. Perched birds, with their striking black and pure white plumage, orange cere, and feathered tarsi, are not likely to be mistaken. In flight, can be confused with several other raptors; look for the gleaming-white leading edge to the wing, which can sometimes be seen at great distances if the bird banks toward the observer. Light morph immature Gray-headed Kite (p. 60) is quite similar but has yellow lores (not black), unfeathered tarsi, and dark irides (not yellow). Immature Ornate Hawk-Eagle shows barring on lower underparts and flanks, and a pointed crest. Black-and-white Hawk-Eagle is rather secretive, usually encountered soaring overhead, occasionally spotted on an exposed canopy perch. Almost never vocalizes, though has been heard to give a series of sharp, rising squeaks in other countries.

ad. 1

ad. 1

imm. 1

ad. 2

ad. 2

ad. and juv. 2

SMALL FALCONS

The smallest falcons encountered in Ecuador are presented here. They are all sexually dimorphic and have narrow, pointed wings. Females are larger than males.

1 AMERICAN KESTREL *Falco sparverius* 25–29cm/10–11.5in

0–4000m. This charming and familiar little falcon is fairly common in open, nonforest habitats throughout much of the highlands, as well as in lowland areas of W and SW. Distinctive facial pattern and rufous tail in all plumages set this species apart from all other falcons and small raptors. In flight, it appears long- and broad-tailed compared to similar species, and its rufous tail is a diagnostic ID feature. American Kestrel is quite conspicuous, perching readily on wires, fence posts, and exposed branches. Flies to the ground to snatch up prey (insects, lizards, mice, etc.); soars readily, hovers frequently when hunting, and can be seen aggressively harassing larger raptors. Called *quilico* in the Ecuadorian highlands based on its *killy-killy-killy-killy* call.

2 MERLIN *Falco columbarius* 27–32cm/10.5–12.5in

0–3000m. A rare boreal migrant to more open country in arid coastal lowlands as well as highlands; recorded from October to early April. A small, staunch, and compact falcon with profusely streaked underparts, distinct malar, and barred tail. Male has slate-gray upperparts; female has brown upperparts. In flight appears compact and dark, with relatively short wings and tail. Peregrine Falcon (p. 84) female and immature are also streaked below but are larger and have a bold face pattern. Merlin is rather inconspicuous, favoring low perches; flight is rapid, powerful, and usually low to the ground as it pursues its prey (mostly birds).

3 BAT-FALCON *Falco rufigularis* 24–28cm/9.5–11in

0–1200m; a few reach 1800m. This handsome falcon is fairly common and widespread in humid and deciduous forest, edge, and clearings; most common in lowlands and foothills but occasionally encountered higher. Quite distinctive within its range and not likely to be mistaken; no overlap with Aplomado Falcon (p. 84), which occurs only at very high elevations in Ecuador. Usually found alone or in pairs, Bat Falcon often perches for protracted periods high atop bare snags, or even antenna towers, where easy to spot. Flight is fast and direct. In keeping with its name, it occasionally hunts bats at dusk. Bat Falcons sometimes join flocks of White-collared Swifts (p. 158), among which they apparently hide as a strategy to hunt swallows and other aerial prey.

Western Ecuador's largest falcons, including the very distinctive Laughing Falcon, are presented here. Females are larger than males.

1 LAUGHING FALCON   *Herpetotheres cachinnans* 46–51cm/18–20in

0–1400m. Fairly common in humid and deciduous forest, edge, and wooded clearings in the lowlands and foothills. Quite unfalcon-like but easily identified, even at great distances, by its owl-like shape and bold dark "bandit" mask, which contrasts with its pale head and underparts. In flight, rounded wings show buff patch at base of primaries, and banded tail is prominent. Encountered alone, often in widely separated pairs, perching stolidly for long periods on an exposed heavy branch or snag. Feeds almost entirely on snakes and other reptiles. Song is loud, far-carrying *aw-aw-aw-aw-AW-AW-AW-AW-AW...*, or *ow-wahow, ow-wahow, OW-WAHOW, OW-WAHOW...*, often given by male and female together.

2 PEREGRINE FALCON   *Falco peregrinus* 38–48cm/15–19in

0–4000m. This bold and powerful falcon is a rare resident in semi-open habitats in the Andean highlands; also a boreal winter visitor from at least September to April nearly throughout; migrants are rare in most of Ecuador but can be locally uncommon along the coast. Austral migrants may also occur. Easily recognized by dark hood and "sideburns," adult has pale, lightly barred underparts. Adult female (not shown) similar to male but more heavily barred below. Immature has a similar head pattern to Aplomado Falcon, but never shows that species' dark vest or rufous belly. Merlin (p. 82) is smaller and lacks a bold facial pattern. Peregrine Falcon hunts on the wing with powerful flight, dive-bombing its prey (primarily birds) with rocket speed, often dispatching it from the sheer impact alone. Peregrines perch conspicuously on any raised vantage point from low mounds to high-rise buildings, and usually nest on cliffs.

3 APLOMADO FALCON   *Falco femoralis* 37–43cm/14.5–17in

2800–4200m. Rare to locally uncommon in open terrain at high elevations, especially páramo. Tawny-rufous lower underparts, postocular line, and dark vest distinguish this species from Peregrine Falcon. In flight, wings appear distinctly long, narrow, and pointed. Aplomado Falcon pursues birds and small mammals in rapid, direct flight, often very low, dropping to the ground to pounce on prey. Tends to perch low, often on a mound, boulder, or fence post.

ad. ♂ 2

imm. 2

3

3

Caracaras are related to falcons; they have conspicuous bare facial skin, long, round-tipped wings, and long tails. They are well-known scavengers but also take live prey given the opportunity. Females are larger than males.

1 NORTHERN CRESTED-CARACARA *Caracara cheriway* 51–59cm/20–23in

0–2000m; occasionally to 3000m. Fairly common in more open, lightly wooded habitats and desert scrub in both dry and humid regions of W and SW; there are also scattered records from the central highlands. Distinctive and usually readily recognizable within its range; in flight, note especially its conspicuous white primary patches, visible even on the duller immature. Regularly perches in the open and often forages on the ground, especially at roadkills along with vultures. Flight is slow and laborious with deep wingbeats; also soars regularly.

2 CARUNCULATED CARACARA *Phalcoboenus carunculatus* 51–56cm/20–22in

3000–4200m. A handsome resident of open páramo and adjacent high-elevation pastures and farmland; uncommon over most of its range, but large numbers can usually be seen in Antisana Ecological Reserve. Boldly patterned adult is not likely to be mistaken, but see Mountain Caracara, which could overlap in S Ecuador. Immature is mostly plain brown, and the white wing and tail markings are much less conspicuous than those of the adult. In flight, immature shows fairly conspicuous, pale primary patches. Carunculated Caracara struts around in loose groups, feeding on carrion or scratching at the ground for insects. Large numbers can congregate around a carcass, occasionally with Andean Condor; often soars high above the ground.

3 MOUNTAIN CARACARA *Phalcoboenus megalopterus* 48–55cm/19–21.5in

2500–3500m. Rare to locally uncommon in habitats similar to those of Carunculated Caracara, which it replaces in S. Adult is very similar to Carunculated, but underparts are plain (unstreaked) black and white. Immature is almost identical in plumage to immature Carunculated, and the two are not reliably separated in the field. Mountain Caracara is usually found alone, occasionally in small numbers; behavior is similar to that of Carunculated Caracara.

4 RED-THROATED CARACARA *Ibycter americanus* 51–56cm/20–22in

0–600m. Very rare and local in W Ecuador; known from dry forest in the hills W of Guayaquil and humid forest in the far NW; few recent sightings. A unique black lowland raptor with white belly and bare red skin on face and throat. Boisterous pairs or small groups range in forest canopy and edge where they raid bee and wasp nests for eggs and larvae. Red-throated Caracara also consumes some fruit; it occasionally forages quite low, even on the ground, and emits a bizarre cacophony of harsh, complaining wails, e.g., *KAH-KAH-KAAWW!*, that can often be heard at considerable distances. Flight is laborious, with deep wingbeats.

ad. 1

ad. 1

imm. 1

ad. 2

ad. 2

imm. 2

ad. 3

imm. 3

Forest-falcons are inconspicuous, forest-dwelling raptors with long legs and colorful bare facial skin; all are quite vocal, but even when heard they are usually very difficult to track down. Females are larger than males.

1 COLLARED FOREST-FALCON *Micrastur semitorquatus* 51–59cm/20–23in

0–2400m. Widespread but uncommon in humid and deciduous forest and woodland throughout W lowlands and foothills; locally occurs up into the subtropics. Large, lanky and polymorphic; only the pale morph is shown. Some birds are buffy rather than white below, and the rare dark morph is entirely sooty black. Immature typically shows tawny or rufous breast and nuchal collar, and thick bars on underparts. Adult can be confused with smaller immature Bicolored Hawk (p. 64), which shows a white superciliary and occasional faint throat streaking. Dark morph can be confused with other dark raptors, but note long tail with three narrow upper bands and six outer tail-feather bands, and olive-yellow facial skin. Despite its large size, this forest-falcon usually remains perched inconspicuously at varying heights inside forest cover, only occasionally venturing out to edge. Its typical song, given primarily at dawn and dusk, consists of well-spaced, deep, hollow *OW* notes; also gives a faster *kuh-kuh-kuh-kuh-kuh-Kuh-KUH-KUH, OW, OW!*

2 SLATY-BACKED FOREST-FALCON *Micrastur mirandollei* 41–45cm/16–17.5in

0–400m. Very rare and local, restricted to primary lowland forest in far NW. Slate-gray upperparts contrast with pale gray underparts; cere and bare facial skin yellow. Immature has coarsely scaled underparts. Lack of nuchal collar separates it from Collared Forest-Falcon; Semicollared Hawk (p. 64) is smaller, more compact, and has orange cere and legs. Slaty-backed Forest-Falcon is a very secretive forest denizen; behavior is much like that of other forest-falcons. Song recalls that of more widespread Laughing Falcon (p. 84). Most common song is a series of slow, almost nasal, down-slurred *ow* notes; also gives a variety of other vocalizations.

3 BARRED FOREST-FALCON *Micrastur ruficollis* 33–38cm/13–15in

0–2000m. Uncommon inside humid and semi-humid lowland forest, and up into the subtropics. Strongly barred adult is very similar to rare Plumbeous Forest-Falcon, but note yellow-orange facial skin and cere (not reddish orange) and two distinct tail bands. Immature Barred shows a conspicuous ear crescent and a variable amount of barring below; apparently always browner and more heavily marked below than immature Plumbeous Forest-Falcon. Smaller Tiny Hawk (p. 64) is superficially similar, but has a gray-barred tail, white throat, and reduced yellow around eyes. Much larger immature Collared Forest-Falcon has a rufous throat and breast and much wider barring. Barred Forest-Falcon usually perches quietly at low to mid levels within forest and only occasionally ventures to forest edge. Hunts a variety of prey including birds, reptiles, and large insects, at times dropping to the ground where it will even pursue its victims on foot. Typical song is a very long series of evenly spaced dog-like yelps; it also gives other variations.

4 PLUMBEOUS FOREST-FALCON

Micrastur plumbeus 31–36cm/12–14in

0–1100m. Rare and local inside humid lowland and forest in NW. Adult (not shown) is very similar to the much more common Barred Forest-Falcon, and the two are often difficult to tell apart; Plumbeous shows only a single tail band, though this is often hard to discern, and its cere and bare facial skin are a deeper reddish orange. Immature Plumbeous is more distinctive: mostly white below (including throat), with sparse barring primarily on breast; tail may show two bands. The species is poorly known; behavior apparently similar to that of Barred. Typical song is virtually identical to Barred's song; other vocalizations are somewhat more distinctive, including a querelous *kwee?* and a series of abrupt, almost sputtered *pik* notes that rises slowly then suddenly falls and accelerates.

imm. **4**

ad. pale morph **1**

imm. **1**

ad. **2**

imm. **2**

ad. **3**

imm. **3**

RAILS AND WOOD-RAILS

Rails are shy, furtive, terrestrial birds that are often frustratingly difficult to see well. They have a hunched posture and often hold their tails cocked up. All species are quite vocal, which can be very helpful when one is attempting to spot one of these skulkers.

1 SPOTTED RAIL *Pardirallus maculatus* 25–27cm/10–10.5in

0–500m. This attractive and distinctively patterned rail is locally fairly common in freshwater marshes, tall damp grassland, rice paddies, and reedbeds in the lowlands; perhaps easiest to find at the La Segua marshes. Profusely spotted plumage is diagnostic; also note yellowish bill with red spot at base of mandible. Furtive, generally remaining undetected, though occasionally can be seen in the early morning or late afternoon when an individual may venture boldly out of dense cover. Vocalizations are quite varied, and include a low thumping, a series of churring squeals, and *piDIT* and *SQWEE, yerrrrrrr* calls.

2 PLUMBEOUS RAIL *Pardirallus sanguinolentus* 28–30cm/11–12in

1500–2000m. Uncommon and very local in damp grassland, sugarcane plantations, and along vegetated borders of slow-flowing streams in the highlands of the far S; perhaps most reliably found in the Vilcabamba area. Combination of dark plumage, turquoise and red base to bill, and red legs is unique in range. Plumbeous Rail generally goes undetected except when calling; occasionally can be seen at dawn and dusk or foraging along slow-moving streams. Song is rather high-pitched, with a buzzy, screechy quality, e.g., *weer-reet, weer-reet, weer-reet-ree-cheet-ree-cheet…*; at close range, soft grunts can be heard while it sings; also gives a sharp *tzeek* note.

3 MANGROVE RAIL *Rallus longirostris* 33–37cm/13–14.5in

Sea level. Uncommon and very local in coastal mangroves; possibly easiest to find in the mangroves and marshes S of Muisne, and on Isla Santay just across the Río Guayas from Guayaquil. Note large size, long orange bill, barred flanks, and streaked back. Wood-rails, which also range in mangroves, never show flank barring or back streaking, and bill color is yellowish to greenish. Mangrove Rail feeds on mudflats, and is more likely to come out to mangrove edge at low tide. Song is a strident, grating, and rhythmic *ch-ch-ch-rrheh, ch-ch-rrheh, ch-ch-rrheh…*, or *CH-RRRHEH, CH-RRRHEH, CH-RRRHEH…*; also gives a growling call. Formerly called **Clapper Rail**.

4 ECUADORIAN RAIL *Rallus aequatorialis* 20cm/8in

1700–3800m. Uncommon and local in marshes, reedbeds, and wet grassland throughout much of the central highlands. The only other rail to share its range and habitat is the very different Sora (p. 92). Immature Ecuadorian Rail (not shown) is mostly sooty brown with much rufous in wings. The species is usually found alone or in well-separated pairs; usually remains within dense cover, but a patient observer stands a decent chance of viewing one through an opening in the vegetation or at edge. Song is harsh, often descending, *shrikshrikshrikshrikshrikshrick…*, with lower grunts included. Sometimes lumped with **Virginia Rail** (*R. limicola*).

5 RUFOUS-NECKED WOOD-RAIL *Aramides axillaris* 29–31cm/11.5–12in

0–1400m. Uncommon to locally fairly common in coastal mangroves; rare and local in deciduous and semi-humid forest in lowlands and foothills (e.g., Jorupe Reserve). Rufous adult is quite distinctive; immature (not shown) is much duller and may almost completely lack any rufous. Immature might be confused with larger Brown Wood-Rail, but never shows that species' distinct separation between gray neck and brown underparts. Mangrove Rail can be found together with Rufous-necked Wood-Rail, but has barred flanks, mostly buffy coloration, and orange bill. Rufous-necked can be readily encountered in a number of coastal mangrove locations, where, at low tide, individuals or even small groups will venture into the open to feed around roots and open mudflats; much more difficult to encounter inside forest. Vocalizations include various very long series of notes, such as *cheeOK, cheeOK, cheeOK…*, and *keeok-kick!, keeok-kick!, keeok-kick!*….

6 BROWN WOOD-RAIL *Aramides wolfi* 32–35cm/12.5–14in

0–600m; old records from higher elevations. Rare and very local in swampy areas and near streams inside humid lowland and foothill forest; there is also one record from coastal mangroves. This large wood-rail is mostly brown with contrasting gray head and neck; also note black belly, flanks, and crissum; immature plumage is unknown. Immature Rufous-necked Wood-Rail is smaller and lacks contrasting gray head and neck. Brown Wood-Rail is usually found in close pairs that walk around on the ground, close to but not necessarily in streams, pools, and other wet areas inside the forest. Song, often given in duet, is a long, loud, and rollicking series of notes, e.g., *woo-CHIT, woo-CHIT, woo-CHIT…*, occasionally interspersed with a series of soft grunts.

SORA AND CRAKES

Crakes are small to very small rails; their diminutive size, preference for dense vegetation, and shy nature make them especially difficult to see. Although it is sometimes called "Sora Rail" by North American birders, the boreal migrant Sora is a crake.

1 SORA *Porzana carolina* 20–23cm/8–9in

0–2800m. A rare to locally uncommon boreal migrant to a variety of wetland areas in the lowlands and highlands; thus far recorded in Ecuador between November and April. Adult easily recognized by short yellow bill, black face and throat, and barred flanks. Immature (not shown) is buffy on the breast and lacks black on face and throat. Sora is more likely to come out to the edge of dense vegetation than other rails and crakes, often at dawn or dusk, though occasionally at other times of day. Typical call given on its wintering grounds is a sharp *keek*. Note: **Yellow-breasted Crake** (*P. flaviventer*; not shown) is considered hypothetical in Ecuador, having been reported on several occasions from the La Segua marshes. It is similar to immature Sora but significantly smaller and has a whitish superciliary, bordered by black lores and crown.

2 UNIFORM CRAKE *Amaurolimnas concolor* 20–22cm/8–8.5in

0–300m. Rare in swampy areas and stream margins in humid lowland forest. A medium-size, all-brown crake with red legs and yellowish bill; no really similar species occurs with it in our region. Rarely encountered; singles or pairs pace quietly, with rather erect posture, under dense forest cover; perhaps more likely to be observed when foraging along the edge of a stream. Song is a series of 20 or more rising, plaintive whistles.

3 WHITE-THROATED CRAKE *Laterallus albigularis* 16cm/6.5in

0–1700m. Fairly common in freshwater marshes, vegetated lake margins, and damp pastures from lowlands to subtropics. An attractive little crake; adult's white throat and breast, rufous sides and neck, and black-and-white-barred flanks are diagnostic in its range. Immature (not shown) has much reduced rufous and might be confused with Gray-breasted Crake, but never shows Gray-breasted's sharp contrast between rufous nape and mantle and mostly gray upperparts. White-throated Crake almost always stays hidden in dense vegetation, often unwilling to come out even if playback is used. Very occasionally comes out to edge to feed, especially at dawn or dusk. Birds occasionally flush out of the grass or even fly across a road. Heard far more often than seen; distinctive song is a loud, long, descending rattle lasting 2–6 sec.

4 PAINT-BILLED CRAKE *Neocrex erythrops* 19cm/7.5in

0–300m. Rare and local in freshwater marshes, rice fields, and wet, overgrown pastures in the lowlands. Brown above, with gray head, neck and underparts, and lower flanks and crissum barred black and white; base of bill broadly scarlet, outer portion blackish above and yellowish green below; legs salmon red. The even rarer Colombian Crake has buffy flanks and crissum with no barring. Paint-billed Crake is rarely seen except occasionally at dawn or dusk, when individuals may venture out of dense cover along a muddy bank or margin of a damp pasture. Vocalizations poorly known in mainland Ecuador, but elsewhere gives a very long series of inflected chirps, a very sharp *cheet*, and a low, drumlike tapping.

5 GRAY-BREASTED CRAKE *Laterallus exilis* 14cm/5.5in

0–500m. This miniscule crake is uncommon in freshwater marshes, grassy lake margins, and damp pastures in the lowlands. Note small size, gray foreparts, rufous nape, and black-and-white-barred flanks and crissum. Immature has reduced rufous on the nape and can be quite similar to immature White-throated Crake (see that species). Behavior is much like that of White-throated. Vocalizations include a dry rattle (usually shorter and slower than White-throated) and a high-pitched series of chips punctuated by clear, piping notes.

6 COLOMBIAN CRAKE *Neocrex colombiana* 19cm/7.5in

0–500m; old records to 1100m. A little-known species in Ecuador, with a few, scattered records in wet pastures and freshwater marshes. Brown above, with gray head, neck, and underparts, and buffy (unbarred) flanks and crissum; bill yellowish green with a black tip and red base; legs salmon red. No suitable photos could be found for this species; apart from its unbarred flanks, it is extremely similar to Paint-billed Crake. Behavior is also very much like that of Paint-billed. Voice is virtually unknown; a mist-netted bird was recorded giving a series of harsh rasps.

Gallinules and coots are plump, bulky-bodied, long-legged wetland birds that can appear duck-like at a distance. Gallinules have long toes adapted for maneuvering over aquatic vegetation, while coots, which seem almost tailless, have lobed toes adapted more for swimming and diving. Sungrebe is a rare inhabitant of wooded swamps, streams, and lagoons.

1   PURPLE GALLINULE   *Porphyrula martinicus*   28–34cm/11–13.5in

0–400m; 2200–3000m. Fairly common in densely vegetated margins of ponds, lakes, and marshes in the lowlands, and locally around highland lakes. Adult is uniquely colorful; azure frontal shield and full white crissum can help separate it from Common Gallinule in difficult light. Immature Purple Gallinule is mostly dull brownish, with wings tinted light blue; note conspicuous white crissum and yellowish bill. Immature Common Gallinule has mostly gray coloration and dusky-pinkish bill. Purple Gallinule seldom swims, and often remains hidden in dense vegetation, though regularly comes into view, when it can be seen perched on or maneuvering clumsily over aquatic vegetation. Flight is awkward, with legs dangling.

2   COMMON GALLINULE   *Gallinula galeata*   33–36cm/13–14in

0–300m; 2200–3000m. Common in freshwater marshes and lakes in lowlands; also found locally on highland lakes. A dark gray gallinule with a brownish back, yellow-tipped red bill, and red frontal shield; note narrow white streaks along sides, flanks, and edge of crissum. Immature could be confused with immature Andean Coot, but coots never show white on sides or crissum. Immature Purple Gallinule is pale brownish below, not slaty or gray. Common Gallinule swims regularly, with tail cocked upward and a characteristic head-bobbing action; often picks food items off the water's surface. Flight is weak and low over the water.

3   ANDEAN COOT   *Fulica ardesiaca*   39–43cm/15.5–17in

2200–4000m; locally near sea level. Ecuador's only extant coot, locally common on highland lakes; a small, lowland population is also resident on Represa El Azúcar near the Santa Elena Peninsula. Adult has slate-colored plumage and a white bill sometimes marked with yellow. Frontal shield ("knob") can be white, yellow, or red. Immature is similar to immature Common Gallinule, but lacks the white on sides and crissum. Andean Coot often congregates in large numbers on larger reed-margined highland lakes, where it swims quietly in open water, and often plunge dives from the surface to feed. Nests are placed on small mounds close to shore. Also called **Slate-colored Coot**. *Note*: **American Coot** (*F. americana*; not shown) formerly occurred on highland lakes in the N, e.g., Laguna Yahuarcocha, but has not been recorded since 1925 and is almost certainly extirpated. Similar to Andean Coot, but adult's frontal shield (always red) is much smaller, and tip of bill marked with dusky.

4   SUNGREBE   *Heliornis fulica*   28–31cm/11–12in

0–300m. A furtive and inconspicuous aquatic species of forest-fringed rivers and lakes in lowlands; very rare in W Ecuador (more common in E). Head and thin neck conspicuously striped black and white; female has cinnamon cheeks, lacking in male. Legs and lobed toes are boldly banded black and yellow, though this is seldom seen. Superficially duck- or grebe-like, but head and neck pattern are unique. Sungrebe swims quietly and stealthily, with body held low to the water and head pumping to and fro. Often hides amidst tangled shoreline vegetation, and only occasionally ventures into open water. Most often heard call is a hollow barking, e.g., *hoe, hoe, hoe.*

1 LIMPKIN *Aramus guarauna* 66–71cm/26–28in

0–300m. This snail-eating wading bird is locally fairly common in lowland marshes. Shape is intermediate between a heron and an ibis; no heron or ibis in Ecuador shows combination of brown plumage, white neck streaking, and thick, only slightly decurved bill. Flight shape is also very distinctive, the bird appearing hunchbacked, with neck outstretched and legs dangling, as it flies with jerky wing strokes. Often quite sedentary, and usually encountered foraging in open, vegetated wetlands or perched on exposed branches. Common calls include a loud *p't't't'yow, GROW* and a dog-like *yap*.

2 BLACK-NECKED STILT *Himantopus mexicanus* 36–39cm/14–15.5in

0–200m. Locally common in freshwater marshes, ponds, rice paddies, coastal lagoons, and inlets in the lowlands. This wading bird is very distinctive, with boldly pied plumage, long coral-red legs, and needlelike bill. Usually seen in small to medium-size flocks, wading quietly, even in deep water, where it forages by picking and probing into mud with its thin bill. *Note:* **White-backed Stilt** (*H. melanurus*; not shown) could occur as a vagrant from the S, and may also hybridize with Black-necked (with which it is sometimes lumped); differs by having a white band across the upper mantle and lacking Black-necked's discrete white patch above eye.

3 AMERICAN OYSTERCATCHER *Haematopus palliatus* 41–45cm/16–17.5in

Sea level. Locally common along the entire coast, especially sandy beaches. Unique in its range, with black-and-white plumage and long, bright orange bill. Flight is strong and direct, showing a bold white wing stripe. Usually encountered in pairs or small groups, often standing still or napping, with bill tucked out of sight. Feeds by prying open seashells with its specially adapted bill. *Note:* **Blackish Oystercatcher** (*H. ater*; not shown) is a very rare vagrant to the coast; its plumage is entirely sooty gray, lacking American Oystercatcher's white underparts.

4 SUNBITTERN *Eurypyga helias* 43–48cm/17–19in

300–1500m. Uncommon and local along forested rivers and streams in the foothills and subtropics. Quite distinctive, with odd, elongate shape, bold white head markings, and profuse banding on body. Displays stunning "sunspot" pattern when wings are spread in flight or during a threat display. Usually encountered walking along the water's edge, head bobbing to and fro, occasionally lunging to nab prey. Flies low with shallow wingbeats interspersed with brief glides. Song is a flat, 1–2 sec. whistle that starts soft and grows in volume, with an ethereal quality; it sometimes abruptly steps up slightly in pitch right at the end.

5 PERUVIAN THICK-KNEE *Burhinus superciliaris* 39–42cm/15.5–16.5in

0–100m. Rare and local in sparsely vegetated desert; almost all recent records are from in and around the Santa Elena Peninsula. Note its huge eyes, stubby black-tipped bill, and the white superciliary bordered above with a black stripe. Mainly nocturnal; by day, pairs or small groups stand erect or crouch, sometimes in the open, but more often in the shade of a small tree or bush; sandy plumage serves as camouflage in their desert environment, and they can be difficult to spot even when standing in the open. Typical call, heard only at night, is a somewhat squeaky *whit* or *whi-di-di-di-dit*. Red eyeshine can be helpful in spotting this species at night.

Wattled Jacana is an attractive wetland species with long toes adapted to moving about with ease over floating vegetation. Lapwings are rather large, boldly patterned plovers that have rounded wings with a carpal spur; short, mostly red bills; and relatively long, red legs. The two *Pluvialis* plovers are nonbreeding boreal migrants to W Ecuador.

1 WATTLED JACANA *Jacana jacana* 22–25cm/8.5–10in

0–300m. Common in freshwater marshes, flooded rice paddies, ditches, and vegetated margins of lakes and sluggish rivers in the lowlands. The distinctive adult is not likely to be confused with any other species (W Ecuador birds have black scapular patches, not evident in this photo). Immature is extremely different from adult and has no similar species: it is all white below and has distinctive black-and-white head stripes. Wattle Jacana forages methodically, in singles, pairs, or scattered groups, over matted and floating vegetation, where generally easy to see. Flight is slow, usually low to ground, with rather stiff wingbeats, legs and long toes protruding way beyond tail; when alighting, wings are often held outstretched, showing off yellow primaries. Can be quite noisy, emitting a series of loud yapping and yelping, cackling notes and churring sounds.

2 ANDEAN LAPWING *Vanellus resplendens* 33–35cm/13–14in

3000–4400m; a few records near sea level. A locally common resident of open, short-grass areas at high elevations, including páramo, pastures, bogs, and lake margins. Sightings from W lowlands may pertain to austral migrants. No really similar bird occurs within Andean Lapwing's range and habitat, but Southern Lapwing is spreading into the highlands and could potentially overlap. Southern Lapwing's conspicuous black throat and breast distinguish it. Andean Lapwing is typically encountered in loosely scattered groups, standing erectly and then rapidly walking short stretches while foraging; easily overlooked within vast, open páramo. Nests are placed on the ground, and angry parents will fly around and scream at any interloper, including a birder. Can be noisy, especially in flight, emitting a hoarse, laughing *GLEE-GLEE-GLEE-GLEE!*

3 SOUTHERN LAPWING *Vanellus chilensis* 33–35cm/13–14in

1400–3200m. Uncommon and local in open habitats such as pastures and lake margins; a recent newcomer to our region, and likely to spread beyond its current mapped range in the near future. Black throat and breast separate it from the otherwise similar Andean Lapwing, with which it may eventually occur. Behavior much like that of Andean; voice is also similar but with longer notes.

4 PIED LAPWING *Vanellus cayanus* 23cm/9in

0–300m. Rare to locally uncommon along banks of larger rivers in the lowlands. This well-named shorebird has long coral-red legs, bold black-and-white foreparts, and black scapular stripes. Killdeer (p. 100) has a similar pattern on underparts but lacks the black face and red legs. Pied Lapwing is encountered alone, in pairs, or in very small groups, standing or scurrying along river edge.

5 AMERICAN GOLDEN-PLOVER *Pluvialis dominica* 24–26cm/9.5–10in

0–200m; 2300–3500m. An uncommon boreal migrant to coastal beaches and grassy areas, as well as lakes and ponds in the highlands; recorded in Ecuador from late July to April. Similar to Black-bellied Plover, which outnumbers it in coastal areas. In alternate plumage (infrequently seen in Ecuador), American Golden-Plover can be distinguished by its all-black lower underparts, dark crown, and golden dorsal flecks. In basic plumage, much more difficult to separate: American Golden-Plover has a thinner bill and slightly warmer-toned plumage that seems less gray. In flight, it lacks the diagnostic black "wingpits," along with white rump and wing patches, shown by Black-bellied Plover. American Golden-Plover is usually encountered alone or in small groups, standing stolidly or resting with a hunched posture; foraging birds walk quickly for a short stretch to snatch up prey from the ground. Whistled call is much shorter than call of Black-bellied and tends to change pitch abruptly rather than smoothly.

6 BLACK-BELLIED PLOVER *Pluvialis squatarola* 28–31cm/11–12in

Sea level. A fairly common boreal migrant to coastal beaches, lagoons, and mudflats; also occasionally grassy areas; can be seen throughout the year. Very similar to American Golden-Plover; see that species for ID details. Behavior is also similar, but Black-bellied Plover is much more common along the coast and can be found in much larger flocks. Call is a clear whistle that falls slightly in pitch and then rises again. Also called **Gray Plover**.

CHARADRIUS PLOVERS

Small and short-billed shorebirds with complete or incomplete breast bands. Plovers are well camouflaged in their surroundings and can be tough to spot if not moving. When foraging, they scurry about, stopping to pick up prey items from the ground.

1 WILSON'S PLOVER *Charadrius wilsonia* 18–20cm/7–8in

0–100m. This stout-billed plover is uncommon to locally fairly common all along the coast on beaches, dry mudflats, shrimp and salt lagoons, and estuaries. Obvious large bill sets it apart from all other small plovers, but also note single, broad breast band and dull, pinkish legs. Usually encountered in pairs or small groups; behavior is much like that of other *Charadrius* plovers, though it is perhaps a bit more sluggish than the smaller species.

2 SEMIPALMATED PLOVER *Charadrius semipalmatus* 17–19cm/6.5–7.5in

0–100m; also in highlands to 3500m. The most frequently encountered small plover in Ecuador; common along the coast on beaches, mudflats, and lagoons; rare around highland lakes. This boreal migrant can be seen year-round but is not known to breed. Combination of complete breast band, orange legs, and pale nuchal collar are diagnostic. In alternate plumage also shows conspicuous yellow base to the bill, but this is reduced or lacking in basic plumage. Usually seen in small to medium-size flocks, though larger concentrations can be seen during migration periods; otherwise similar in behavior to other *Charadrius*.

3 COLLARED PLOVER *Charadrius collaris* 15–16cm/6–6.5in

0–300m. Uncommon to locally fairly common along sandy riverbanks, beaches, and mudflats in the lowlands. The only small plover to lack a white nuchal collar; also note adult's rufous-tinged crown and nape, and pink legs. Immature (not shown) is duller but still lacks nuchal collar. Collared Plover is usually encountered alone or in pairs, though occasionally seen in larger flocks.

4 KILLDEER *Charadrius vociferus* 24–26cm/9.5–10in

0–100m; locally to 1200m. The largest *Charadrius*; locally fairly common in open habitats including desert, grassy fields, farmland, and riverbanks in the lowlands; an isolated population in dry valleys N of Ibarra. Double breast bands are diagnostic; in flight appears long-winged and long-tailed, and shows prominent white wing stripe and bright rusty-cinnamon rump. Encountered singly or in pairs, often standing in the open. Call, is a squeaky whistle, sometimes (but not always) rising, e.g., *weer?* or *k'deer?*

5 SNOWY PLOVER *Charadrius nivosus* 16cm/6.5in

Sea level. An uncommon to locally fairly common breeding resident along SW coast, where it inhabits sandy beaches and salt lagoons, especially on the Santa Elena Peninsula. Pale plumage, incomplete breast band (often showing as just dark spots on side of neck) and gray legs differentiate it from all other small plovers. Female (not shown) and immature are paler than adult male. Encountered most often in pairs; otherwise behavior is similar to that of other *Charadrius*.

ad. ♂ (right), imm. (left) **5**

Seedsnipes are quail-like or ptarmigan-like terrestrial birds. Snipes are chunky, long-billed "shorebirds," though two of Ecuador's species are not associated with water at all. Snipes are furtive, wary, and cryptic, which makes them very hard to see without a concerted effort, an abundance of luck, or both. They engage in noisy, aerial displays (winnowing) at dawn and dusk that can draw attention to their presence.

1 RUFOUS-BELLIED SEEDSNIPE *Attagis gayi* 27–30cm/10.5–12in

4000–4600m. Uncommon and very local in cold, windswept páramo at very high elevations. Size, shape, rufous belly, and intricately patterned plumage make this bird unique in its range. Easily overlooked, as singles, pairs, or small coveys move about methodically. It often crouches, barely noticeable, among rocks and tussock plants; can even be curious, peering over stunted vegetation to see who is approaching. When startled, birds may either scurry off or burst up in powerful, direct flight. Call is a series of short whistles, often given by several birds at once in a loud cacophony. Birds from Ecuador are sometimes split as the endemic **Ecuadorian Seedsnipe** (*A. latreillii*).

2 LEAST SEEDSNIPE *Thinocorus rumicivorus* 17cm/6.5in

0–100m. Very rare in barren or at most sparsely vegetated desert on the Santa Elena Peninsula; last recorded there in 2010. Small and quail-like. Male has diagnostic black "wishbone" on breast. Female (not shown) is similar but lacks black mark, and breast is mottled brown. Pairs or small groups walk slowly or feed inconspicuously on the ground, where they easily escape detection even at close range. When approached, may just walk away in an unhurried manner, but when startled can flush upward and fly away strongly. Most common vocalization is a fast series of low, soft *woop* or *tuck-a-woop* calls.

3 NOBLE SNIPE *Gallinago nobilis* 30–32cm/12–12.5in

2900–4100m. Uncommon in high-elevation bogs and marshy páramo lake edge. Note large size. Similar to other snipes; best field marks are white belly, long, buff dorsal streaks, and cinnamon tinge to rump; these features are often most visible in flight. Habitat is also a strong clue, as Andean Snipe is usually found in drier grassland. Also see the rare vagrant Wilson's Snipe. Noble Snipe is usually encountered singly, and often only when flushed. It forages deliberately, probing soft ground with its long bill, regularly crouching down when approached, making it even harder to detect. Winnowing display sound is a rapid series of toneless, airy pulses. Also gives a series of harsh *chak* notes; when flushed, utters a loud *ki-ki-ki-ki-kit*.

4 WILSON'S SNIPE *Gallinago delicata* 25–28cm/10–11in

1200(?)–2600m. A rare boreal vagrant to marshes and vegetated lake margins. There are several documented records from Lago San Pablo near Otavalo (February), and sight records from the Mindo area (December–January). In our region, it might occur together with notably robust Noble Snipe. Wilson's is smaller, has a shorter bill and more conspicuous white on the trailing edge of the wing, and usually shows little or no white on the edge of the tail. When flushed, gives a harsh *zheet!*, quite different from Noble Snipe's call.

5 ANDEAN SNIPE *Gallinago jamesoni* 29cm/11.5in

3100–4400m. Uncommon in grassy páramo and scrubby edge of temperate forest and *Polylepis* woodland. Best told from similar-size Noble Snipe by entirely barred underparts, relatively unstreaked back, and, in flight, lack of cinnamon or rufous tinge to rump and tail. Noble Snipe also favors wetter terrain and is not typically found in the drier grassland that Andean prefers. Andean's general behavior is similar to that of Noble Snipe. Gives a *pit-where, pit-where, pit-where...* during winnowing display, as well as quick series of short, sharp whistles. When flushed, gives a quick series of dry *chak* notes.

6 IMPERIAL SNIPE *Gallinago imperialis* 29–31cm/11.5–12in

2700–3800m. Rare and local in temperate and elfin forest at high elevations; nearly all sightings in our region come from the Yanacocha Reserve. The only forest-based snipe in Ecuador, and the only one with upperparts and breast scaled rufous and black. This species is rarely encountered except when displaying, remaining hidden inside dense undergrowth during the day; on extremely rare occasions, especially on foggy early mornings and late afternoons, one might venture out into the open at forest edge or along muddy trails. Most reliably seen at known winnowing sites, where one or two birds may display just before dawn or after dusk, giving a long series of harsh *wi-ti-chit...* calls ending in a bizarre buzzing reminiscent of a large swarm of bees; may also give a series of evenly spaced *chak* calls.

MIGRANT SHOREBIRDS

These shorebirds are boreal migrants and do not breed in Ecuador, though some are present year-round.

1 SHORT-BILLED DOWITCHER *Limnodromus griseus* 25–28cm/10–11in

Sea level. A locally common boreal migrant to coastal mudflats and saltwater lagoons. Most common in August and September, but small numbers can be seen throughout the year; alternate plumage birds can be seen from May to August. Best distinguished by its long, straight bill, chunky shape, and foraging behavior; in flight, shows a distinct white stripe down back. Godwits are larger, less compact, and have slightly upturned bills with pink bases. Stilt Sandpiper (p. 110) has longer legs, shorter bill, and a rufous face patch (rufous can be faint in basic plumage). Short-billed Dowitcher tends to congregate in fairly large, compact groups. Foraging behavior is quite characteristic: feeding birds move about with hunched-over posture, often belly deep in water, probing with a constant, rhythmic up-and-down motion (often likened to a sewing machine). Call is a very rapid, whistled *whi-dit!* or *whi-di-dit!* Note: There are at least three records of **Long-billed Dowitcher** (*L. scolopaceus*; not shown) from the highlands; any dowitcher seen in the highlands should be carefully observed and documented. The two dowitchers are very difficult to tell apart except by voice: Long-billed gives a much longer series of whistles than Short-billed.

2 HUDSONIAN GODWIT *Limosa haemastica* 38–40cm/15–15.5in

0–100m; a few records from the highland lakes. A rare boreal migrant to coastal mudflats, salt lagoons, and high-Andean lakes; records are scattered throughout much of the year. Note long upswept bill with pink base and, in flight, white tail with dark tip. In basic plumage, compare to basic Willet (p. 106; straighter, all dark bill, pale underparts, and mostly white tail). In alternate plumage, Hudsonian Godwit is quite similar to Marbled Godwit, but Marbled tends to be buffy-cinnamon below (never chestnut) and has a relatively plain tail; the Hudsonian alternate plumage photo here shows several birds in various stages of molt. Hudsonian Godwit is usually found alone, occasionally in very small groups. It often wades out in fairly deep water, probing face down.

3 MARBLED GODWIT *Limosa fedoa* 43–48cm/17–19in

Sea level. A rare boreal migrant to coastal mudflats and salt lagoons, recorded from at least late July to March. In recent years, small numbers have regularly been seen near the town of Bahía de Caráquez. Note long, upswept bill and buffy-cinnamon coloration, which is retained year-round. Underparts are usually not as bright as those of alternate Hudsonian Godwit; sometimes best separated by tail pattern: Marbled has a rather plain, finely barred tail, not the bold black-and-white tail Hudsonian always shows. Behavior is similar to that of Hudsonian Godwit.

4 UPLAND SANDPIPER *Bartramia longicauda* 28–31cm/11–12in

0–100m; 2800–4200m. A rare boreal migrant to open, grassy areas; most often encountered at high elevations (especially páramo), but there are scattered records from the lowlands. Encountered mainly on southward passage from August to October, and occasionally on northbound return in March–April. Best identified by shape: long, slender neck, large eye, short yellowish bill, and erect posture give this species a rather distinctive appearance. In flight, note contrasting blackish primaries. Pectoral Sandpiper (p. 110) has a duller bill with yellow only at the base, shorter legs, and a less vertical posture. Upland Sandpiper is generally encountered singly or in small numbers. Note: **Buff-breasted Sandpiper** (*Calidris subruficollis*; not shown), a boreal migrant, is a vagrant to W Ecuador; appears as a small, short-necked version of Upland Sandpiper but with a distinctly buffy breast.

5 WHIMBREL *Numenius phaeopus* 38–43cm/15–17in

0–100m. Common throughout the year along and near the coast, on rocky and sandy beaches, mudflats, and lagoons; rare any distance inland. No other Ecuadorian shorebird has such an obviously decurved bill. Singles or pairs are found scattered about, often seen running away from the incoming tide, picking up food items off the ground.

bas. 1

alt. 1

bas. 2

alt. 2

3

4

MIGRANT SHOREBIRDS

More boreal migrant shorebirds are presented here; none breed in Ecuador, but some are present year-round.

1 GREATER YELLOWLEGS *Tringa melanoleuca* 30–33cm/12–13in

0–4000m. A boreal migrant to aquatic habitats in both lowlands and highlands; common along the coast but uncommon in the Andes. Can be seen throughout the year, though it is much scarcer during boreal summer months. Note especially the long, yellow legs and thin bill. Very similar to Lesser Yellowlegs, but bill is significantly longer than head, may be slightly paler at base (not all black), and may be slightly upswept (Lesser has a very straight bill). Pectoral Sandpiper (p. 110) has shorter legs and shorter, slightly decurved bill. Wandering Tattler has shorter legs, thicker bill, and is restricted to rocky coastlines. Greater Yellowlegs is often encountered in small concentrations, foraging by strolling about, in or out of water, picking prey items off the ground or swaying bill from side-to-side in shallow water. Flight call is a ringing *klee-klee-klee*, each note sounding distinctly two-tone, as compared to call of Lesser Yellowlegs.

2 LESSER YELLOWLEGS *Tringa flavipes* 25–28cm/10–11in

0–4000m. A fairly common boreal migrant to aquatic habitats nearly throughout W Ecuador; can be seen year-round, but numbers are reduced during boreal summer. Similar to Greater Yellowlegs; see that species for ID details. Behavior is also similar. Common call is a *tew-tew* or *tew-tew-tew*; individual notes lack the two-tone quality of Greater Yellowlegs.

3 WANDERING TATTLER *Tringa incana* 27–29cm/10.5–11.5in

Sea level. Uncommon along rocky coastlines; a boreal migrant, present in small numbers throughout the year. Mostly uniform leaden gray, but has profuse underpart barring in alternate plumage; note straight, medium-length bill and short yellow legs. Yellowlegs have longer legs, thinner bills, and are not so uniformly gray (showing more white on abdomen); basic Spotted Sandpiper (p. 108) is brown above (not gray) and white below, lacking gray flanks. Surfbird (p. 112) shares the same rocky habitat but has a dark breast and very different bill shape. Wandering Tattler's plumage coloration blends in well with rocky surroundings. Easily overlooked, it forages rather inconspicuously on rocks, probing crevices with its bill and teetering with distinctive up-and-down hind-part motion.

4 SOLITARY SANDPIPER *Tringa solitaria* 20–22cm/8–8.5in

0–4000m. An uncommon boreal migrant to freshwater rivers, lakes, and marshes nearly throughout W Ecuador; recorded from late July through April. Fairly small; distinguished from Spotted Sandpiper (p. 108) by white speckling on wings and back, unmarked wings in flight, and "normal" flight lacking the jerky quality of Spotted's flight. Separated from both yellowlegs by shorter and much duller legs. Solitary is (aptly so) most often encountered alone, characteristically bobbing or nodding.

5 WILLET *Tringa semipalmata* 35–38cm/14–15in

Sea level. A common boreal migrant to beaches and mudflats all along the coast; found in Ecuador year-round. In both basic and alternate plumages, readily identified by combination of large size, gray plumage, and straight, stout, moderately long bill. In flight, displays a bold black-and-white wing pattern and white rump and upper tail. Basic Hudsonian Godwit can look somewhat similar, but has longer, upswept bill with pink base and white tail with broad black tip. Willet is usually encountered singly or in small groups, foraging by picking food items off the ground or probing soft sand or mud; may perch or roost in mangroves. *Note:* Only **Western Willet** (*T. s. inornatus*) has been recorded in Ecuador thus far.

alt. **5**

Among these small boreal migrant sandpipers, those in the genus *Calidris* are often referred to as "peeps."

1 SPOTTED SANDPIPER *Actitis macularia* 18–20cm/7–8in

0–3500m. A fairly common boreal migrant to aquatic habitats nearly throughout our region; can be seen year-round, but rare from May to July. Note its forward-tilted posture and habitat of "teetering" (bobbing hind-parts up and down); in flight, shows white wing stripes and flies with very stiff, jerky wingbeats. Can be confused with Solitary Sandpiper (p. 106), but lacks that species' white spotting on back and wings, and in flight shows white wing stripes and different flight motion. Wandering Tattler (p. 106), of rocky coastlines, also teeters and has yellow legs, but is larger, longer-billed, and more uniformly gray; in alternate plumage, the tattler's underparts are more speckled, not distinctly spotted. Spotted Sandpiper is usually encountered singly or in dispersed groups. Calls include clear, piping *weep!-weep!* or *chee-deep!* whistles.

2 SEMIPALMATED SANDPIPER *Calidris pusilla* 16cm/6.5in

Sea level; vagrant elsewhere. A fairly common to locally abundant boreal migrant to mudflats and lagoons along the coast; very rare inland. Can be seen throughout the year but is much less numerous in May and June. In all plumages, note especially black legs and fairly short bill. Extremely similar to Western Sandpiper and not always separable in the field; bill of Semipalmated averages slightly shorter and straighter, with less "droop" toward the tip, but there is significant overlap in bill length and shape between species. In alternate plumage, Semipalmated shows only a hint of rust on head and wings, not the obvious bright markings of Western. Also easily confused with Least Sandpiper; see that species for details. Semipalmated Sandpipers congregate on mudflats, sometimes in huge numbers; often intermixed with other sandpipers, foraging by probing their bills into mud and shallow water. Flight calls are somewhat raspy *tchrf* notes.

3 WESTERN SANDPIPER *Calidris mauri* 16cm/6.5in

Sea level; vagrant elsewhere. Boreal migrant; fairly common to common on mudflats and lagoons; very rare inland; found throughout the year, but scarce from April to June. Extremely similar to Semipalmated Sandpiper as well as Least Sandpiper (see those species for ID details). Behavior is also similar, but when foraging Western may wade out into slightly deeper water than Semipalmated. Flight call is a thin *cheet*.

4 LEAST SANDPIPER *Calidris minutilla* 15cm/6in

0–500m; 2300–4000m. A fairly common boreal migrant in a variety of aquatic habitats in both the lowlands and highlands; seen throughout the year, though quite rare in June. Note small size, yellow legs, and short, thin bill. Legs, when covered with mud, may appear dark, and then Least is easily confused with both Western and Semipalmated Sandpipers, but breast of Least is usually more heavily marked, appearing darker. Alternate plumage (not shown) is intermediate between basic and immature plumages. General behavior is similar to that of other peeps, though Least Sandpiper often favors more vegetated ground. Flight call is a rising, slightly trilled *trrreeep?*

5 SANDERLING *Calidris alba* 19–21cm/7.5–8.5in

Sea level; vagrant elsewhere. Fairly common on beaches, mudflats, and lagoons along the entire coast; very rare inland. A boreal migrant recorded throughout the year, but numbers are smaller from May to July. In basic plumage, pale coloration, dark legs, black patch on wing coverts, and, in flight, bold white wing stripes, help separate this species from other peeps. Immature (not shown) is similar but spangled above with black and buff. Alternate plumage, rarely seen in Ecuador, is similar to basic, but with rufous tinge to upperparts and foreneck; the bird shown is beginning to attain alternate plumage. Sanderling is often encountered in small groups feeding in the surf, walking into the ocean as the surf recedes and then springing away as a wave crashes ashore.

bas. 5   alt. 5

bas. 1
alt. 1
bas. 2
alt. 2
bas. 3
alt. 3
bas. 4
imm. 4

Two more peeps, as well as several larger sandpipers, are treated here. All are boreal migrants, though many species can be seen in small numbers any time of the year.

1 WHITE-RUMPED SANDPIPER *Calidris fuscicollis* 18cm/7in

0–3800m. Very rare, and most often seen on southward passage from August to October. Records come from coastal lagoons and mudflats as well as marshy areas in the Andean highlands. Very similar to Baird's Sandpiper; as in that species, legs and bill are black, and wings extend beyond tail. White rump, usually visible only in flight, is the best ID feature; if rump cannot be seen, faint streaking extending down sides onto flanks can separate it from Baird's at close range. Some White-rumpeds show a faint yellowish patch at the base of the bill (lacking in Baird's), but this feature is hard to see in the field; it can help confirm a White-rumped, but can't exclude a Baird's. Only basic plumage is shown; immature has rufous scapulars and crown; alternate plumage is more streaked below but very unlikely to be seen in Ecuador. Stilt Sandpiper also has a white rump, but has longer legs and a notably longer, droopy bill. White-rumped Sandpiper is usually found alone in Ecuador, or at most in very small numbers, foraging rather inconspicuously.

2 BAIRD'S SANDPIPER *Calidris bairdii* 18cm/7in

0–4000m. Fairly common in coastal marshes and mudflats as well as around highland lakes and in marshy páramo. Most common on passage from August to November and again in March–April, though there are records throughout the year. Note horizontal posture, black bill and legs, and wings that extend beyond tail. Only basic plumage is shown here; immature and alternate adult are similar but brighter, with more of a scaly appearance. Very similar to the rare White-rumped Sandpiper; Baird's lacks the white rump (usually visible only in flight) and has unstreaked flanks. Pectoral Sandpiper is larger, stands more erect, and has yellow or olive legs. Baird's Sandpiper can be seen alone or in small flocks, often on grassy and muddy lake margins, where it can be quite inconspicuous, picking prey off the ground.

3 PECTORAL SANDPIPER *Calidris melanotos* 19–23cm/7.5–9in

0–3600m. Uncommon along margins of lagoons, mudflats, marshes, and flooded grassland, in the lowlands as well as the highlands and páramo. Most records are from late July to November, and March–April. Male is larger than female. Larger size, longer, streaked neck and breast, which contrast strongly with white lower underparts, separate it from the peeps; also note yellowish legs. Lesser Yellowlegs (p. 106) has much longer legs; Stilt Sandpiper has a very different bill shape. Pectoral Sandpiper is usually encountered alone in Ecuador, occasionally in small flocks, which, when flushed, may take off in unison with zigzagging flight.

4 STILT SANDPIPER *Calidris himantopus* 20–22cm/8–8.5in

0–3500m. Locally fairly common on coastal mudflats and lagoons, especially on the Santa Elena Peninsula, where small numbers can be seen throughout the year. Uncommon inland along major rivers, and very rare in the highlands. Combination of yellow legs and long droopy-tipped bill help ID basic plumage birds; may also show a faint rusty auricular patch. Alternate plumage (usually seen only in August) is profusely marked below and very distinctive. In flight, note dark, unmarked wings and white rump. Basic Short-billed Dowitcher (p. 104) is similar in behavior, but bill is notably long, straight, and thick, and legs are shorter. Yellowlegs (p. 106) have longer legs and lack the droopy tip to the bill. Stilt Sandpiper can congregate in large flocks; it forages much as dowitchers, often belly deep in water, probing with a "sewing-machine" action.

5 RED KNOT *Calidris canutus* 25–27cm/10–10.5in

Sea level. Very rare, with scattered records from coastal lagoons and beaches between August and May. Medium-long legs and bill black. Basic plumage birds are plain gray and lack strong features, though often show a faint superciliary and flank scaling. In flight, note faint white wing stripe and lack of white rump. Alternate plumage is distinctive but rarely seen in Ecuador. Dowitchers (p. 104) have longer, straighter bills. Stilt Sandpiper has longer legs, a longer, droopy bill, and a white rump. Baird's and White-rumped Sandpipers are browner and have a more slender, elongate appearance. Red Knot is encountered alone or in small flocks in Ecuador, often probing shallow water.

MIGRANT SHOREBIRDS

A selection of widely different boreal migrant shorebirds found primarily along the coast or offshore. None of these birds breeds in Ecuador, though a few species can occur in small numbers year-round.

1 RUDDY TURNSTONE *Arenaria interpres* 21–23cm/8.5–9in

Sea level. This common shorebird can be seen year-round; it favors rocky shorelines and sandy beaches. Distinctive and unlikely to be mistaken; unique breast and facial pattern, short, orange or reddish legs, and short, slightly upswept bill. In flight, heavily patterned with white above. The alternate plumage bird shown here is molting into basic plumage. Full alternate plumage (seen only briefly in Ecuador during boreal spring) is brighter overall with darker face and breast markings. Ruddy Turnstone is usually encountered in small groups that pick prey from crevices in rocks and off sandy ground.

2 WILSON'S PHALAROPE *Phalaropus tricolor* 21–24cm/8.5–9.5in

0–3500m. By far the most commonly seen phalarope in Ecuador, and the only one regularly encountered in alternate plumage; most likely to be found in coastal lagoons, though also regularly seen on highland lakes. Present year-round, but very scarce in June and July. Basic plumage birds can be separated from other phalaropes by the relatively long, slender bill and rather weak facial pattern, with often faint postocular line. Alternate plumage is distinctive: in flight, note dark, unmarked wings and white rump. Varying numbers (up to many thousands at the Ecuasal salt lagoons) can be found swimming, often spinning characteristically, or occasionally foraging along the shore, picking lightly at the ground or water's surface.

3 RED-NECKED PHALAROPE *Phalaropus lobatus* 18–19cm/7–7.5in

Sea level. Uncommon and encountered predominately well offshore; only rarely seen from land, where most sightings are from the Santa Elena Peninsula. Encountered year-round, but very rare in May and June. In basic plumage, similar to Wilson's Phalarope but note darker and bolder facial pattern, with black cap extending to hind-crown and a wider postocular line. Red-necked can be distinguished from Red Phalarope by all-black bill, lacking a pale base, and presence of white dorsal scaling. In alternate plumage (not shown), Red-necked has a distinctive rufous stripe extending from face to sides of neck and breast, and a white throat. Offshore, rafts of hundreds may gather to feed on the ocean surface, with characteristic spinning behavior; on the mainland usually seen alone.

4 RED PHALAROPE *Phalaropus fulicarius* 20–22cm/8–8.5in

Sea level. Like Red-necked Phalarope, this species is primarily pelagic in Ecuador, occasionally sighted from the Santa Elena Peninsula. Only basic plumage is likely to be seen in Ecuador; see Red-necked for comparisons with that species. Short bill should preclude confusion with Wilson's Phalarope. Alternate plumage Red Phalarope (not shown) is rufous with pale face and black crown. Usually encountered singly or in small numbers; regularly associates with other phalaropes.

5 SURFBIRD *Calidris virgata* 23–26cm/9–10in

Sea level. A short-legged, chunky shorebird of rocky shorelines; uncommon in Ecuador mainly from August to April; very rare in other months. Note combination of short, stout bill with orange base, yellowish legs, and white, sparsely streaked lower underparts. Alternate plumage (not shown; rarely seen in Ecuador) is darker, more strongly marked, with rusty scapulars. In flight, note white wing stripe, rump, and base of tail. Basic plumage Wandering Tattler (p. 106) is longer-billed, lacks streaking on lower underparts, and is plain-winged in flight. Surfbird forages slowly and is generally inconspicuous in its rocky habitat; often associates with turnstones and Wandering Tattler.

bas. **5**

bas. 1

alt. 1

bas. 2

alt. 2

bas. 3

bas. 4

Gulls are a familiar group found throughout the world. Most species have a variety of age-related plumages that often make ID a challenge. A number of species occur as very rare vagrants and are not covered in this book (see p. 425). Any strange gull should be carefully documented and photographed if possible.

1 ANDEAN GULL *Chroicocephalus serranus* 46–48cm/18–19in

2300–4200m. The only resident highland gull, locally fairly common around lakes, farmland (especially freshly plowed fields), and páramo. Highland range alone should clinch this species' ID, but beware of vagrant gulls, especially Laughing and Franklin's (p. 116). In all plumages, Andean Gull shows ample black underwing with bold white primary patch near wing tips. Laughing Gull and immature Franklin's Gull have entirely dark wing tips; adult Franklin's Gull has white underwing with reduced black near the tip. Andean Gull is encountered singly, in pairs, or in small to large flocks; often flies quite high and swims regularly.

2 GRAY-HEADED GULL *Chroicocephalus cirrocephalus* 41–43cm/16–17in

0–100m. Uncommon to locally common, favoring coastal salt lagoons, shrimp ponds, and adjacent beaches. Adult's red legs and bill and flashy black-and-white forewing patch are diagnostic within its range. Alternate plumage adults have a distinctive gray hood; gray much reduced in basic plumage. Immature (not shown) lacks gray hood and has pinkish legs and bill, which may have a dark tip; wing pattern much less conspicuous. In all plumages, wings show far more conspicuous white compared to corresponding plumages of Laughing and Franklin's Gulls (p. 116). Gray-headed Gull congregates in moderate numbers along shores and beaches; generally flies at fairly low heights. Also called **Gray-hooded Gull**.

3 KELP GULL *Larus dominicanus* 61–66cm/24–26in

Sea level. Ecuador's largest resident gull, locally fairly common on beaches, lagoons, and mudflats along the S and central coasts. Adult is white (including entire tail), with black upperwing and mantle, yellowish legs, and heavy yellow bill with red spot on lower mandible. Kelp Gull takes three years to attain adult plumage. Immatures vary based on age, but all have a broad black tail tip and black (or black-tipped) bill. The immature shown is a typical first-year bird; younger birds are browner, and older birds gradually begin to resemble adult. Kelp Gull is the only large gull to be expected within its range, though various vagrants may accidentally show up. It is a typical scavenger, usually encountered singly or in small, scattered numbers.

GULLS

1 LAUGHING GULL *Leucophaeus atricilla* 38–43cm/15–17in

0–250m; 2300–4000m. A common and widespread boreal migrant along the entire coast, occurring in smaller numbers on inland rivers and wetlands, with scattered highland records. Found throughout the year, but numbers are lower in the boreal summer months. Similar to Franklin's Gull; Laughing is somewhat larger and has a slightly longer, droopy-tipped bill, but this is not always discernible in the field. In alternate plumage best separated in flight, when Laughing always shows solid black wing tips with no white. In basic and immature plumages, Laughing never shows the bold, dark triangle from eye to nape that Franklin's always has. In highlands, see Andean Gull (p. 114). Laughing is usually the most numerous gull in Ecuador during the boreal winter and the most likely to turn up in unexpected locations.

2 FRANKLIN'S GULL *Leucophaeus pipixcan* 35–38cm/14–15in

0–200m; vagrant to highlands. An uncommon to locally common boreal migrant along the coast; in smaller numbers to inland rivers and wetlands; very rare in the highlands. Mainly seen from October to April, though there are scattered records from other months. Very similar to Laughing Gull; see that species for separation details. Also see Andean Gull (p. 114), though Franklin's Gull is never expected in the highlands. Usually encountered in small numbers, though transients can appear in larger groups, often intermixed with more common Laughing Gull.

3 GRAY GULL *Leucophaeus modestus* 44–46cm/17.5–18in

Sea level. Uncommon to locally fairly common on sandy shores and saltwater lagoons along the S coast; occasionally slightly inland near Guayaquil; can be seen year-round, but most common in Ecuador from June to November. This well-named gull is almost all gray; in alternate plumage shows a contrasting white head. Basic plumage (not shown) is similar to immature, but is more uniformly gray and may show a white eye-ring. No other Ecuadorian gull is so uniformly gray, including tail and wings. Encountered in small groups, foraging along the shoreline, often with other gull species; tends not to soar high.

4 SWALLOW-TAILED GULL *Creagrus furcatus* 53–59cm/21–23in

Sea level. This exquisite gull is mostly pelagic but can be seen from shore on rare occasions. In all plumages, note black bill with white tip and forked tail. Only alternate plumage adult is shown. Basic plumage adult and immature lack the dark hood but have a small, dark periocular patch and may show a small auricular spot. In flight, wings display broad white trianglular area. Mostly nocturnal and rather inactive by day; encountered swimming and resting on the ocean's surface.

5 SABINE'S GULL *Xema sabini* 27–33cm/10.5–13in

Sea level. Sightings of this boreal migrant have increased in recent years. Mainly pelagic, but can be seen in fair numbers in August and September from the Santa Elena Peninsula (especially La Chocolatera); rare during the rest of the boreal winter. Bold black-and-white wing markings are diagnostic, and adult has a yellow bill tip year-round. Only adult molting into basic plumage is shown (these gulls often look like this when seen in Ecuador); adult in full basic plumage and immature lack the dark hood; immature additionally has an all-black bill and black tip to the tail. Swallow-tailed Gull has black on wings restricted to tips and a very different head and bill pattern.

alt. 4

bas. 5

alt. 1

bas. 1

imm. 1

alt. 2

imm. 2

bas. 2

alt. 3

alt. 3

imm. 3

TERNS

Terns are superficially gull-like, though more slender, and have longer, more pointed bills, and forked tails. Most Ecuadorian terns are migrants. They forage over water and plunge dive to catch their prey.

1 ROYAL TERN *Thalasseus maximus* 46–51cm/18–20in

0–100m. This boreal migrant is Ecuador's most common tern, found year-round along the entire Pacific coast on beaches, mudflats, and salt ponds, and regularly flying along the ocean shoreline. Large size and stout, orange-red bill set it apart from most other terns. Elegant Tern is very similar, but has a thinner, more daggerlike bill that is paler, especially at tip. In basic plumage, Royal Tern usually shows a shaggy hind-crest, which Elegant normally has only in alternate plumage. Royal Tern often rests in large flocks, along with other terns and gulls, on sandy beaches, rocky outcroppings, etc. Regularly seen cruising offshore with strong direct flight, slowing only to plunge dive for fish, then continue along. *Note:* There have been recent sightings of **Caspian Tern** (*Hydroprogne caspia*; not shown) at the La Segua marshes; it is similar to Royal Tern but bulkier, with heavy, black-tipped red bill and black crown; crown streaked with white in basic plumage.

2 ELEGANT TERN *Thalasseus elegans* 41–43cm/16–17in

Sea level. An uncommon boreal migrant to Ecuador's entire Pacific coastline; much less numerous than Royal Tern, compared to which, Elegant has a thinner bill that appears sharper and more droopy. In alternate plumage, Elegant's bill is just as red as Royal's but may show a yellowish tip. In basic plumage, bill is paler than Royal's and usually has a distinct yellow tip. Hind-crest is quite shaggy in alternate plumage but usually appears comparatively smoother than Royal Tern's crest in basic plumage. Behavior is similar to that of Royal, though Elegant Tern tends not to venture great distances from the shore.

3 SANDWICH TERN *Thalasseus sandvicensis* 41–43cm/16–17in

0–100m. A fairly common boreal migrant along the entire coast; occasionally found farther inland at shrimp ponds. Black bill with yellow tip is diagnostic if seen, but may look all black at a distance or under poor viewing conditions. Elegant and Royal Terns are similar in size and shape but have orange or red bills. Gull-billed Tern (p. 122) has a shorter, heavy all-black bill, and a shorter, less forked tail. The smaller *Sterna* terns (p. 120) all have red legs as well as shorter bills that lack a yellow tip. Sandwich Tern can gather in fairly large flocks, especially during migration periods. Otherwise behavior is similar to that of Royal Tern. Sandwich Tern is sometimes split; birds in Ecuador are then called **Cabot's Tern** (*T. acuflavidus*).

alt. 3

bas. 3

bas. 1

alt. 1

1

alt. 2

bas. 2

TERMS

1 PERUVIAN TERN *Sternula lorata* 22–24cm/8.5–9.5in

Sea level. An austral migrant to sandy beaches, ponds, estuaries, and mudflats along W and SW coasts; found in Ecuador from at least July to October. Large numbers can occur seasonally on Isla Jambelí in July and August; elsewhere it is rare. Note small size, yellow feet, grayish underparts; in all plumages can be identified by thin bill with yellow base and dark tip. Only alternate plumage is shown; basic plumage is similar but with reduced black on crown; immature shows even less black (reduced to a dark postocular line) and is rather blotchy underneath. The very rare Least Tern is similar in size but has white (not gray) underparts, and in basic plumage has dark bill and legs. Away from its nesting area, Peruvian Tern is usually encountered singly or in very small groups; feeds by plunge diving into shallow water.

2 LEAST TERN *Sternula antillarum* 21–23cm/8.5–9in

Sea level. A very rare boreal migrant, with a few scattered records along the coast. Very small, with a thin bill; bill and legs are yellow in alternate plumage. In basic plumage (not shown), bill and legs are dark, and white on head is more extensive, extending from forehead to crown. Distinguished from similar Peruvian Tern by white (not gray) underparts. Has been encountered alone or in very small groups; feeds by plunge diving into shallow water.

3 ARCTIC TERN *Sterna paradisaea* 33–38cm/13–15in

Sea level. An uncommon boreal migrant, usually well offshore, rarely coming close to land. Mainly recorded as a transient from August to October, and in smaller numbers in April–May. Very similar to Common and South American Terns; Arctic on average has shorter bill and legs, but this is not often evident. In immature (not shown) and basic plumage adult, Arctic's carpal bar is not as dark; from above, flight feathers, especially secondaries, are paler than those of Common. Alternate plumage (not shown) is similar to alternate of South American, but Arctic has grayer breast set off from black crown by a narrow white line. Behavior much like that of other terns, but rarely comes close to shore.

4 COMMON TERN *Sterna hirundo* 33–38cm/13–15in

Sea level. Boreal migrant along the entire Pacific coastline to sandy beaches, ponds, and adjacent lagoons. Usually uncommon, but large numbers can sometimes be seen on the Santa Elena Peninsula; occurs throughout the year, but very scarce from March to May. Very similar to both South American and Arctic Terns; bill of Common Tern averages slightly larger than Arctic and slightly smaller than South American, but this is not always a reliable feature. In basic plumage, Common Tern can sometimes be easily recognized by its very dark carpal bar, noticeable both perched and in flight; it also has a dark bill, whereas basic South American Tern retains its red bill. In alternate plumage, ID can be challenging. Common usually shows a dark tip to its red bill, while South American, in full alternate plumage, has an all-red bill. In flight, alternate Common Tern shows less contrast between wing tips and dark trailing edge to primaries, often giving the impression of all-dark wing tips. Arctic Tern is more of a pelagic species and rarely seen from land; see that species for ID details. Common Tern generally remains close to shore; flies gracefully but pauses to hover and plunge dive.

5 SOUTH AMERICAN TERN *Sterna hirundinacea* 41–43cm/16–17in

Sea level. A fairly common breeder in and around the Santa Elena Peninsula from April to September (when it is the most common *Sterna*); there are very few records from other months, suggesting that it migrates southward, out of Ecuador, after nesting. Note rather large red bill in all adult plumages but black bill in immatures. Juvenile is extensively marked with black and white. Similar to both Common and Arctic Terns; see those species for ID details. Behavior is much like that of Common Tern.

alt. 5

juv. 5

TERNS AND BLACK SKIMMER

1 GULL-BILLED TERN *Gelochelidon nilotica* 33–38cm/13–15in

0–100m. A fairly common breeding resident on coastal lagoons, salt and shrimp ponds, and marshes all along the coast; much scarcer in NW. The only tern to show a thick, all-black bill in all plumages; also note black legs and short, only slightly forked tail. Sandwich Tern (p. 118) can look similar, but tail is deeply forked, bill is distinctly thinner and yellow-tipped (though this last feature may be difficult to discern); all other dark-billed terns have much thinner bills. Behavior rather distinctive for a tern: does not seem to plunge dive, instead feeds by hawking insects in the air or picking a variety of prey items off the ground or water's surface.

2 BLACK TERN *Chlidonias niger* 23–26cm/9–10in

0–100m. A boreal migrant to coastal waters and adjacent lagoons and marshes; most records are from July through March. During most years it is rare, but occasionally larger numbers are found, especially on the Santa Elena Peninsula and at the La Segua marshes. In basic plumage identified by dark gray wings and upperparts, conspicuous dark pectoral patches, and black head pattern described as "skullcap and earmuffs." Alternate plumage bird (not shown; very rare in Ecuador) has head and almost all of underparts black. This small tern flies gracefully and usually only picks prey off the water's surface instead of plunge diving.

3 INCA TERN *Larosterna inca* 41–43cm/16–17in

Sea level. This beautiful tern used to be rare in Ecuador but appears to be increasing. It is now seen fairly regularly along the Santa Elena Peninsula, where it can occur in large numbers in August to September. It is much less likely to be encountered elsewhere along the coast. Snazzy "mustached" adults are nearly unmistakable; immature (not shown) is mostly gray but still usually shows at least a hint of the white mustache; immature might be mistaken for Gray Gull (p. 116), but shape and flight are typically tern-like. Inca Tern's flight is buoyant on rather stiff wings; hovers briefly then drops to pick food off the water's surface.

4 BLACK SKIMMER *Rynchops niger* 41–47cm/16–18.5in

Sea level. Rare in W Ecuador; recent sightings come from the Santa Elena Peninsula and La Segua marshes (as well as surrounding areas). At least formerly occurred in the Gulf of Guayaquil and northward along major rivers, but lack of any recent records suggests it may be extirpated from that region. Odd and vaguely tern-like; easily identified by striking black-and-white plumage and oversize black and orange bill, with lower mandible notably longer than upper. Immature (not shown) is similar but slightly duller. Flight is buoyant, close to water while bird skims the surface with lower mandible. Found only in very small numbers in our region, though elsewhere this species can gather in large flocks.

Large, arboreal pigeons of canopy and edge; usually found in pairs, but some species such as Band-tailed Pigeon occur in large flocks. Flight is strong and direct.

1 SCALED PIGEON *Patagioenas speciosa* 32cm/12.5in

0–800m. This attractive pigeon is uncommon to locally fairly common in humid and deciduous forest, edge, and lighter woodland in lowlands and foothills. No other similar pigeon occurs in Ecuador. At a distance could be confused with Pale-vented Pigeon, which has a black bill; Scaled Pigeon's red bill often stands out even when the scaled plumage cannot be discerned. Scaled Pigeon is usually encountered alone or in pairs, but on rare occasions flocks of a dozen or more can be seen. Regularly perches conspicuously on an exposed canopy branch or snag. Song is a deep *wooo, hoo-oo-ooo, hoo-oo-ooo, hoo-oo-oo…*; typically lower and huskier than song of Pale-vented Pigeon.

2 BAND-TAILED PIGEON *Patagioenas fasciata* 36cm/14in

1000–3600m. Often common in humid montane forest, but its occurrence in some areas seems to be very erratic, and it is sometimes present in abundance and other times not present at all; may engage in elevational migration that is not yet understood. Yellow bill and narrow white nuchal collar are diagnostic; grayish tail band is evident usually only in flight. Band-tailed Pigeon is typically encountered perched high in the canopy, and often congregates in large flocks that fly conspicuously among tall trees. Song is a deep *uh-wooOO*, often repeated quite quickly; the first note is inaudible except at close range.

3 PALE-VENTED PIGEON *Patagioenas cayennensis* 30cm/12in

0–1000m. Fairly common in forest edge, light woodland, agricultural areas, and river and lake margins in the lowlands and foothills. Grayish-green head and underparts contrast with purplish-red back, wings, and neck; also note red irides and black bill. Two-tone plumage separates it from most other pigeons within its range, though at great distances it may be confused with Scaled Pigeon, which has a conspicuous red bill. Pale-vented Pigeon is found alone, in pairs, and sometimes in fairly large flocks; often perches in the open on a high, bare branch or even on wires; avoids forest interior, but may be found along edge, especially near water. Song is a *WOW, wuh-wu-wow, wuh-wu-wow, wuh-wu-wow, wuh-wu-wow…*, clearer and more insistent than song of Scaled Pigeon; a low growl is also given.

4 PLUMBEOUS PIGEON *Patagioenas plumbea* 32cm/12.5in

1000–2400m; down to 600m in SW. Fairly common in humid foothill and subtropical forest and edge. Similar to Ruddy Pigeon but much grayer, with darker, more contrasting wings and pale irides; in poor light, iris color may be the only reliable way to separate silent birds in the areas of overlap. Plumbeous Pigeon is usually encountered in pairs, perched or foraging quietly in forest canopy, often well hidden within vegetation; pairs tend to fly through or just above canopy. Song is lazy, slurred *who-cooks-foo-ood!*, or sometimes a more mellow *cooks-for-you*.

5 RUDDY PIGEON *Patagioenas subvinacea* 30cm/12in

0–1700m. Common in humid lowland and foothill forest and edge, locally up into the subtropics. Plumage uniform rufous-brown; red irides. Plumbeous Pigeon is grayer, with darker wings and pale irides; Dusky Pigeon has gray head and underparts. In poor light, song is often the best clue. Behavior is much like that of Plumbeous Pigeon. Typical song is a quick, rhythmic four-note *what-BOTH-ers-you!*

6 DUSKY PIGEON *Patagioenas goodsoni* 27cm/10.5in

0–1000m. Uncommon in humid lowland and foothill forest and edge in NW. Overlaps completely with Ruddy Pigeon, from which it can be distinguished in good light by gray head and breast; note small bill. In poor light, it is best to go by song. No overlap with Plumbeous Pigeon. Behavior similar to that of Plumbeous. Song is a quick *whah, whip-whip*, repeated every couple of seconds; very different from song of Ruddy Pigeon.

ROCK PIGEON AND DOVES

Rock Pigeon is a familiar cosmopolitan species of urban zones. *Zenaida* doves are medium-size arboreal and terrestrial inhabitants of open and wooded situations. *Leptotila* species are fairly large, stocky, and furtive forest- and woodland-based doves that forage mainly on or near the ground; all show white tail tips.

1 ROCK PIGEON *Columba livia* 33–36cm/13–14in

0–2800m. Introduced; this widespread, familiar, and highly gregarious urban pigeon inhabits many villages, towns, and cities almost throughout the country. While a "typical" individual is shown, plumage color and patterns are extremely variable. Despite this variety, large size and urban habitat preference make this species rather uncomplicated to ID. Often encountered in large numbers in plazas, city streets, gardens, and on rooftops, wherever human population has taken hold.

2 EARED DOVE *Zenaida auriculata* 26cm/10in

0–3500m. Common in most nonforest habitats in W, SW, and in the Andean highlands; abundant in Quito and more arid coastal areas. A plain-looking dove; note narrow black postocular and malar streaks, wings with distinctive black tertial spots, and graduated, broadly white-tipped tail. White-tipped Dove lacks black facial and wing markings and has a broader tail with white tips only on outer tail feathers. Eared Dove can be very common and conspicuous around towns and cities, but also along roadsides and in fields in more open country. Song is a soft *cooOOO, oo-oo-ooo*.

3 WEST PERUVIAN DOVE *Zenaida meloda* 29cm/11.5in

0–200m; locally to 700m. Locally fairly common in arid lowlands and foothills near W coast and in the far SW, where it inhabits desert scrub, dry woodland, and adjacent fields. No other Ecuadorian dove has conspicuous white wing patches; also note blue periocular skin. Generally encountered alone or in small flocks; forages on the ground but perches atop trees and bushes. Song is a soft, deep *gr, groo-dooDOO* or *who, hooDOOooh*, repeated every few seconds.

4 WHITE-TIPPED DOVE *Leptotila verreauxi* 28cm/11in

0–3000m. Fairly common and very widespread in light woodland, forest edge, and overgrown clearings nearly throughout W; avoids interior of dense forest. Separated from Pallid Dove by brown tinge to nape, and brown (not cinnamon) wings, rump, and tail. Also similar to Eared Dove, but has plain wings and face and a rounder tail with white only at the corners. White-tipped Dove is usually found alone or in pairs; walks on the ground, often under thick cover, but regularly ventures out into clearings and along roads in the early morning and afternoon. When flushed, flies up to a low branch, usually just in from forest edge; flies low to the ground. Song is a low, hollow *hu-oooOOOOOOOooo*; at a distance the first note is inaudible

5 PALLID DOVE *Leptotila pallida* 27cm/10.5in

0–1400m. Fairly common in humid and semi-humid forest and lighter woodland in the lowlands and foothills. Easily confused with White-tipped Dove; Pallid Dove has a distinct cinnamon tinge to wings, rump, and tail, and has a grayer head lacking brown on the nape. Behavior is also similar, but Pallid Dove is much less likely to venture into the open. Song is a simple, drawn-out *whooooo*, slightly higher and more resonant than that of White-tipped, and repeated every 10 sec. or so.

6 OCHRE-BELLIED DOVE *Leptotila ochraceiventris* 26cm/10in

0–1700m. Rare to locally uncommon inside semi-humid and deciduous forest in W and SW; apparently engages in seasonal movements, which are not understood. Rich ochraceous with purplish wash on crown, nape, and mantle; bright coloration should preclude confusion with other doves. Similar to other *Leptotila* in behavior, except it is especially shy and almost never ventures out of forest cover, making it even harder to see. Sometimes visits feeders at the Jorupe Reserve during the January–April rainy season. Song is a deep hoot that rises abruptly and then falls, e.g., *hWOOOooo*, repeated every few seconds.

QUAIL-DOVES AND GROUND-DOVES

Quail-doves are shy inhabitants of forest interior. They are mainly terrestrial, usually seen walking on the forest floor, feeding on fallen seeds and fruits, but may perch higher after being flushed or while singing. Ground-doves are small, short-tailed doves of more open country. They forage mainly on the ground, although most species readily perch in shrubs and trees, and at least some perch on wires. Most are sexually dimorphic.

1 OLIVE-BACKED QUAIL-DOVE *Leptotrygon veraguensis* 24cm/9.5in

0–300m. Rare inside primary and mature secondary humid forest in far NW. Very similar to Purple Quail-Dove, especially when looked down upon in the dark forest understory. Olive-backed Quail-Dove has gray to grayish-brown back, lacking rufous tones, is darker below, and lacks the coppery neck patch of Purple Quail-Dove. Olive-backed is generally encountered alone, walking quietly on the forest floor; may favor the vicinity of streams; shy and easily flushed but tends not to fly far and may perch in view on a low branch. Song is a short, explosive, croaking *Grroo* or *woo*, repeated every few seconds.

2 PURPLE QUAIL-DOVE *Geotrygon purpurata* 24cm/9.5in

0–1100m. Uncommon inside humid lowland and foothill forest in NW. Colorful and stunning when seen well but easily mistaken for Olive-backed Quail-Dove if seen poorly, especially if the bird is walking away from the observer. Purple Quail-Dove has mostly white underparts, rufous wings, and coppery patches on the sides of the neck. Behavior is similar to that of Olive-backed. Song is a very soft *WOOoo*, higher pitched than songs of other quail-doves, and sometimes with a slightly buzzy quality. Formerly called **Indigo-crowned Quail-Dove**.

3 WHITE-THROATED QUAIL-DOVE *Zentrygon frenata* 32cm/12.5in

800–3200m. Fairly common inside humid forest from the foothills to the temperate zone. Large size and white throat bordered by conspicuous black scaling is usually distinctive. If seen poorly, might be confused with Ruddy Quail-Dove, which also has a white throat but is redder, lacks black scaling on the neck and breast, and has a brown malar clearly bordered with white. White-throated is like other quail-doves in behavior, though it tends to be less shy, walking calmly away when approached and occasionally venturing out of forest cover to adjacent clearings or roadsides; sometimes even visits feeders. Song is a repeated, very low-pitched *WOOOoo*.

4 RUDDY QUAIL-DOVE *Geotrygon montana* 23cm/9in

0–1700m. Fairly common inside humid lowland and foothill forest, locally occurring up into the subtropics. If seen well, rufous plumage and distinctive facial pattern, with brown malar bordered above by a white line, should rule out all other species. Behavior is like that of other quail-doves, though Ruddy is especially shy and hard to approach. Song is a repetitive, deep, hollow *WHOOOoo* that descends ever so slightly.

5 COMMON GROUND-DOVE *Columbina passerina* 16cm/6.5in

1300–3000m. Locally fairly common in arid scrub and agricultural land in dry inter-Andean valleys. The only ground-dove in most of its range; scaly breast and conspicuous rufous patches in primaries (usually seen only in flight) are diagnostic. Croaking Ground-Dove (p. 130), which may overlap N of Quito, has a distinctive black and yellow bill and black primaries. Common Ground-Dove is encountered in pairs or small groups that forage on the ground, often hidden in scrubby vegetation, though sometimes in the open along quiet roadsides or in fields; most often seen in fast, low flight, when rufous flight feathers flash distinctively. Song is a slow-paced series of rising *whooo?* or *pyooo?* notes.

6 PLAIN-BREASTED GROUND-DOVE *Columbina minuta* 15cm/6in

0–500m. Uncommon, local, but possibly spreading in humid and semi-humid lowlands, where it prefers open habitats such as rice paddies and pastures. Small and very plain; male shows a faint violet tinge to breast, and may show a slightly contrasting crown and nape in fresh plumage. Female (not shown) is dull and browner, lacking any strong markings. Both sexes show conspicuous rufous in primaries (obvious only in flight). Easily confused with the more common Ecuadorian Ground-Dove (p. 130); that species shows more extensive and bolder black wing markings, and black primaries. Plain-breasted Ground-Dove is usually encountered alone, in pairs, or in small flocks, foraging on the ground in the open. It sometimes mixes with Ecuadorian or Croaking Ground-Doves. Song is a fast-paced, steady series of short *hoop?* notes.

GROUND-DOVES

1 ECUADORIAN GROUND-DOVE *Columbina buckleyi* 18cm/7in

0–2000m. Fairly common in a wide variety of open and lightly wooded habitats, and in parks in humid and semi-humid regions. Most likely confused with Plain-breasted Ground-Dove (p. 128), but Ecuadorian shows bolder and more extensive black markings on wings and black primaries (usually visible only in flight). Distinguished from Croaking Ground-Dove by the all-dark bill lacking yellow base. Usually found in pairs or small flocks feeding on the ground, often in the middle of a quiet dirt road, and flushing to a low perch when approached. Song is a leisurely series of *woo* or *puwoo* notes.

2 CROAKING GROUND-DOVE *Columbina cruziana* 17cm/6.5in

0–2500m. Common in open habitats, scrub, and agricultural settings in more arid zones. Mostly found at lower elevations in W and SW, but ranges higher in inter-Andean valleys in S; recently also found in dry valleys N of Quito. Bicolor yellow and black bill is diagnostic. Female is shown; male is very similar but grayer. Behavior is similar to that of Ecuadorian Ground-Dove (the two species locally occur together). Distinctive song is a weird, frog-like croak, repeated every few seconds.

3 BLUE GROUND-DOVE *Claravis pretiosa* 21cm/8.5in

0–1000m. Uncommon to locally fairly common, and somewhat nomadic, in deciduous and humid forest and edge. Markedly sexually dimorphic; handsome blue-gray male unlikely to be confused with any other species. Female is distinguished from other ground-doves by rufous wing markings and cinnamon rump and tail (often conspicuous in flight). Female Maroon-chested Ground-Dove (little range overlap) is very similar, but note buffy throat and face, darker wing markings, and white tail corners. Blue Ground-Dove is found in pairs or small flocks, and usually stays inside the forest, occasionally venturing out to edge, clearings, or quiet roadsides to feed on the ground. Regularly seen in rapid, low flight. Song is a distinctive and far-carrying *boop*, repeated every few seconds.

4 MAROON-CHESTED GROUND-DOVE *Claravis mondetoura* 22cm/8.5in

500–3500m. Very rare and highly nomadic in humid and semi-humid montane forest; apparently wanders widely in search of seeding *Chusquea* bamboo. Male is similar to male Blue Ground-Dove (the two species may occur together in the SW foothills around Jorupe), but has an obvious maroon chest and should not be mistaken if seen well. Female Maroon-chested differs from very similar female Blue Ground-Dove by its buffy throat and face, darker wing markings, and white tail corners. Maroon-chested Ground-Dove is rarely seen and is very inconspicuous, usually remaining inside dense cover, only rarely coming to feed at the edge of a forest-lined clearing or road, usually in the vicinity of *Chusquea* bamboo. Song is an evenly spaced series of deep, two-syllable *pu'WOOO* notes. At a distance, the first syllable will not be audible.

Parakeets are small to medium-size parrots with pointed, often long tails. Most species are noisy and gregarious.

1 RED-MASKED PARAKEET *Psittacara erythrogenys* 34cm/13.5in

0–2200m. Fairly common in deciduous and semi-humid forest, lighter woodland, and adjacent scrubby clearings and fields; range is expanding northward into more humid areas of NW. Large size, long tail, and red face are enough to ID Red-masked Parakeet in most of its range, but it overlaps with the rare Scarlet-fronted Parakeet; see that species for distinguishing details. Immature Red-masked (not shown) has reduced red on face. Usually encountered in flocks containing from a few birds to 50 or more. Calls include a rather low, nasal *kenh-kenh-kenh...*, or a series of higher, more musical *Screeh-screeh-screeh...* calls with lower-pitched grunts mixed in.

2 SCARLET-FRONTED PARAKEET *Psittacara wagleri* 39cm/15.5in

1000–2500m. Rare and poorly known in montane forest and scrub in SW, perhaps favoring acacia-dominated habitats. Extremely similar to the far more common Red-masked Parakeet, but red is restricted to forecrown and does not descend below eye. However, immature Red-masked has reduced red and can look nearly identical to Scarlet-fronted. Positive ID can come from seeing several birds well, with no Red-masked Parakeets present. Calls are very similar to those of Red-masked, but tend to be slightly higher pitched and less guttural or nasal.

3 MAROON-TAILED PARAKEET *Pyrrhura melanura* 24cm/9.5in

0–1700m. Fairly common in humid forest, edge, and adjacent clearings from the lowlands to the subtropics. Slender and long-tailed. The only parakeet in most of its range; overlaps very locally with Red-masked Parakeet, which is larger, has red mask, and lacks breast scaling. Small, noisy groups of usually 6 to 12, occasionally more, are most often encountered flying swiftly through forest canopy or low over roads or clearings. Flocks forage quietly on fruit and seeds on leafy branches in the subcanopy, where they can blend in quite well and be hard to spot; often confiding, allowing fairly close approach. Typical call, usually given in flight, is a series of shrill, grating *chrreeet!* notes. Birds in W Ecuador and SW Colombia are sometimes split as **Chocó Parakeet** (*P. pacifica*).

4 EL ORO PARAKEET *Pyrrhura orcesi* 23cm/9in

600–1200m. Known from only a few humid foothill forest sites in SW; nearly all sightings come from the Buenaventura Reserve. In its tiny range, confusion is possible only with Red-masked Parakeet, which is larger, has more red on the head (but beware immature birds), and lacks the faint scaling on breast and neck. Behavior and voice are similar to those of Maroon-tailed Parakeet.

5 GRAY-CHEEKED PARAKEET *Brotogeris pyrrhoptera* 20cm/8in

0–1000m. A small, short-tailed parakeet of deciduous and semi-humid forest, edge, and wooded clearings in lowlands and foothills; also found sparingly in some urban parks and gardens. Gray cheeks and throat distinguish it from all other parakeets and parrotlets (p. 134). Generally encountered in pairs or small groups; usually favors forest and woodland canopy or subcanopy, but may descend lower at edge; feeds primarily on seeds and flowers; flight is undulating. Calls include scratchy, fairly high-pitched *chweet* and *chrirt* notes interspersed with gravelly churrs.

6 WHITE-WINGED PARAKEET *Brotogerus versicolurus* 22cm/8.5in

0–100m. Introduced; a population has become established in and around the city of Guayaquil, where large flocks can be found in some city parks and suburban neighborhoods. Consequences of this invasion could be dire for the native Gray-cheeked Parakeet, due to competition and possible interbreeding; both species have been seen together at Cerro Blanco Protected Forest W of the city. Extensive yellow and white wing patch immediately separates White-winged Parakeet from Gray-cheeked. Voice is similar to that of Gray-cheeked.

PARROTLETS AND HIGHLAND PSITTACIDS

An assortment of small to medium-size psittacids (members of the family Psittacidae, which includes all parrots, macaws, parakeets, and parrotlets). Only Pacific Parrotlet is common; the others are scarcer and rarely encountered. *Note:* **Yellow-eared Parrot** (*Ognorhynchus icterotis*) is widely regarded as extirpated in Ecuador and thus is not treated in this book; however, there are rumors that it may persist in remote areas of the NW Andes. If seen, large size and yellow face and forehead will render it unmistakable; it is highly tied to wax palms (*Ceroxylon* spp.).

1 PACIFIC PARROTLET *Forpus coelestis* 13cm/5in

0–1600m. Common in a wide variety of lightly wooded and scrub habitats, even city parks, at lower to mid elevations. The only small, all-green parrot in our range. Gray-cheeked Parakeet has a distinctive gray face, longer graduated tail, and orange in wing. Pacific Parrotlet occurs in noisy pairs, sometimes large flocks; feeds from mid to upper levels in fruiting trees, and often perches in the open, even on wires and antennas; occasionally descends to the ground to feed. Flight is fast, with a bounding motion. Call is a sharp, high-pitched and crackling *chrrittt*, sometimes in a series, *chrrrttt, chrrritt, chrrrritt....*

2 BLUE-FRONTED PARROTLET *Touit dilectissimus* 17cm/6.5in

400–2300m. Uncommon in humid foothill and subtropical forest, edge, and adjacent clearings. Small and chunky; combination of small size, red facial patch, and yellow throat is diagnostic; male also shows a conspicuous red wing patch. Encountered in pairs or small groups, usually inconspicuous inside forest canopy. Rarely seen perched, and usually spotted in low, noisy, fast, twisting flight. Pairs nest in a cavity dug into a termite nest. Typical flight call is an odd, metallic *twee*, given once, twice, or in a series.

3 GOLDEN-PLUMED PARAKEET *Leptosittaca branickii* 35–38cm/14–15in

2400–3400m. Rare and local in humid temperate forest; mainly an E slope species, but spills over locally W of the divide at various locations. The only large, long-tailed parakeet in its range and habitat. The golden face plumes may not be obvious at a distance. Usually found in medium-size flocks, often perching on exposed limbs and treetops where it clambers about acrobatically as it feeds. Calls are shrill, harsh, and possess a metallic quality.

4 RED-FACED PARROT *Hapalopsittaca pyrrhops* 21–23cm/8.5–9in

2700–3500m. Rare and local in humid temperate forest; mainly an E slope species, but occurs locally W of the divide. No other highland parrot has a red face; also note red wing coverts and short tail. Very inconspicuous, usually encountered in pairs or small flocks flying over forest, then disappearing into canopy, where it is difficult to locate. Calls are usually metallic and squeaky, e.g., *kwEEP*; a lower *coo*, *CUH-CUCK* is also given.

5 BARRED PARAKEET *Bolborhynchus lineola* 18cm/7in

1100–3600m. An unpredictable and somewhat nomadic species of montane forest; usually seen only as high-flying specks. Only the luckiest birder ever sees this species perched; the small size and black barring should make it easy to ID. The photo of the perched bird is of a captive individual and has been digitally manipulated to give it a more natural background. In flight, note short, graduated tail and voice. Usually noted when noisy bands are heard and then glimpsed as they cross the sky high overhead. This species may be nomadic based on seeding cycles of *Chusquea* bamboo, though it does not feed exclusively on it. Flight calls are shrill, though sweet in quality, e.g., *shoowee* or *chrweee* notes.

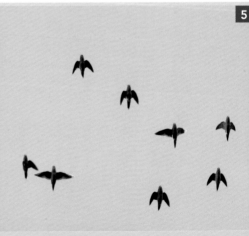

Rose-faced Parrot is small, compact, and somewhat inconspicuous in humid lowland and foothill forest canopy. *Pionus* are medium-size, rather compact parrots with a red crissum that contrasts with the body plumage. They range in pairs, small groups, or fairly large flocks, and often perch on exposed branches and snags in forest canopy and edge; flight is strong, steady, and distinctive: wings drop very deeply on the downward swing, but come up only to body level on the upswing. Flight calls can be useful for ID; like most parrots, these can make a wide variety of other sounds that are not described here.

1 ROSE-FACED PARROT *Pyrilia pulchra* 21–23cm/8.5–9in

0–1500m. Uncommon in humid lowland and foothill forest and edge, mostly in the NW but also occurs locally as far S as Buenaventura Reserve. A small, chunky, and square-tailed parrot with a unique rose-colored face; no other similar species occurs in range. Inconspicuous and most often seen in rapid flight through forest canopy or clearings. Usually encountered in pairs or small flocks; which perch in the open rarely at forest edge or in clearings, but most often remain undetected as they forage methodically in the forest canopy. Typical flight calls are high-pitched, grating screeches.

2 BLUE-HEADED PARROT *Pionus menstruus* 27–29cm/10.5–11.5in

0–1100m. Fairly common in humid forest, edge, and clearings in the lowlands and foothills. No other W Ecuador parrot is green with a blue head; note black cheek patch and mostly black bill with red base. Red-billed Parrot of higher elevations is vaguely similar but has much reduced blue on the head and an all-red bill. Blue-headed Parrot's flight calls are distinctive, up-slurred screeches, e.g., *chrrEET!, chrrEET!…*, and are often accompanied by other grating churrs.

3 RED-BILLED PARROT *Pionus sordidus* 27–29cm/10.5–11.5in

1200–2400m. Fairly common in humid forest, edge, and clearings, mainly in the subtropics, but locally down into the foothills. Mostly green with blue on the breast and crown, and a red bill. Blue-headed Parrot is a lower-elevation species and has a mostly black bill, extensive blue head, and black cheek patch. Red-billed is very noisy, especially in flight, when birds emit a cacophony of screeches intermixed with lower, more guttural calls.

4 WHITE-CAPPED PARROT *Pionus seniloides* 28–30cm/11–12in

1500–3600m. Uncommon in humid subtropical and temperate forest, edge, and clearings. Conspicuous white forecrown and white-speckled face instantly ID this species; otherwise it is mostly green, with violet breast, neck, and hind-crown, and an ivory-colored bill. Flies with somewhat shallower wing strokes than other *Pionus*. Flight calls are somewhat similar to those of Red-billed Parrot, but the screeches are more querulous, and White-capped does not give the lower, guttural calls. Sometimes lumped with Plum-crowned Parrot (*P. tumultuosus*; not found in Ecuador) and then called **Speckle-faced Parrot**.

5 BRONZE-WINGED PARROT *Pionus chalcopterus* 28cm/11in

0–1500m. This uniquely colored parrot is fairly common in humid lowland and foothill forest, edge, and clearings. Dark blue plumage is unique in range, but it often appears black in poor light or at great distances; under such conditions, the pinkish breast often stands out as a pale patch against the otherwise dark bird. Noisy bands exuberantly emit crackling screeches and down-slurred jeers, e.g., *DJEE!-DJEER-DJEER-djeer.*

AMAZONS AND MACAWS

These long-lived parrots mate for life and thus are usually found in pairs even when in flocks. Amazons are large, stocky, square-tailed, and mostly green parrots that fly with distinctive shallow wingbeats and show a conspicuous red wing speculum in flight. Macaws are large to huge and have long, pointed tails, bare facial skin, and raucous calls.

1 RED-LORED AMAZON *Amazona autumnalis* 31–35cm/12–14in

0–700m. Uncommon and local in both humid and deciduous lowland forest, edge, light woodland, and mangroves. Red forehead and lores along with pale yellow-green cheeks and lavender crown distinguish this species from the larger and more widespread Mealy Amazon. The subspecies *lilacina* (sometimes split as **Lilacine Amazon**) is endemic to our region and has a red superciliary; subspecies *salvini*, which may reach extreme NW Ecuador, lacks the superciliary. Red-lored Amazon is found in pairs or small flocks, and is more likely to be seen early in the morning or late in the afternoon as it flies between its feeding and roosting grounds. Very vocal; birds give a large variety of screeches, barks, and yodels.

2 MEALY AMAZON *Amazona farinosa* 38–41cm/15–16in

0–900m. Uncommon to locally fairly common in humid forest, edge, and adjacent wooded clearings in the lowlands and foothills. Large, chunky, and mostly pale green, with a whitish frosting on upperparts and a white eye-ring. Red speculum in wing usually visible only in flight. Distinguished from smaller Red-lored Amazon by plain face and whitish wash on upperparts; not always separable if seen in flight at a great distance. Behavior and vocalizations similar to those of Red-lored.

3 SCALY-NAPED AMAZON *Amazona mercenarius* 31–33cm/12–13in

1200–3300m. Uncommon in subtropical and temperate forest and edge. Mostly uniform green; red patches in wing and tail and yellow tail tip hard to see even in flight. Found at higher elevations than other amazons, so confusion possible only with *Pionus* parrots (p. 136); along with plumage differences, flight pattern is noticeably different: Scaly-naped Amazon flies in pairs with very shallow wingbeats, while *Pionus*, less likely to pair up, fly with very deep, downward wing strokes. Scaly-naped Amazon is usually seen flying very high in pairs (or paired groups) over montane forest; tends to remain under cover when perched. Calls include a variety of barks, squawks, and yodels; a tripled *kow-kow-kow* is perhaps given most often.

4 GREAT GREEN MACAW *Ara ambiguus* 76–84cm/30–33in

0–800m. This huge parrot is now rare and local; found mainly in humid lowland forest in far NW, with an isolated population in deciduous forest at Cerro Blanco Protected Forest W of Guayaquil. In flight, underwing and tail appear yellowish. Confusion possible only with Chestnut-fronted Macaw, which is much smaller, with a whiter face and maroon rather than bright red on forehead, and shows reddish underwing and tail when in flight. Great Green Macaw is usually seen in pairs, occasionally escorting a single offspring, or in paired groups of up to 10 birds. Deep, raucous calls are unique in its range.

5 CHESTNUT-FRONTED MACAW *Ara severus* 43–46cm/17–18in

0–600m. Uncommon in humid lowland forest, edge, and clearings; now quite local due to deforestation. Distinguished from the rare Great Green Macaw by much smaller size, whiter facial skin, and maroon forehead. In flight from below, Chestnut-fronted Macaw shows reddish, not yellow, underwing and tail. Behavior similar to that of Great Green Macaw. Calls are harsh, grating screeches, much higher pitched than those of Great Green.

lilacina 1

lilacina 1

salvini 1

2

2

3

4

CUCKOOS

Medium-size to large birds with long, graduated tails. Color of bill, eye-ring, and underparts is often useful for ID. Most species are shy and tend to remain hidden in dense vegetation.

1 SQUIRREL CUCKOO *Piaya cayana* 41–46cm/16–18in

0–2500m. Fairly common in most wooded habitats from lowlands through the subtropics. The largest arboreal cuckoo, with an ostentatiously long tail. Size alone is usually enough to ID it, but see Little Cuckoo, which is notably smaller and has a red (not yellow) eye-ring. Squirrel Cuckoo is typically found alone or in pairs; often seen scurrying over branches and through canopy vegetation, but may perch and peer out through leaves from time to time; occasionally glides conspicuously across a clearing with its spectacular graduated tail flared out. Vocalizations include a characteristic, sharp *Whik, weeyr!*, a dry, descending cackle, and a long, raptor-like series of evenly spaced *wheep* notes.

2 LITTLE CUCKOO *Coccycua minuta* 25cm/10in

0–1600m. A small, furtive cuckoo of forest edge and dense thickets, often near water; found mainly in the lowlands and foothills, rarely to the subtropics. A miniature version of the widespread Squirrel Cuckoo, with which it can easily be confused. Note Little Cuckoo's small size, shorter tail, more rufous underparts, and red (not yellow) eye-ring. Little Cuckoo is encountered alone or in pairs, most often skulking about in low, dense vegetation, and usually hard to see. Occasionally one will climb higher into trees, especially in response to playback. Most common vocalizations are a croon followed by a chuckle, *croooooh, cu-cucucucuccu*, and a scratchy *djit!*, which is sometimes followed by a *djeer*.

3 GRAY-CAPPED CUCKOO *Coccyzus lansbergi* 27cm/10.5in

0–1300m. Breeds in dense deciduous scrub and woodland in lowlands and foothills; postbreeding movements not well understood, but some years this species can turn up just about anywhere at lower elevations of W Ecuador. Rich chestnut plumage, with gray crown and coral bill; unlike any other cuckoo. Encountered alone, or in pairs when breeding, typically skulking in dense undergrowth and probably often overlooked. Song a rapid, guttural *coh-coh-coh-coh-coh-coh-cohcoh*; a strange, buzzy *drrruuuhh* note is sometimes given.

4 PEARLY-BREASTED CUCKOO *Coccyzus euleri* 26cm/10in

0–1300m. A rare and little-known bird in Ecuador; recorded from humid lowland and foothill forest, edge, and clearings in NW; records in Ecuador are mainly between March and September, suggesting it may be an austral migrant, but there is circumstantial evidence that it may actually breed here. No other cuckoo has pure white underparts, yellow lower mandible, and lacks rufous in wings. Stays in dense canopy vegetation, where inconspicuous and difficult to see well, perhaps overlooked. Vocalizations include a series of guttural *Gyowh* notes and a series of quick rattles. *Note:* **Yellow-billed Cuckoo** (*C. americanus*; not shown) is a vagrant to W Ecuador with few recent records. It is nearly identical to Pearly-breasted Cuckoo, but has contrasting rufous primaries.

5 BLACK-BILLED CUCKOO *Coccyzus erythropthalmus* 28cm/11in

0–1200m; occasionally to 2800m. A rare boreal migrant to a variety of wooded habitats; mainly occurs in the lowlands and foothills, but occasionally seen as high as Quito. Mostly encountered during northward passage in March–April, with occasional sightings from October to February. Dark bill and mostly white underparts separate it from other cuckoos. Eye-ring is usually red, but can be gray or yellowish in some birds. While Black-billed Cuckoo can show a buffy tinge on throat, it never shows the extensive buff found on underparts of Dark-billed Cuckoo. Black-billed is usually solitary; rarely encountered in small, loose groups. Skulks about silently in dense vegetation at varying heights.

6 DARK-BILLED CUCKOO *Coccyzus melacoryphus* 27cm/10.5in

0–1400m; occasionally to 2800m. Rare to uncommon in dense forest edge and overgrown clearings mainly in the lowlands and foothills; locally higher; appears to be seasonal and/or erratic in many areas. Black bill, buffy underparts, and blackish mask distinguish this species from other similar cuckoos. Solitary and retiring, often very hard to see as it moves inconspicuously in dense, low vegetation. Very quiet; song (rarely heard in Ecuador) is a soft, descending *drow-drow-drow-drow-drow*.

Anis are black cuckoos of open country with long, rounded tails and distinctive bills. Striped Cuckoo possesses an expressive crest and distinctive vocalizations. Banded Ground-Cuckoo, perhaps the most sought-after of all Chocó endemics, is very rare and frustratingly hard to find.

1 SMOOTH-BILLED ANI *Crotophaga ani* 35cm/14in

0–1700m. Common and widespread in humid lowlands and foothills; inhabits clearings, roadsides, agricultural areas, pastures, scrub, and can even be found in cities and towns. Very similar to Groove-billed Ani; not always easy to tell the two apart. Groove-billed prefers drier habitats, but there is significant overlap. Smooth-billed lacks grooves on the bill and usually has a more arched culmen; however, bill size and shape vary greatly among individuals, and the presence of bill grooves can be indiscernible except at close range. Smooth-billed tends to hang about lethargically in loose groups, congregating conspicuously on shrubs, fences, low tree branches, and wires, with tail hanging; groups often fly in single file, with awkward, stiff flight consisting of a few flaps and short glides; tail is usually flicked up upon alighting. Call is a shrill and up-slurred squeak, e.g., *wooo-EEEEK!*

2 GROOVE-BILLED ANI *Crotophaga sulcirostris* 32cm/12.5in

0–2500m. Common and widespread in drier parts of W and SW, but also expanding northward into more humid areas of NW. Found in all types of open habitats including fields, pastures, roadsides, and scrub, and also often around cities and towns. Prefers drier areas than Smooth-billed Ani, but the two occur together in a number of areas. Groove-billed usually has a smaller, grooved bill with a less arched culmen, but there is much individual variation in bill shape. Especially in the NW, where Groove-billed is rare, ID should be based on seeing the grooves in the bill or by voice. Behavior similar to that of Smooth-billed Ani. Typical call is shorter and weaker than Smooth-billed's, and often preceded by a sharp *pit*; e.g., *pit-week!*

3 GREATER ANI *Crotophaga major* 47cm/18.5in

0–300m; occasionally higher. Rare and very local in the lowlands of W Ecuador, especially around wooded streams and lake margins. Tends to wander and can turn up in very unexpected locations. Size, huge bill, yellow irides, and greenish-purple iridescent sheen sets this species apart from the other anis. Great-tailed Grackle (p. 362) looks vaguely similar but has a totally different bill shape. Greater Ani is almost always found near water, often in large, noisy groups that clamber through dense vegetation. Vocalizations are hard to describe; often consist of a raucous jumble of clucks and grunts given collectively by an entire flock, followed by a very long, guttural growl given by several birds perched beak to beak, seemingly staring at each other.

4 STRIPED CUCKOO *Tapera naevia* 29cm/11.5in

0–1500m; locally higher in SW. Fairly common in scrub, overgrown clearings, and forest edge at lower elevations. Note expressive crest, facial pattern, and dark brown streaking on upperparts; no similar species in its range. Immature (not shown) is similar but duller overall. Solitary, usually remains in dense cover, but occasionally one perches in the open atop a shrub, post, wire, etc., where it will often slowly raise and lower its crest and flare out its alula (a small, thumb-like feather group near the bend of the wing). Occasionally, individuals or even small groups are encountered dust-bathing on little-traveled tracks. Most common call is a ventriloquial, two-note whistle, with the second note a half-step higher. Song is a series of querulous whistles, e.g., *fuh?-fuh?-fuh?-fuh-uh.*

5 BANDED GROUND-CUCKOO *Neomorphus radiolosus* 48cm/19in

0–1200m. This magnificent jungle "roadrunner" is very rare inside humid lowland and foothill forest in the NW. Usually only the luckiest of birders ever have a chance to see this amazing creature, but since 2012, two or three birds have occasionally visited Un Poco del Chocó Nature Reserve (NE of Milpe Bird Sanctuary); it remains to be seen whether these birds will continue to delight visitors. ID is easy enough, assuming the bird is seen well. Banded Ground-Cuckoo is most often found around large swarms of army ants, where it can be surprisingly difficult to see as it maneuvers deftly through dark undergrowth, snapping up insects, lizards, snakes, and anything else that is scared off by the marauding ants; it may occasionally perch on low open branches in the understory, especially when singing its long, rising, and low-pitched *booooooooooooo...* song; it also produces loud bill snaps around ant swarms.

Owls are familiar birds of prey found nearly worldwide; most are nocturnal. They belong to two different families, the barn owls (Tytonidae), and the "typical" owls (Strigidae). Only one barn owl species occurs in the Americas.

1 BARN OWL *Tyto alba* 38cm/15in

0–4000m. Widespread but uncommon in open areas, especially around human habitation. No other Ecuadorian owl has white underparts; also note heart-shaped outline to face and lack of ear tufts. Striped Owl (p. 146) has bold dark streaking on underparts and has ear tufts. Nocturnal; usually encountered alone, except near active nests, often perched in the open on posts and wires; usually roosts and nests in abandoned buildings, barns, and caves. Hunts by flying very low over fields and other open ground, searching for small rodents. Call is a harsh, hissing burst of pure noise.

2 GREAT HORNED OWL *Bubo virginianus* 48–56cm/19–22in

3200–4500m. A robust owl with prominent ear tufts; scarce at high elevations, where it prefers wooded páramo edge and *Polylepis* groves. Female is significantly larger than male. Very large size, prominent ear tufts, and coarse underpart barring are diagnostic. Great Horned Owl is usually encountered alone, and although it is nocturnal, the open nature of its preferred habitat means it can often be spotted by day, roosting inconspicuously, occasionally facing harassment by smaller birds. Usual song is a very deep, muffled *who,WHOO-who*; a louder, hoarser, and higher-pitched version is also given.

3 SHORT-EARED OWL *Asio flammeus* 38cm/15in

3000–4000m. Uncommon and local in open country and páramo throughout much of the highlands. Round head lacking obvious ear tufts and diurnal habits are the best ID features, though also note yellow irides and, in flight, dark carpal patch and pale base of primaries. Any large owl seen actively hunting during the day is likely to be Short-eared. Other large highland owls are nocturnal and have obvious ear tufts. Mottled Owl (p. 146) is similar but the two species do not occur together. Short-eared Owl flies over open terrain with characteristic buoyant flight, seeming somewhat hawk- or harrier-like; most often encountered at dawn, dusk, and on dark, cloudy days, perching low, often on the ground, a fence post, or at a roadcut. Rarely vocalizes, though may emit a harsh scream or grunt.

4 STYGIAN OWL *Asio stygius* 42cm/16.5in

1700–3100m. This dark, long-eared owl is rare and local in semi-humid forest, light woodland, and urban parks in the highlands; known only from scattered locations, though likely more widespread and simply overlooked. Large size, very dark plumage heavily marked tawny on belly, and distinctive ear tufts should ID this owl within its range and habitat. Mottled Owl (p. 146) shows distinct streaks on lower underparts. Stygian Owl is generally encountered alone, tending to stay under fairly thick cover, though will emerge to an open perch in response to playback. Most common call is a short (½ sec.), high-pitched screech, though it also gives a deeper, more owl-like *WOOO*.

5 SPECTACLED OWL *Pulsatrix perspicillata* 46cm/18in

0–1200m. A large, boldly patterned owl, widespread but uncommon in both humid and deciduous lowland and foothill forest. Easily recognized by its bold facial pattern and dark breast band. Immature is mostly white with contrasting blackish mask; gradually attains adult plumage. Spectacled Owl is nocturnal, though it is not unusual to accidentally flush one from a day roost. Encountered alone, occasionally in pairs; may respond aggressively to playback, perching boldly in the open, unintimidated by human presence. Song is a muffled *BUHBUHBUHBUH*, like the sound of sheet metal flexing back and forth, and often given as a duet by a pair (female pitch slightly higher); also gives a querulous scream.

LARGE OWLS AND BURROWING OWL

Strix owls in the neotropics are sometimes placed in the genus *Ciccaba*.

1 CRESTED OWL *Lophostrix cristata* 41cm/16in

0–1100m. Uncommon in humid and semi-humid forest in lowlands and foothills. Large, with diagnostic long, white facial tufts. These tufts are sometimes laid back but always appear as a distinct white V over the eyes. Juvenile is mostly white, with rusty mask, brown wings, and white facial tufts. Crested Owl is usually encountered alone or in pairs in subcanopy, where it feeds mainly on large insects. Roosts by day under dense, low cover inside forest. Song is a short, throaty *grow!*

2 MOTTLED OWL *Strix virgata* 33cm/13in

0–2000m. Uncommon in humid forest, edge, and adjacent wooded clearings from lowlands to subtropics. Identified by combination of unmarked brown breast and bold, brown streaks on lower underparts. Rufous-banded Owl, despite its name, is much more mottled below and lacks streaking. Mottled Owl usually stays quite high in forest canopy, but occasionally comes to forest edge or into isolated trees in clearings. Song is a series of four to eight evenly spaced, somewhat muffled hoots; also emits a rising, whining cry that may fall in pitch toward the end.

3 RUFOUS-BANDED OWL *Strix albitarsis* 36cm/14in

1900–3600m. Uncommon in subtropical and temperate forest, edge, and wooded clearings. Heavily mottled, with indistinct breast band and tawny facial disk. Mottled Owl has distinct black underpart streaks, uniform dark breast, and brown facial disk. Rufous banded's behavior is similar to that of Mottled Owl. Its typical song is a gruff, throaty *who-who-who-who-who-who,WHOO!*; also gives a variety of one to three clear, more resonant *hoo!* notes as well as other hoarser, low hoots.

4 BLACK-AND-WHITE OWL *Strix nigrolineata* 38cm/15in

0–2300m. Uncommon in humid forest, edge, and clearings in the lowlands and foothills; found very locally in the subtropics. No other owl in our range has black-and-white-barred underparts; also note black mask and yellow bill. Black-and-white Owl tends to perch, in singles or pairs, on exposed limbs in subcanopy, sometimes lower at edge. It is sometimes found near streetlights, preying on the insects they attract. Typical song is a rising *hu-hu-hu-hu,WOO!*; also gives a low *huWOH!* note, either alone or in a short series, as well as a rising and falling scream.

5 STRIPED OWL *Pseudoscops clamator* 36cm/14in

0–700m. Uncommon in open, lightly wooded habitats and agricultural areas, even near human habitations; not a forest bird. Combination of white face conspicuously bordered with black, and black-and-white-striped underparts is diagnostic. Sits conspicuously on exposed branch, wire, post, or other perch; also may occasionally hang around streetlights along quiet roads. Roosts low by day, even on the ground, in dense vegetation; hunts both on the wing in low flight or by pouncing on its prey from a perch. Common call is a piercing, down-slurred *EEEeeear*; also gives harsh screeches and low hoots.

6 BURROWING OWL *Athene cunicularia* 23cm/9in

0–3200m. A small, partially diurnal, and terrestrial owl of open, arid terrain in W and SW lowlands as well as arid valleys in the highlands. Distinctly spotted; has yellow irides and long legs. No other Ecuadorian owl has such extensively spotted plumage or is remotely similar in habitat or behavior. Frequently seen during the day perched adjacent to nest burrow, on the ground, or on a low post or other low perch. When disturbed, individuals may bob up and down or twist head sideways. Typical song is a very harsh, rasping *djerrrr, djit-djit-djit-djit-djit*.

ad. **1**

ad. (left), juv. (right) **1**

2

3

4

5

6

PYGMY-OWLS

Small, similarly patterned, and primarily diurnal owls with rounded heads and false eyespots on their napes. Location, elevation, and voice are more useful for ID than plumage; most species cannot be separated in the field by sight alone. The songs of some species can attract mobs of angry small birds that incessantly harass them. Birders who use playback or a whistled imitation may elicit the same behavior (or even attract a pygmy-owl).

1 PACIFIC PYGMY-OWL *Glaucidium peruanum* 16cm/6.5in

0–2400m. W Ecuador's most common and conspicuous pygmy-owl; found in virtually any wooded habitat, and even in urban areas, in W and SW; also spreading northward into more humid zones (e.g., Tinalandia Nature Reserve and Río Palenque Science Center). Brown and grayish-brown birds are shown, but rufous morphs also occur. May overlap locally with Andean Pygmy-Owl in the SW highlands; the two species usually can be distinguished only by voice. Pacific Pygmy-Owl is generally encountered alone or in pairs at almost any forest level, and also readily perches on wires, antennas, and even buildings. Often responds aggressively to whistled imitations or playback, and regularly attracts a mobbing horde of passerines and other smaller birds. Song is a rapid series (too fast for most people to easily imitate) of liquid notes, e.g., *whip'whip'whip'whip'whip'whip'whip'whip…*, sometimes interspersed with a few screeched whinnies. Also called **Peruvian Pygmy-Owl**.

2 CLOUD-FOREST PYGMY-OWL *Glaucidium nubicola* 15cm/6in

1100–2000m. Uncommon in humid foothill and subtropical forest and edge in the NW. Occurs mainly at lower elevations than Andean Pygmy-Owl, but there may be a very narrow zone of overlap at around 2000m elevation. In these areas, the two species can be reliably separated only by voice (behavior is similar). Cloud-forest Pygmy-Owl's song is a very long, simple series of toots, usually but not always given in couplets, e.g., *woop-woop, woop-woop, woop-woop…*; a proficient whistler can easily imitate it.

3 CENTRAL AMERICAN PYGMY-OWL *Glaucidium griseiceps* 14cm/5.5in

0–400m. Rare in humid forest in the lowlands of the extreme NW. No other pygmy-owl is currently known to occur with Central American Pygmy-Owl, though in the future Pacific Pygmy-Owl could potentially expand into its range. A rufous morph is shown, but grayish-brown plumage is much more common. This pygmy-owl is more scarce and less vocal than most, meaning it is less likely to attract mobbing birds. Song is an evenly spaced series of 3 to 12 soft, hollow *woot* notes.

4 ANDEAN PYGMY-OWL *Glaucidium jardinii* 15cm/6in

2000–3600m. Uncommon in humid subtropical and temperate forest and edge. Both rufous and brown morphs are regularly encountered. The only pygmy-owl present in most of its range, but may overlap in a narrow elevational zone with Cloud-forest Pygmy-Owl in the NW, and with Pacific Pygmy-Owl in the SW. In these areas, voice is usually the only sure way to ID it to species. Single birds are usually located either by voice or by the presence of a mobbing flock of smaller birds. Song consists of a series of easily imitated *woop* notes, usually preceded by one or more *woo-diddle-oot* phrases.

brown morph 4

grayish-brown morph 1

brown morph 1

2

rufous morph 3

brown morph 4

rufous morph 4

SCREECH-OWLS AND BUFF-FRONTED OWL

Four species of screech-owl occur in forested areas of W Ecuador. Only one occurs in most areas, making range and elevation excellent ID clues, along with voice. The beautiful Buff-fronted Owl is rare and local in montane forest.

1 WEST PERUVIAN SCREECH-OWL *Megascops roboratus* 20cm/8in

0–1700m. Uncommon in deciduous forest in W and SW. No other screech-owl occurs with it. There are two distinct color morphs, rufous and gray. Usually encountered alone or in fairly close pairs, often perching at rather low heights. Primary song is a 2–4 sec. trill that rises gradually, and sometimes falls slightly toward the end. Single screeches and a short series of yelps may also be given.

2 COLOMBIAN SCREECH-OWL *Megascops colombianus* 27cm/10.5in

1200–2400m; down to 500m in coastal range. Uncommon in humid foothill and subtropical forest; locally also occurs in the coastal range (e.g., Bilsa Biological Station), where it is sympatric with Chocó Screech-Owl. Colombian Screech-Owl can be distinguished by dark (not yellow) irides and white scapular markings, as well as voice. A rufous-morph bird is shown, but gray-brown morphs also occur. Mostly encountered alone, and often quite shy even in response to playback, tending to keep to dense cover. Most commonly heard song is a very long (17 sec. or longer) series of evenly spaced, soft *boop* notes; also gives a shorter, more halting series of barks, and a soft wail. Sometimes lumped with **Rufescent Screech-Owl** (*M. ingens*).

3 WHITE-THROATED SCREECH-OWL *Megascops albogularis* 26cm/10in

2400–3600m. A chunky screech-owl found in humid temperate forest; uncommon but probably under-recorded, since it inhabits areas that are often inconvenient to visit at night. Darker plumage, white throat, and yellow irides separate it from Colombian Screech-Owl, though the species are not known to overlap in our region. White-throated is often found in fairly close pairs, perching at low to medium heights, and responds aggressively and vocally to playback. Male initiates with a short series of low toots, and female responds with a similar but higher-pitched outburst; individual toots are often doubled, especially when birds are excited.

4 CHOCÓ SCREECH-OWL *Megascops centralis* 21cm/8.5in

100–1100m. Uncommon in humid lowland and foothill forest, mostly in the NW, but with a few records as far S as the Buenaventura Reserve. A smaller version of Colombian Screech-Owl; the two species overlap only very locally in the coastal range. Chocó's yellow irides and white scapular markings are diagnostic; plumage coloration varies between brown and rufous. Quite inconspicuous; usually encountered alone inside forest cover, perching at low to medium height. Song is a soft, 1–2 sec. trill that rises and then falls. Sometimes lumped with **Vermiculated Screech-Owl** (*M. vermiculatus*).

5 BUFF-FRONTED OWL *Aegolius harrisii* 20cm/8in

600–3100m. This stunning owl is very rare and local in dry and semi-humid montane forest and lighter woodland. There are recent sightings from Pululahua Geobotanical Reserve and Jerusalem Recreational Park, N of Quito, as well as from Yunguilla and Jorupe Reserves in the SW; it is likely more widespread, but easily overlooked. Buff underparts and striking facial pattern render this owl unmistakable. It is encountered only rarely, usually alone, and tends to perch low. Song, quite reminiscent of that of a screech-owl, is a rapid, 7–10 sec. trill that rises and then levels out near the end; it has a ventriloquial quality, starting almost imperceptibly and gradually becoming louder.

gray morph 1

rufous morph 1

rufous morph 2

3

4

5

Nighthawks are highly aerial, cryptically patterned, insectivorous nightjars. They are crepuscular, feeding only during a very short period around dawn and dusk, and spending the rest of the day sleeping on a tree branch. When perched, long wings that reach or extend past tail help separate nighthawks from all nightjars except male Lyre-tailed and Swallow-tailed Nightjars (p. 154).

1 SHORT-TAILED NIGHTHAWK *Lurocalis semitorquatus* 20cm/8in

0–1300m. Uncommon over humid forest and adjacent clearings in the lowlands and foothills. When seen in flight, note white throat; otherwise appears rusty and short-tailed; underparts are finely barred, but this is usually not apparent. Easily mistaken for a bat in flight and can appear nearly identical to larger Rufous-bellied Nighthawk; the two species are not known to overlap. Common and Lesser Nighthawks have narrower wings with white primary marks, and different flight behavior. Short-tailed Nighthawk's flight is rapid and twisting, interspersed with bouts of gliding. Call is a very short whistle repeated about once per second.

2 RUFOUS-BELLIED NIGHTHAWK *Lurocalis rufiventris* 24cm/9.5in

1500–3100m. Uncommon over humid forest and adjacent clearings in the subtropical and temperate zones. Similar to the smaller Short-tailed Nighthawk, but less barred and slightly more rufous below; Short-tailed occurs at lower elevations and the two species are not known to overlap in our region. Rufous-bellied Nighthawk appears rather bat-like, and can be observed briefly at dawn or dusk flying low over the forest, either alone or in pairs. Occasionally spotted by day roosting lengthwise on a horizontal mossy branch. Song is a whistled *fwee-fwee-fwah-fwo*, each note lower than the previous, that can be easy to imitate; hoarse *wroh* notes are also sometimes given.

3 LESSER NIGHTHAWK *Chordeiles acutipennis* 21cm/8.5in

0–800m; locally to 2000m. Fairly common in open, nonforest habitats in more arid areas; mainly occurs in lowlands and foothills, but also locally in arid inter-Andean valleys. When perched, long wings that reach tail tip separate it from nightjars (pp. 154–156) in its range. Males are shown; female is similar but has buff throat and primary bars. Common Nighthawk is very similar (though less likely to be found in the arid habitats that Lesser prefers). In flight, Lesser Nighthawk has primary bar about two-thirds of the way between bend of wing and wing tip, whereas Common Nighthawk has it about halfway between. When perched, wing tips just barely reach the tail tip on Lesser, but wing tips extend beyond the tail on Common. Lesser Nighthawk's flight appears light and graceful; it glides with wings held in a shallow dihedral, and sometimes with stiff, jerky wingbeats. It is more likely to be found roosting during the day, due to the sparsely vegetated habitat it prefers.

4 COMMON NIGHTHAWK *Chordeiles minor* 23cm/9in

0–3400m. A rare boreal migrant to both lowlands and highlands; most likely to be seen during the March–April and September–October migration periods. Very similar to Lesser Nighthawk; see that species for ID details in the areas of overlap. When perched, long wings that extend past tail can be helpful to separate Common Nighthawk from most nightjars. Behavior similar to that of Lesser Nighthawk, though more often observed flying very high above the ground; roosts lengthwise along branches, often high up in a tree.

Nightjars are wholly nocturnal and cryptically patterned; they are often best distinguished by range, habitat, and voice. They sally out from the ground, cliff ledge, or branch to snatch up flying insects. All are sexually dimorphic; females tend to be more plainly patterned than males, with buff replacing white in wing, tail, and throat. Look for reflective red eyeshine when illuminated. *Note:* The flight shots were digitally generated, since no suitable photos could be found.

1 BAND-WINGED NIGHTJAR *Systellura longirostris* 21cm/8.5in

1800–4000m. Fairly common in subtropical and temperate forest edge, clearings, lightly wooded areas, and even tall buildings in towns and cities; often heard even in the center of Quito. In flight, separated from other, sympatric nightjars by pale wing bands and tail corners (much reduced in female; not shown). Perched bird shows a faint, rufous nuchal collar. Both sexes distinguished from female Swallow-tailed and Lyre-tailed Nightjars by large white and buffy spots on wing coverts. Band-winged Nightjar is usually encountered singly or in pairs; roosts and nests on the ground, rock faces, and walls; occasionally sits in roads. Song is a high-pitched, rather piercing *SEEEEEuuuu* or *SEEEEEuuuEE*.

2 WHITE-TAILED NIGHTJAR *Hydropsalis cayennensis* 20cm/8in

1400–2000m. Uncommon and local in arid valleys N of Ibarra. Only male is shown; female has buffy rather than white underparts and head markings. In flight, male shows broad white tips to most tail feathers; at least some birds found in Ecuador seem to lack white or buff in primaries, but elsewhere in their range they appear to always show this feature. It is unlikely that other nightjars occur together with it in its very restricted range and arid habitat. White-tailed Nightjar seems to favor rocky, shrubby areas, and is not observed sitting on roads. Song is one or two high-pitched *tzp* notes followed by a rapidly descending whistle, e.g., *tzp, tzp-seeeeeeeeer*.

3 ANTHONY'S NIGHTJAR *Nyctidromus anthonyi* 19cm/7.5in

0–700m. Uncommon to locally fairly common in deciduous woodland and arid scrub in the coastal lowlands; also found locally inland in the far SW. Sexes are fairly similar. In flight, shows narrow white wing crescents and white edges on some of the outer tail feathers. Few nightjars share its desert habitat; male Pauraque (p. 156) shows similar wing and tail markings in flight, but is much larger and longer tailed. Lesser Nighthawk (p. 152) shares the same habitat, but wings are much longer, reaching tail tip when perched. Anthony's Nightjar is encountered singly, in pairs, or in loose groups, often perching in the open on the ground or a low perch. Song, heard most often during the rainy season, is a clear, whistled *trEEEooh*, repeated regularly; also gives a rasping *brt-kuwat*. Also called **Scrub Nightjar**.

4 LYRE-TAILED NIGHTJAR *Uropsalis lyra* 24–95cm/9.5–37.5in

1200–2000m. Uncommon at edge of humid subtropical forest, especially near cliffs, roadcuts, landslides, and along forested mountain streams. Male's remarkable tail is even longer than Swallow-tailed Nightjar's; that species typically occurs at higher elevations, and lacks white tail tips. For female, see Swallow-tailed and Band-winged Nightjars for separation details. Behavior is similar to that of Swallow-tailed Nightjar. Song is rolling *woh-widdEEyou, woh-widdEEYOU, WOH-WIDDEEYOU...*, usually lasting 3–6 sec.

5 SWALLOW-TAILED NIGHTJAR *Uropsalis segmentatus* 21–74cm/8.5–29in

2200–3600m. Uncommon at edge of humid temperate forest, especially near cliffs, landslides, and roadcuts. Male, with its spectacularly long tail, could be confused only with longer-tailed Lyre-tailed Nightjar, which occurs mainly at lower elevation and has white tips to its tail. Female lacks the nuchal collar of female Lyre-tailed, and plumage is much more broadly mottled than finely barred. See also Band-winged Nightjar. Swallow-tailed Nightjar feeds over clearings and roads, swooping out to catch insects, and occasionally sits on roads. Song is a rising and falling *wrrrrRREEEEEEEeerrrr* with a very buzzy quality; a rising *whip* is also given.

Additional nightjars, along with two other nocturnal species. All give off reflective eyeshine when immersed in the beam of a strong light. *Note:* The flight shots were digitally generated, since no suitable photos could be found.

1 PAURAQUE *Nyctidromus albicollis* 28cm/11in

0–1700m. The most frequently encountered nightjar in most of Ecuador; common in forest edge, clearings, and lightly wooded terrain from the lowlands to subtropics. Note long, round-tipped tail, black-spotted scapulars, white throat, and rufous cheeks. In flight, male is distinctive, with white primary bar and extensive white in tail; female (not shown) is duller, wings have only a faint buff primary bar and tail only slightly tipped white. Size, long tail, range, and habitat should help to distinguish this species from other nightjars, but see especially the smaller Anthony's Nightjar (p. 154) of arid zones. Pauraque perches on the ground, in brush piles and on low shrubs, from which it tends to hunt with brief sallies. In the lowlands and foothills, it is the nightjar most likely to be seen sitting in the road, and occasionally may be approached very closely. Often-heard song is an explosive *phwWEEEoh!*; other calls include a liquid *wup?*

2 CHOCÓ POORWILL *Nyctiphrynus rosenbergi* 21cm/8.5in

0–900m. Uncommon inside humid lowland and foothill forest in NW. Sexes are fairly similar. Very dark, with white wing-covert spots and tail tip; throat also white (not evident in photo). In flight, shows no wing markings, but white tail tip may be evident. Not likely mistaken within its limited range and habitat; female Pauraque can also look plain-winged in flight, but is larger, longer-tailed, and tends to avoid deep forest. Chocó Poorwill usually stays inside forest and is easily overlooked; occasionally one may come out to a small clearing, or flush from the ground along a forest trail. Best located by its song, a series of three to five rising whistles, the last note more drawn out, e.g., *tu-tru-tru-TREEOO*; also gives a frog-like *drt!*

3 COMMON POTOO *Nyctibius griseus* 35–40cm/14–15.5in

0–2400m. W Ecuador's only potoo; fairly common and widespread in forest, edge, and adjacent clearings from the lowlands to the subtropics. When perched, vertical posture and long tail immediately distinguish it from other night birds. In flight, resembles Oilbird, but has a square rather than graduated tail and a very direct point-to-point flight, not the erratic and searching flight of Oilbird. Common Potoo roosts by day at the end of a vertical broken-off snag or post, but is easily overlooked even if unobscured. When seen perched in the middle of a branch, it may be on eggs or brooding chicks. Potoos forage by sallying out after large insects, which they engulf in their huge open gape. Song, most often heard on moonlit nights, is a haunting, whistled *Waooooh-woooh-wooh-oooow*; each note is lower than the previous, and the song can be imitated.

4 OILBIRD *Steatornis caripensis* 43–47cm/17–18.5in

700–2800m. Uncommon and infrequently seen away from its colonies, which are placed in caves and forested ravines from the foothills to the temperate zone. Individuals wander widely in search of fruit and can turn up in very unexpected places. Large and rufous, with white spotting; note distinctly hooked bill and prominent rictal bristles. Appears quite hawk-like in flight; note long, pointed wings, graduated tail, and erratic flight. Nightjars and nighthawks (pp. 152–154) have darker plumages and tiny bills; Common Potoo is fairly large but distinctly grayer, with a tiny bill, square tail, and more direct flight. Away from its colony, Oilbird sometimes perches very awkwardly in trees, tending to teeter back and forth. It forages at night by hover-plucking fruit, especially from palms and a variety of Lauraceae (laurel family) trees. It navigates by echolocation clicks, which can easily be heard from the flying bird. Very noisy at colonies, where it gives a loud mix of grating screeches and growls.

LARGER SWIFTS

Swifts are a confusing family of fast-flying, highly aerial insectivorous birds. ID is challenging and frequently impossible in poor light, in which the subtle differences in rump and underpart pattern and coloration are impossible to detect. With experience, shape and flight pattern can often be helpful, but some species are so similar they usually cannot be safely identified in the field except by voice.

1 WHITE-COLLARED SWIFT *Streptoprocne zonaris* 21cm/8.5in

0–4200m. Ecuador's largest and most frequently encountered swift; fairly common from the lowlands to the páramo. Complete white collar is diagnostic, but may be invisible at great distances. White-chested Swift can look similar, but is less bulky, with narrower, more sickle-shaped wings, and white chest patch does not extend to sides of neck. Also note White-collared's flight pattern, alternating between strong shallow flapping and "fighter jet" glides. Often occurs in large flocks, in which birds soar about in lazy circles; roosts and nests on forested cliffs and also behind waterfalls. Flight call is a rollicking up-and-down series of squeaks.

2 CHESTNUT-COLLARED SWIFT *Streptoprocne rutila* 13cm/5in

200–3300m. Fairly common over forested areas at mid elevations in the Andes, but regularly wanders higher and lower. Rufous collar is diagnostic if seen, but may be invisible in poor light, and may not even be present on immature birds. Quite vocal, and calls are often the safest way to ID the species; gives a rapid, buzzy series of notes with an electric quality, e.g., *bzz-bzz-bzz-bzz-bzz-bzz....* Notably smaller than White-collared Swift, and larger with less fluttery wingbeats than *Chaetura* swifts (p. 160). Most likely confused with the three *Cypseloides* swifts, especially Spot-fronted, which is almost identical in shape. White-chinned Swift is slightly chunkier than Chestnut-collared, and White-chested has a more slender shape. *Cypseloides* may also show faint pale feathering around the feet. Chestnut-collared Swift is usually encountered in medium to large flocks, flying with steady, fast wingbeats, interspersed with glides, and tending to make several passes over the same area before moving on. It tends to fly lower than other swift species that may be in the same flock.

3 SPOT-FRONTED SWIFT *Cypseloides cherriei* 14cm/5.5in

300–2400m. Uncommon and local over humid forest in the foothills and subtropics; may wander to drier areas. Most frequently found in our region in the upper parts of the Tandayapa Valley. White "headlights" are diagnostic but extremely difficult to see in the field, and the species is usually safely identified only by voice: a rapid twitter interspersed with down-slurred notes, e.g., *ti-ti-ti-ti-ti-ti-tyer-ter.* The rare White-chinned Swift is slightly chunkier. Also see Chestnut-collared Swift and White-chested Swift. Spot-fronted Swift is usually encountered in small groups, often with other swift species, in which direct comparison is occasionally possible. Flight is similar to that of Chestnut-collared, but Spot-fronted tends to fly higher.

4 WHITE-CHINNED SWIFT *Cypseloides cryptus* 15cm/6in

300–2000m. Rare over humid forest; distribution poorly known. A uniformly dark, chunky swift; note heavy body and relatively broad wings, though this may be evident only in direct comparison with other swifts flying near it. Lower belly may appear pale, though some Spot-fronted and White-chested Swifts share this feature. White chin and forecrown are nearly impossible to see in the field, and voice is often the only reliable method by which to ID White-chinned Swift. Voice is a series of soft, toneless *pit* notes that suddenly bursts into a rapid, churred jumble, e.g., *pit, pit, pit, pit-djerdjerdjerdjertitititit.* Flight is characterized by long bouts of rapid flapping intermixed with long glides.

5 WHITE-CHESTED SWIFT *Cypseloides lemosi* 14cm/5.5in

400–1700m. Status uncertain; primarily an E slope species, but recently recorded over humid lowland and foothill forest in NW. Amount of white on chest is very variable; some birds show a conspicuous white triangle, but on most birds it is at best just a faint, whitish frontal collar. Could be easily confused with White-collared Swift at a distance if size can't be judged accurately; White-collared is bulkier, and bulging primaries give its wings less of a sickle shape; White-chested Swift's collar never extends up the sides of the neck, though this can be hard to discern. Some birds (immatures?) may show no white at all, in which case they may be identified only by voice. Gives a series of sharp *pit* notes, each one at a different pitch, interspersed with occasional louder or harsher notes.

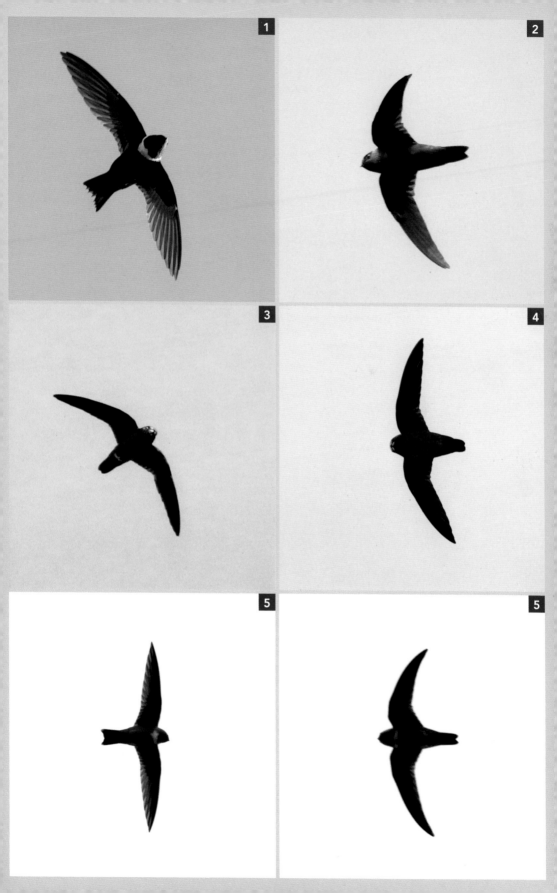

White-tipped and Lesser Swallow-tailed Swifts are relatively easy to ID in comparison to the four *Chaetura*, which may be distinguished by careful observation of the presence, extent, shape, and tonality of rump patch. As a group, *Chaetura* can often be distinguished from other swifts by their faster, more fluttery and bat-like wingbeats, but this is not always easy to discern without significant field experience.

1 WHITE-TIPPED SWIFT *Aeronautes montivagus* 12cm/4.5in

1300–2700m. Fairly common but very local throughout much of the Andes; seems to favor areas with deep canyons or sheer rock faces. The only swift with a white bib and ventral band; white tail tip is not always visible from below. Lesser Swallow-tailed Swift is a lowland species and lacks white ventral band. White-tipped Swift is usually encountered in tight, fast-flying groups, occasionally accompanying other swift species. Flocks will sometimes rocket down a canyon in single file along a chosen trajectory, repeating the routine over and over again. Call is a rapid, gravelly churr.

2 LESSER SWALLOW-TAILED SWIFT *Panyptila cayennensis* 13cm/5in

0–1600m. Uncommon over forest and adjacent clearings throughout the humid lowlands and foothills, occasionally wandering higher. Long, forked tail is almost always held closed, appearing sharply pointed. This shape, combined with white throat and flank patches, makes it one of the easiest swifts to ID, even at great distances. Usually encountered alone or in pairs or small, loose groups, occasionally with other swifts; usually flies quite high, with rapid, shallow wing strokes. Its nest is a cottony cylinder placed on a tree trunk or under an overhang. Rather quiet, but occasionally gives rapid, high-pitched notes interspersed with short buzzes.

3 GRAY-RUMPED SWIFT *Chaetura cinereiventris* 11cm/4.5in

0–1700m. Fairly common throughout much of the humid lowlands and foothills, becoming scarce in the subtropics; also occasionally over deciduous forest (though there mostly replaced by Short-tailed Swift). Uniform gray below, blacker above with a slightly contrasting dark gray rump. Band-rumped Swift has a narrower and brighter rump patch; Short-tailed Swift appears distinctly short-tailed and long-winged; rare boreal migrant Chimney Swift is larger and darker, with a slightly paler throat and, at most, a slightly brown rump patch. Gray-rumped Swift is encountered in flocks varying from small to very large; it has a rapid, fluttery bat-like flight with a twisting motion, and often flies quite low. Voice is a chatter with a stuttered and warbling quality.

4 BAND-RUMPED SWIFT *Chaetura spinicaudus* 11cm/4.5in

300–1500m. Uncommon to locally fairly common over humid lowland and foothill forest and adjacent clearings in NW, occasionally wandering higher. Best told by its narrow, white rump patch, which can give this slender species a long-tailed look; other small swifts have wider, less contrasting rump patches. Usually encountered in small to medium-size flocks. Tends to fly relatively high above the ground, and may join flocks of other swifts. Voice is similar to that of Gray-rumped Swift, but individual notes are sharper and less slurred together.

5 SHORT-TAILED SWIFT *Chaetura brachyura* 11cm/4.5in

0–1000m. Uncommon and local over deciduous forest and adjacent clearings in W and SW. Distinctive shape is diagnostic; appears almost tailless in the field, with long, bow-shaped wings. Rump, tail, and entire hindquarters are gray. Usually encountered in small groups, often flying quite low. Flight is fast, with rapid wingbeats and occasionally long, swooping glides. Call is a soft, jumbled twitter. Birds in W Ecuador and NW Peru are sometimes split as **Tumbes Swift** (*C. ocypetes*).

6 CHIMNEY SWIFT *Chaetura pelagica* 13cm/5in

0–2800m. A rare boreal migrant, recorded from September to March, from scattered locations in the lowlands, foothills, and central valley; probably frequently overlooked. The largest *Chaetura*, but hard to ID with certainty; best ID features are rump that shows little, if any, contrast with rest of upperparts, and pale throat that contrasts with rest of underparts. Can be found alone, in large flocks, and/or with other swifts. Flight seems more deliberate, compared to other *Chaetura*, with short bouts of rapid wingbeats alternating with short glides. Chimney Swift is not known to vocalize in Ecuador.

Hummingbirds are one of the most well-known and best represented families in W Ecuador, and range in size from miniscule, insect-like woodstars (pp. 192–194) to the enormous Giant Hummingbird (p. 184). They feed primarily on flower nectar, but also take small insects and other arthropods. Voice is only occasionally useful for ID, so is not described for most species. Hermits are inconspicuous hummingbirds that usually favor the dark forest understory. Many species feed primarily on *Heliconia* flowers by "traplining," or moving from flower to flower along an established route. Males gather at leks, where they sing simple songs while constantly wagging their tails.

1 BRONZY HERMIT *Glaucis aeneus* 9cm/3.5in

0–600m. Uncommon in humid lowland forest in NW. Identified by combination of cinnamon underparts and rounded tail with white tip and rufous base; note faint facial pattern. Band-tailed Barbthroat (p. 164) is gray below, with rufous only on throat, and has white base to tail. Other hermits have long, pointed central tail feathers. Bronzy Hermit is usually encountered alone at flowering *Heliconia*; easily overlooked, as individuals fly rapidly through dark forest understory between flowering plants; also gleans insects from vegetation.

2 WHITE-WHISKERED HERMIT *Phaethornis yaruqui* 12cm/4.5in

0–1500m. Fairly common in humid lowland and foothill forest, edge, and adjacent clearings. Dark green plumage and lack of tawny on rump separate it from other similar hermits. Female (not shown) is very similar to male but has grayer underparts. Rather bold for a hermit, regularly emerges to more open areas, visiting feeders and sometimes even entering buildings. Listen for its characteristic flight call, a clear whistled *wheeep!* Song at lek is a soft, repeated squeak.

3 LONG-BILLED HERMIT *Phaethornis longirostris* 13cm/5in

0–1300m. Uncommon in deciduous and semi-humid forest in lowlands and foothills; locally occurs in more humid forest (e.g., Río Palenque Science Center). Large, with grayish underparts, pale green upperparts, and tawny rump. White-whiskered Hermit is much darker and lacks the tawny rump; Stripe-throated Hermit is markedly smaller. No overlap with Tawny-bellied Hermit of higher elevations. Generally shy, Long-billed Hermit stays inside dark forest understory and only rarely comes out to edge. Occasionally visits feeders. Gives a long series of evenly spaced *twee* notes at lek sites. Formerly called **Western Long-tailed Hermit**. Birds in W Ecuador and NW Peru are sometimes split as **Baron's** (or **Ecuadorian**) **Hermit** (*P. baroni*).

4 TAWNY-BELLIED HERMIT *Phaethornis syrmatophorus* 13cm/5in

1300–2800m. Uncommon inside humid forest from foothills to the temperate zone. Lighter coloration along with tawny underparts and rump distinguish it from White-whiskered Hermit, with which it can occur in the upper foothills. Also see Speckled Hummingbird (p. 164), which has a similar facial pattern but is speckled below and has a shorter tail. Tawny-bellied Hermit, similar in behavior to Long-billed Hermit, only rarely visits feeders and tends not to linger long. Song at lek is a high *tseep* repeated over and over.

5 STRIPE-THROATED HERMIT *Phaethornis striigularis* 8cm/3in

0–1300m. Fairly common inside humid and semi-humid lowland and foothill forest; occasionally comes out to edge. Tiny size and narrow, graduated, white-tipped tail are enough to ID this species. Bronzy Hermit is larger, more rufous below, and has a rounded tail. No overlap with Gray-chinned Hermit. Behavior much like that of Long-billed Hermit, but Stripe-throated has not been seen visiting feeders in Ecuador. Song at lek is a variable series of high-pitched chirps and warbles.

6 GRAY-CHINNED HERMIT *Phaethornis griseogularis* 8cm/3in

600–2500m. Restricted to SW foothills and subtropics, where uncommon in deciduous and semi-humid forest and scrub. Rufous rump and pale cinnamon underparts contrast with green upperparts; tail is tipped white and has long, spiky central feathers. This small hermit is unique in its range. Behavior and voice are very similar to those of Stripe-throated Hermit. Birds in SW Ecuador and NW Peru are sometimes split as **Porculla Hermit** (*P. porcullae*).

The first three species are related to the hermits (p. 162), and are similar in behavior. Lancebills and starthroats have long, straight bills, though are otherwise rather different in plumage, habitat, and behavior. Speckled Hummingbird is a hermit-like species of montane forest edge.

1 WHITE-TIPPED SICKLEBILL *Eutoxeres aquila* 12cm/4.5in

0–1300m. Uncommon inside humid lowland and foothill forest. No other bird in W Ecuador has such a curved bill; also note extensively streaked underparts and graduated, white-tipped, tail. Usually encountered alone, clinging to *Heliconia* and probing the flower with its unique bill; inconspicuous, often difficult to detect even when right in front of the observer. Sicklebills do not usually hover feed, and never visit feeders. Song is a long series, e.g., *CHEEP-sit, CHEEP-sit...*, or *tsit-p'dit, psit-p'dit...*, sometimes interspersed with a short, fast series of *tsip* notes.

2 BAND-TAILED BARBTHROAT *Threnetes ruckeri* 10cm/4in

0–900m. An inconspicuous hermit-like hummingbird; uncommon inside humid lowland and foothill forest, only occasionally coming to edge. Orange-tinged throat-patch combined with face and tail pattern are unique in range. Bronzy Hermit (p. 162) is larger, has more extensive rufous on the underparts and base of tail; other hermits have graduated tails with elongate, white-tipped central tail feathers. Band-tailed Barbthroat is solitary, feeding on flowers in understory of forest interior; may perch for long periods giving a high-pitched, buzzy, warbling song.

3 TOOTH-BILLED HUMMINGBIRD *Androdon aequatorialis* 10cm/4in

100–1100m. Rare to locally uncommon inside humid forest in lowlands and foothills of NW. No other hummingbird shows combination of streaked underparts and long, straight bill. Usually encountered alone, foraging at varying heights within the forest; usually remains inside the forest, only rarely encountered in clearings or at edge. Birds sometimes perch for very long periods giving an incessant, high-pitched *seep-seep-seep-chip...* series that continues for many minutes.

4 GREEN-FRONTED LANCEBILL *Doryfera ludovicae* 10cm/4in

1100–2400m. Uncommon in humid foothill and subtropical forest and edge, especially near streams. Long, slightly upswept bill and short, rounded tail are diagnostic; also note contrasting coppery hind-crown. Inconspicuous and solitary; usually encountered at forest edge probing long, tubular flowers or catching insects over streams and small pools; visits feeders only rarely.

5 LONG-BILLED STARTHROAT *Heliomaster longirostris* 10cm/4in

0–1500m. Uncommon to fairly common in both deciduous and humid forest edge, woodland, clearings, and gardens, mainly at lower elevations. Long, straight bill, white rump streak, and distinctive facial pattern are diagnostic; should not be mistaken if seen well. Female (not shown) is very similar to male but has less blue on the crown and a smaller gorget. Usually found alone or in small groups feeding high in flowering trees; often perches high on exposed branch. Occasionally visits feeders.

6 SPECKLED HUMMINGBIRD *Adelomyia melanogenys* 9cm/3.5in

1400–3600m; down to 500m in coastal range. Common in forest, edge, and wooded clearings in the subtropical and temperate zones. The only hummingbird with a dark facial stripe and speckled underparts. The facial pattern may suggest a hermit, but no hermits in range have speckled underparts or such a short tail. Speckled Hummingbird can be common at feeders; otherwise is usually encountered alone or in small numbers, foraging low on flowers at shrubby forest edge and roadsides; often clings to flowers, vines, or branches while feeding. Song is a very long, simple series of high-pitched *seet* notes; also emits rasping *trrrrt* calls while foraging, and occasionally a complicated series of squeaks and buzzes that may recall the song of Tanager Finch (p. 406).

Violetears include three medium-size Andean hummingbirds that share glittering violet-blue auricular tufts and a subterminal tail band. Coronets are cloud-forest hummingbirds with relatively short, straight bills, and tails that flash buff or white.

1 GREEN VIOLETEAR *Colibri thalassinus* 9cm/3.5in

1200–2300m. Fairly common in humid subtropical forest edge and clearings. It appears to undertake seasonal movements that are not understood, and in some areas it is completely absent for a few months of the year. Distinguished from the larger Sparkling Violetear, with which it often occurs, by the lack of blue throat and belly. While several may congregate at a feeder, Green Violetear is otherwise rather solitary. Often encountered on a high, exposed twig, singing an endlessly repetitive *kr-CHIT, kr-CHIT*…; sometimes omitting the leading *kr*.

2 SPARKLING VIOLETEAR *Colibri coruscans* 12cm/4.5in

1100–3500m. Common in a wide variety of habitats throughout much of the Andes, including forest edge, montane scrub, agricultural land, cities, towns, and gardens. Very seasonal in more humid forest at its lower elevation limit, where it may be present only part of the year. Larger size combined with blue throat and belly distinguish it from Green Violetear. Encountered alone, or in small groups that may congregate at flowering trees, often harassing smaller species. A regular but often seasonal visitor to feeders, where aggressive and conspicuous. Song, usually given from an exposed perch, is a monotonous, seemingly unending *tzik-tzik-tzik-tzik*…; in display flight, ascends rapidly into the sky, returning in almost free fall, with tail flared, uttering a crackling trill.

3 BROWN VIOLETEAR *Colibri delphinae* 9cm/3.5in

500–2100m. Uncommon to locally fairly common in humid montane forest edge and clearings, mostly in the NW, but also found locally in the SW (e.g., Buenaventura Reserve) and along the coastal range. Combination of brown plumage, blue auricular tufts, and green gorget is unique, and Brown Violetear is unlikely to be mistaken. Regularly visits feeders in a number of areas, and rarely encountered away from them. Away from feeders it is quite solitary, though several may gather at a flowering tree. Its song, usually given from a prominent perch, consists of a long series of rather unmusical chirps regularly interspersed with short pauses.

4 VELVET-PURPLE CORONET *Boissonneaua jardini* 11cm/4.5in

800–2000m. A stunning but uncommon hummingbird of humid forest, woodland, and edge in the foothills and subtropics of the NW; also found in the SW at Buenaventura Reserve. Note glittering purple lower underparts, with glittering turquoise and shining green on flanks, and white outer tail feathers. Distinctive when seen in good light; otherwise it can appear nearly black, though the white in the tail is usually conspicuous and may be a helpful clue. Scarce and rarely encountered away from feeders, though can be overlooked at flowering trees, where single birds may remain perched inside thick vegetation, only to emerge briefly to feed or chase other hummers away. Coronets typically hold their wings open for a moment after alighting, showing off rufous underwing coverts. Velvet-purple Coronet is easiest to see at various feeders in the Tandayapa-Mindo area, where often very tame, allowing close approach.

5 BUFF-TAILED CORONET *Boissonneaua flavescens* 11cm/4.5in

1500–2800m. Fairly common in canopy and edge of humid subtropical and temperate forest. Plain and easily mistaken; good marks include buffy undertail and pectoral tufts, white tibial puffs, and white postocular spot. The typical coronet habit of holding wings open briefly after alighting is also a great clue for ID. Glittering dark green head and breast separate it from Fawn-breasted Brilliant (p. 176); white tibial puffs may also suggest a puffleg (p. 186), but no puffleg shares its buffy markings. Buff-tailed Coronet can be abundant around feeders, especially in the Tandayapa Valley, chasing off other species. Otherwise it is encountered alone, foraging on flowers high in the canopy, where flaring buff tail can draw attention.

Sexually dimorphic hummingbirds found mainly at lower elevations. The two woodnymphs are now lumped with **Crowned Woodnymph** (*Thalurania colombica*) by most authorities.

1 GREEN-BREASTED MANGO *Anthracothorax prevostii* 11cm/4.5in

0–600m; occasionally wanders higher. Fairly common in humid and semi-humid forest edge, woodland, and clearings. Both sexes have a purplish tail, which is usually obvious only when the tail is fanned. Male can appear all dark in the field, in which case the large size and thick, slightly decurved bill are useful features. Female is very distinctive, with white-bordered broad black vertical stripe on underparts. Tends to feed quite high, and large numbers may congregate in the canopy of freshly flowering trees. *Note:* The subspecies in W Ecuador, *iridescens*, is sometimes placed with **Black-throated Mango** (*A. nigricollis*).

2 GREEN-CROWNED WOODNYMPH *Thalurania fannyi* 8–10cm/3–4in

0–1700m. Fairly common in forest, edge, light woodland, and clearings from the lowlands to the subtropics in W and NW. Stunning male could be confused only with Violet-bellied Hummingbird, which is smaller, with green on throat not extending to breast, and lacks violet-blue wing coverts. Female Green-crowned Woodnymph is slightly smaller and less colorful than male, but no other hummer in range has combination of pale gray bib and blue wing coverts; not known to overlap with Emerald-bellied Woodnymph. Green-crowned is common at feeders in some areas (e.g., Milpe Bird Sanctuary and Mindo); otherwise usually encountered alone at low to mid heights; often attracted to large flowers.

3 EMERALD-BELLIED WOODNYMPH *Thalurania hypochlora* 8–10cm/3–4in

0–1600m. Uncommon to locally fairly common (e.g., Buenaventura Reserve) in humid lowland and foothill forest and edge in SW. Male is stunning in good light, with glittering green head and underparts and violet-blue wing coverts. Smaller female is best identified by pale gray underparts and blue wing coverts. Other similar species such as female Violet-bellied Hummingbird and female Ecuadorian Plumeleteer (p. 172) lack the blue wing coverts. No known overlap with Green-crowned Woodnymph; behavior is similar.

4 VIOLET-BELLIED HUMMINGBIRD *Damophila julie* 7cm/3in

0–1100m. Uncommon in humid forest, edge, and wooded clearings in lowlands and foothills. Male is similar to larger Green-crowned Woodnymph, but green on throat does not extend to breast, it lacks violet-blue wing coverts, and may show red lower mandible. Female can be confusing, but she lacks the blue wing coverts of woodnymphs, and has much more extensive green and blue scaling on sides and flanks than other pale-bellied hummingbirds, such as Ecuadorian Plumeleteer (p. 172). Some birds, possibly immature males, show green and blue specking on breast, leading to possible confusion with Blue-chested Hummingbird (p. 174), which has a grayer belly and crissum. Violet-bellied Hummingbird is generally encountered alone at low to mid levels, but small numbers can congregate at flowering trees, and it is a regular visitor to feeders in some locations (e.g., Buenaventura Reserve).

Five dissimilar hummingbirds that do not fit well elsewhere; they have little in common apart from the general characteristics of the family.

1 WHITE-NECKED JACOBIN   *Florisuga mellivora*   9cm/3.5in

0–1800m. Fairly common in humid lowland and foothill forest, edge, and clearings. Colorful male is distinctive, and white nape is unique. Female is duller and can be confusing; key field marks include gray face, green breast scaling, and white tips to the tail feathers. Female brilliants (p. 176) show a white malar and postocular spot. White-necked Jacobin can be encountered singly in the forest, where it defends flowers from interlopers, but it also congregates with other hummers at flowering trees and feeders.

2 PURPLE-CROWNED FAIRY   *Heliothryx barroti*   9cm/3.5in

0–1400m; occasionally wanders higher. This beautiful hummer is uncommon in humid forest edge, clearings, and gardens in the lowlands and foothills. Striking snowy-white underparts contrast with shining pale green upperparts and black mask; no really similar species in its range. Female is shown; male is very similar but has more extensive purple on crown. Purple-crowned Fairy is usually encountered alone, foraging on flowers, hovering with tail cocked horizontally, often flashing its white outer tail feathers; regularly hovers to snap up flying insects or glean them from foliage. It rarely visits feeders.

3 BLUE-HEADED SAPPHIRE   *Hylocharis grayi*   9cm/3.5in

1200–2200m. Uncommon and local in scrub, light woodland, and gardens in arid inter-Andean valleys in far N. Male unique in range, with red bill and blue head. Female is more confusing, though in its very restricted range is the only hummer with conspicuously scaled underparts; faint reddish base of lower mandible can also be a clue. Similar Humboldt's Sapphire does not overlap in range. Blue-headed Sapphire is usually encountered alone, feeding on and defending flowering trees, and tending to perch conspicuously. Not currently known to visit feeders.

4 HUMBOLDT'S SAPPHIRE   *Hylocharis humboldtii*   9cm/3.5in

0–100m. Rare in mangroves and adjacent humid woodland in far NW between Las Peñas and the Colombian border. Male can be recognized by its mostly red bill, blue crown and throat, and white stripe on lower underparts. Female lacks bold characteristics, but no other midsize hummer within its small range has white underparts spangled green on sides and throat, and a reddish base to the bill. Not well known in Ecuador, but behavior is apparently similar to that of Blue-headed Sapphire. Humboldt's Sapphire is sometimes lumped with Blue-headed.

5 TUMBES HUMMINGBIRD   *Leucippus baeri*   10cm/4in

0–1200m. This large, drab hummer is uncommon and local in arid scrub and sparse deciduous woodland in the far SW; in some areas it seems to be only an erratic visitor. Sexes are very similar, both dusky green above with gray underparts, white tail tips, and a white postocular spot; no similar species occurs in the species' range and habitat. Usually found alone, sometimes even in extremely dry areas that seem to be devoid of flowering plants. Imitating or playing back song of Pacific Pygmy-Owl (p. 148) can often attract a Tumbes Hummingbird seemingly out of nowhere.

Plumeleteers have restricted ranges in W Ecuador; one occurs in the extreme N, the other in the extreme S. Green Thorntail's white rump band makes it unique in our region. Western Emerald ranges from the highlands to the foothills in varied habitats.

1 ECUADORIAN PLUMELETEER *Chalybura intermedia* 10cm/4in

500–1800m. Rare to locally uncommon in humid foothill and subtropical forest and edge in the SW. Male is only hummer in range with mostly glittering blue-green underparts and white crissum. Female is more difficult, with pale gray underparts that contrast only slightly with white crissum; female Emerald-bellied Woodnymph (p. 168) shows shining blue wing-covert patches; smaller female Violet-bellied Hummingbird (p. 168) has more extensive green on sides; Andean Emerald (p. 174) has immaculate white underparts. Ecuadorian Plumeleteer is generally encountered feeding alone at low heights. Most often seen in and around the Buenaventura Reserve, where it occasionally visits feeders. This species is lumped by various taxonomical authorities with either **White-vented Plumeleteer** (*C. buffonii*) or Bronze-tailed Plumeleteer (below); we have chosen to split it until more data come to light.

2 BRONZE-TAILED PLUMELETEER *Chalybura urochrysia* 10cm/4in

0–800m. Uncommon in humid lowland and foothill forest and edge in extreme NW. Combination of fluffy white crissum and bright pink feet is diagnostic in both sexes; photo of male is of a subspecies from outside of Ecuador, digitally modified to resemble NW Ecuador birds. Female is perhaps most similar to smaller female Green-crowned Woodnymph (p. 168), which differs by having a distinctive pale bib and blue wing-covert patches. Behavior similar to that of Ecuadorian Plumeleteer, but Bronze-tailed is not known to visit feeders anywhere in Ecuador.

3 GREEN THORNTAIL *Discosura conversii* 7–10cm/3–4in

100–1400m; occasionally wanders higher. This delightful little hummer is fairly common in humid lowland and foothill forest, where it inhabits forest edge, wooded clearings, and gardens. White rump band is diagnostic in both sexes. Male shows distinctively long, deeply forked tail; female has white malar and flank patches. Green Thorntail is sometimes found alone, but large numbers can congregate at feeders or areas with an abundance of flowers; tends to perch high, on thin exposed bare limbs. Flight is slow and methodical, with blurred wingbeats.

4 WESTERN EMERALD *Chlorostilbon melanorhynchus* 7cm/3in

600–2700m; occasionally down to lowlands. Fairly common in light woodland, scrub, and gardens in valleys in the N highlands; also occurs locally in more humid areas on the W slope of the Andes (e.g., the Tandayapa Valley, where it visits feeders). Male is stunning glittering golden-green, with a very short, forked tail; the only small, all-green hummingbird in our range. Female has pale gray underparts and black-and-white facial pattern; Speckled Hummingbird (p. 164) has a similar facial pattern, but is notably speckled below. Singles or small concentrations of Western Emeralds are encountered foraging in flowering shrubs, hedgerows, and gardens, where they tend to remain low and often under cover; feed higher in adjacent flowering trees.

Amazilia is a widespread genus of midsize hummingbirds; bills show varying amounts of red, and underparts have at least some white or gray. All species tend to favor more open habitats and forest edge.

1 RUFOUS-TAILED HUMMINGBIRD *Amazilia tzacatl* 9cm/3.5in

0–2500m. Common in humid forest edge, clearings, and gardens, from lowlands to subtropics; spreading into inter-Andean valleys in N. Sexes are very similar. No other hummer in range has a red bill, rufous tail, and almost entirely green plumage (grayer on belly). A conspicuous species of lightly wooded areas, avoiding forest interior; very prevalent at feeders throughout its range. Quite vocal, emitting an often constant staccato chattering while feeding.

2 ANDEAN EMERALD *Amazilia franciae* 9cm/3.5in

300–2300m. Fairly common in humid foothill and subtropical forest edge and clearings; also occurs locally in the coastal range. Sexes are similar. Entirely pure white underparts separate this species from nearly all other hummers that share its range; female Booted Racket-tail (p. 178) is decidedly smaller, shorter-billed, and has a distinct malar streak; female Emerald-bellied Woodnymph (p. 168); only in SW) is more gray-toned below and has violet patches on shoulders. Andean Emerald is a regular visitor to feeders throughout its range; otherwise not very conspicuous, feeding on flowering trees and shrubs at edge and clearings.

3 PURPLE-CHESTED HUMMINGBIRD *Amazilia rosenbergi* 8cm/3in

0–1100m. Uncommon to locally fairly common in humid lowland and lower foothill forest and edge in NW, occasionally wandering slightly higher (e.g., Milpe Bird Sanctuary). Extremely similar to Blue-chested Hummingbird; best separated from that species by snowy-white crissum in both sexes; also bill of Purple-chested shows very little red, often appearing all black in the field. Male additionally has greener lower underparts, compared to grayish in most Blue-chested. Females may not always be safely identified if crissum cannot be seen, but Purple-chested female's throat and breast usually show less white than Blue-chested. Purple-chested Hummingbird feeds inconspicuously at low to mid levels; most easily seen at forest edge or in clearings. Male gives a series of four to seven chip notes from regular song perches. Can be seen at feeders in the Río Canandé Reserve.

4 BLUE-CHESTED HUMMINGBIRD *Amazilia amabilis* 8cm/3in

0–350m. Fairly common in humid lowland forest, edge, lighter woodland, and clearings. Best distinguished from similar Purple-chested Hummingbird by mostly gray crissum; Blue-chested also may show more extensive red in the lower mandible. See Purple-chested for additional details. Behavior also similar to that of Purple-chested, but Blue-chested males gather in dispersed leks, singing a high-pitched, squeaky *pee-pit-pit-pit*....

5 AMAZILIA HUMMINGBIRD *Amazilia amazilia* 9cm/3.5in

0–2500m. Common in deciduous and semi-humid woodland, scrub, and gardens in W and SW. Subspecies *dumerilii* is found in most of mapped range, and is identified by combination of white breast, rufous vest, and red base to bill. SW highland birds (*alticola*; sometimes split as **Loja Hummingbird**) are somewhat variable, but typically have a bright rufous rump and tail and much less rufous on the underparts than *dumerilii*. Amazilia Hummingbird feeds conspicuously on a variety of flowering bushes and trees; *dumerilii* occasionally visits feeders, but *alticola* is not known to do so.

dumerilii 5

alticola 5

Brilliants are rather large, sexually dimorphic, stout-billed hummingbirds of foothill and subtropical zone forest. They often appear flat-headed, and facial feathering extends distinctively onto base of bill, imparting a somewhat fierce visage. Females are smaller than males, and have a narrow white malar stripe. Wedge-billed Hummingbird is a scarce and seldom seen cloud-forest denizen.

1 FAWN-BREASTED BRILLIANT   *Heliodoxa rubinoides*   10–11cm/4–4.5in

1200–2500m. Uncommon to fairly common in humid forest and edge in foothills and subtropics. Lacks strong plumage features; best identified by combination of buffy tinge to underparts, thick, slightly decurved bill, and bulky shape. Male has pinkish throat spot, lacking in female. Sometimes confused with Buff-tailed Coronet (p. 166), but that species is almost completely green below and has a straight bill. Fawn-breasted Brilliant regularly visits feeders, but away from them tends to be rather inconspicuous, feeding quietly at flowering trees and shrubs at forest edge and vegetated roadside banks.

2 GREEN-CROWNED BRILLIANT   *Heliodoxa jacula*   10–13cm/4–5in

300–1800m. Fairly common in humid forest, edge, and clearings with scattered trees in foothills and subtropics. Note large size, chunky shape, and relatively short tail. Male has a purple throat patch, absent in female. Most similar to Empress Brilliant, but lacks that species' long tail and golden sheen to underparts. Female lacks strong field marks, but note white malar and postocular spot. Immature male (not shown) much like female, but with conspicuous orange-buff malar patch. This brilliant tends to forage at low to medium heights at forest edge and in clearings, and regularly visits feeders.

3 EMPRESS BRILLIANT   *Heliodoxa imperatrix*   12–16cm/4.5–6.5in

1100–2200m. Uncommon in humid foothill and subtropical forest in NW; rarely seen away from feeders. Large and robust, with long, deeply forked tail (usually appears pointed tailed). Male has a glittering pink throat patch, lacking in female. Both sexes can be separated from the otherwise similar Green-crowned Brilliant by longer tail and golden sheen on underparts. Immature (not shown) like female but shows a rufous malar. Empress Brilliant is usually solitary away from feeders, but on rare occasions several may gather at a flowering tree. Even at feeders, tends to arrive only sporadically and not remain long.

4 WEDGE-BILLED HUMMINGBIRD   *Schistes geoffroyi*   8cm/3in

700–2200m. A unique, inconspicuous hummingbird of humid foothill and subtropical forest interior (rarely comes to edge). Bill straight and pointed. Male identified by narrow white breast band (sometimes appearing as two separate patches), glittering green forecrown and gorget (often appears dark), and blue and violet patches on sides of breast. Female has white throat, expanding to sides of breast, otherwise much like male. Gorgeted Sunangel (p. 180) also has a narrow white breast band but gorget is purple, and it lacks colorful breast patches. Wedge-billed Hummingbird feeds on flowers at all levels, sometimes clinging to puncture the flower base; rarely visits feeders. Sometimes can be located on a song perch by listening for its very high-pitched, repeated *tseep?* notes.

Three cloud-forest hummingbirds well known for the male's marvelous tails.

1 VIOLET-TAILED SYLPH *Aglaiocercus coelestis* 10–19cm/4–7.5in

800–2400m. Fairly common in humid foothill and subtropical forest and edge; by far the most common sylph in the heavily birded areas around Tandayapa and Mindo. Similar to Long-tailed Sylph; male Violet-tailed is best distinguished by violet throat patch and buffier (less green) underparts; tail color varies based on lighting conditions, but it typically appears turquoise and purple-violet, not green or turquoise like that of Long-tailed. Female Violet-tailed differs from female Long-tailed by white breast patch and glittering blue crown. Violet-tailed Sylph male, with its fabulous tail, is quite conspicuous as it forages at varying heights, tending to come lower at edge and clearings; female is rather inconspicuous, feeding mainly in lower growth. Violet-tailed Sylph regularly comes to feeders at several lodges and reserves in NW.

2 LONG-TAILED SYLPH *Aglaiocercus kingii* 10–18cm/4–7in

1800–2600m. Humid subtropical and temperate zone forest and edge in NW; fairly common in the far N but rare at the S limit of its mapped range. Male lacks Violet-tailed Sylph's violet throat patch and has greener underparts and tail; iridescent tail can look green or turquoise depending on light; tail length varies among individuals. Female Long-tailed lacks the white breast patch and glittering blue crown of female Violet-tailed. See also trainbearers (p. 188). Behavior of Long-tailed Sylph is similar to that of Violet-tailed, but it is not known to visit feeders in our region.

3 BOOTED RACKET-TAIL *Ocreatus underwoodii* 7–11cm/3–4.5in

900–2400m. Fairly common (sometimes abundant around feeders) in humid foothill and subtropical forest, edge, and wooded clearings. Tiny and rather short-billed; male's tail and conspicuous "cotton ball" tibial puffs make it easy to ID. Female lacks long tail and has smaller leg puffs and a white malar streak; she is most similar to female Purple-bibbed Whitetip (p. 180) but, at least in W, has mostly white underparts with green spangles restricted to sides. Andean Emerald (p. 174) is larger and lacks a malar streak. Booted Racket-tail often forages high in canopy with tail cocked up. Aggressive males hover face to face, with tails flared outward and puffs expanded. Female is quite inconspicuous, except around feeders. Can be quite vocal when feeding, emitting a descending, musical *tidididdoo*.

A variety of Andean hummingbirds from several different habitats. ID is usually straightforward; even the less colorful females have strong field marks.

1 PURPLE-BIBBED WHITETIP   *Urosticte benjamini*   8cm/3in

700–2400m. Uncommon in foothill and subtropical forest and edge. Male distinctive, with white central tail spot and postocular streak, glittering green throat, and purple chest patch. Female best distinguished by combination of white postocular streak and green spots on underparts; also note white malar stripe and tail tips. Female can be confused with female Booted Racket-tail (p. 178), which (in W) is mainly white below, lacks postocular streak, and shows green spangling only on flanks. Purple-bibbed Whitetip is solitary and inconspicuous, usually staying inside forest, occasionally coming to edge to visit a feeder or a flowering bush or tree. Small numbers regularly visit feeders at various sites in the Tandayapa-Mindo area.

2 PURPLE-THROATED SUNANGEL   *Heliangelus viola*   11cm/4.5in

1800–3300m. Fairly common in open woodland, forest edge, overgrown clearings, and patches of scrub in S Andes. Bold purple throat and glittering blue forecrown diagnostic in its range; can appear all dark in poor light, in which case the relatively long tail can be a helpful clue. Female is shorter-tailed and duller, but always shows some purple on the throat and usually shows at least a hint of the glittering blue crown. Purple-throated Sunangel is usually encountered alone at forest edge, foraging by hovering or clinging to flowers at medium to upper heights, charateristically holding wings outstretched after perching or while cling-feeding. A regular visitor to feeders in the Utuana Reserve.

3 GORGETED SUNANGEL   *Heliangelus strophianus*   9cm/3.5in

1700–3000m. Uncommon in subtropical and temperate forest and edge. Narrow white pectoral band and glittering, rosy gorget ID this species. Female (not shown) is very similar to male, but has a slightly smaller gorget. Collared Inca (p. 182) is vaguely similar, but has conspicuous white in the tail and a white bib instead of narrow collar. Behavior is similar to that of Purple-throated Sunangel; Gorgeted is a regular visitor to feeders in the Tandayapa Valley.

4 WHITE-TAILED HILLSTAR   *Urochroa bougueri*   12cm/4.5in

1100–2000m. Rare to locally uncommon in humid subtropical forest, especially along rushing streams. Sexes alike; large and dull-colored, with glittering blue throat and breast, and inconspicuous rufous malar; white in tail sometimes hard to see when perched. Not likely confused with any other species within its range; immature brilliants (p. 176) may show a rufous malar, but none show all-blue throat and breast. White-tailed Hillstar is solitary and unobtrusive inside forest, occasionally foraging at edge; rarely visits feeders in the Tandayapa Valley.

5 ECUADORIAN HILLSTAR   *Oreotrochilus chimborazo*   12cm/4.5in

3600–4600m. A robust hummingbird restricted to very high elevation páramo; can be fairly common in areas with large patches of *Chuquiragua jussieui*, a small shrub with spiky orange flowers, but otherwise is rare in W Ecuador. Gorgeous male is unique in range. Female is totally different, but can be identified by large size, dull plumage, decurved bill, and white in tail; Giant Hummingbird (p. 184) is much larger, browner, and has a straight bill. The widespread *jamesonii* subspecies of Ecuadorian Hillstar is shown; male of the *chimborazo* subspecies, endemic to the Chimborazo volcano, is similar but has a glittering green throat; females of both subspecies are similar. Ecuadorian Hillstar characteristically cling feeds on *Chuquiragua jussieui* stems to extract nectar from the flowers, but also hover feeds on other types of flowers.

INCAS AND STARFRONTLETS

Large Andean hummingbirds with long, straight bills. All are sexually dimorphic to varying degrees, and prefer long tubular flowers.

1 BROWN INCA *Coeligena wilsoni* 10cm/4in

1100–2400m. Uncommon to fairly common in forest and edge in foothills and subtropics. Combination of brown plumage and white neck patches is unique in W Ecuador; note inconspicuous glittering violet gorget (reduced in female). Brown Inca is an inconspicuous hummingbird of forest interior, though regularly comes to edge to feed; a familiar visitor to feeders in the Tandayapa-Mindo area.

2 COLLARED INCA *Coeligena torquata* 11cm/4.5in

1800–3000m; occasionally higher. Fairly common in humid subtropical and temperate forest and edge. Dapper and distinctive, with large white bib and conspicuous white tail feathers; note small glittering blue crown patch. Gorgeted Sunangel (p. 180) is vaguely similar but has narrow white breast band, a violet gorget, and lacks white in the tail. Collared Inca feeds conspicuously, flashing about as it forages on a variety of larger flowers. A regular visitor to feeders in the Tandayapa Valley.

3 BUFF-WINGED STARFRONTLET *Coeligena lutetiae* 11cm/4.5in

2700–3600m. Fairly common to common in temperate forest and edge. Sexually dimorphic, but both sexes are easily recognized by their conspicuous buff wing patches. Feeds on a wide variety of flowers at almost any height, and often perches high, with bill held at an upward angle. The most common feeder visitor at the Yanacocha Reserve.

4 RAINBOW STARFRONTLET *Coeligena iris* 12cm/4.5in

2000–3300m. This spectacular hummingbird is fairly common in humid forest, edge, and shrubby clearings in S Andes. Male is slightly brighter on throat and crown than female. No other hummingbird is mostly rufous with a green hood. S subspecies *iris* is shown; N subspecies *hesperus* is very similar but with more extensive green on underparts. Rainbow Starfrontlet frequents flower patches at forest edge as well as more open shrubby areas; it is often hard to see well, as it forages rapidly and moves quickly from flower to flower. Finally getting a good look at a perched male in perfect light is a truly unforgettable experience. A daily visitor to feeders at the Utuana Reserve.

LARGE HIGH-ANDEAN HUMMINGBIRDS

Distinctive hummingbirds of the Andean highlands, including the world's largest. All are easy to ID.

1 SWORD-BILLED HUMMINGBIRD *Ensifera ensifera* 20cm/8in

2500–3600m. Uncommon in temperate forest, edge, wooded clearings, and gardens. Exceptionally long bill, matching the length of its body, renders this unique bird unmistakable. When it is perched against vegetation, bill may be mistaken for a long twig. Generally found alone, usually feeding methodically with a back-and-forth hovering motion at flowering plants, especially those with elongate flowers, including the so-called angel's trumpets often found in highland gardens. It flies quite high above the ground, appearing like a rocket-propelled hypodermic needle. One or two birds can usually be seen visiting feeders at the Yanacocha Reserve.

2 SHINING SUNBEAM *Aglaeactis cupripennis* 12cm/4.5in

2600–4000m. Fairly common in scrub, light woodland, and forest edge at high elevations. Tawny cinnamon below (birds in N are paler than the one shown), with brown upperparts and ear coverts. Male has glittering violet, green, and yellow lower back and rump; female duller, with little or no dorsal glitter; the bird shown is of undetermined sex, since upperparts are mostly hidden. No really similar species, but the overall coloration is reminiscent of the much larger Giant Hummingbird. Shining Sunbeam regularly perches atop bushes and low trees, especially near large flower patches; dives about to feed, often clinging to flowers while holding its wings open; keeps wings extended briefly upon perching. Can be quite confiding, allowing close approach.

3 GIANT HUMMINGBIRD *Patagona gigas* 18cm/7in

2000–3800m. The world's largest hummingbird; uncommon in dry scrub, agricultural areas, and gardens in the highlands. Monstrous size, mostly brown plumage, and white rump are enough to ID it; its size and very slow wingbeats can make it appear as something completely different (e.g., a swallow or swift), until the typical hummingbird shape can be seen. Bold, with notably slow and powerful wingbeats; often perches on exposed branches, stalks, and even wires. Feeds on a wide variety of flowers, but tends to favor freshly blooming agave when present; occasionally visits feeders. Call is a characteristic high-pitched, grosbeak-like *peek!*

4 GREAT SAPPHIREWING *Pterophanes cyanopterus* 15cm/6in

3000–3600m. This huge hummingbird is fairly common in humid temperate forest and edge. Large size and shining blue wings make it easy to ID. Female has cinnamon underparts and reduced blue in wings; young male is intermediate in plumage between male and female adults. Great Sapphirewing is found alone or in small groups congregating at flowers or feeders; regularly hover feeds, though also may feed from a perch. Wingbeats are slow and laborious when hovering; flight is often high and bounding. A regular visitor to the feeders at the Yanacocha Reserve.

PUFFLEGS

Andean hummingbirds with relatively short, straight bills and prominent tibial puffs.

1 SAPPHIRE-VENTED PUFFLEG *Eriocnemis luciani* 12cm/4.5in

2500–3700m. Fairly common in temperate forest, edge, and isolated wooded areas. Sexes alike; the only puffleg in our range with shining blue forecrown and glittering blue crissum; also note lack of throat patch. Usually encountered alone or in small groups congregating at feeders or large flower patches, where it vigorously chases away smaller hummingbirds. Hovers or cling feeds on a wide variety of flowering plants; a common visitor to feeders at the Yanacocha Reserve.

2 GOLDEN-BREASTED PUFFLEG *Eriocnemis mosquera* 12cm/4.5in

3000–3600m. Uncommon in temperate forest, edge, and adjacent shrubbery. Combination of coppery-golden breast and lack of blue in plumage is diagnostic. Behavior is similar to that of Sapphire-vented Puffleg, but Golden-breasted is not as common and is less aggressive around flowers and feeders. Small numbers visit the feeders at Yanacocha Reserve.

3 BLACK-BREASTED PUFFLEG *Eriocnemis nigrivestis* 9cm/3.5in

2800–3600m. A small, very rare, and critically endangered Ecuadorian endemic. Found inside humid temperate forest and edge in the NW; most often seen at the Yanacocha Reserve, where it has even visited feeders on a few occasions. Male is very dark; all-dark head and blue back separate it from other pufflegs. Female is rather different, but no other puffleg has blue throat patch bordered by a pale whisker, and gold-spangled underparts. Poorly known, but usually encountered alone, feeding on small, tubular flowers at low to mid levels at edge of forest.

4 BLACK-THIGHED PUFFLEG *Eriocnemis derbyi* 8cm/3in

3000–3500m. Uncommon and restricted to the far N, where it is found in temperate forest edge and scrub near tree line; perhaps most easily seen near Cerro Mongus and the nearby Guandera Biological Station. Tibial puffs (black in male, white in female), are inconspicuous and hard to see. Best identified by glittering green rump and crissum in both sexes. Glowing Puffleg has violet-blue crissum and conspicuous white puffs. Black-thighed Puffleg is usually seen alone, foraging actively at low flowers.

5 HOARY PUFFLEG *Haplophaedia lugens* 9cm/3.5in

1500–2300m. Rare and inconspicuous inside humid subtropical forest in NW. Dull and brownish-looking; scaled breast and small white tibial puffs are the best ID features. No other puffleg occurs with it, but see Buff-tailed Coronet (p. 166), which is much brighter green, lacks scaling on breast, and has a buff tail. Not often encountered, Hoary Puffleg tends to remain inside forest, often near streams, where single birds may be seen feeding on a variety of flowering shrubs, small trees, vines, and epiphytes.

6 GLOWING PUFFLEG *Eriocnemis vestita* 9cm/3.5in

2800–3300m. Uncommon and local in humid temperate forest and edge. Mainly an E slope species, but occurs in our region near the continental divide, e.g., Pasochoa Reserve. Both sexes show violet crissum and bright glittering green rump; male has violet throat patch; female (not shown) has blue throat patch and a buffy tinge to the breast. Behavior is much like that of other small pufflegs.

THORNBILLS AND TRAINBEARERS

Thornbills have very short "thumbtack" bills, while trainbearers are distinctively long-tailed. All species on this page are found mainly at high elevations in the Andes.

1 PURPLE-BACKED THORNBILL *Ramphomicron microrhynchum* 8cm/3in

2500–3700m. Unpredictable and possibly nomadic in humid temperate forest and edge; it may be fairly common at a site for a few weeks only to seemingly vanish for months. Stunning male not likely to be mistaken if seen well. Female is not as colorful, but no other hummer has combination of very short bill, white underparts heavily spangled with green, and white-tipped tail. Usually encountered alone, foraging from mid heights to canopy; occasionally small numbers congregate at flowering trees, where they feed on small composite flowers, hovering or even walking over them as they probe for nectar.

2 BLUE-MANTLED THORNBILL *Chalcostigma stanleyi* 12cm/4.5in

3600–4200m. Uncommon to fairly common in páramo and temperate forest edge near tree line. Male has long, narrow glittering green and purple gorget; no other high-elevation, long-tailed hummer is so uniformly dark. Female is duller and lacks gorget; it is told from female Rainbow-bearded Thornbill by lack of rufous forecrown. Paler female Ecuadorian Hillstar (p. 180) has a much longer, decurved bill. Blue-mantled Thornbill often clings to small flowers as it feeds, and even occasionally perches on the ground in páramo. It can be rather inconspicuous until it flies off rapidly to feed elsewhere.

3 RAINBOW-BEARDED THORNBILL *Chalcostigma herrani* 10cm/4in

2800–3700m. This attractive, rufous-crowned thornbill is uncommon in temperate forest edge and scrub, often around rocky outcrops and cliffs. Easily identified by tiny bill and rufous forehead and crown stripe, along with conspicuous white tips to tail. Male has narrow gorget that appears dark at most angles, only to burst into color as the bird turns his head. Solitary, usually seen perching unobtrusively atop a shrub or cling-feeding on relatively small flowers.

4 GREEN-TAILED TRAINBEARER *Lesbia nuna* 11–17cm/4.5–6.5in

1700–3600m. Uncommon in humid temperate forest edge, light woodland, and scrubby roadsides, seasonally descending to the subtropics. Smaller than Black-tailed Trainbearer, with a straighter, stiffer tail, but usually best identified by bill shape in areas of overlap: Green-tailed Trainbearer has a short, thin, and almost straight bill, compared with Black-tailed's longer, thicker, and noticeably decurved bill. Green-tailed feeds at all heights; usually solitary, but small groups may congregate where flowers are in abundance. Displaying male emits a crackling sound with tail.

5 BLACK-TAILED TRAINBEARER *Lesbia victoriae* 13–24cm/5–9.5in

2300–3800m. Common throughout much of the high Andes in lightly wooded areas, scrub, edges of fields, gardens, parks, and even in cities. Fully adult male has a spectacularly long tail that curves slightly upward when the bird is either perched or in flight. Immature male (with shorter tail) and female are easily confused with Green-tailed Trainbearer, which can also show much black in the tail. Bill shape is usually the best feature: Black-tailed has a thicker, noticeably decurved bill, while Green-tailed has a shorter, thinner, almost straight bill. Black-tailed Trainbearer forages at all heights, even high up in flowering *Eucalyptus*. Displaying male emits a crackling sound with tail.

VELVETBREAST AND METALTAILS

High Andean hummingbirds that show strong sexual dimorphism. Mountain Velvetbreast has a distinctive decurved bill; metaltails are smaller and have relatively short, straight bills.

1 MOUNTAIN VELVETBREAST *Lafresnaya lafresnayi* 9cm/3.5in

2400–3600m. Uncommon in temperate forest and edge. No other high-Andean hummingbird has such a decurved bill; also note white in tail, which can be conspicuous in flight. Male has a black belly; female has mostly white underparts. Solitary; tends to remain low in shrubbery, moving very quickly from flower to flower; flashes tail with rapid open-and-shut action as it feeds. Occasionally visits feeders, but very skittish and usually does not stay long.

2 TYRIAN METALTAIL *Metallura tyrianthina* 8cm/3in

2500–4100m. The most widespread metaltail, common in temperate forest edge and scrubby clearings throughout the Andean highlands. Both sexes have shining coppery tail. Male has glittering green gorget; lower underparts are much paler than those of Viridian Metaltail. Female Tyrian has distinctive cinnamon-buff throat and breast. Single birds or small groups forage actively at flower patches, and regularly use holes punched by flowerpiercers (pp. 396–398) in larger flowers; often clings to flowers rather than hover feed.

3 VIRIDIAN METALTAIL *Metallura williami* 8cm/3in

2600–4000m. Limited distribution in W on Páramo El Angel and near the continental divide; also a recent record at the Utuana Reserve. Locally uncommon in páramo, shrubby clearings, and temperate forest edge. Tail in both sexes blue above and green below, but often looks dark in the field. Viridians appear uniform and dark in the field; male shows glittering dark green gorget in N (*primolina*) or black gorget in S (*atrigularis*; not shown). Female lacks gorget and has buffy throat scaling; short bill and mostly uniform plumage also help distinguish it from other species. Viridian Metaltail is usually encountered alone, feeding low on flowering bushes, occasionally perching high atop a tree or shrub.

4 VIOLET-THROATED METALTAIL *Metallura baroni* 8cm/3in

3000–3900m. Endemic to Ecuador; found only in and around El Cajas National Park W of Cuenca, where it inhabits páramo, scrub, shrubby edges to pastures, and *Polylepis* woodland. Easily identified in its tiny range by combination of its bronzy-brown coloration, violet throat, small size, and short bill. Behavior much like that of Viridian Metaltail; Violet-throated can be quite inconspicuous, but is also confiding and frequently allows close approach.

♂ 1 ♀ 1
♂ 2 ♀ 2
♂ primolina 3 ♀ primolina 3

ASSORTED WOODSTARS

Woodstars are tiny, beelike hummingbirds distributed throughout Ecuador; most species have two white or buffy lateral dorsal spots. All species show strong sexual dimorphism, and females can be challenging to ID. Woodstars feed on flowers at varying heights, but tend to perch on bare branches atop a shrub or even the canopy of a tall tree.

1 PURPLE-THROATED WOODSTAR *Calliphlox mitchellii* 6–7cm/2.5–3in

800–2300m; occasionally wanders lower. Fairly common in humid foothill and subtropical forest edge and adjacent clearings. Note prominent white lateral dorsal spot. Adult male is distinctive, with purple gorget, white collar, and long narrow tail; female and young male are more difficult and not always safely identified; note white throat (often flecked with green) and collar, which contrast strongly with rufous lower underparts and narrow postocular line. Female White-bellied Woodstar (p. 194) usually (but not always) has a more distinct, white belly and wider postocular line. Female Little Woodstar (p. 194) shows entirely cinnamon-buff underparts and postocular line and an all-cinnamon tail base. Purple-throated Woodstar forages at varying heights, though often perches high on exposed branches in canopy. This species is a regular visitor to feeders in the Tandayapa-Mindo region; numbers vary depending on season, but it usually outnumbers White-bellied Woodstar there.

2 SHORT-TAILED WOODSTAR *Myrmia micrura* 6cm/2.5in

0–800m. This tiny, almost tailless woodstar is uncommon in desert scrub, deciduous forest edge, and occasionally even parks and gardens in W and SW (also Isla de la Plata). Male displays a unique facial pattern, with a white postocular streak and narrow white whisker bordering the upper edge of the gorget. Female is buffy white below and, unlike other woodstars that could occur with it, does not show a distinctive facial pattern. Short-tailed Woodstar forages at low heights, often on sparsely flowered shrubs, managing to survive even in nearly barren areas.

3 PURPLE-COLLARED WOODSTAR *Myrtis fanny* 6–7cm/2.5–3in

1400–2800m. Uncommon to locally fairly common in arid inter-Andean valleys, where it inhabits light woodland, scrub, parks, and gardens. Large and stocky compared to other woodstars, it has a long, slightly decurved bill and lacks dorsal spots. Male is unique, with mostly mostly glittering azure gorget bordered below by a glittering purple collar; in poor light the gorget will look all dark. Female is very plain and often does not even look like a woodstar; note the white tail tips and decurved bill; no other similar hummingbird regularly occurs with it. Purple-collared is usually found alone, foraging on low flowering shrubs; lacks the characteristic beelike flight of other woodstars. Males seasonally engage in impressive deep U-shaped display flights.

♂ 3   ♀ 3

Chaetocercus is a genus of miniscule hummingbirds; all species are strongly sexually dimorphic and have two white or buffy lateral dorsal spots. Females cannot always be safely identified in the field. These woodstars forage at varying heights depending on flower location, and sometimes perch on exposed branches high in the canopy. They also engage is seasonal movements that are poorly understood.

1 WHITE-BELLIED WOODSTAR *Chaetocercus mulsant* 6–7cm/2.5–3in

1100–3500m. Fairly common in a wide range of elevations and habitats, from humid forest edge to city parks and gardens, though avoids forest interior. Very seasonal; apparently breeds in the highlands and then disperses to lower elevations. Larger and stockier than other woodstars, with a potbellied appearance. Male's pure white belly separates it from other woodstars typically found with it; Esmeraldas Woodstar, which only very rarely wanders to the Andes, has longer outer tail feathers. Female White-bellied Woodstar varies from white to rufous in belly color; rufous-bellied birds can be very similar to both Purple-throated (p. 192) and Little Woodstars; see those species for details. White-bellied Woodstar is usually encountered alone, though several may congregate at feeders. Flying male creates distinctive ringing by whirring its wings that can help draw attention to its presence.

2 LITTLE WOODSTAR *Chaetocercus bombus* 6–7cm/2.5–3in

0–2000m. Rare and unpredictable in both humid and deciduous forest, preferring edge and clearings. Found mostly in lowlands and foothills, but seasonally moves up into the subtropics. Male in full alternate plumage is rarely encountered. In male, cinnamon-buff wash to the pectoral collar is diagnostic. Female is mostly cinnamon buff below and has tail cinnamon with black subterminal band; if seen, unbroken cinnamon base of tail separates female from other woodstars in range. Female Esmeraldas Woodstar is slightly paler on throat and has a whiter postocular line. Female White-bellied usually (but not always) shows a whiter belly, and has a whiter postocular line and green central tail feathers. Little Woodstar is usually found alone, tending not to congregate at flowering trees; on rare occasions, females visit feeders in the Tandayapa-Mindo area.

3 GORGETED WOODSTAR *Chaetocercus heliodor* 6cm/2.5in

1500–2200m(?). Very rare; range and status in W uncertain; known from only a few records of females in humid foothill and subtropical forest. The birds shown were photographed in E Ecuador, where the species is much more common. Male distinguished from other woodstars by "handlebar" gorget that extends nearly to breast, mostly dark underparts, and lack of a bright white collar. Female's rufous rump is diagnostic; otherwise very similar to several other female woodstars. Gorgeted Woodstar is usually found alone; behavior is similar to that of other small woodstars.

4 ESMERALDAS WOODSTAR *Chaetocercus berlepschi* 6–7cm/2.5–3in

0–200m; vagrants to 2000m. Rare and local in semi-humid and deciduous forest edge and clearings; range is poorly known, but most records come from within 40km (25mi) of coast, especially from the Ayampe area and in the nearby coastal hills. There are also scattered records from higher elevations on the W slope. Male's all-white lower underparts separate it from other woodstars in its normal range and habitat. Female is very similar to female Little Woodstar but typically has a whiter throat and postocular line, an elongate auricular patch, and a rufous tail base broken by darker central tail feathers. Esmeraldas Woodstar is known to wander to higher elevations, where it could overlap with White-bellied Woodstar; male Esmeraldas has longer outer tail feathers; females cannot always be safely separated in the field. Esmeraldas Woodstar is sometimes observed perching on low twigs above a favored flowering shrub.

♂ 4

♀ 4

QUETZALS AND SMALL RED-BELLIED TROGONS

Quetzals and trogons make up a family of large and colorful forest birds. All are sexually dimorphic; tail pattern and eye-ring shape and color are often important ID keys. These birds perch quietly for long periods on their surprisingly small feet, turning their heads ever so slowly from side to side, occasionally sallying out to pluck fruit from branches or to snatch up a large insect.

1 GOLDEN-HEADED QUETZAL *Pharomachrus auriceps* 34cm/13.5in

1000–2600m. Fairly common in humid forest, edge, and wooded clearings from foothills to the temperate zone. Male separated from Crested Quetzal by black underside of tail, golden sheen on head, and lack of crest. Female Golden-headed very similar to Crested, but lacks white barring on outer tail feathers and has a greener (less brown) head. Golden-headed Quetzal is usually encountered alone or in pairs, but occasionally several birds will congregate at a fruiting tree; found at mid levels to subcanopy; generally quite lethargic. Song (easily imitated) is a series of paired whistles: *kaa-wooo, kaa-wooo, kaa-wooo, kaa-wooo*. Also emits a descending cackle, often in flight.

2 CRESTED QUETZAL *Pharomachrus antisianus* 33cm/13in

1500–2500m. Uncommon in humid subtropical and temperate forest, edge, and wooded clearings. Male's laterally compressed frontal crest and white underside of tail distinguish it from Golden-headed Quetzal. Female Crested has white barring on the outer tail feathers and a browner head than female Golden-headed. Red irides in both sexes of Crested is also a useful ID feature if it can be seen. Behavior similar to that of Golden-headed. Song is a series of paired whistles, shorter and sharper than in Golden-headed, e.g., *ku-WOAW, ku-WOAW, ku-WOAW*...; also gives a cackle similar to that of Golden-headed.

3 COLLARED TROGON *Trogon collaris* 25cm/10in

0–1600m. Fairly common in humid forest, edge, and wooded clearings from lowlands to subtropics. Male can be separated from the very similar Masked Trogon by wide and even black-and-white barring on the undertail that can still be seen at a distance; female distinguished from Masked by broken white eye-ring, dark culmen, and lack of distinct black face mask. Lethargic; encountered alone or in pairs from lower levels to subcanopy. Song a series of three to six soft whistles with the first one doubled, e.g., *kwitit-kwo-kwo-kwo-kwo*; also gives a crisp, descending churr as tail is sharply raised and then lowered.

4 MASKED TROGON *Trogon personatus* 25cm/10in

1500–3600m; locally down to 1100m. Fairly common in habitats similar to those occupied by Collared Trogon, but occurs mainly at higher elevations. In the zone of overlap, male Masked can be distinguished by the fine black-and-white undertail barring; in poor light, at a distance, or without a scope, barring can be invisible. Female shows a distinct black face mask, white postocular mark, and an all-yellow bill. Behavior as in Collared Trogon. Song is a soft, very slow series of 2 to 10 *woh* notes; also gives a churr call similar to that of Collared.

LARGE RED-BELLIED TROGONS

Large trogons found mainly at lower elevations; these species all have solid black undertails and red bellies. They overlap only minimally, so location and habitat are helpful for ID.

1 CHOCÓ TROGON *Trogon comptus* 28cm/11in

300–1200m. Fairly common in humid lowland and foothill forest and edge in NW. Male separated from other green and red trogons by white irides, yellow bill, and lack of both an eye-ring and a white breast band. Female is very similar to female Ecuadorian Trogon (little or no overlap) but has more extensive gray underparts and never has a breast band. Chocó Trogon avoids the deciduous and semi-humid forest that Ecuadorian Trogon prefers; usually encountered alone or in pairs, mostly from mid levels to subcanopy. Typical song is an evenly paced series of 8 to 30 mellow *kow* notes; calls include a rapid, descending *cwa-cwa-cwa-cwa-cuh-cuh* and a soft cackle. Also called **Blue-tailed Trogon**.

2 SLATY-TAILED TROGON *Trogon massena* 32cm/12.5in

0–200m. Uncommon in humid lowland forest and edge in far NW near the Colombian border. Male's orange bill is diagnostic; female can be identified by her two-tone orange and gray bill, and brown (not pale) irides. Behavior is much like that of Chocó Trogon. Song is a long series of *kow* notes; the notes start soft and muffled but quickly become loud and strident, lacking the mellow quality of other similar species; also gives a faster but much quieter series.

3 ECUADORIAN TROGON *Trogon mesurus* 32cm/12.5in

0–800m; locally to 2000m in SW. Fairly common in deciduous and semi-humid forest and edge, mostly in lowlands and foothills, but locally higher; uncommon and local in more humid areas of NW. Male is the only green and red trogon with yellow bill, red eye-ring, and white breast band; note gray-white irides. Female is very similar to female Chocó Trogon (little or no overlap), but has less extensive gray on underparts and may show a hint of a white breast band. Behavior of Ecuadorian Trogon is similar to that of other large trogons, but especially in drier areas it can be quite conspicuous and more apt to appear at forest edge. Song is a series of *kow* notes that starts out soft, increases in pitch, and becomes quite loud, then drops off again at the end; also gives a soft, rapid *cho-cho-cho-cho-cho-cho-cho-cho* call.

YELLOW-BELLIED TROGONS

These species overlap widely in the lowlands and foothills of NW. Tail pattern along with coloration, size, and shape of the eye-ring are helpful ID clues.

1 WHITE-TAILED TROGON *Trogon chionurus* 28cm/11in

0–900m. Fairly common in humid forest and edge in lowlands and foothills. Male can be identified by blue head, broad milky-white eye-ring, and all-white undertail. Female is very similar to female Gartered Trogon, but is larger and has a complete, unbroken eye-ring and more extensive undertail barring. White-tailed Trogon is encountered at varying heights inside forest, though most often at mid levels, and is often seen at forest edge and in clearings. Typical song is a series of 20 or so down-slurred *kwoh* notes that starts very softly and gradually becomes louder; also gives a much faster series that slowly rises and falls in pitch and can go on for a minute or more. A soft *chup* is also given, either alone or repeated several times.

2 BLACK-THROATED TROGON *Trogon rufus* 25cm/10in

0–800m. Uncommon inside humid lowland and foothill forest. Color combination of both sexes is unique; male is the only green and yellow trogon in our range, and female is the only brown and yellow trogon. Male might be confused with Gartered Trogon in difficult light, but Black-throated has a contrasting black face and throat. Black-throated inhabits forest interior and is less likely to come to forest edge than other trogons; favors lower forest strata. Song is an even-paced series of 4 to 10 *cwoh* notes, much slower than the songs of the other trogons on this page; call is a drawn-out, down-slurred churr.

3 GARTERED TROGON *Trogon caligatus* 23cm/9in

0–900m. Fairly common and widespread in both humid and deciduous forest and edge in lowlands and foothills. Male's blue head and yellow eye-ring are diagnostic, though in some lighting conditions it might be confused with Black-throated Trogon; Gartered lacks a distinct throat and face patch. Female Gartered is very similar to the larger female White-tailed Trogon, but note broken eye-ring and mostly black center to undertail. Behavior is similar to that of larger White-tailed. Song is a fast, 5–7 sec. series of evenly spaced *tu* notes; call is a stuttered, descending churr. Formerly called **Northern Violaceous Trogon**.

KINGFISHERS

Familiar fish-eating birds with bushy crests and thick, elongate bills. Kingfishers hunt by plunge diving, usually from a perch located over water, though occasionally will hover dive for prey. All species nest in burrows in banks.

1 RINGED KINGFISHER *Megaceryle torquata* 40cm/15.5in

0–2800m. Ecuador's largest kingfisher, found in aquatic habitats nearly throughout W Ecuador; common at lower elevations, but scarce and local higher in the Andes. Large size, blue-gray upperparts, and largely rufous underparts separate it from other kingfishers (but see note). Usually encountered alone or in well-spaced pairs, often perched conspicuously; can sometimes be seen flying high overhead emitting a series of harsh, rattled *CHEK* notes. *Note*: **Belted Kingfisher** (*M. alcyon*; not shown) is a vagrant to W Ecuador (one record); it is similar in color to Ringed but smaller; male has rufous on underparts restricted to narrow chest band and flanks; female shows no rufous at all.

2 GREEN KINGFISHER *Chloroceryle americana* 19cm/7.5in

0–1400m. The most common small kingfisher in W Ecuador, found along streams, rivers, lake margins, marshes, and mangroves throughout the lowlands and foothills. Male can be distinguished from other small kingfishers by all-white lower underparts with rufous restricted to breast; female is the only green kingfisher with no rufous. Rather solitary, usually seen perched on a low branch or rock close to the water's surface or flying low over the water. Gives a soft *tik-tik* or a crackling rattle.

3 AMERICAN PYGMY KINGFISHER *Chloroceryle aenea* 13cm/5in

0–700m. Rare and local along dark, wooded streams, riverbanks, ponds, and swamps in the lowlands and foothills. White mid-belly and crissum separate it from the even rarer Green-and-rufous Kingfisher. Male Green Kingfisher has all-white lower underparts and whiter throat and neck. The tiny pygmy kingfisher is easy to overlook as it often perches inside tangled vegetation along the water's edge; it is usually encountered alone, perching low, sometimes very close to the water's surface. Flies rapidly, low over the water, often giving a short, sharp *djeet* as it goes. Rarely heard song is a series of soft crackles and short, descending trills.

4 GREEN-AND-RUFOUS KINGFISHER *Chloroceryle inda* 22cm/8.5in

0–200m. Now very rare in W due to deforestation; probably found only in far NW lowlands along sluggish wooded streams and in swampy forest. A chunky version of the smaller American Pygmy Kingfisher, from which both sexes differ by lack of white belly and crissum. Green-and-rufous Kingfisher often remains in dense cover and can easily be overlooked. It is rather solitary, usually perching low over the water. Call, usually given in flight, is a sharp, raspy, and down-slurred *djeuw*.

♂ 4

♀ 4

Motmots are colorful birds with long tails ending in two central "rackets." They perch upright, often swishing their tails from side to side in a pendulum motion. Jacamars have iridescent plumage and long bills that can impart a hummingbird-like appearance. Motmots and jacamars feed primarily on large insects and nest in burrows in earthen banks. Lanceolated Monklet is a small, distinctive puffbird (see p. 206).

1 RUFOUS MOTMOT *Baryphthengus martii* 43–46cm/17–18in

0–1700m. Fairly common in humid forest, edge, and lighter woodland in the lowlands and foothills; also ranges locally into the subtropics. Similar to Broad-billed Motmot, but has a smaller breast spot and more rufous on the underparts, extending about three-quarters of the way down from the chin to the belly; note narrow bill. Rufous Motmot is usually encountered perched unobtrusively at low to mid heights inside forest or at edge, often swishing its tail; occasionally visits feeders (e.g., Milpe Bird Sanctuary). Gives a deep, resonant *whoo-doop*, or a longer series of *whoo* notes. Vocalizations are most often heard at dawn or dusk.

2 BROAD-BILLED MOTMOT *Electron platyrhynchum* 33–36cm/13–14in

0–1700m. Fairly common in humid lowland, foothill, and subtropical forest and edge, broadly overlapping with the larger Rufous Motmot. Broad-billed Motmot can be distinguished by its larger black breast spot and rufous on underparts extending only halfway from the chin to the belly. Behavior similar to that of Rufous Motmot. Typical vocalization of Broad-billed is a hoarse and grating *graaw*, given alone or in a long series.

3 WHOOPING MOTMOT *Momotus subrufescens* 39–41cm/15.5–16in

0–1000m; to 1800m in SW. Fairly common in deciduous and semi-humid forest, edge, and adjacent clearings; uncommon and local in more humid forest. Very different from other W Ecuador motmots; note mostly green plumage and conspicuous bright turquoise-blue crown bordered by black. Behavior is like that of other motmots, but Whooping can be more conspicuous, occasionally even perching on telephone wires and fences. Most commonly heard call is a single, low-pitched *whoop?*, given every few seconds, and also occasionally a faster *pu-pu-pu-pu-pu-pu…* series. Formerly included with **Blue-crowned Motmot** (*M. coeruliceps*).

4 RUFOUS-TAILED JACAMAR *Galbula ruficauda* 24cm/9.5in

0–800m. Fairly common in humid lowland and foothill forest, edge, and wooded clearings. Female (not shown) is very similar to male but has a cinnamon throat. Iridescent plumage and long, slender bill can suggest an enormous hummingbird. The larger Great Jacamar lacks green on the breast and has a shorter, thicker, and decurved bill. Rufous-tailed Jacamar is encountered alone or in pairs, sometimes perched side by side, often sitting quietly on an exposed branch; preys primarily on butterflies and moths taken in swooping sallies, and often returns to the same perch. Song is a series of sharp squeaks that accelerates into a very loud, fast trill; call is just a single squeak that may be repeated every few seconds.

5 GREAT JACAMAR *Jacamerops aureus* 30cm/12in

0–500m. Rare and local in subcanopy of humid lowland forest in the far NW. Male (not shown) is very similar to female but has a white throat. Distinguished from the smaller and much more common Rufous-tailed Jacamar by the rufous (not green) breast and shorter, thicker, decurved bill. Great Jacamar is easily overlooked, as it perches inconspicuously in upper forest strata, remaining motionless for long periods, making occasional short sallies to capture prey. Best located by voice; song is a mournful, descending *KEEEyooooo*; also gives a strange, catlike growl followed by a soft whistle.

6 LANCEOLATED MONKLET *Micromonacha lanceolata* 13cm/5in

0–1400m. The smallest puffbird; rare to uncommon in humid lowland and foothill forest and edge. Shape, heavy bill, and dark breast streaks help ID this species; White-whiskered Puffbird (p. 206) is larger, longer-tailed, and has an orange-rufous breast. Lanceolated Monklet often escapes detection, perching unobtrusively on a horizontal branch at varying heights, occasionally sallying out to catch prey or flying rapidly to another perch. Song is a series of thin, up-slurred *seep?* notes that gradually accelerate and become louder.

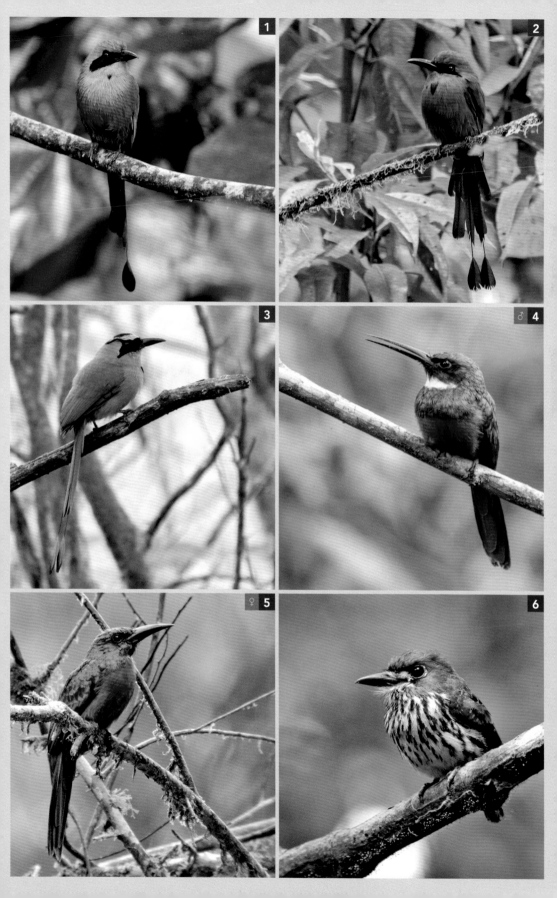

PUFFBIRDS

Puffbirds are stocky, large-headed forest birds; the sexes are alike, except in White-whiskered Puffbird. Most are found in lowlands and foothills, but White-faced Nunbird is a rare Andean puffbird found at higher elevations. Puffbirds tend to perch motionless for long periods of time, occasionally sallying out to catch large arthropods and small vertebrates.

1 WHITE-NECKED PUFFBIRD *Notharchus hyperrhynchus* 25cm/10in

0–600m. The largest puffbird in our region; uncommon in humid and semi-humid lowland forest and lighter woodland. Distinguished from other black-and-white puffbirds by large size, bold white forehead patch that extends over eyes, and complete white collar that extends from throat to nape. Singles, pairs, or family groups usually stay high in the canopy, often perching on exposed branches. Song is a long, flat trill, *pi'pi'pi'pi'pi'pi'pi...*, lasting 6 sec. or longer.

2 BLACK-BREASTED PUFFBIRD *Notharchus pectoralis* 20cm/8in

0–200m. Restricted to the extreme NW near the Colombian border, where it is uncommon in humid lowland forest, edge, and light woodland. Identified by its entirely black head with white throat separated from hind-collar. Similar to White-necked Puffbird in behavior but more likely to perch lower. Very long song begins with a series of soft *wip* notes that gradually become longer and higher, and ends with a louder, descending *WIT-where-weeyr-weer-wer-wer-WIT-wit-WER-wit-WER....*

3 PIED PUFFBIRD *Notharchus tectus* 15cm/6in

0–500m. Uncommon in humid lowland forest, edge, and light woodland. Separated from other black-and-white puffbirds by small size, narrow white superciliary that does not extend over forecrown, spotted crown, and white wing patches. Similar to Black-breasted Puffbird in behavior, and the two are often together where their ranges overlap. Typical song is a high, piping *t't't, peee, pi'p'p'p'pee-pity-pity-pity-pity-pity-pity...*, descending toward the end.

4 BARRED PUFFBIRD *Nystalus radiatus* 22cm/8.5in

0–1500m. Uncommon in humid lowland and foothill forest, edge, and clearings with scattered trees. Cinnamon and buff plumage with black barring and scaling distinguishes it from all other puffbirds in its range. Usually found alone or in widely spaced pairs that perch quietly at mid to upper forest levels. Most easily seen at forest edge, and can be far more difficult to spot inside forest. Often the key to locating the bird is its song, a slow, mournful, wolf whistle: *whiiiiip?......wooOOOooh.*

5 WHITE-WHISKERED PUFFBIRD *Malacoptila panamensis* 19cm/7.5in

0–1200m. Uncommon to fairly common inside humid forest in lowlands and foothills. Recognized by orange-rufous bib, dusky-streaked belly, and stiff white rictal bristles that form a "mustache". Female (not shown) is lighter brown than male and lacks white lores. Singles or pairs perch unobtrusively at low levels. This puffbird is easily overlooked; occasional quick sallies may draw attention to its presence. Occasionally joins mixed-species flocks and attends army ant swarms. Typical call is a very high-pitched, down-slurred whistle, e.g., *tseeeeeeew.* Also sometimes gives a series of high-pitched rasps intermixed with lower grunts.

6 WHITE-FACED NUNBIRD *Hapaloptila castanea* 23cm/9in

1300–2400m. Rare in humid subtropical forest; occurs at higher elevations than other puffbirds. Note rufous underparts and conspicuous white forecrown and throat; no similar species occur with it. Not often encountered; most records in our region come from the Tandayapa-Mindo area. Solitary, and most often encountered perched quietly from mid levels to subcanopy. Song is a series of rising, mellow whistles, given at a pace of about one per second.

Barbets are colorful forest birds, closely related to the toucans. The smaller species show strong sexual dimorphism. Sexes are similar in the larger Toucan Barbet, now placed in a separate family.

1 RED-HEADED BARBET *Eubucco bourcierii* 16cm/6.5in

100–2000m. Fairly common in humid forest, edge, and wooded clearings in the foothills and subtropics; locally down into lowlands. Male has striking red head and yellow bill. Female is very different, but plumage is still unique in our range; note especially the thick yellow bill and orange, blue, and black head pattern. Often encountered in pairs; regularly joins mixed-species flocks, especially with tanagers, foraging rather acrobatically, stretching and hanging upside down, as it plucks fruit and searches foliage and dead leaf clusters for insects. Visits feeders at various sites, e.g., the Tandayapa Valley, Milpe Bird Sanctuary, and Tinalandia Nature Reserve. Song is a fast, soft, and low-pitched *oo'oo'oo'oo'oo'oo'oo'oo'o o'oo'oo'oo'oo*, given by male as he perches stationary with head pointing sharply downward.

2 ORANGE-FRONTED BARBET *Capito squamatus* 18cm/7in

0–900m. Fairly common in humid lowland and foothill forest, lighter woodland, edge, and adjacent clearings. Combination of black-and-white plumage and orange forecrown is diagnostic; also note typical large barbet bill. Female differs from male by black throat and breast. Male Five-colored Barbet (restricted to extreme NW) has yellow lower underparts and extensive red on crown and nape. Behavior of Orange-fronted is similar to that of Red-headed Barbet, but it is perhaps somewhat less acrobatic. Song is a very soft, low, and guttural gargle, lasting up to 7 sec. or longer; also gives a series of creaking rasps.

3 FIVE-COLORED BARBET *Capito quinticolor* 17cm/6.5in

0–300m. Rare to locally fairly common in humid lowland forest in extreme NW. Male can be separated from Orange-fronted Barbet by yellow lower underparts, black flank spots, and mostly red crown (not white and orange). Female is best identified by typical barbet shape and extensive spotting on underparts. Five-colored Barbet is usually encountered alone or in pairs, feeding on fruit in the canopy, occasionally joining mixed-species flocks. Song is a soft, low-pitched series of eight or more evenly spaced *ooh* notes; typical call is a series of rasping grunts.

4 TOUCAN BARBET *Semnornis ramphastinus* 21cm/8.5in

1100–2400m. A spectacular, multicolor denizen of humid subtropical forest, edge, and adjacent clearings; also occurs locally down into the foothills (e.g., Milpe Bird Sanctuary). Large size, thick bill, and unique coloration render this bird easily identifiable. Encountered alone, in pairs, or in small groups, often congregating at fruiting trees with other birds; also regularly joins mixed-species foraging flocks (especially with tanagers), and even comes to feeders in some areas (e.g., Paz de las Aves Refuge, Tandayapa Valley). Although large and bulky, Toucan Barbet can still be quite acrobatic while foraging. Distinctive song is a series of nasal *honk* calls that starts softly and quickly becomes louder. Both members of a pair often sing at the same time in a raucous, off-tempo duet; also gives sharp, toneless bill claps and clucks.

4

Small, attractively patterned forest toucans. Yellow-eared Toucanet is strikingly sexually dimorphic; in other species plumage is nearly identical, but males have longer bills than females. All species discussed here are mostly frugivorous, but regularly take insects, reptiles, amphibians, and even birds and bird eggs. Both aracaris are often lumped with **Collared Aracari** (*Pteroglossus torquatus*).

1 PALE-MANDIBLED ARACARI *Pteroglossus erythropygius* 41–43cm/16–17in

0–1600m. Common in humid and semi-humid lowland and foothill forest, edge, and clearings with scattered trees. Note black and yellow plumage with dark belly band and breast spot; bill is pale with a black stripe along bottom of upper mandible and black on tip of lower. Stripe-billed Aracari (restricted to far NW) is identical in plumage, but differs by having an all-black lower mandible. Immature Pale-mandibled (not shown) may show a dusky lower mandible but never the glossy black of Stripe-billed. Pale-mandibled Aracari usually ranges through forest canopy and subcanopy, sometimes descending lower at edge, in small bands of up to eight individuals. Common vocalizations include squeaking hiccup or "sneezing" notes.

2 STRIPE-BILLED ARACARI *Pteroglossus sanguineus* 41–43cm/16–17in

0–800m. Restricted to the far NW, where it is uncommon to fairly common in humid lowland and foothill forest and edge. Essentially identical to Pale-mandibled Aracari except for entirely black lower mandible. Behavior and vocalizations of both species are quite similar, and they are often treated as the same species.

3 CRIMSON-RUMPED TOUCANET *Aulacorhynchus haematopygus* 36cm/14in

300–2200m. Fairly common in humid foothill and subtropical forest, edge, and lightly wooded clearings. The only green toucan in W Ecuador (but see note below), and therefore easy to ID. Usually encountered in pairs, sometimes in larger groups at freshly fruiting trees. Blends in with foliage and often not spotted until it moves or flies between trees. Song is a long series of evenly spaced, nasal *quenk* notes, or a deeper, throaty croaking *crrruh-crruh-crrruh-crrruh....* Note: **Emerald Toucanet** (*A. atrogularis*; not shown) ranges widely in E, and may locally spill over W of the continental divide, especially in S; it is easily distinguished from Crimson-rumped by bill showing bright yellow culmen.

4 YELLOW-EARED TOUCANET *Selenidera spectabilis* 36–38cm/14–15in

0–300m. Very rare in humid forest and edge in extreme NW, with very few records in recent years; any sightings of this beautiful species in Ecuador should be reported. Very colorful and unlike any other toucan in our region. Female is shown; male is similar but has large yellow ear tufts and a black (not chestnut) crown and nape. This species is usually encountered alone or in pairs, usually at upper strata of the forest. It occasionally gives a mechanical, rasping *t-krrrrt, t-krrrrt, t-krrrrt, t-krrrrt....*

LARGE TOUCANS

Spectacular and iconic birds of humid forest. Sexes have almost identical plumage, but males have longer bills than females.

1 PLATE-BILLED MOUNTAIN-TOUCAN *Andigena laminirostris* 43–46cm/17–18in

1600–2600m; occasionally as low as 1000m and as high as 3600m. One of the "star" birds of our region. Locally fairly common in humid forest and edge, sometimes venturing into clearings with fruiting trees. Mostly found in the subtropics, but rarely wanders down into the foothills or up into the temperate zone; most easily seen along the upper parts of the Paseo del Quinde (Nono-Mindo) Ecoroute. Spectacular and unmistakable, given a decent view; immature has reduced yellow "plate" on bill; no overlap with Gray-breasted Mountain-Toucan. Usually encountered in pairs in the forest canopy, though larger numbers may congregate at fruiting trees. Often first detected by its distinctive song, a far-carrying *YEAAAH,YEAAAH,YEAAAH…*; notes are often preceded by a short grating rattle.

2 GRAY-BREASTED MOUNTAIN-TOUCAN *Andigena hypoglauca* 43–46cm/17–18in

2500–3300m. This is mainly an E slope species, but it occurs very locally on the W slope, S of Cuenca. It is as spectacular as Plate-billed Mountain-Toucan, but the species do not overlap, so there should be no confusion. Behavior is similar to that of Plate-billed, though Gray-breasted is generally more lethargic. Its song is a slow, drawled *AAAAWWWWNNH?*, repeated several times; short yelps and rattles are also given.

3 CHOCÓ TOUCAN *Ramphastos brevis* 43–46cm/17–18in

0–1500m. Fairly common in humid forest and edge in the lowlands and foothills. Distinguished from the similar Yellow-throated Toucan by the black (not chestnut) lower part of the bill and by voice; the two species overlap broadly in range, and at great distance or under poor viewing conditions may be safely separated only by voice. Chocó Toucan is generally encountered in pairs, though groups may gather at fruiting trees. It usually roams the canopy, but occasionally descends to lower levels at forest edge. Song is a croaking, frog-like *krreeeek, krreeeek, kreeeek, krreeeek…*, given while the bird jerks its head back and tail upward, usually from a conspicuous perch high in the canopy.

4 YELLOW-THROATED TOUCAN *Ramphastos ambiguus* 53–56cm/21–22in

0–1500m. Fairly common in humid forest and edge in the lowlands and foothills. Can be separated from Chocó Toucan (wide overlap) by chestnut coloration of the lower part of the bill, and by voice. Keep in mind that in poor viewing conditions the chestnut on the bill may appear black, so voice can be the safest way to ID the species. Behavior is much like that of Chocó Toucan, but vocalizations differ markedly; song is a yelping *TEE-YEEEP, TE-YOOP, TE-YOOP!*, with slight variations. Birds W of the Andes were formerly split as **Chestnut-mandibled Toucan** (*R. swainsonii*).

ad. 1

imm. 1

2

3

3

Woodpeckers are a family of insectivorous and mainly arboreal birds with stiff, graduated tails adapted for clinging to and hitching up tree trunks, allowing them to peck vigorously at crevices, bark, and wood with chisel-like bills. All are sexually dimorphic. Piculets are tiny woodpeckers that do not use their tails for support.

1 ECUADORIAN PICULET *Picumnus sclateri* 9cm/3.5in

0–1600m. Fairly common in deciduous and semi-humid forest, light woodland, and scrub in W and SW. Strongly patterned, brownish, and distinctive; female of SW subspecies *sclateri* is shown; male has yellow spots on forehead instead of white. W subspecies *parvistriatus* is very similar but has narrower barring and streaking. Unlikely to be mistaken if seen well; Olivaceous Piculet (very limited overlap) lacks strong markings on underparts and inhabits more humid regions. Encountered alone, in pairs, or in small family groups, often accompanying mixed-species foraging flocks. Forages at varying heights, actively working dead twigs, narrow branches, and vines. Most common vocalization is a high-pitched *p't't't'sip'sip*.

2 OLIVACEOUS PICULET *Picumnus olivaceus* 9cm/3.5in

0–1300m. Fairly common in humid forest and edge in lowlands and foothills. Rather plain olivaceous, but profusely spotted black crown and blurry olive streaking on underparts help ID this species. Female (not shown) very similar to male but has white spots on forecrown instead of yellow. Ecuadorian Piculet (little overlap) is much more strongly patterned below. Xenops (p. 230) are similar in size and behavior but have a short, pointy, and slightly upturned bill, and white superciliary and malar streak. Behavior of Olivaceous Piculet is similar to that of Ecuadorian. Typical song is a very fast, high-pitched trill that trails off near the end.

3 BLACK-CHEEKED WOODPECKER *Melanerpes pucherani* 19cm/7.5in

0–1000m. W Ecuador's only midsize, black-backed woodpecker; common in lightly wooded habitats (including towns and gardens) and forest edge throughout the humid lowlands and foothills. No similar bird occurs in our region. Usually found in pairs, but small and noisy family groups are regularly encountered and can be quite confiding. This species forages at all levels and often perches conspicuously on dead snags; it will even visit feeders in some areas. Song is a harsh and rapid *t'-d'dit!*, given alone or repeated several times in succession.

4 CINNAMON WOODPECKER *Celeus loricatus* 20cm/8in

0–1100m. A handsome woodpecker of humid forest and edge in the lowlands and foothills. Distinctive in our range; no other woodpecker in W has barred upperparts, scaled underparts, and a hammerhead shape; male has red malar. This species is rather shy and favors upper forest levels, where it can be hard to spot from the ground; the tower at Río Silanche Bird Sanctuary can be a great place to see it. Usually encountered alone or in pairs, though occasionally joins mixed-species foraging flocks, and is heard more often than seen. Typical call (song?) is a loud, shrill *PEE-PEE-PEE-pih-pit* (number of notes varies); also gives a raspy *t't't't't'jyer*.

5 LITA WOODPECKER *Piculus litae* 18cm/7in

0–800m. Rare inside humid lowland and foothill forest in far NW. Yellow face and white throat are diagnostic in our range. Female (not shown) differs from male by golden-olive crown and malar, with red restricted to a tiny patch on nape. Vaguely similar to Golden-olive Woodpecker (p. 218), but that species has a white face and black throat. Lita Woodpecker is usually inconspicuous and hard to see in subcanopy of mature forest. Singles or pairs work larger branches and sometimes join mixed-species foraging flocks. Typical call is a very harsh, hissing scream, but also gives a soft *whit-whit-whit*, sometimes extended into a longer series.

Small woodpeckers; most are golden olive above and distinctly barred below; all are sexually dimorphic, with female having little or no red on crown. *Veniliornis* woodpeckers forage singly or in pairs, usually at mid to upper forest levels, and often join mixed-species foraging flocks.

1 BAR-BELLIED WOODPECKER *Veniliornis nigriceps* 17cm/6.5in

2600–4000m. Uncommon in humid temperate and elfin forest and edge, and in *Polylepis* woodland. No other high-elevation woodpecker shares combination of golden-olive upperparts and coarse black-and-white-barred underparts; note blackish cheeks, delineated by white malar stripe and superciliary. Female has black crown and nape. Yellow-vented Woodpecker, found at lower elevations, shows similar facial pattern but has a plain, unbarred yellow belly and black throat. Bar-bellied's song is long series of short notes that first rises and then slowly falls; also gives a squeaky chatter.

2 YELLOW-VENTED WOODPECKER *Veniliornis dignus* 16cm/6.5in

1700–2500m. Uncommon in subtropical and temperate forest in NW; fairly common in areas near the Colombian border. Similar to Bar-bellied Woodpecker of higher elevations, but note the unbarred yellow belly and black throat. Yellow-vented Woodpecker gives a variety of soft trills, ranging from a short, 1–2 sec. burst to a drawn-out 3–5 sec. series that may rise and fall. Other calls include soft *pek* notes and rattles.

3 SCARLET-BACKED WOODPECKER *Veniliornis callonotus* 14cm/5.5in

0–1800m. Fairly common in deciduous and semi-humid forest and woodland in W and SW; also occurs locally in more humid habitats in NW (e.g., Mindo and the Milpe Bird Sanctuary). Very distinctive, with its scarlet upperparts contrasting strongly with the white, very lightly barred underparts. Birds of SW subspecies *major* tend to show more barring and have more white behind the eye compared to W and NW subspecies *callonotus*. Not likely to be confused with other species, but see larger Crimson-mantled Woodpecker (p. 218) of higher elevations. Vocalizations of Scarlet-backed Woodpecker include a very long trill, a rollicking, squeaky chatter, and a single *pek* note, sometimes doubled.

4 RED-RUMPED WOODPECKER *Veniliornis kirkii* 16cm/6.5in

0–1200m. Fairly common in semi-humid and humid forest, edge, and lightly wooded areas in lowlands and foothills. Red rump is diagnostic if seen, but is often hidden under the folded wings; also note plain face and yellow nuchal collar. Confusion is possible with the rare Chocó Woodpecker; see that species for details. No overlap with Yellow-vented and Bar-bellied Woodpeckers. Female (not shown) has black instead of red on crown. Common vocalization (song?) is a slow series of inflected squeaks.

5 CHOCÓ WOODPECKER *Veniliornis chocoensis* 16cm/6.5in

200–700m. Rare and local in humid foothill forest in far NW. This species must be identified with care as it can occur together with the much more common Red-rumped Woodpecker, which very often shows no sign of its diagnostic red rump when perched. The underpart barring of Chocó Woodpecker tends to be coarser, imparting a scaly appearance, and perhaps most important, the breast is suffused with a rusty-brown tinge lacking in Red-rumped. Chocó also tends to have less yellow on the nape. Chocó Woodpecker favors wetter, less disturbed forest. Song is a short series of metallic, piping notes, *p-pi-pi-pi-pi-pi-pi-pi-pi-pik*; typical call is a series of soft, high-pitched squeaks.

♀ 5

♂ 5

Small to medium-size woodpeckers found in a variety of wooded habitats. *Colaptes* woodpeckers are related to flickers, and show a distinctive unmarked facial area that contrasts with the rest of the head.

1   SMOKY-BROWN WOODPECKER   *Picoides fumigatus*   18cm/7in

300–2500m. Fairly common in humid foothill and subtropical forest and edge. Small and brown; male has red crown, lacking in female. No other woodpecker in our region is so plain and unmarked, and confusion is unlikely if seen reasonably well. Usually found alone or in pairs, inconspicuously foraging at lower to mid heights, occasionally higher, picking and probing, with light taps, on branches, limbs, and narrow trunks. Regularly joins mixed-species flocks. Vocalizations include a squeaky *chwhee-chwhee-chwhee…*, a high, fast whinny, and a sharp *pek*; drum is very fast and rather soft.

2   GOLDEN-OLIVE WOODPECKER   *Colaptes rubiginosus*   23cm/9in

0–2100m. Fairly common and widespread from the lowlands to the subtropics. Inhabits deciduous and humid forest, light woodland, forest edge, and clearings with scattered trees. In humid areas, it avoids forest interior. Combination of white face, golden-olive upperparts, and strongly barred underparts is diagnostic. Lita Woodpecker (p. 214) has a yellow (not white) face. Golden-olive is one of the most frequently encountered woodpeckers, mostly found singly or in loose pairs, foraging on trunks and thick branches at mid levels and up into canopy, occasionally lower. Typical vocalization (song?) is a rapid, harsh trill lasting about 3 sec. Also gives a grating *krih-krih-krih-krih-krih-krih-krih* and a single, descending *chew!*

3   CRIMSON-MANTLED WOODPECKER   *Colaptes rivolii*   24cm/9.5in

1700–3600m. This stunning montane woodpecker is fairly common throughout much of the Andes in subtropical and temperate forest and edge, including lightly wooded areas such as parks and gardens. Note the diagnostic crimson upperparts and yellowish-white facial area; no similar bird regularly occurs with it, though it may overlap very locally in the SW with the smaller Scarlet-backed Woodpecker (p. 216), which has mostly white underparts. Behavior is similar to that of Golden-olive Woodpecker, but Crimson-mantled often forages inconspicuously along mossy and epiphyte-laden trunks and branches, and frequently consumes fruit as well as insects. Common calls include an abrupt staccato trill (often given in flight) and a single (or repeated) querulous *sweeet?* note.

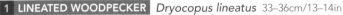

LARGE WOODPECKERS

Large, spectacular woodpeckers with distinctive bushy crests; most have bold white back markings. Flight in all species is strongly undulating. Often detected by their loud vocalizations and powerful drumming.

1 LINEATED WOODPECKER *Dryocopus lineatus* 33–36cm/13–14in

0–1500m. Fairly common and widespread in the lowlands and foothills; found in both humid and deciduous forest, lighter woodland, and edge. Male larger than female; both sexes differ from other large woodpeckers in having parallel white "suspenders" on back that do not form a V, and narrow white facial stripe. Female Guayaquil Woodpecker can appear similar, especially if back stripes are obscured, but note Lineated's narrower facial stripes and dark gray face patch that extends well behind the eye (and to forehead on female). Male Powerful Woodpecker (little or no overlap) differs from female Lineated by rufous cast to lower underparts. Lineated Woodpecker singles or pairs work thick trunks and heavier limbs for insect larvae and beetles; occasionally seen on narrow branches when feeding on fruit. Usually conspicuous, though sometimes remains hidden in dense forest canopy. Song is a loud, far-carrying, *EH-EH-EH-EH-EH-EH-EH-EH-EH-EH...!*; calls include a *tchee-drrrrrr*; territorial drum is a rapid, decelerating series, usually of at least 10 strikes. Birds in W Ecuador and NW Peru are sometimes split as **Dusky-winged Woodpecker** (*D. fuscipennis*).

2 GUAYAQUIL WOODPECKER *Campephilus gayaquilensis* 34cm/13.5in

0–1400m. Widespread but uncommon in lowlands and foothills; inhabits deciduous and humid forest, edge, and even light woodland if a few larger trees remain. Male's combination of nearly completely red head and white V on back is diagnostic. Female could be confused with Lineated Woodpecker (wide overlap; see that species for details) or Powerful Woodpecker (no known overlap; note color of lower underparts). Guayaquil Woodpecker is usually encountered singly or in pairs; behavior is quite similar to that of Lineated, though Guayaquil is less likely to be found far from forest. Typical vocalization is a repeated, rich *hick* call note, sometimes given in a fast series that can seem like maniacal laughter. Drum is similar to that of Lineated Woodpecker, but shorter, usually fewer than 10 strikes.

3 POWERFUL WOODPECKER *Campephilus pollens* 33cm/13in

1500–3600m. Rare to locally uncommon in humid subtropical and temperate forest and edge. No other large woodpecker regularly occurs within its range and habitat, but there is potential overlap with Guayaquil or Lineated Woodpeckers at its lower elevation limit. Black head of female is unique; male might be confused with Lineated or female Guayaquil, but note distinct rufous tones to lower underparts. Powerful has a white rump, though this is usually conspicuous only when seen in flight. This scarce and often shy forest woodpecker is usually found alone or in pairs, sometimes in small family groups, foraging at any height, though often low; it is hard to locate in dense cloud forest. Typical song is a series of sneezing *TCHyoo!* notes, sometimes quickening to a rapid and harsh chatter; also gives a quick series of nasal *chup* notes. Drum is a loud, abrupt, double knock, occasionally a triple knock.

4 CRIMSON-BELLIED WOODPECKER *Campephilus haematogaster* 34cm/13.5in

100–1400m. A rare and stunning woodpecker of humid lowland and foothill forest. Distinguished from all other large woodpeckers in our range by unmarked black mantle, deep crimson underparts, and buff malar and postocular stripe. Female (not shown) is very similar to male, but buff on face continues as a solid line down the neck. Inconspicuous; individuals or pairs forage inside forest, quite low to the ground, on thick trunks. Typical vocalizations include an abrupt, throaty, *pek*, a very rapid whinny, and a long series of wheezy gasps. Drum is usually a double knock, but occasionally a longer series of raps. Birds in W Ecuador, W Colombia, and Panama are sometimes split as **Splendid Woodpecker** (*C. splendens*).

HIGH-ANDEAN FURNARIIDS

Furnariidae is a large and diverse neotropical family of cryptically colored and patterned insectivorous birds. Members of this family are often called "furnariids" or "ovenbirds." Shades of brown, gray and black dominate, and ID in some groups can be a challenge; it is helpful to note elevation, habitat, behavior, size, and vocalizations. Sexes are nearly alike. All species on this page are restricted to high elevations in the Andes. The two cinclodes are mainly terrestrial inhabitants of open páramo terrain; both are brownish, with rufous wing markings, a prominent white throat, and a narrow superciliary.

1 CHESTNUT-WINGED CINCLODES *Cinclodes albiventris* 18cm/7in

3200–4300m. Fairly common in páramo, adjacent shrubby areas, plowed fields, and edge of *Polylepis* woodland. Quite similar to Stout-billed Cinclodes and often found with it. Note Chestnut-winged's smaller size and short, thin, and nearly straight bill. Terrestrial; encountered alone or in pairs, walking, briefly running about, or perching up on a rock, shrub, or tussock; regularly cocks tail. Nests in burrows that are often found in roadcuts and earthen banks. Song is a long, dry trill, e.g., *trrrrrrrrrrrrrr*, customarily accompanied by wing fluttering; a variety of short, high-pitched *tikik* calls are also given. This species, along with two others found elsewhere in South America, were formerly lumped as **Bar-winged Cinclodes** (*C. fuscus*).

2 STOUT-BILLED CINCLODES *Cinclodes excelsior* 20cm/8in

3300–4500m. This stocky cinclodes ranges throughout the páramo and adjacent scrub and forest edge; tends to favor wet, boggy areas, though is not restricted to them. Very similar to Chestnut-winged Cinclodes; distinguished by its larger size and thicker, longer, and more decurved bill. Behavior is similar to that of Chestnut-winged. Song of Stout-billed is a rather squeaky trill that rises first then falls off at the end, often accompanied by wing fluttering; also emits a single *tcheeoo* call note.

3 ANDEAN TIT-SPINETAIL *Leptasthenura andicola* 17cm/6.5in

3200–4200m. Fairly common in páramo, *Polylepis* woodland, and edge of temperate forest throughout much of the high Andes. Streaked plumage, long, blackish, spiky tail, and pale superciliary are distinctive. Canasteros (p. 224) lack superciliary and show conspicuous rufous in wings and tail; thistletails (p. 224) lack distinct streaking. Charming and acrobatic, Andean Tit-Spinetail is usually encountered in pairs or small groups that forage actively and methodically inside shrubs and dense foliage, often hanging upside down and coming into view from time to time to look around before moving on. Song is a very long, high-pitched trill; calls include various *tsip*, *tink*, and *krik* notes, given alone or in quick series.

4 SLENDER-BILLED MINER *Geositta tenuirostris* 18cm/7in

3300–4000m. Known in Ecuador from only a few sites in high-elevation páramo near the continental divide in the central highlands (e.g., Quilotoa volcano). Look for the long, thin, and distinctly decurved bill, faint breast markings, rufous in wings, and short tail. Cinclodes have shorter bills and longer tails, contrasting white throats and plain breasts. Slender-billed Miner is usually encountered singly or in pairs that walk and run about on the ground. Song is a sharp, descending *kek-kek-kek-ke-ke-ke-ke-ke-ke…*, continuing for up to 15 sec. or longer, and often preceded by a squeak.

4

A set of high-Andean furnariids with rufous, chestnut, or brown spiky tails, found in tree line forest and páramo, though White-browed Spinetail ranges slightly lower into temperate forest as well.

1 MANY-STRIPED CANASTERO *Asthenes flammulata* 16cm/6.5in

3200–4400m. Common in high-elevation páramo grassland. Profusely streaked plumage is most similar to that of Andean Tit-Spinetail (p. 222), which lacks rufous in wings and tail, has bolder white superciliary and yellow chin. Streak-backed Canastero, usually found in more arid terrain, is unstreaked below. Many-striped Canastero is usually found alone, often difficult to see as it runs along the ground under tall grass or dense shrubbery; more easily seen when singing from atop a bush or tussock. Song is quite long (4–8 sec.), starting with a series of buzzy notes, then ending in staccato chatter; also gives a complaining *wheer*.

2 STREAK-BACKED CANASTERO *Asthenes wyatti* 17cm/6.5in

2700–4400m. Fairly common but very local in drier páramo and on arid, scrubby slopes above inter-Andean valleys. Distinguished from the more widespread Many-striped Canastero by plain underparts and lack of white streaking on upperparts. Similar to Many-striped Canastero in behavior, though often more difficult to spot due to the dense, scrubby vegetation in which is often found. Song is a short, rising, and accelerating trill; most common call is a short, musical churr repeated once.

3 WHITE-CHINNED THISTLETAIL *Asthenes fuliginosa* 19cm/7.5in

2800–4000m. Uncommon at the edge of temperate forest and in dense, scrubby vegetation at the edge of páramo. The only plain, unstreaked, and long-tailed bird in its range and habitat. Mouse-colored Thistletail replaces it in the S Andes (no known overlap). White-chinned Thistletail is normally encountered singly or in pairs, foraging methodically well inside dense vegetation, moving slowly and carefully while examining branches and leaves for insects. When one does finally emerge into view, it can be very confiding and almost oblivious to human presence. Song is a sharp, ringing series that rises slightly then gradually falls and accelerates toward the end; also gives a short series of two to five *pi'di'dit* calls.

4 MOUSE-COLORED THISTLETAIL *Asthenes griseomurina* 19cm/7.5in

2800–4000m. Replaces White-chinned Thistletail in similar habitats in the S Andes (no known overlap). Mouse-colored Thistletail is mainly an E slope species, but is locally fairly common in W at a few sites near the continental divide. The two species are very similar, but Mouse-colored has a brown (not chestnut) back and a more well-defined eye-ring. Typical song is a rising trill that starts slowly but accelerates rapidly.

5 WHITE-BROWED SPINETAIL *Hellmayrea gularis* 13cm/5in

2500–3700m. An odd, wren-like spinetail that is fairly common in dense vegetation at the edge of temperate forest. Combination of white spectacles and throat, along with lack of streaking, is unique in its range. Singles or pairs forage unobtrusively and methodically inside dense vegetation close to the ground; occasionally joins mixed-species flocks. Vocalizations include a high-pitched, chippering *tsip-tsip-tsipsipsipsipt't't't't't'dit*, a flatter, staccato chatter, and a weak *pit*.

SYNALLAXIS SPINETAILS

Synallaxis comprises a large number of small furnariids found throughout much of the neotropics and well represented in W Ecuador. All have long, spiky tails, and stay low in dense undergrowth, where they are often hard to see well. They are typically found alone or in pairs and do not usually join mixed-species flocks. Their distinctive vocalizations are often the first sign of their presence.

1 AZARA'S SPINETAIL *Synallaxis azarae* 17cm/6.5in

1500–3400m; down to 600m in SW. Common and widespread in dense vegetation at forest edge, overgrown clearings, and hedgerows in the Andes. Paler overall appearance, longer, more rufous tail and dark throat patch bordered by white separate it from Slaty Spinetail. Widespread *media* subspecies is shown; SW subspecies *ochracea* is similar but somewhat paler and may show a vague, whitish superciliary. This spinetail's distinctive and often-heard song is a sharp *pit-SWEET!*, repeated every few seconds.

2 SLATY SPINETAIL *Synallaxis brachyura* 17cm/6.5in

0–1700m. Fairly common in brushy forest edge, overgrown clearings, hedgerows, and other secondary habitats throughout the humid lowlands and foothills, and locally up into the subtropics. Similar Azara's Spinetail is paler and has a longer, brighter rufous tail and white edges to dark throat patch. Blackish-headed Spinetail is restricted to deciduous forest and has a black crown and sooty tail. Behavior is similar to that of Azara's, but Slaty regularly forages in isolated bushes, and is more likely to climb higher, making it a little less difficult to see. Song is a hard, guttural, descending rattle lasting about 1 sec.

3 RUFOUS SPINETAIL *Synallaxis unirufa* 17cm/6.5in

1900–3200m. Fairly common in humid subtropical and temperate forest and edge; seems to favor areas with extensive *Chusquea* bamboo. Mostly uniform rufous, with black lores and a long, graduated tail. Plumage is much more similar to that of Rufous and Sepia-brown Wrens (p. 332) than to other spinetails, but note longer, unbarred tail and plain wings. Song is a rather relaxed *pt-where?*

4 BLACKISH-HEADED SPINETAIL *Synallaxis tithys* 14cm/5.5in

0–1100m. Rare to locally uncommon in understory of deciduous forest in W and SW. Mostly dark gray, with a black face, contrasting rufous wing coverts, and a sooty tail. Slaty Spinetail is similar, also with dark tail, but is larger, has a rufous crown, and inhabits more humid zones. Blackish-headed Spinetail has similar behavior to other members of the genus, though it can be somewhat easier to see through the leafless vegetation during the dry season. Vocal repertoire is surprisingly varied; typical song is a short, harsh *t't't't't't't'tirit!*, with the last few notes higher; some calls include a squeaky *dwe'we'weet*, an extended, wheezy series of gasping whistles, and single *kwee-dit*, *krrt*, and *tick* notes.

5 NECKLACED SPINETAIL *Synallaxis stictothorax* 13cm/5in

0–200m. Restricted to very arid lowland regions of W and SW, where it is locally common in desert scrub and deciduous woodland. This attractive bird is unique in its range and habitat, and its streaked breast and rusty wing patches separate it from other desert species such as Superciliated Wren (p. 334). Much like other *Synallaxis* in behavior, though can be easier to see, especially during the dry season when leafless vegetation offers little or no cover for hiding. Usual song is a crisp, chattered *tit't't't't't't'treep-treep*, though a longer version intermixed with squeaks and chatters is occasionally given. Calls include a single *weet* and a soft *chit*.

Cranioleuca is a genus of arboreal spinetails; they are usually found in the canopy, making them more easily seen than other spinetails. Tuftedcheeks have bold white or buff facial tufts that facilitate ID. Double-banded Graytail is a strange, but rarely encountered furnariid of NW forests.

1 RED-FACED SPINETAIL *Cranioleuca erythrops* 14cm/5.5in

700–1800m; locally down to 100m along the central coast. Fairly common at forest edge and in lighter woodland in more humid foothills and subtropics, locally occurring in the lowlands. Adult is dingy grayish brown with contrasting rufous face, wings, and tail. Stripe-faced immature may recall Line-cheeked Spinetail, which is found only in SW (the two species do not overlap). Red-faced Spinetail is usually encountered in pairs that actively and acrobatically examine leaves, epiphytes, tangles, and mossy branches at varying heights, though they tend to favor mid to upper strata. Regularly joins mixed-species flocks. Frequently given song is a rapid, high-pitched series of chips that is quite variable in length, and usually descends and accelerates at the end, e.g., *sip-tsip-tsip-tsip-tip'tip'ti'ti't't't't't*.

2 LINE-CHEEKED SPINETAIL *Cranioleuca antisiensis* 14cm/5.5in

800–2600m. Fairly common in lighter woodland, scrub, and forest edge in highlands of SW, where found in both dry and humid zones. Prominent white spectacles together with rufous cap, wings, and tail are diagnostic in our range; immature (not shown) may lack rufous crown. Behavior is very similar to that of Red-faced Spinetail (the two species do not overlap). Song of Line-cheeked is a metallic *zeep-JEET-jeet-zit't't't't*; call is an extended series of squeaky notes that are sometimes doubled.

3 STREAKED TUFTEDCHEEK *Pseudocolaptes boissonneautii* 21cm/8.5in

1900–3600m. A fairly common and entertaining denizen of subtropical and temperate forest and edge. Puffy white throat and facial tufts, which can be flared out aggressively, make this species easy to ID in most of its range. Overlaps only very locally (note elevation ranges) with Pacific Tuftedcheek, which has smaller buff-tinged tufts, darker underparts, and plainer upperparts. Singles, pairs, or small groups of Streaked Tuftedcheek are most often encountered amidst mixed-species flocks at mid to upper forest levels, clambering along thick mossy branches, regularly probing bromeliads and tangles. Most commonly heard vocalization is a series of *chak* calls followed by a decelerating, chippered trill.

4 PACIFIC TUFTEDCHEEK *Pseudocolaptes johnsoni* 20cm/8in

700–2000m. Uncommon and local in humid foothill and subtropical forest and edge, preferring exceptionally lush, epiphyte-laden cloud forest. A lower-elevation replacement of Streaked Tuftedcheek, though the species do occur together at a couple of locations. Pacific Tuftedcheek has smaller, buffier facial tufts, darker underparts, and a plain mantle. Behavior and vocalizations are similar, but Pacific's trill often rises and falls in pitch and is intermixed with squeaks. Sometimes lumped with **Buffy Tuftedcheek** (*P. lawrencii*).

5 DOUBLE-BANDED GRAYTAIL *Xenerpestes minlosi* 11cm/4.5in

0–500m. This odd furnariid, appearing more like a warbler or wren, is very rare in wet lowland and foothill forest and edge in the NW. Mostly gray and white, with white superciliary, unbarred tail, and white wing bars. Gray-mantled Wren (p. 332), which can occur with it in forest canopy, lacks the superciliary and wing bars, and has a barred tail (usually the key feature when looking up at the bird from far below). Behavior also differs: Gray-mantled Wren tends to creep along branches, while Double-banded Graytail clings to leaves, gleaning insects from them. It is generally found singly or in pairs, often with mixed-species flocks, staying high in the trees, where often difficult to see well from the ground. Song is a very long, dry trill, sometimes with a stuttering quality, and often lasting 10 sec. or more.

Small forest furnariids. Spotted Barbtail and treerunners often climb up branches and trunks in a manner similar to that of woodcreepers. Xenops clamber about and pick off insects in viny tangles and along tiny twigs.

1 SPOTTED BARBTAIL *Premnoplex brunnescens* 13cm/5in

700–2500m; lower in coastal range. Fairly common in humid foothill and subtropical forest. Mostly brown, with tawny-buff throat and underpart spotting; note short, straight bill. Rusty-winged Barbtail has contrasting rufous wings and tail, and a more conspicuous pale superciliary. Wedge-billed Woodcreeper (p. 236) is also similar, but has a shorter, wedge-shaped bill, and streaks restricted to throat and breast. Spotted Barbtail is usually encountered alone or in pairs in the forest understory, occasionally joining mixed-species flocks. Tends to remain fairly low, clinging to thin, mossy trunks and branches, and sometimes uses its tail to hitch upward. Vocalizations include a dry, sputtered trill, and a series of three to seven *seep* notes.

2 RUSTY-WINGED BARBTAIL *Premnornis guttuliger* 14cm/5.5in

1300–2500m. Uncommon and somewhat local in humid subtropical forest. Combination of contrastingly rufous wings and tail, pale superciliary, and whitish breast streaking separate it from other similar sympatric species (but see foliage-gleaners, pp. 232–234). Singles or pairs of Rusty Barbtail are usually seen with mixed-species flocks at mid levels inside forest, actively and methodically exploring dense vine tangles, moss-covered branches, and dead leaf clusters. Song is a moderately fast series of flat, evenly spaced *tik* notes; typical call is a high-pitched chip repeated regularly.

3 PEARLED TREERUNNER *Margarornis squamiger* 15cm/6in

1800–4000m. This stunning furnariid is common and widespread in humid subtropical and temperate forest and edge, as well as in *Polylepis* groves in páramo. Boldly patterned; entirely rufous back, wings, and tail, contrasting white throat and postocular stripe, and bold white "pearls" eliminate other species. Usually found in pairs or small groups, joining mixed-species flocks, conspicuously hitching along mossy trunks and branches, often clinging upside down to the undersides. Vocalizations include a variety of high-pitched, chippered trills.

4 STAR-CHESTED TREERUNNER *Margarornis stellatus* 15cm/6in

1200–2300m. Very rare except at a few sites near the Colombian border, where it can be locally uncommon (e.g., the Chical road); inhabits wet, mossy subtropical forest. Combination of mostly uniform chestnut plumage, white throat, and black-rimmed white spots on throat and breast is diagnostic. Behavior is much like that of Pearled Treerunner; this seldom-encountered bird is nearly always found with mixed-species flocks. Song is a short burst of rather erratic high-pitched notes; typical call is a very high *seep-seep-seep-seep*. Also called **Fulvous-dotted Treerunner**.

5 PLAIN XENOPS *Xenops minutus* 12cm/4.5in

0–1400m. Fairly common in humid and semi-humid forest, edge, and light woodland in the lowlands and foothills. Note bill shape and pale facial markings. White chin with streaks restricted to a very small area on the throat distinguish it from the more heavily marked Streaked Xenops. Singles or pairs forage actively in tangles, on thin, bare branches, and on vines at mid to upper heights, often dangling precariously from the tips of thin twigs; frequently joins mixed-species flocks. Song is a fairly rapid, gravelly trill that rises in pitch after the first couple of notes.

6 STREAKED XENOPS *Xenops rutilans* 12cm/4.5in

0–2000m. Fairly common and widespread in deciduous and humid forest, woodland, and edge. Similar to Plain Xenops, but much more strongly marked on underparts; keep in mind that Plain Xenops often shows very faint throat streaking, but never as extensive as on Streaked. Behavior of the two species is also very similar, though Streaked Xenops is perhaps even more likely to be found with mixed-species flocks. Song is a fairly slow series of sharp notes that rises briefly then falls in pitch, e.g., *tseep'tseep'tsee p'seep'seep'seep'seep'sip'sip*.

Treehunters are hefty foliage-gleaners found in montane forest. Foliage-gleaners are forest furnariids with predominantly brown plumage, often with various amounts of streaking; almost all have rufous tails.

1 UNIFORM TREEHUNTER *Thripadectes ignobilis* 19cm/7.5in

1000–1800m. Uncommon in humid foothill and subtropical forest and edge. Mainly uniform dark rufous brown; note tawny eye-ring, faint postocular streak, and blurry streaking on throat, upper breast, and sides of neck. Streak-capped Treehunter has a dusky, streaked crown; Lineated Foliage-gleaner has a buffy throat and more prominent streaking; Western Woodhaunter (p. 234); little or no overlap) lacks a distinct eye-ring and has a different bill shape. Uniform Treehunter is usually encountered alone, sometimes with mixed-species flocks; rummages through dense vegetation, along mossy branches and vine tangles, picking at leaf litter and other debris. Song is somewhat variable, but typically a rising then falling series of 4 to 15 sharp *tchip!* notes; call is a single *tchak*.

2 STREAK-CAPPED TREEHUNTER *Thripadectes virgaticeps* 21cm/8.5in

1500–2300m. Fairly common in humid subtropical forest and edge. Combination of dusky crown and nape; chestnut back, wings, and tail; and streaking on head, throat and neck separates it from other similar species. Uniform Treehunter is darker overall and lacks dusky crown and head and nape streaking; Striped Treehunter shows prominent buff streaking on mantle and breast; Lineated Foliage-gleaner has a pale buffy throat. Streak-capped's behavior is similar to that of Uniform Treehunter. Song is a calm, squeaky *tzeep, tseep, tzeep-tzeep-tzup*; also gives an abrupt, loud chatter.

3 STRIPED TREEHUNTER *Thripadectes holostictus* 21cm/8.5in

1800–3200m. Fairly common in humid subtropical and temperate forest and edge, especially where there is extensive *Chusquea* bamboo. Mostly brown with rufous wings, chestnut tail, and bold buff streaking above and below. The similar Flammulated Treehunter is larger and more boldly striped buff, contrasting sharply against darker brown base coloration. Streak-capped Treehunter has streaking only on head, nape, and throat. Lineated Foleage-gleaner has a distinctive buffy throat and smaller bill. Behavior is similar to that of other treehunters; tends to skulk in dense cover. Song is a rapid, often descending, rattling trill lasting about 1–2 sec. Distinctive call is a sharp *pi-di-di-dit!*

4 FLAMMULATED TREEHUNTER *Thripadectes flammulatus* 24cm/9.5in

2200–3600m. Rare in humid subtropical and temperate forest and edge; often found in *Chusquea* bamboo. Broadly striped tawny buff above and below; wings, rump, and tail chestnut brown. Smaller Striped Treehunter shows less contrast between narrow buff streaks and dark brown base coloration. It is usually a challenge to observe Flammulated Treehunter, as it remains under dense cover and rarely emerges into the open; otherwise behavior is much like that of other treehunters. Typical song is a 2–3 sec. rapid, grating trill that barely rises and then falls slightly at the end; can also give a much longer and more drawn-out version. Call is a snappy *p'DIT!*

5 LINEATED FOLIAGE-GLEANER *Syndactyla subalaris* 18cm/7in

1000–2300m. Fairly common in humid forest, lighter woodland, and edge in the foothills and subtropics. Note pale buffy throat; sharp streaking on head, neck, and underparts; and rufous wings and tail. No other similarly streaked species shows such a contrasting pale throat. Usually encountered singly or in pairs, often with mixed-species flocks, and often hard to see well as it actively searches through dense tangles and along mossy limbs, inspecting dead leaf clusters and debris. Song is metallic, accelerating, and rising, e.g., *dit-dit-di-di-di'd'd'd'd'd'd'd'd*. Call is a raspy, toneless *tcht't*.

6 RUFOUS-NECKED FOLIAGE-GLEANER *Syndactyla ruficollis* 18cm/7in

600–2700m. Uncommon and local in semi-humid and humid foothill and subtropical forest and edge in SW. A brighter rufous version of Lineated Foliage-gleaner (no overlap); distinctive orange-rufous superciliary and sides of neck are diagnostic within its small range. Singles or pairs often accompany mixed-species flocks at varying heights and in dense tangles, including in *Chusquea* bamboo, where they inspect vine tangles, ferns, mossy branches, bromeliads, and other epiphytes for arthropods. Song is similar to that of Lineated Foliage-gleaner, but falls off in a raspy growl at the end, e.g., *dit-dit-di-di-di-di-di'd'd'd'd'd'd'd'd'drrrrrr*. Call is a sharp, metallic *djit*.

Several genera of brown, rufous, and buff-toned forest furnariids, all with rufous tails. Except for Ruddy Foliage-gleaner, the birds on this page are regularly encountered with mixed-species flocks.

1 WESTERN WOODHAUNTER *Automolus virgatus* 17cm/6.5in

0–1100m. Uncommon inside humid lowland and foothill forest. Lacks strong markings, but very faint streaking on head, throat, and breast is the best plumage feature. Lineated Foliage-gleaner (p. 232) is more sharply streaked and has a buffy throat; Ruddy Foliage-gleaner is darker and lacks streaking. Perhaps most similar to Uniform Treehunter (p. 232), but the two species are not known to overlap; note different bill shape and the treehunter's more buffy plumage tones and more distinct eye-ring. Western Woodhaunter is furtive and a challenge to see well; singles or pairs carefully inspect and probe vine tangles, dead leaves, and epiphytes on trunks and along branches, often joining mixed-species foraging flocks. Typical song is a sharp, evenly paced, and somewhat nasal *tyew, tyew, tyew, tyew, tyew, tyew, tyew, tyew*; harsh *tchreep* notes are also given. This species is sometimes lumped with **Eastern Woodhaunter** (*A. subulatus*) from E of Andes, and then called **Striped Woodhaunter**.

2 BUFF-FRONTED FOLIAGE-GLEANER *Philydor rufum* 19cm/7.5in

300–1700m. Fairly common and conspicuous in humid foothill and subtropical forest and edge. Bright and distinctive, with rufous wings and cinnamon-buff throat and superciliary that contrast with gray crown. Russet Antshrike (p. 244) is similar and best distinguished by its stout bill, short tail, and pale throat and superciliary. Singles, pairs, or small groups of Buff-fronted Foliage-gleaner regularly accompany mixed-species flocks, acrobatically gleaning foliage and dead leaves along limbs and branches in mid to upper forest strata, though occasionally dropping lower. Song is a long (3–5 sec.), rapid, metallic *PEE-KEE-KEE-kee-kee-keekeekeekeekeekee...* that descends slightly and fades toward the end; typical call is a toneless *djit*.

3 SCALY-THROATED FOLIAGE-GLEANER *Anabacerthia variegaticeps* 17cm/6.5in

500–1700m. Fairly common in humid foothill and subtropical forest and edge. W Ecuador's most striking foliage-gleaner; bold buff spectacles, along with streaked throat and underparts, are diagnostic. Typically encountered alone or in pairs from mid levels to subcanopy, usually with mixed-species flocks; works along small branches and twigs, peering around regularly to probe at the underside; also investigates dead leaf clusters and vine tangles. Gives both a slow and fast song. Slow song is a series of 3 to 10 well-separated metallic *chak* notes; fast song has a more raspy quality, e.g., *djik-djik-djik-djik-djik-djik-djik-djik...*.

4 RUDDY FOLIAGE-GLEANER *Clibanornis rubiginosus* 18cm/7in

0–1300m. Uncommon in dense undergrowth of humid lowland and foothill forest. Mostly dark olive brown with a rufous throat; tail is edged with black; note especially the pale eye-ring, which is often the only feature visible in the dark forest understory it inhabits, and helps separate it from similar species. It can even resemble an antbird (pp. 250–254) in the shady undergrowth, and voice is usually the best way to ID it. The photo shown is from E Ecuador; W birds show more black in the tail and head, and have a more prominent eye-ring. This is the ultimate skulker; pairs remain frustratingly hidden in dense undergrowth, foraging close to or even on the ground. They don't typically join mixed-species flocks, and often the only clue to their presence is their distinctive song, which is a low, harsh, questioning *uhhhh-ER?*, repeated over and over.

5 BUFF-THROATED FOLIAGE-GLEANER *Automolus ochrolaemus* 19cm/7.5in

0–1000m. Uncommon and very furtive in undergrowth of humid and semi-humid lowland forest; rare in foothills. Mostly olive brown; conspicuous puffy white throat, and buffy eye-ring and postocular streak separate it from other foliage-gleaners. Singles or pairs lurk in dense tangles fairly close to the ground and regularly join mixed-species understory flocks; usually difficult to see well as they rummage about and cling to epiphytes, tangled branches, and vines, characteristically probing dead leaf clusters. Song is a series of nasal notes that descends slightly, e.g., *WEH-WEH-WEH-weh-weh-weh-weh-weh-weh-eh*; a short, guttural churr is also given.

6 SLATY-WINGED FOLIAGE-GLEANER *Philydor fuscipenne* 17cm/6.5in

0–600m. Rare and local in humid lowland and lower foothill forest; most recent sightings are from Buenaventura Reserve, Río Palenque Science Center, and Río Ayampe Reserve. Rich tawny and rufous overall with dark postocular line bordered with buff; the distinctive, contrasting dark wings set it apart from all other foliage-gleaners in its range. Usually encountered alone or in pairs, almost always accompanying mixed-species flocks at varying heights; difficult to see well, as it seldom pauses while foraging. Rather quiet, but some vocalizations include a slow, sharp rattle and an abrupt, toneless *tchit!*

A variety of furnariids that do not fit well elsewhere, along with W Ecuador's two smallest woodcreepers; see p. 238 for general information on woodcreepers.

1   SCALY-THROATED LEAFTOSSER   *Sclerurus guatemalensis*   18cm/7in

0–1100m. Uncommon inside humid lowland and foothill forest. Plumage is mainly dark brown, with a white-scaled throat; bill is fairly long and straight. Tawny-throated Leaftosser has a more decurved bill and a tawny, unscaled throat. Scaly-throated Leaftosser is usually encountered alone, occasionally in pairs, probing the ground and flicking leaves back and forth; does not join mixed-species flocks. Typical song is a descending and then ascending series that also accelerates in pace, and may be repeated many times without pause, e.g., *pik…pik…pik-pik-pi-pi-p'p'p'p'pppidl….* Call is a sharp, inflected *weep!*

2   TAWNY-THROATED LEAFTOSSER   *Sclerurus mexicanus*   17cm/6.5in

0–1800m. Rare to locally uncommon inside humid forest from lowlands to subtropics. Note long, slender, decurved bill and rich tawny throat. Scaly-throated Leaftosser has a straight bill and white throat with dark scaling; Ruddy Foliage-gleaner (p. 234) has a different shape, heavier bill, longer tail, and faint eye-ring. In behavior Tawny-throated Leaftosser is much like Scaly-throated. Song is a descending, piping series of about four to eight notes, e.g., *pee-pee-pee-pee-pee-pee-pee*; call is a sharp *pik!*

3   HENNA-HOODED FOLIAGE-GLEANER   *Clibanornis erythrocephalus*   21cm/8.5in

0–2000m. Uncommon and local in deciduous and semi-humid forest and woodland in W and SW; Jorupe Reserve and Cerro Blanco Protected Forest are two of the best places to find it. Orange-rufous hood, wings, and tail contrast with brownish-gray mantle and underparts. Quite unique within its restricted range. Singles or pairs forage close to or on the ground, often joining mixed-species flocks; it frequently rummages around in leaf litter and along fallen logs and branches, picking, probing, and prying away at bark and debris. Most vocal during the rainy season (January–May); song is a dry, metallic rattle repeated every couple of seconds.

4   PACIFIC HORNERO   *Furnarius cinnamomeus*   19cm/7.5in

0–2500m. Widespread and familiar in open habitats almost throughout, including fields, towns, parks, and roadsides. Common at lower elevations but quite scarce at its upper limit. Along with terrestrial habits, note especially the chunky shape and strong contrast between cinnamon upperparts and buffy-white underparts; cinnamon wing stripe is obvious only in flight. Singles, pairs, or small groups strut about on the ground in the open, where quite confiding; readily perch in shrubs and trees, where they place their oven-like clay nests. Song is a laughing and descending *syahsyahsyahsyahsyahsyah….* Sometimes lumped with **Pale-legged Hornero** (*F. leucopus*).

5   WEDGE-BILLED WOODCREEPER   *Glyphorynchus spirurus*   14cm/5.5in

0–1700m. The smallest woodcreeper; common in humid lowland and foothill forest, and locally reaching subtropics. Combination of small size, wedge-shaped bill, and throat streaking are diagnostic. Olivaceous Woodcreeper lacks streaking and has a straight bill; Streaked Xenops (p. 230) has a white throat and much stronger facial markings. Wedge-billed behaves like a typical woodcreeper, usually hitching along fairly broad tree trunks, favoring lower forest strata; sometimes joins mixed-species flocks. Typical song is a short (ca. 1 sec.), soft, rising series of soft notes with a whipping quality. Common call is a rasping *tch-tch-tch-tch*.

6   OLIVACEOUS WOODCREEPER   *Sittasomus griseicapillus*   16cm/6.5in

0–1100m; to 2000m in SW. Fairly common in deciduous and semi-humid forest and woodland in W and SW; uncommon and local in more humid areas in NW. Mainly plain grayish olive with mostly rufous wings and tail; the only small, unmarked woodcreeper in its range. Usually encountered alone or in pairs, occasionally with mixed-species flocks, clinging to and hitching up trunks and limbs at varying heights; not especially wary. Typical song is a rapid trill that rises and then falls; also emits an extended rattle and a short series of soft squeaks.

MIDSIZE WOODCREEPERS

Woodcreepers use their stiff, spike-tipped tails to hitch up tree trunks, limbs, and branches while they pick and probe for prey. They are primarily brown, with rufous wings and tail, and many species are also variably streaked or spotted. These markings (or their lack), along with bill size and shape and vocalizations, are critical for ID. Elevation and habitat can also provide helpful clues. Sexes are nearly alike. They were formerly treated as a separate family (Dendrocolaptidae) but have now been merged with the Furnariidae.

1 BLACK-STRIPED WOODCREEPER *Xiphorhynchus lachrymosus* 24cm/9.5in

0–800m. Locally fairly common in humid lowland and foothill forest in the NW. The most boldly patterned woodcreeper; its strong black and buff markings separate it from all others; also note the mostly straight bill. Singles or pairs are usually seen accompanying mixed-species flocks at varying heights, working trunks and large limbs. Song is a fairly long, rapid, and usually descending series of up to 30 or so soft *tew* notes. Calls, which are usually heard more often, include an accelerating *chew-ew-ew-ew-up* and *chew-EEP!*

2 SPOTTED WOODCREEPER *Xiphorhynchus erythropygius* 23cm/9in

0–2000m. Fairly common in humid forest and edge from lowlands to subtropics. Spotted (not streaked) underparts separate it from other woodcreepers in range; also note buff eye-ring and straight, bicolor bill. Behavior is similar to that of other woodcreepers; tends to remain on trunks and larger limbs. Song is a series of descending whinnies, repeated two or three times at progressively lower pitch. Also gives a down-slurred, burry *cheer!*

3 STREAK-HEADED WOODCREEPER *Lepidocolaptes souleyetii* 20cm/8in

0–1400m; to 1800m in SW. Common and widespread in deciduous, semi-humid and humid forest edge, light woodland, plantations, gardens, and scrub, from lowlands to subtropics. Narrow, slightly decurved bill is distinctive in its range; also note streaked crown, nape, and underparts. Replaced at higher elevations by Montane Woodcreeper (little or no overlap), which lacks crown and nape streaking. Streak-headed is a rather confiding woodcreeper that forages at varying heights, including quite low on trunks and along branches, often clinging to and hitching along the underside of the branch. Frequently heard song is a sharp descending and ringing trill, *trrrre'e'e'e'ew*. Most common call is a warbled, descending *tcheer*.

4 MONTANE WOODCREEPER *Lepidocolaptes lacrymiger* 20cm/8in

1500–3000m. Fairly common in humid subtropical and temperate forest. Note especially the narrow, decurved bill; also has faintly spotted crown (can appear unmarked at a distance), indistinct postocular streak, and white-streaked underparts. Streak-headed Woodcreeper, of lower elevations, differs by distinctly streaked crown and nape; larger Spotted Woodcreeper has a straight, two-tone bill and buff spotting below. Behavior of Montane Woodcreeper is similar to that of Streak-headed. Song is typically a thin, high-pitched *tsip-tsip-tsip-tsip-seeeu-soo-soo-sip*, though it is quite variable; also gives a sharp chatter and an extended series of high-pitched *tsip* and *tsee* notes.

5 TYRANNINE WOODCREEPER *Dendrocincla tyrannina* 25cm/10in

1400–3600m. Uncommon in subtropical and temperate forest and edge. Large and almost totally unmarked, but may show extremely faint streaking on forecrown and throat. Plain-brown Woodcreeper (very little overlap), is similar, but has a pale face patch and dark malar. Behavior of Tyrannine is much like that of other woodcreepers; it tends to forage at mid heights. Song is a long (15 sec. or longer), rapid series of *tip* notes that builds to a slight crescendo and then slows before fading at the end. Most common call is a quick, harsh whinny.

6 PLAIN-BROWN WOODCREEPER *Dendrocincla fuliginosa* 20cm/8in

0–1400m; occasionally to 1700m. Fairly common in humid and semi-humid forest, mainly in the lowlands and foothills; rare and local (or seasonal) in subtropics. Uniform brown, with paler face and dusky malar; almost all other sympatric woodcreepers have streaking or spotting. Tyrannine Woodcreeper (very limited overlap) lacks the pale face and dark malar. Plain-brown is usually found alone or in pairs, often joins mixed-species flocks, and regularly attends army ant swarms; it usually remains at low heights and often clings motionless to a trunk for long periods. Song is a very long mechanical-sounding chattering, briefly stuttering from time to time, giving a choppy effect; also gives a shorter and harsher version that slows and descends; also a loud and very sharp *PEET!* call.

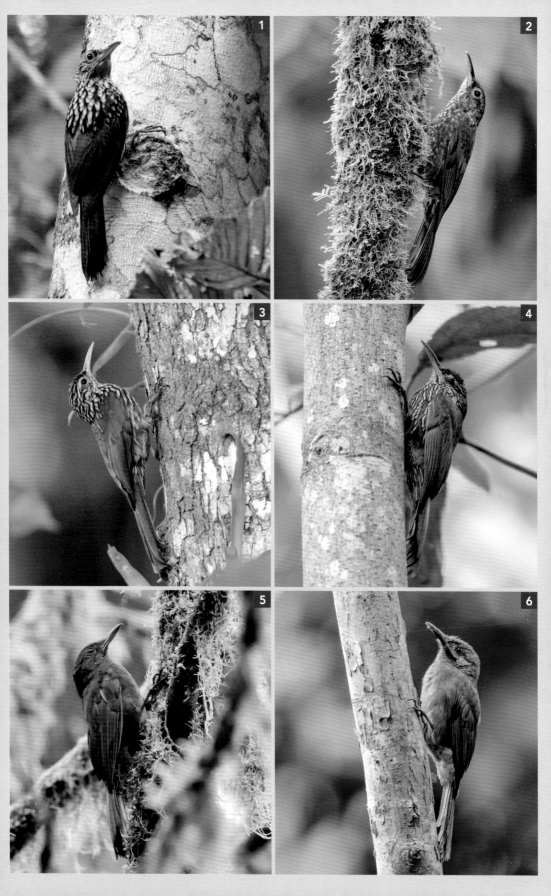

Western Ecuador's largest woodcreepers are presented here, along with the distinctive scythebills, which are woodcreepers with exceptionally long, thin, and strongly sickle-shaped bills.

1 STRONG-BILLED WOODCREEPER *Xiphocolaptes promeropirhynchus*
28–30cm/11–12in

600–3000m. This large and robust woodcreeper is uncommon in humid subtropical and temperate forest and edge; also found in deciduous forest at lower elevations in SW. Large size and stout decurved bill are the best ID features, but also note narrowly streaked underparts, head, and mantle. Usually encountered alone or in pairs at lower to mid levels, often accompanying mixed-species flocks. At some sites in the Tandayapa-Mindo area, can be encountered in the early morning, feeding on insects and other creatures that have been attracted to lights during the night. Song is a curious squealing, hiccuping phrase, repeated up to 10 times, each at a lower pitch, e.g., *weé-kyew, weé-kyew, weé-kyew, weé-kyew, weé-kyew, weé-kyew*.... Calls include a drawn-out *squeeeee-CHUK!* and various squeals and grunts.

2 NORTHERN BARRED-WOODCREEPER *Dendrocolaptes sanctithomae*
27cm/10.5in

0–1000m. Uncommon inside humid lowland and foothill forest, mainly in the NW. Mostly tawny brown, narrowly and evenly barred above and below; note almost straight, thick black bill. The only woodcreeper in our range with barred instead of streaked or plain plumage, but keep in mind that at a distance or in poor light the barring may not be visible; in these situations, bill shape and tawny foreparts are good clues. Singles or pairs forage on thick trunks at low to mid levels of the forest, often clinging motionless and easily overlooked. Readily attend army ant swarms, at which several birds may congregate. Song is a series of clear, rising notes, sometimes with a whipping quality, e.g., *whee-whee-whee-whee-wee-weih?*; the series sometimes ends in a rattling crescendo. Calls include a long rattle and a whining *TCHwhere*.

3 GREATER SCYTHEBILL *Drymotoxeres pucheranii* 29cm/11.5in

2000–2800m. Very rare in humid subtropical and temperate forest. In W Ecuador, it has been recorded only a few times in the highlands W of Quito; likely occurs farther N as well. Superficially much like Strong-billed Woodcreeper, but note distinctive facial pattern (lacking in Strong-billed) and much thinner bill. Forages from low to mid heights on mossy trunks, and sometimes joins mixed-species flocks. Usually quiet; vocalizations include a weak, up-slurred squeal, e.g, *eeeee-eeh!*, and a series of whiny, piping notes.

4 RED-BILLED SCYTHEBILL *Campylorhamphus trochilirostris* 24cm/9.5in

0–600m; to 1700m in SW. Fairly common in deciduous and semi-humid forest and edge; uncommon and local in humid forest edge and woodland, where there is possible overlap with Brown-billed Scythebill. The two species are almost identical in appearance; Red-billed Scythebill usually has a redder and longer bill, but length and color are variable, so these are not reliable ID features. Voice and habitat are more helpful. Brown-billed is not present in dry forest, where Red-billed is fairly common. In humid zones, Brown-billed is found in tall, wet epiphyte-laden forest, and Red-billed favors disturbed forest, even isolated patches of trees. Red-billed Scythebill is usually encountered alone or in pairs at low to medium heights, often with mixed-species flocks; forages on trunks and branches, also bamboo, often probing moss and crevices. Typical song begins with a chatter, then slows into a series of clear, upward notes, e.g., *ch'ch'ch'ch-twee-twee-twee-twee-twee-tew-tew*; sometimes lacks the initial chatter.

5 BROWN-BILLED SCYTHEBILL *Campylorhamphus pusillus* 24cm/9.5in

100–2100m. Uncommon in humid forest, mainly in the foothills but locally in the lowlands and subtropics as well; mostly restricted to the NW but also occurs in the SW at Buenaventura Reserve. Almost identical to Red-billed Scythebill; see that species for details, and note that bill color is not a reliable ID feature. Behavior much like that of Red-billed. Song is a long (ca. 5 sec.) series of clear whistles that mostly descend but are interspersed with longer, higher-pitched notes, e.g., *pi'pi'pi'pi'WEE'pi'pi'pi'pi'WEE-WEE'pi'pi'pi*....

ANTSHRIKES

Antbirds form a very diverse neotropical family of small to medium-size insectivorous birds. Antshrikes, among the largest members, differ in characteristics depending on genus; most have fairly thick, hooked bills and fairly short tails; those on this page all show marked sexual dimorphism.

1 FASCIATED ANTSHRIKE *Cymbilaimus lineatus* 18cm/7in

0–500m. Uncommon in humid lowland forest and edge; often around tree falls. Both sexes are profusely barred above and below and are unlike any other bird in our region. Fasciated Antshrike is usually encountered in furtive pairs that skulk in thick vine and branch tangles in the mid-story and subcanopy, where often difficult to see well; they often join mixed-species flocks. Song is a mellow series of four to eight up-slurred low whistles; calls include a single down-slurred whistle and a loud chatter.

2 GREAT ANTSHRIKE *Taraba major* 20cm/8in

0–1300m; to 1600m in SW. The region's largest antshrike. Fairly common and widespread in dense undergrowth of deciduous and humid forest edge and clearings, mostly in the lowlands and foothills but ranging higher in S. Both sexes have intense red irides and crest; male is striking and distinctive, with pied plumage; female is rufous above, whitish or pale buff below, and has a dusky mask. Encountered in pairs that move through dense undergrowth and vines, occasionally joining mixed-species flocks. Song is a fairly long accelerating, bouncy series of hollow notes that ends in a curious growl: *bwoh-bwoh-bwoh-bwoh-bwohbohbohbohbohboh-brrrrraaaah*. Also gives a long, decelerating series of harsh clucks.

3 WESTERN SLATY-ANTSHRIKE *Thamnophilus atrinucha* 15cm/6in

0–1300m. Fairly common in semi-humid and humid lowland and foothill forest, edge, and overgrown clearings. Male is mostly gray and black, while female is brown and tan. Thick, hooked bill and bold wing and tail markings (white in male; buff in female) separate the species from all other antbirds in W Ecuador. Western Slaty-Antshrike is usually encountered in pairs, foraging at low to mid levels; regularly joins mixed-species flocks. Song is a series of nasal notes that ends in a final higher-pitched and slightly louder note: *wu- wu- wu- wu- wu- wu- wu- wu-wu-wu-wu-WHAN!* Calls include various nasal grunts and whines. Sometimes called **Black-crowned Antshrike**.

4 UNIFORM ANTSHRIKE *Thamnophilus unicolor* 15cm/6in

700–2200m. Uncommon in humid foothill and subtropical forest and edge. Both sexes have pale irides, though this feature is often not obvious. Male is uniform gray; female is rufous brown with gray face and throat. Male Esmeraldas Antbird (p. 252) has white wing spots and red irides; male Zeledon's Antbird displays bare bluish-white periocular skin. Uniform Antshrike is encountered mainly in pairs that forage from understory to mid levels, and only occasionally join mixed-species flocks. Song is a slow, soft, and somewhat nasal series of two to four notes, e.g., *anh-anh-anh-anh*. Calls include various churrs and low chatters.

Three very dissimilar antshrikes and Streak-headed Antbird, a slender, long-tailed antbird strongly associated with *Chusquea* bamboo; all but Russet Antshrike show strong sexual dimorphism.

1 COLLARED ANTSHRIKE *Thamnophilus bernardi* 17cm/6.5in

0–1500m. Fairly common in deciduous forest and scrub, mostly in the lowlands, but reaches higher elevations in SW. Male is striking with black hood contrasting with white neck and lower underparts. Female is brown and buff, with black grizzled face. Not likely to be confused with any other species if seen well. Animated pairs forage in tangled lower and middle growth, raising and lowering their crests and often pumping their tails. Song is a rapid, nasal series ending in an abrupt *coh!*; calls include a snarled growl and an abrupt *puk!*

2 RUSSET ANTSHRIKE *Thamnistes anabatinus* 14cm/5.5in

100–1300m. Fairly common in humid lowland and foothill forest. Sexes are similar. Note combination of stout, hooked bill, rufous upperparts, pale superciliary, and dusky postocular line. Can be confused with larger Buff-fronted Foliage-gleaner (p. 234), which has longer tail, gray crown, rufous superciliary, and a thinner bill. Singles or pairs of Russet Antshrike forage actively along branches and in foliage in canopy and subcanopy, often with mixed-species flocks. Song is a series of fairly high-pitched whistled notes, e.g., *tsheew-tsheew-tsheew-tsheew-tsheew-tsheew-tsheew*.

3 CHAPMAN'S ANTSHRIKE *Thamnophilus zarumae* 15cm/6in

800–2600m. Locally fairly common in semi-humid foothill and subtropical forest, edge, and scrub in the SW. No similar bird occurs in range. Male has strong black-and-white barring. Female is very different: chestnut crown, upperparts, and tail contrast with buffy underparts; also note black-and-white facial mottling. Chapman's Antshrike is encountered alone or in pairs that forage about in dense tangles at lower to mid levels, regularly accompanying mixed-species flocks. Song is a fairly rapid series of notes that ends in a stutter, e.g., *pu-pu-pu-pu-pu-pu-pu-pu-pu-pu-pu-pih-dih-di'd'd'd*.

4 STREAK-HEADED ANTBIRD *Drymophila striaticeps* 15cm/6in

1400–2600m; down to 700m at S limit of range. Fairly common in subtropical and temperate forest, where almost always encountered in *Chusquea* bamboo thickets; locally ranges down into the foothills, where more likely to be found away away from bamboo. This slender, long-tailed, and heavily streaked antbird is distinctive and unique in our range. Female is a buffier version of the male. Pairs forage close together in thick lower growth and dense bamboo, where they can easily hide from view; do not join mixed-species flocks. Their antiphonal song consists of the male's brisk buzzy *tchip! tchip! dzew-dzew-dzew*, often followed by the female's shorter *chip chip tew-tew-tew*. This species, along with three others found elsewhere in South America, were formerly lumped as **Long-tailed Antbird** (*D. caudata*).

Small, short-tailed antbirds found in humid forest. All are sexually dimorphic.

1 SPOT-CROWNED ANTVIREO *Dysithamnus puncticeps* 12cm/4.5in

0–800m. Uncommon in humid lowland and foothill forest in the NW. Both sexes have pale gray irides and stout, hooked bills. Male is gray with small white spots on crown and wings; female is mostly brown with faint buff edges to wing coverts and rufous and gray streaks on crown. Small size, chunky shape, and wing and crown markings help separate both sexes from other antbirds. Singles or pairs are typically found in mid-story or subcanopy, and often join mixed-species flocks. Song is a rapid, ringing 3–4 sec. series of notes that descends and accelerates somewhat near the end. Call is a short, dry, metallic trill.

2 PLAIN ANTVIREO *Dysithamnus mentalis* 12cm/4.5in

0–1800m. Fairly common in deciduous and humid forest, from lowlands well up into the subtropics. Note dusky auriculars and dark irides in both sexes. Male is mostly gray, with yellowish-olive belly, wing coverts edged whitish. Female is an olivaceous-brown version of male, with rufous crown and whitish eye-ring. Tawny-crowned Greenlet (p. 322) is similar to female but has thinner bill and white irides. Pairs forage in tangled lower growth, regularly joining mixed-species flocks. Song is a low, descending and accelerating series, e.g., *pih, pih, pih, pih, pih-pipipipipipidipih*.

3 CHECKER-THROATED ANTWREN *Epinecrophylla fulviventris* 10cm/4in

0–900m. Fairly common in understory of humid lowland and foothill forest. Both sexes have narrow buff wing bars and pale irides. Male, with its distinctively black-and-white-checkered throat, is unique in its range. Female is much like male but lacks bold checkered throat and is buffier below. Female White-flanked Antwren (p. 248) has dark irides, grayer head, pale flanks, and whitish throat; female Slaty Antwren (p. 248) has unmarked wings. Pairs or small groups of Checker-throated Antwren join mixed-species flocks in dense, vine-tangled lower growth, where they glean foliage and dead leaf clusters. Vocalizations include a rapid *tsip-tsip-tsip-tsip-tsip...*, a slower *see-see-see-see*, and a single squeak.

4 DOT-WINGED ANTWREN *Microrhopias quixensis* 12cm/4.5in

0–1200m. Fairly common in humid lowland and foothill forest. Combination of bold spots on wing coverts, which form a broad white line on the folded wing, and broadly white-tipped tail is diagnostic; male otherwise all black; female has rufous-chestnut underparts. Animated pairs work actively and conspicuously through foliage and tangles at varying heights, often fanning their tails; sometimes join mixed-species flocks. Song is a clear, short series of descending notes. Calls include a short *tyew*, and an extended musical chatter.

5 RUFOUS-RUMPED ANTWREN *Euchrepomis callinota* 11cm/4.5in

900–1800m. Uncommon in humid foothill and subtropical forest. Both sexes have a rufous rump, but this is often hard to see in the field. Male has black crown, yellow wing bars, faint white superciliary, and dark postocular line. Female is a duller version of male, with grayer underparts and fainter wing bars and facial markings. No other antwren in our range has a rufous rump and yellow wing bars. Pairs forage from mid levels to canopy, almost always within mixed-species flocks, appearing rather warbler-like as they actively glean foliage and branches. Song is a very high-pitched, rising, and accelerating chippered trill.

Five antwrens of lowland and foothill forest (one ranges into the subtropics). All are sexually dimorphic.

1   WHITE-FLANKED ANTWREN   *Myrmotherula axillaris*   10cm/4in

0–900m. Fairly common inside humid lowland forest. Both sexes have white flanks, which are diagnostic when seen but often inconspicuous in female. Male is black with white-dotted wing bars and white-tipped tail feathers. Female is mostly brown, with a grayish head, faint buff wing bars, and whitish throat. Pairs, or small groups, regularly join mixed-species understory flocks, foraging actively in lower and middle growth, especially vine tangles, often flicking their wings and flashing the white flanks. Song is a descending series of sharp, evenly spaced, breathy whistled notes *whee! whee! whee! whee! whee, whee.*

2   SLATY ANTWREN   *Myrmotherula schisticolor*   10cm/4in

200–1800m. Fairly common inside humid lowland, foothill, and subtropical forest. Male is dark slate, with black bib, and wing coverts narrowly tipped white. Female is gray above, tawny below, with wing coverts faintly tipped rufous. Female Checker-throated Antwren (p. 246) has pale eyes and obvious buffy wing bars. Behavior of Slaty is much like that of White-flanked Antwren. Song consists of single, inflected *sweep* notes repeated somewhat randomly; also a short, squeaky, downward-slurred *skweee.*

3   PACIFIC ANTWREN   *Myrmotherula pacifica*   9cm/3.5in

0–1400m. Fairly common in secondary forest edge, overgrown clearings, gardens, and plantations in humid lowlands and foothills. Male is profusely black-and-white striped; female has distinctive orange-buff head and breast. No other antbird is similar, though male is vaguely reminiscent of longer-tailed Black-and-white Warbler (p. 358), which is more slender and displays very different, woodcreeper-like behavior. Pacific Antwren is usually found in pairs or small groups, foraging at varying heights at forest edge or in isolated trees and shrubs; not found with mixed-species flocks. Song is a fast series of about 10 to 16 slightly ascending *chip* notes.

4   MOUSTACHED ANTWREN   *Myrmotherula ignota*   8cm/3in

0–600m. Uncommon in humid lowland forest in the NW. Tiny, appearing almost tailless; crown, upperparts, and sides of breast heavily streaked black and white; face and throat white, with black eye stripe and broad malar stripe; remaining underparts pale yellow. Female (not shown) is similar to male but buffier, especially on face. No really similar species occurs in our range. Usually encountered in pairs, sometimes with mixed-species flocks, foraging at high levels where it can be hard to see well. Song is a rapid series of ca. 20 clear notes that accelerates and descends toward the end; a clear down-slurred *tyew* call is also given. Birds in W Ecuador are sometimes called **Griscom's Antwren**.

5   RUFOUS-WINGED ANTWREN   *Terenura callinota*   12cm/4.5in

0–400m. Rare to uncommon and very local in humid forest and edge; in W Ecuador, known only from a few scattered locations (e.g., Río Palenque Science Center). Note bold rufous wing patch, white superciliary, and black eye stripe. Crown is black in male and rufous in female (not shown). Rufous-winged Tyrannulet (p. 266) also has a rufous wing patch, but has white underparts and much less black on the face. Pairs of Rufous-winged Antwrens are usually seen with mixed-species flocks, from mid levels to canopy, appearing somewhat warbler-like. Song is a short, 1–2 sec. sputtered trill that rises and falls in pitch.

♂ 5

LOWLAND ANTBIRDS

Four sexually dimorphic antbirds found mainly in lowland forest. All are quite shy and can be difficult to see.

1 DUSKY ANTBIRD *Cercomacroides tyrannina* 14cm/5.5in

0–800m; locally to 1400m. Fairly common in humid lowland and foothill forest edge and overgrown clearings. Both sexes have a white dorsal patch that is usually hidden unless the bird is excited. Male is medium gray, with wing coverts and tail feathers narrowly tipped white. Female is olive brown above, with wing coverts and tail feathers narrowly tipped tawny buff; underparts tawny buff. Male differs from female Jet Antbird (little overlap) by lack of white streaking on underparts. Western Slaty-Antshrike (p. 242) is larger, more compact, and has a stouter hooked bill and bolder wing markings. Dusky Antbird is usually encountered in pairs that move furtively through dense thickets in the understory, gleaning prey from leaves and stems. Song is a rapid, piping rising-falling series: *peepee-peepee-PEEPEEPEEPEE-peepee*; also gives a sharp *chyew!* call note.

2 JET ANTBIRD *Cercomacra nigricans* 15cm/6in

0–500m. Uncommon and local in deciduous and semi-humid forest and edge in the lowlands; also inhabits shade-grown cacao plantations. Both sexes have a semi-concealed white dorsal patch. Male is glossy black with bold white wing and tail markings. Female is grayer, with white streaking on throat and breast; similar male Dusky Antbird has weaker white markings on wings and tail and lacks breast streaking; male White-backed Fire-eye has no white wing or tail markings. Jet Antbird's behavior is much like that of Dusky, but it may forage a bit higher in cacao groves. Song is a creaky-sounding *chk-uh, chk-uh, chk-uh*; also gives a short series of *chk* notes.

3 STUB-TAILED ANTBIRD *Myrmeciza berlepschi* 14cm/5.5in

0–700m. Uncommon and local in humid lowland forest and edge in NW. Male is black with a relatively short tail and small, usually obscured white dorsal patch. Female similar, but with white spots on wings, throat, and breast. Deep red irides usually look dark in the field. Other all-black antbirds have brighter red irides, stronger wing markings, or blue periocular skin. Typically found alone or in pairs, foraging low in dense vegetation, and does not associate with mixed-species flocks; frequently pumps tail downward. Song is a series of falling and then rising notes, *see, syew, syew, su, su, syew, see, see.*

4 WHITE-BACKED FIRE-EYE *Pyriglena leuconota* 18cm/7in

0–1300m. Uncommon and local in undergrowth of deciduous and humid forest and edge in lowlands and foothills. Both sexes have a large (often concealed) white dorsal patch and bright red eyes. Male is all jet black; female has brown upperparts, grayish-buff underparts, and a dusky tail. Other antbirds that occur with it have wing markings or periocular patches. White-backed Fire-eye is often encountered in pairs, foraging through low branches and dense vegetation; sometimes attends army ant swarms with other antbirds; often pumps tail downward. Heard far more often than seen; song is a hurried, 3 sec. long, slightly rising and falling series of sharp, piping whistles: *pipipipiPIPIPIPIPIpipipi*; also gives a variety of chatters and chirps. (Female photo digitally modified from another species.)

MYRMECIZA ANTBIRDS

Myrmeciza is a diverse genus of medium-size to fairly large understory antbirds; all are sexually dimorphic. Stub-tailed Antbird (p. 250) is included in this genus.

1 CHESTNUT-BACKED ANTBIRD *Myrmeciza exsul* 14cm/5.5in

0–1400m. Common in humid lowland and foothill forest. Combination of pale blue periocular skin and white wing markings is diagnostic in its range. Female Esmeraldas Antbird lacks the periocular skin and has red irides and pale throat scaling. Vocal pairs or small groups of Chestnut-backed Antbird roam the forest understory, often independent of other birds but sometimes attending army ant swarms; habitually pumps tail in a downward motion. Often-heard song is a clear, whistled *FEH, few*, or *FEH, FEH, few*; also gives a whining churr and dry chatter.

2 ESMERALDAS ANTBIRD *Myrmeciza nigricauda* 14cm/5.5in

400–1500m. Uncommon in humid foothill forest, especially in damp ravines and on steep slopes above streams. Male is uniform gray, with dotted white wing bars and red eyes. Female is similar but has chestnut back, wings, and tail, and brown flanks and crissum; throat is scaled whitish. Female best distinguished from Chestnut-backed Antbird by her red irides and lack of pale blue periocular skin. Esmeraldas Antbird is mostly encountered alone or in pairs and usually remains very near the forest floor, where tough to see in the gloom. Song is a shrill, breathy, falling and rising *SWEE, swee-swee-swee-swee-SWEE, SWEE*; also gives chatters and churrs. (Female photo digitally modified from another species.)

3 ZELEDON'S ANTBIRD *Myrmeciza zeledoni* 18cm/7in

0–2000m. Fairly common in humid forest and edge from lowlands to subtropics. Note conspicuous pale blue periocular skin; male is glossy black; female is chestnut brown, with dusky face, throat, and tail. White-backed Fire-eye (p. 250) lacks bare periocular skin, irides are red, and it sometimes shows a white dorsal patch. Zeledon's Antbird is encountered alone or in pairs; usually forages low in dense undergrowth; sometimes attends army ant swarms. Song is an evenly spaced (two notes per second), slightly descending series of clear, forceful down-slurred whistles: *pyew-pyew-pyew-pyew-pyew-pyew…*; also gives several chirps in rapid succession. Formerly lumped with Blue-lored Antbird (*M. immaculata*; not found in Ecuador) and called **Immaculate Antbird**.

4 GRAY-HEADED ANTBIRD *Myrmeciza griseiceps* 13cm/5in

600–2600m. Rare and local in humid montane forest with extensive *Chusquea* bamboo in the far SW. Cinnamon-brown mantle, wings, flanks, and crissum; two white black-bordered wing bars; tail blackish, feathers broadly tipped white. Male has head and underparts slaty; female (not shown) is similar but paler gray on head and underparts. Quite furtive and difficult to see as it moves through dense, bamboo-tangled undergrowth. Song is a hard, descending chattered trill, *tchrrrrrrrrr*; also gives a thin scrapy *dzjee-dzjih* call.

The three antbirds treated here habitually follow army ant swarms. The antthrushes are shy, terrestrial birds that walk deliberately about on the forest floor, usually with tail cocked, in a rather rail-like fashion. They are heard far more often than seen.

1 SPOTTED ANTBIRD   *Hylophylax naevioides*   12cm/4.5in

0–400m. This small, attractive antbird is uncommon inside humid lowland forest in the far NW. Strongly patterned male is distinctive. Female is duller and browner looking, but no other antbird in its range shows a combination of dusky breast band and tawny wing bars. Usually encountered in pairs, though small groups may congregate at ant swarms; regularly clings to vertical stems, spreading and flicking its tail. Song is a shrill, rollicking series that rises slightly then falls, e.g., *weeee-di-wee-di-wee-di-wee-di-wee-di-wee*; calls include a sharp *pit-pit-pit* and a short rattle.

2 BICOLORED ANTBIRD   *Gymnopithys bicolor*   14cm/5.5in

0–900m. Uncommon inside humid lowland and foothill forest. Combination of white central underparts bordered by black, brown upperparts, and bluish-gray periocular region is diagnostic. Highly tied to army ant swarms, at which several birds invariably congregate, remaining close to the ground, regularly clinging to vertical stems and dropping to the forest floor to snatch up prey. Quite vocal, especially at ant swarms; song is a *TWEE-TWEE-TEE-ti-ti't't'ti- tjer* that rises and then falls in pitch; also gives an incessant grating down-slurred churr.

3 OCELLATED ANTBIRD   *Phaenostictus mcleannani*   19cm/7.5in

0–800m. A large, stunning antbird; uncommon inside humid lowland and foothill forest in the NW. This spectacular species will not be mistaken if seen well. Almost always found at army ant swarms, where it dominates other species present; usually perches on a low branch or thin sapling, sallying out or dropping to the ground to grab arthropod prey. Song is a 4–5 sec. series of shrill, rising notes that speeds up and descends abruptly at the end. Most common call is a down-slurred *tcheeer*.

4 BLACK-HEADED ANTTHRUSH   *Formicarius nigricapillus*   18cm/7in

0–900m. Uncommon to locally fairly common inside humid lowland and lower foothill forest. Dark gray, with rufous back, tail, and crissum and a pale bluish eye-ring. No really similar species; no known overlap with Rufous-breasted Antthrush of higher elevations. Entirely terrestrial; singles or pairs walk about on the forest floor with tail usually cocked up. Very shy and usually first detected by voice, and even then difficult to observe in the dark forest understory. Song is a 4–5 sec. rapid series of ringing whistles that accelerates, drops slightly in pitch, and then slows and rises at the end, e.g., *pipipipipipipipipupupupupupu pupupupupupep-pep-pep, pep, puh, puh, puh, puh, puh*. Usual call is a sharp *wihDIT!*

5 RUFOUS-BREASTED ANTTHRUSH   *Formicarius rufipectus*   19cm/7.5in

900–2000m. Uncommon to locally fairly common inside humid foothill and subtropical forest. Rufous and gray plumage combined with pale, broken eye-ring is unique in range. Black-headed Antthrush replaces this species at lower elevations (the two are not known to overlap). Behavior is similar to that of Black-headed Antthrush, though Rufous-breasted is more likely to walk along forest trails, especially at dawn and dusk. Song is easily imitated and consists of two clear piping notes, the second is higher and flatter, e.g., *fih, FEH!*; typical call is a guttural *kra-kra-kra-kra-kra-kra*.

5

Antpittas are plump, short-tailed, long-legged, and mostly terrestrial birds of dense forest undergrowth. They are dressed in earthen tones and are notorious for being hard to observe, though a number of species now come to feeders at various lodges and reserves.

1 UNDULATED ANTPITTA *Grallaria squamigera* 23cm/9in

2500–3700m. This large antpitta is uncommon in humid temperate forest. Tawny below, profusely scaled with black; white malar is bordered by a black stripe. The larger Giant Antpitta of lower elevations is similar but much richer rufous below and lacks malar. Undulated is a very secretive and seldom-seen species, though occasionally can be encountered along muddy trails during damp and foggy early mornings. Song is a 5–7 sec. deep, screech-owl-like trill that rises gradually, then drops very slightly in pitch on the last note.

2 GIANT ANTPITTA *Grallaria gigantea* 24cm/9.5in

1400–2400m. The largest antpitta in W Ecuador, rare to locally uncommon inside humid subtropical forest. Rich rufous underparts are narrowly barred in black. Undulated Antpitta is much less richly colored below and shows white malar bordered below by black. Despite its size, this species is very secretive, seldom seen away from the Paz de las Aves Refuge, where one or more visit a worm feeder. Song is similar to that of Undulated Antpitta, but continuously rises and does not drop on the last note.

3 MOUSTACHED ANTPITTA *Grallaria alleni* 17cm/6.5in

1700–2300m. Uncommon and very local inside humid subtropical forest. Much like the more widespread Scaled Antpitta; differs by whiter malar and creamy-white belly. The paler belly is the most reliable plumage ID feature, but it can be extremely hard to see, and the two species are best separated by voice in their area of overlap. Like most other antpittas, Moustached is shy and difficult to see, hopping on the ground or occasionally singing from an elevated but very hidden perch. Easier to see at some sites, such as the Paz de las Aves Refuge, where habituated birds come in to feed on earthworms. Song is a rising, hollow, 3–4 sec. series of low whistles.

4 SCALED ANTPITTA *Grallaria guatimalensis* 16cm/6.5in

300–1800m; to 2200m in the SW. Uncommon and very local inside humid forest in a wide range of elevations. Extremely similar to Moustached Antpitta, with which it overlaps locally in the subtropics. Scaled has a buffier malar and lacks a pale belly; these features are difficult to distinguish in the dark forest understory, and it is usually best to go by voice. Plain-backed Antpitta is superficially similar though more uniformly colored and has an indistinct, buffy malar. Behavior is similar to that of Moustached. Song is also similar, but briefly slows down toward the end, which gives it a stuttering quality.

5 YELLOW-BREASTED ANTPITTA *Grallaria flavotincta* 17cm/6.5in

1500–2400m. This attractive antpitta is uncommon and local inside humid subtropical forest. Yellow throat and breast are distinctive in range. Behavior is similar to that of Moustached Antpitta, and Yellow-breasted likewise can be seen coming in to feed on earthworms at the Paz de las Aves Refuge. Song consists of three clear whistled notes (sometimes the first is difficult to hear), e.g., *fih-fee-fwee* or *can't see me*; call is a screeching *eeeeeee-yit!*

6 PLAIN-BACKED ANTPITTA *Grallaria haplonota* 16cm/6.5in

700–1500m. Uncommon and local inside humid foothill and subtropical forest; known only from a few sites in the NW (e.g., the Mashpi area and ridges above Mindo), as well in the SW at Buenaventura Reserve. A plain version of Scaled Antpitta, it differs mainly by its more uniform plumage (lacking gray upperparts) and very indistinct malar streak. Behavior is similar to that of Moustached Antpitta. On very rare occasions, Plain-backed Antpitta may feed on a muddy trail in predawn light. Song is a slow, hollow series of low whistles that rises and then falls, e.g., *who, who, who, whO, WHO, WHO, WHO, WHO, WHO, Who, who, who, who.*

1 CHESTNUT-CROWNED ANTPITTA *Grallaria ruficapilla* 19cm/7.5in

1600–3100m. This attractive antpitta is fairly common and widespread inside humid subtropical and temperate forest. No really similar species within most of its range, but Watkin's Antpitta is sympatric with it in the far SW Andes. Watkin's shows paler overall coloration, whitish face, and chestnut restricted to crown and nape. Chestnut-crowned Antpitta is usually found alone or in pairs, hopping stealthily around the forest floor and sometimes singing from an elevated perch. Occasionally one may emerge to feed in the open along a trail or roadside in predawn hours. It sometimes visits a worm feeder as Paz de las Aves Refuge. Song is a well-enunciated three-note, whistled *Not so close!*, with the second note lowest; call is a descending *EEEyer*.

2 WATKIN'S ANTPITTA *Grallaria watkinsi* 18cm/7in

0–1800m. Uncommon to locally fairly common in deciduous and semi-humid forest in W and SW; found mainly in lowlands and foothills; locally up to the subtropics in far SW, where it is sympatric with Chestnut-crowned Antpitta. Watkins's Antpitta is a pale version of Chestnut-crowned, lacking its chestnut hood (chestnut restricted to crown and nape). Behavior is similar to that of Chestnut-crowned, though Watkin's Antpitta is easier to see during the dry season, when vegetation is leafless and leaf litter can crunch noisily as the bird hops along. Song is a series of several loud whistles, the last of which slurs distinctly upward, e.g., *too-too-too-too-too, toowee?*; shorter versions are also given. Typical call is *titooLER?*

3 CHESTNUT-NAPED ANTPITTA *Grallaria nuchalis* 19cm/7.5in

2600–3500m. Rare and local inside humid temperate forest. The bird shown is from E Ecuador; W birds have a gray crown, with chestnut restricted to nape. No other antpitta in our range is similar; under poor light conditions white eye-ring and chestnut nape usually stand out more than other features. Behavior similar to that of Chestnut-crowned Antpitta. Song is an ascending series of hollow whistles reminiscent of Morse code, e.g., *peet, pididit, pidadit-dit-dit-di-di-dih*. Call is a series of about 10 evenly spaced whistles.

4 TAWNY ANTPITTA *Grallaria quitensis* 16cm/6.5in

3000–4500m. By far the most easily observed antpitta; common in páramo, wooded borders of agricultural areas, and edge of temperate forest. Plain brownish above and ochraceous buff below. Smaller Rufous Antpitta is uniformly rich rufous and usually stays inside forest. Tawny Antpitta frequently emerges from dense cover to forage boldly in open areas. It often runs, with surprising speed, then suddenly stops and stands still with a vertical posture. Often sings from an exposed perch atop a shrub or mound. Song is a three-note whistle, the first note highest pitched, e.g., *fwee-too-too*; call is a sharp, down-slurred *TCHyoo*.

5 RUFOUS ANTPITTA *Grallaria rufula* 14cm/5.5in

2600–3700m. The smallest *Grallaria*; fairly common inside temperate forest. Mostly uniform rufous, with a slightly paler belly. Tawny Antpitta is larger and mostly brown and tawny, not rufous. Behavior is similar to that of Chestnut-crowned Antpitta, though Rufous Antpitta is more likely to feed boldly along a trail at almost any time of the day. It has a wide vocal repertoire: A typical short song is a quick, bouncing *pit, pididit*; also occasionally gives a much longer, descending series, followed by several bursts similar to the short song. Most common call is a rapid, descending *pid'd'd'd'd'd'dih*.

6 STREAK-CHESTED ANTPITTA *Hylopezus perspicillatus* 14cm/5.5in

0–800m. Rare to locally uncommon in humid lowland and foothill forest in the NW. Note boldly black-streaked breast and flanks, prominent ochraceous eye-ring, and black malar; there is no similar species in range. Behavior is similar to that of Chestnut-crowned Antpitta, though Streak-chested Antpitta may attend army ant swarms, and sometimes rocks its body from side to side. Song, often given from a slightly elevated perch, is a series of clear and easily imitated whistles; the first note is low pitched and the remaining descend gradually, e.g., *poh-pee-pee-pee-pee-peh-pah-poh*. Other calls include a descending, whinnying *wee-wowowowowowowowo* and a long, guttural staccato trill. Sometimes called **Spectacled Antpitta**.

1 OCHRE-BREASTED ANTPITTA *Grallaricula flavirostris* 10cm/4in

800–2000m. Locally fairly common inside humid foothill and subtropical forest. Two subspecies occur; NW subspecies *mindoensis* has ochraceous breast, eye-ring, and throat; heavy dark streaking on underparts; and bicolor bill. SW subspecies *zarumae* is much more ochraceous, less streaked below, and has an all-yellow bill. No known overlap with Rusty-breasted Antpitta. Ochre-breasted Antpitta is not terrestrial, but is usually found singly or in pairs within a few meters of the ground, perching quietly for long periods, and sometimes twisting its chest from side to side. It makes abrupt sallies to pick off prey, and often returns to the same spot. Most common vocalization is a single down-slurred, whistled note, e.g., *sweeoh*.

2 RUSTY-BREASTED ANTPITTA *Grallaricula ferrugineipectus* 11cm/4.5in

1800–2600m. Known in Ecuador only from a number of widely separated locations both in the N and far S (e.g., Pululahua Geobotanical Reserve and Utuana Reserve), where it is uncommon to fairly common in *Chusquea* bamboo patches. Note brown upperparts, tawny underparts, and white postocular spot; does not overlap with any similar species. Behavior is similar to that of Ochre-breasted Antpitta, but Rusty-breasted may perch much higher when inside tall bamboo patches. Song is an evenly spaced series of level chips, e.g., *choo-chip-chip-chip-chip-chip-chip-chip-chip-chip-chip*. The taxonomy of this species is in need of revision; birds from Ecuador and NW Peru could prove to be undescribed subspecies and species.

3 RUFOUS-CROWNED ANTPITTA *Pittasoma rufopileatum* 16cm/6.5in

100–1100m. Rare and local inside humid lowland and foothill forest in NW. Rufous crown and throat, broad black superciliary, and dense barring on underparts render this bird easy to ID if seen well. Female (not shown) is similar to male but with fainter barring. Mainly terrestrial and very shy; regularly attends army ant swarms, at which it can be somewhat more approachable. Runs about rapidly and adeptly, sometimes pausing in a frozen stance, then resuming, usually disappearing out of sight; may flush to an exposed perch when startled. Song is a single mid-tone, slightly down-slurred *tyeeoo*, repeated every 1–2 sec.

4 OCELLATED TAPACULO *Acropternis orthonyx* 22cm/8.5in

2200–3600m. One of the most spectacular of all Andean birds. Locally fairly common in dense undergrowth in humid temperate forest and edge, favoring *Chusquea* bamboo. While scarce in many areas, good numbers inhabit roadside bamboo thickets in the upper reaches of the Tandayapa Valley. This unique skulker will not be mistaken if seen well. Mostly encountered alone or in pairs, scratching in leaf litter with its extended hind claws or hopping along mossy branches in dense vegetation. Song is a clear, loud, and far-carrying whistled note, e.g., *FWEER!*, repeated at regular intervals; also a shorter *WHEN!* call is given.

5 ELEGANT CRESCENTCHEST *Melanopareia elegans* 14cm/5.5in

0–2300m. Locally fairly common in arid scrub and deciduous forest edge; in recent years, it has been expanding into deforested areas of the NW. This strikingly patterned bird is easy to ID when seen well. Male has more contrasting plumage and larger black bib than female. Singles or pairs skulk in dense tangles, where they can be hard to see, especially in the rainy season after the vegetation leafs out. Usually heard before seen; song is series of ca. 10 to 20 snappy tick notes, e.g., *puh, pih-pih-pit-pit-pit-pit-pit-pit-pit-pit*; call is a rapid *pi'ti'tit* with a dripping quality.

♂ 5

♀ 5

mindoensis 1

zarumae 1

2

♂ 3

4

SMALL TAPACULOS

Scytalopus tapaculos are small, mouse-like birds that skulk in forest understory. Species look the same and can be separated only by their vocalizations, distributions, and elevation ranges, so photos refer to multiple species, and plumage is not described in detail. Ash-colored Tapaculo is similar to *Scytalopus* species but longer tailed.

1 NARIÑO TAPACULO *Scytalopus vicinior* 13cm/5in

1300–2100m; to 2400m in far NW. Fairly common in humid foothill and subtropical forest. Overlaps marginally with Spillmann's Tapaculo. Typical song is a 3–15 sec. series of rapid squeaky chips, though not nearly as fast as Spillmann's; individual notes can almost be counted in Nariño's song, whereas it is impossible to count notes in Spillmann's beyond the first several. Other calls include a sharp *peek!* and a short songlike burst of four or five notes.

2 SPILLMANN'S TAPACULO *Scytalopus spillmanni* 13cm/5in

2100–3500m. Fairly common in humid subtropical and temperate forest. Overlaps marginally with Nariño Tapaculo. Song initiates with a rising, accelerating series of fast notes, then becomes a very long, rattled trill that may continue for 10 sec. or longer. Other calls are a 1 sec. rising, metallic trill repeated several times; a 1 sec. rising and falling series of higher-pitched notes; and various sharp squeaks and churrs.

3 CHOCÓ TAPACULO *Scytalopus chocoensis* 11cm/4.5in

200–1200m. Uncommon inside humid lowland and foothill forest in the far NW. No other tapaculo shares this species' range. Usual song is a 4–30 sec. leisurely series of squeaky chips; it often starts faster before slowing down. Also gives a descending series of chip notes that starts off very loud and sharp but quickly becomes quieter; also emits a quick series of down-slurred notes, e.g., *chu-chu-chu-chu*.

4 EL ORO TAPACULO *Scytalopus robbinsi* 11cm/4.5in

700–1200m. Rare and local in humid foothill forest in the SW (e.g., Buenaventura Reserve). No other tapaculo shares its range. Song can be very long (up to 45 sec.); it starts with a short series of softer single notes, which then become doubled (e.g., *clidup*) as the song gradually increases in volume; notes are given about five per second in mid-song. Other calls include a rising, buzzy *chwEET!* and a falling *cheeuu*. Also called **Ecuadorian Tapaculo**.

5 BLACKISH TAPACULO *Scytalopus latrans* 12cm/4.5in

2300–3800m; 1600–3300m in SW. Fairly common in humid temperate forest; ranges down into the subtropics in SW. Song of N subspecies *latrans* starts out as a rather slow series of erratic yapping notes; eventually the notes become faster, louder, and evenly spaced; the whole series can last 30 sec. or longer; common call is a rising frog-like *wert?* S subspecies *subcinereus* gives a wide variety of vocalizations. Some songs are similar to those of *latrans*, but it also gives a lower-pitched, more forceful series consisting of bursts of 4 to 15 evenly spaced notes; other vocalizations include a series of sharp, frog-like notes, a sharp *wit*, and a rising *wert?* This species was formerly lumped with **Unicolored Tapaculo** (*S. unicolor*) of NW Peru. (Male and female photos digitally modified from another species.)

6 PÁRAMO TAPACULO *Scytalopus canus* 11cm/4.5in

3000–4000m. Mainly an E slope species, but uncommon in scrub and temperate forest edge in Páramo El Angel near the Colombian border; it also spills over W of the continental divide locally in other locations. Male similar to Blackish Tapaculo; female (not shown) has brownish upperparts. Song is a long, very rapid, dry, insect-like trill; also gives a descending series of squeaks, a short burst of 4 to 10 notes, a short metallic trill, and a metallic *jeeRIT*. (Male photo digitally modified from another species.)

7 ASH-COLORED TAPACULO *Myornis senilis* 14–15cm/5.5–6in

2300–3600m. Uncommon in humid subtropical and temperate forest. Adult mostly gray; may show a brownish wash to plumage, especially on crissum. Long tail helps separate it from Blackish Tapaculo. Juvenile (not shown) is faintly barred, rusty brown above, buffier below, with pale throat and belly. This tapaculo skulks in dense understory, and is often found in or near *Chusquea* bamboo. Typical song is a series of sharp chips that start well spaced, then become closer together, doubled, then tripled, etc., until finishing in a fast, descending trill. Other vocalizations include a very long trill reminiscent of that of Spillmann's Tapaculo but lower pitched; a dry 1 sec. trill; and a lone sharp, chip.

ad. 1–4

imm. 1–4

♂ 5 & 6

♀ 5

7

Phyllomyias tyrannulets are small arboreal flycatchers with stubby bills; most have wing bars. Marble-faced Bristle-Tyrant is superficially similar, but has a thinner bill and tends to perch more upright and stay lower in the forest. Most of these species regularly join mixed-species flocks of tanagers, barbets, other flycatchers, etc.

1 SOOTY-HEADED TYRANNULET *Phyllomyias griseiceps* 10cm/4in

0–1200m. Fairly common in humid secondary forest and edge in lowlands and foothills. Plain; gray head and olive-brown upperparts contrast with mostly yellow underparts. Note whitish superciliary, faint dark line through the eye, and vertical posture; lack of wing bars is best ID feature for this species, though beware possible confusion with Greenish Elaenia (p. 270), which is larger and has much paler, faintly streaked underparts. Brown-capped Tyrannulet (p. 268) is distinctly smaller and shorter-tailed. Chocó Tyrannulet (p. 268) has extensive yellow in wings and face. Sooty-headed Tyrannulet is usually found in pairs away from mixed-species flocks. Song a rollicking, staccato series of short notes, e.g., *dih-dih-DIH-dih, dih-dih-DIH-dih, dih-dih-dih-dih*.

2 BLACK-CAPPED TYRANNULET *Phyllomyias nigrocapillus* 11cm/4.5in

2300–3500m. Uncommon in high-Andean temperate forest and edge. White superciliary and wing bars contrast strongly with black cap, dark upperparts, and mostly yellow underparts. Tawny-rumped Tyrannulet is browner, with pale tawny wing bars, whiter underparts, and tawny rump. White-banded and White-tailed Tyrannulets (p. 266) have white underparts and much paler upperparts. Black-capped Tyrannulet is usually seen singly or in pairs, often with mixed-species flocks. Often utters a series of high-pitched buzzy notes, e.g., *tsee-tsee-dj-dj-djit*.

3 TAWNY-RUMPED TYRANNULET *Phyllomyias uropygialis* 11cm/4.5in

2100–3500m. Uncommon in subtropical and temperate forest and edge. No other small flycatcher has a tawny rump, but it can be hidden by the folded wings. Upperparts dark brown, with pale tawny wing bars; underparts whitish with a slight yellowish tinge; faint, pale superciliary and dark lores. White-banded, White-tailed (both p. 266), and Black-capped Tyrannulets all have much paler wing bars, sometimes tinged yellowish, but never pale tawny. Tawny-rumped is encountered singly or in pairs, occasionally with mixed-species flocks. Often-heard song is a high-pitched, sibilant *TSEE-TSEE-tsip*.

4 WHITE-FRONTED TYRANNULET *Phyllomyias zeledoni* 11cm/4.5in

500–1500m. Rare in humid foothill forest; must be identified with great care. Note especially the pale base to the short, stubby bill, white brows that meet on forehead (can be very indistinct on some birds), pale yellow wing bars, and indistinct facial markings with lack of ear crescent. Other similar foothill-zone flycatchers either show ear crescents, lack wing bars, or have all-dark bills. Voice is a simple, strident *PEE*, either given singly or in a rapid series of eight or more notes. Usually found singly or in pairs amid mixed-species flocks. Sometimes lumped with **Rough-legged Tyrannulet** (*P. burmeisteri*).

5 ASHY-HEADED TYRANNULET *Phyllomyias cinereiceps* 11cm/4.5in

800–2400m. Fairly common in foothill and subtropical forest, edge, and wooded clearings. Note rather stubby bill, blue-gray crown, dark ear crescent, and yellow underparts with smudgy olive streaks on breast; thin white wing bars contrast strongly with otherwise dark wings. Easily confused with thinner-billed Marble-faced Bristle-Tyrant, which lacks blue tinge to crown (only evident in good light) and has a cleaner breast and wider, yellower wing bars and wing edging. Slaty-capped Flycatcher (p. 266) has tan wing bars. Ashy-headed's song is a high-pitched, ca. 1 sec. long *TSEE-trrreee* or *TSEE-d'd'd'eeee*.

6 MARBLE-FACED BRISTLE-TYRANT *Phylloscartes ophthalmicus* 11cm/4.5in

1000–2000m. Fairly common in foothill and subtropical forest, edge, and wooded clearings. Very similar to Ashy-headed Tyrannulet; note thinner bill, cleaner breast, and thicker, yellower wing bars; feathers between wing bars edged yellow (not all black). Slaty-capped Flycatcher (p. 266) has brownish-buff wing bars and a thicker bill. Marble-faced Bristle-Tyrant is almost always seen with mixed-species flocks in low to mid forest levels; often in pairs. Usually perches upright. Often-heard song: *tsip…t't't 't't't't't't't't't't't't't't'-tsip-tsip-tsip*.

MECOCERCULUS AND OTHER SMALL FLYCATCHERS

Mecocerculus tyrannulets are small, warbler-like flycatchers found mainly in the Andes. All have wing bars and frequently join mixed-species flocks. Southern Beardless-Tyrannulet is common and widespread; its bushy crest sets it apart from most other similar species. Slaty-capped Flycatcher is a cloud-forest species more similar to some of the tyrannulets on the preceding two pages.

1 WHITE-THROATED TYRANNULET *Mecocerculus leucophrys* 14cm/5.5in

2800–4000m. Common in temperate forest and edge; also locally occurs up into *Polylepis* woodland and scrubby areas in páramo. A well-named species: the striking white throat and the rusty wing bars separate this bird from all other similar species in its range and habitat. Perches vertically and is often seen with mixed-species flocks. Song is a long, rapid, and slightly descending series of *tik* notes.

2 WHITE-TAILED TYRANNULET *Mecocerculus poecilocercus* 11cm/4.5in

1500–2400m; slightly higher in SW. Common in humid subtropical forest and edge. Size, shape, horizontal posture, and active habits give it a rather warbler-like appearance. Look for combination of off-white wing bars (never pure white), white undertail, and white superciliary. Occurs mostly below the range of the similar White-banded Tyrannulet, which has pure white wing bars and dark undertail. Usually seen with mixed-species flocks. Song is a high-pitched *pee-pee-pee-pee*, sometimes followed by a series of ticking notes. Note: **Sulphur-bellied Tyrannulet** (*M. minor*; not shown) occurs very locally on the W slope near the Colombian border (e.g., the Chical road and near Maldonado); it is similar to White-tailed but has all-yellow underparts, buffy wing bars, and lacks white in the tail.

3 WHITE-BANDED TYRANNULET *Mecocerculus stictopterus* 13cm/5in

2400–3600m. Common in humid temperate forest and edge. Pure white (not off-white) wing bars and dark undertail separate this species from the very similar White-tailed Tyrannulet of lower elevations (at most they have a very narrow zone of overlap). White-banded is also very warbler-like, perching horizontally and actively gleaning insects from leaves; usually seen with mixed-species flocks. Most often-heard vocalization is one or two short, wheezy notes followed by a *ti-ti-ti-ti-chew-WIT*.

4 RUFOUS-WINGED TYRANNULET *Mecocerculus calopterus* 11cm/4.5in

500–2000m; occasionally lower. Uncommon to fairly common in humid foothill and subtropical forest, edge, and adjacent clearings. Distribution is poorly understood; most regularly encountered in humid areas of the SW, but seasonally fairly common in the NW as well. It may undertake seasonal movements; it can disappear from some areas in the NW for extended periods. Resembles White-tailed Tyrannulet (with which it can occur) but has obvious rufous wing patches; the two are not likely to be mistaken if seen well. Also resembles male Rufous-winged Antwren (p. 248; little overlap), which has black (not gray) crown, yellow underparts, and bolder line through eye. Rufous-winged Tyrannulet is similar in behavior to White-tailed Tyrannulet. Frequently heard call is a *pik-PEK* (second note louder and higher pitched), sometimes followed by a quick series of lower notes.

5 SOUTHERN BEARDLESS-TYRANNULET *Camptostoma obsoletum* 10cm/4in

0–3000m. A common and widespread species in lighter woodland, forest edge, scrub, and gardens; does not occur inside dense forest. The perky, bushy crest (almost always raised) combined with small size, gray plumage, tannish wing bars, and short, mostly pale bill are usually enough to ID this species. Gray-and-white Tyrannulet (p. 268), which occurs in only a few coastal desert areas and the far SW, always shows a white crest patch. Elaenias (p. 272) can have similar plumage characteristics but are significantly larger. Song of Southern Beardless-Tyrannulet is a series of five or six querulous *pee* notes; call a burry *wheeee*.

6 SLATY-CAPPED FLYCATCHER *Leptopogon superciliaris* 13cm/5in

0–1700m. Fairly common in humid foothill forest and edge; uncommon and local in the lowlands and subtropics. Look for brownish-buff wing bars and dark, smudgy ear crescent on face. It is most similar to Marble-faced Bristle-Tyrant and Ashy-headed Tyrannulet (p. 264), but those species always have paler yellow or white wing bars, and are also brighter overall with more distinct ear crescents. Slaty-capped Flycatcher is usually found at low to mid forest levels and frequently joins mixed-species flocks. Voice includes an often-heard *SQUEE-ik*, like the sound of a dog toy being squeezed and released.

MISCELLANEOUS TYRANNULETS

Small flycatchers from a variety of habitats. Chocó Tyrannulet and Loja Tyrannulet were once lumped with Golden-faced Tyrannulet (see note in Chocó Tyrannulet account, below), but have been split due to significant vocal disparity as well as more subtle plumage differences and genetic variances.

1 CHOCÓ TYRANNULET *Zimmerius albigularis* 11cm/4.5in

0–1500m. Fairly common in humid forest and edge, from lowlands through to the subtropics. Note olive upperparts, pale gray-white underparts, distinct yellow line from bill to just behind eye, and bright yellow edging to most of the wing feathers. Singles or pairs typically perch high, atop outer canopy leaves, occasionally joining mixed-species flocks. Common call is a soft, repeated *wet* or *ti-WET*; song a rapid, rising *tu-we-we-we-weh*. *Note*: **Golden-faced Tyrannulet** (*Z. chrysops*; not shown) was recently found in far NW near the Colombian border. It occurs only above ca. 1500m (above range of Chocó Tyrannulet), and most sightings are from the Chical road and near Maldonado. Golden-faced looks nearly identical to Chocó Tyrannulet, but voice differs, typically a slow *chu-wi-dit*, or occasionally a longer, faster series.

2 LOJA TYRANNULET *Zimmerius flavidifrons* 11cm/4.5in

800–2500m. Replaces Chocó Tyrannulet in the SW, where it is locally fairly common in both humid and deciduous forest in foothills and subtropics. The two species are not known to occur together, but may do so in the area where their mapped ranges meet. Loja Tyrannulet is very similar to Chocó Tyrannulet but has grayer upperparts and fainter yellow wing markings. Behavior is very similar as well, but voice is very different; Loja's most common call is a lazy *sooooooooWEE*.

3 YELLOW TYRANNULET *Capsiempis flaveola* 11cm/4.5in

0–1600m. Fairly common in humid secondary forest, edge, and overgrown clearings, from lowlands to subtropics. Olive upperparts; otherwise mostly yellow: underparts, superciliary, and wing bars. Wing bars can be faint on birds with very worn plumage. Inhabits low, dense vegetation, and seems especially common in bamboo patches; usually found in pairs, and away from mixed-species flocks. Song, often given as a duet, is a long, rapid, rollicking series such as *d-DIH-di-di-d-DIH-di-di...*, repeated over and over; also gives a drawn-out rattle.

4 BROWN-CAPPED TYRANNULET *Ornithion brunneicapillus* 8cm/3in

0–800m. Fairly common in canopy of humid lowland and foothill forest. Tiny, short-tailed, and lacking wing bars; note plain olive, yellow, and brown plumage with a very bold white superciliary. Sooty-headed Tyrannulet (p. 264) is similar in plumage but has thinner superciliary, longer tail, and a more vertical posture. Singles or pairs of Brown-capped Tyrannulet forage high in canopy, occasionally joining mixed-species flocks. Song is distinctive, a repeated, high-pitched *deeh?, dee-dee-dee-dee*, first note rising in pitch, others falling.

5 GRAY-AND-WHITE TYRANNULET *Pseudelaenia leucospodia* 13cm/5in

0–200m. Uncommon and local in sparsely vegetated areas in coastal deserts in W and SW; also Isla de la Plata. Mostly plain gray, with only indistinct wing bars. Within its limited range this species is easily identifed by its distinctive crest: large, splayed out on the sides, and always showing white in the center. Southern Beardless-Tyrannulet (p. 266) never shows white in the crest, is smaller, and has tannish wing bars. Plumage may also recall an elaenia (p. 272), though none shares Gray-and-white Tyrannulet's desert habitat. Utters a variety of squeaks, squeals, and *chak* notes.

6 TORRENT TYRANNULET *Serpophaga cinerea* 11cm/4.5in

400–3000m; locally lower or higher. Fairly common along rushing streams and rivers from the foothills to the temperate zone; also occurs locally around lakes, marshes, or even flooded pastures. No other small bird has the combination of pale gray underparts and mantle contrasting with slaty back, wings, and tail. White-capped Dipper (p. 324) frequently occurs with it but is much larger, chunkier, and always shows at least some white on the crown. Typical song of Torrent Tyrannulet is a series of five or six abrupt sputters; call is a high-pitched *pik* note, given alone or in a rapid series.

Three more tyrannulets: one from humid forest and a very similar pair from drier habitats. *Myiopagis* elaenias are small, round-headed flycatchers found in a variety of wooded habitats.

1 YELLOW-CROWNED TYRANNULET *Tyrannulus elatus* 10cm/4in

0–1300m. Fairly common in humid forest, edge, and lighter woodland in lowlands and foothills. Short, stubby bill, white wing bars, and contrasting pale throat help separate it from other similar small flycatchers. Yellow crown patch is usually hidden, only rarely seen in the field. Singles and pairs forage actively in canopy for insects, only occasionally joining mixed-species flocks. Frequently heard call is a soft, languid *free-beer*.

2 TUMBESIAN TYRANNULET *Phaeomyias tumbezana* 12cm/4.5in

0–2000m. Locally fairly common in deciduous forest edge, light woodland, and desert scrub in W and SW. A dull flycatcher that lacks strong field marks. Mostly grayish-brown, slightly paler on throat and belly, with whitish or gray superciliary and faint, but usually discernible, pale brownish wing bars. Most birds are noticeably brown above, which can be the most useful ID feature, since other similar species have either grayish or olive upperparts. Bran-colored Flycatcher (p. 276) has a streaked breast and shorter superciliary. Tumbesian Tyrannulet usually stays hidden, but occasionally pops up on top of a small bush or exposed tree branch, especially in response to a pygmy-owl imitation. Song is a jumbled series of buzzy squeaks and *tik* notes. Sometimes lumped with Mouse-colored Tyrannulet.

3 MOUSE-COLORED TYRANNULET *Phaeomyias murina* 12cm/4.5in

1000–2400m. In W Ecuador, restricted to light woodland in dry, inter-Andean valleys of N, where uncommon. Almost identical in plumage to Tumbesian Tyrannulet (no overlap), and the two are often considered the same species. Confusion is possible with Bran-colored Flycatcher (p. 276), but that species has distinct breast streaking and a shorter superciliary. Behavior similar to that of Tumbesian. Song is a rapid series of *dit* notes that rises in pitch until the final note, which descends: *di-di-di-di-Di-Di-DI-DI-dit*.

4 GRAY ELAENIA *Myiopagis caniceps* 12cm/4.5in

0–1000m. Uncommon in humid lowland and foothill forest and edge; quite scarce in more disturbed secondary forest. Sexually dimorphic. Male is gray, paler below, with white wing bars and white crown stripe (usually hidden). Female is very different and somewhat variable; mostly olive yellow, with a pale throat, varying amounts of gray on the head, yellowish wing bars, and yellow crown stripe (usually not visible). Both sexes lack long superciliary (though may have faint, pale lores); this is a useful feature, as virtually all similar species have a longer, more distinct superciliary. Female can be confusing, but look for combination of faint wing bars, pale throat, and lack of long superciliary. Usually found in pairs, Gray Elaenia stays high in canopy, and frequently joins mixed-species flocks. Song is a descending trill that starts very slowly then quickly accelerates: *tik-tik-tik-ti-t-t-t-t-t-t-t-t-t-t-t-t-t-t*; the first notes are dry, the song becomes more "musical" toward the end.

5 GREENISH ELAENIA *Myiopagis viridicata* 14cm/5.5in

0–1500m. Fairly common in humid and semi-humid secondary forest edge and light woodland from the lowlands to the subtropics. Mostly olive yellow, with a gray head and pale throat; breast often appears faintly mottled or streaked. Lacks wing bars, and shows only a short, white superciliary that does not continue past eye. Yellow crown stripe is usually concealed. Can look quite similar to Pacific Elaenia, but that species usually shows a long superciliary that continues well behind eye as well as some faint wing markings. Sooty-headed Tyrannulet (p. 264) is smaller and has brighter yellow and cleaner underparts. Greenish Elaenia is usually seen singly or in pairs; generally not with mixed-species flocks. Calls include a variety of fairly high-pitched buzzy whistles, such as *PEEeer*, *pee-yeeer*, or *pee-wee*.

6 PACIFIC ELAENIA *Myiopagis subplacens* 14cm/5.5in

0–1800m. Fairly common in semi-humid and deciduous forest and edge from lowlands to subtropics. Much like Greenish Elaenia, including the semi-concealed yellow crown stripe, but usually shows faint wing bars as well as a longer pale superciliary that continues well behind eye. However, individuals in worn plumage can sometimes lack both these features, so voice can be helpful. Pacific Elaenia frequently gives a distinctive *WHI-tit.........prrrrrup*. Forages singly or in pairs in mid to upper forest levels; often mobs pygmy-owls.

The notoriously difficult genus *Elaenia* is represented in our region by four species, all of which have crests, white crown patches (rarely visible in the most challenging species), and wing bars. Voice can often be the best way to ID the more difficult species, and silent birds cannot always be identified with certainty. Elaenias feed on both insects and small fruits. The last two species presented are rather distinctive flycatchers unlike any others in W Ecuador.

1 YELLOW-BELLIED ELAENIA *Elaenia flavogaster* 16cm/6.5in

0–1600m. Common and widespread from lowlands to subtropics in sparsely wooded areas such as clearings, pastures, and forest edge. The most distinctive elaenia in W; large size, yellow belly, bushy crest showing some white, and habitat preference should be enough to separate it from other elaenias, though voice can also be a useful clue. Distinctive calls, sometimes given by a pair as a duet, include a drawn-out, burry *wheeeer*, or *pr-wher-peer*, often given in a rollicking series.

2 WHITE-CRESTED ELAENIA *Elaenia albiceps* 14cm/5.5in

1700–3500m. Fairly common in the subtropical and temperate zones; inhabits montane scrub, forest edge, and light woodland. The palest of W Ecuador's elaenias, it never shows distinct yellow on the underparts, though birds in fresh plumage can show a somewhat warm coloration on sides and flanks. Crest is usually apparent and more pointed than the crests of Sierran and Lesser Elaenias. White-crested gives a variety of short, abrupt whistles, including a burry "police whistle," as well as other rattling calls.

3 SIERRAN ELAENIA *Elaenia pallatangae* 14cm/5.5in

1000–3000m. Uncommon to fairly common in humid subtropical and temperate forest, edge, and wooded clearings; rare in the foothills. Only slightly crested, and often appears round-headed; faint white crown patch is usually invisible. Birds in fresh plumage have underparts entirely pale yellow, with slightly brighter yellow on belly. In worn plumage, underparts show at most a yellow tinge, and this species can be inseparable from Lesser Elaenia, except by voice, but even some of their calls are similar. Sierran Elaenia utters a variety of short whistles, either clear or burry and often doubled, usually repeated every few seconds, as well as a rapid series of burry trills and squeaks.

4 LESSER ELAENIA *Elaenia chiriquensis* 13cm/5in

700–2000m. Rare to locally fairly common in light woodland, forest edge, and wooded clearings in the foothills and subtropics. Extremely similar to Sierran Elaenia (especially birds with worn plumage), and silent birds cannot always be identified. Lesser Elaenia is always dull, showing only a hint of yellow on the lower underparts and never showing yellow on throat. Calls include a short, abrupt, squeaky whistle repeated every few seconds; a very soft, burry whistle (sometimes doubled) repeated every few seconds; and a burry *doo-whit-t't't't't't*.

5 ORNATE FLYCATCHER *Myiotriccus ornatus* 12cm/4.5in

100–2000m. Fairly common in humid foothill and subtropical forest and edge; uncommon and local in the lowlands. A conspicuous, often confiding and distinctive flycatcher; yellow rump and white "headlights" make it easy to ID. Perches singly, in pairs, or in family groups at lower to mid levels of forest, often even at forest edge, occasionally sallying out to catch insects. Frequently emits a soft, dry *pik*, either alone or in a short, rapid series.

6 SUBTROPICAL DORADITO *Pseudocolopteryx acutipennis* 11cm/4.5in

2600–3500m. Known only from dense reedbeds around a few lakes and marshes in the central valley, e.g., Lago San Pablo near Otavalo, where it is fairly common. The combination of dull, yellowish plumage, warbler-like shape and behavior, and distinctive habitat rules out any other resident species. Yellow Warbler (p. 354) could possibly wander into the Subtropical Doradito's habitat during migration; the female warbler is rather similar but brighter overall, with a distinctly yellow eye-ring and yellowish legs and feet (black in the doradito). Voice is a series of soft ticks, sometimes ending in a guttural note.

Tit-tyrants are small, charming, and easy to ID Andean flycatchers found only at high elevations. *Mionectes* are small forest flycatchers of lower to mid elevations; they are often found with mixed-species flocks and eat mainly fruit.

1 TUFTED TIT-TYRANT *Anairetes parulus* 11cm/4.5in

2500–3500m. By far the most common and widespread tit-tyrant in Ecuador; it is locally common in montane scrub and edge of temperate forest and woodland in the high Andes. Note streaked underparts, wing bars, yellow irides, and thin crest (which can be invisible at a distance). Usually found in pairs or small groups, actively flitting through the bushes while foraging for insects. Voice includes a variety of trills and squeaks.

2 AGILE TIT-TYRANT *Uromyias agilis* 13cm/5in

2400–3700m. Uncommon and local, found only in or near patches of *Chusquea* bamboo in temperate forest at high elevations. Lacks the pointed crest of other tit-tyrants; at a distance, it might be confused with Tufted Tit-Tyrant, but look for plain wings, dark eye, and black crown bordered by long, white stripes. Usually found singly or in pairs, moving actively through bamboo or nearby vegetation; occasionally joins mixed-species flocks. Voice is quite similar to that of Tufted, though the two are separable with experience.

3 BLACK-CRESTED TIT-TYRANT *Anairetes nigrocristatus* 13cm/5in

2400–2700m. In Ecuador, known only from montane scrub in the Utuana area in the SW Andes, where it is uncommon. This very handsome black-and-white flycatcher is boldly streaked on its mantle and underparts, and displays a black crest with a bold white basal patch. No other similar species occurs in its miniscule Ecuadorian range. Usually found alone, occasionally in pairs, often perched conspicuously at the top of a bush. Occasionally gives a descending series of squeaks or a long, descending trill.

4 OCHRE-BELLIED FLYCATCHER *Mionectes oleaginous* 13cm/5in

0–1000m; rarely higher. Uncommon in humid lowland and foothill forest. Rather plain, with olive upperparts, slightly darker wings, and pale ochre underparts; bill has a pink base and dark tip. While the throat and breast can sometimes appear to have very faint streaking, this species never shows the obvious, bold streaking of Olive-striped or Streak-necked Flycatchers. Ochre-bellied Flycatcher is a shy, solitary species that usually remains in the dark forest understory, though it occasionally joins other species at a fruiting tree. Its song is very distinctive: *wip-wip-wip-wip-wip-wip-dur-dur-dur-dur...*; the *dur* notes have an electronic quality, and there can be 20 or more of them. Also gives short, rapidly descending, squeaky *PEEyer*.

5 OLIVE-STRIPED FLYCATCHER *Mionectes olivaceus* 13cm/5in

0–1600m. Fairly common in humid lowland and foothill forest. Overlaps with the very similar Streak-necked Flycatcher between about 1300 and 1600m. In this zone, the two are not easily separated except by voice. Olive-striped Flycatcher often shows a more conspicuous postocular spot, less yellow on the belly, and bolder streaking on the underparts. Found regularly with mixed-species flocks, usually in mid to upper forest levels, where it consumes mostly small berries, often hovering in place while plucking them off. Its song, very different from that of Streak-necked, is a very high-pitched *Seeezi-zip, Seeezi-zip...*, repeated over and over from a low perch. Occasionally also gives a high-pitched, descending *Tseeee*.

6 STREAK-NECKED FLYCATCHER *Mionectes striaticollis* 13cm/5in

1300–2700m. Fairly common in subtropical and temperate forest and edge. A small flycatcher with plain olive and gray upperparts, unmarked wings, distinct streaking on underparts, and a small, white postocular spot. Confusingly similar to Olive-striped Flycatcher, which occurs mainly at lower elevations. In the narrow zone of overlap, they are not easy to separate in the field except by voice. Streak-necked typically has a smaller postocular spot, brighter yellow belly, and finer underpart streaking (making the throat appear grayer). Behavior similar to that of Olive-striped. Song of Streak-necked is a long series of squeaks, each note varying slightly in pitch. Other calls include a rapid, jumbled series of buzzy squeaks. All vocalizations are much lower pitched than any given by Olive-striped.

Miscellaneous small flycatchers from a variety of habitats. With the exception of Handsome Flycatcher, the birds on this page typically do not join mixed-species flocks. Males of *Myiophobus* and *Nephelomyias* have a bright orange or yellow crown patch, but it is usually mostly or entirely hidden from view.

1 FLAVESCENT FLYCATCHER *Myiophobus flavicans* 12cm/4.5in

1600–2600m; lower in SW. Fairly common in humid subtropical and temperate forest and edge. Note the distinct broken yellow eye-ring and cinnamon wing bars. Male has yellow crown patch, usually hidden. Singles or pairs forage actively in lower to mid levels of the forest, but usually do not join mixed-species flocks. Commonly heard call is a dry *chip*, sometimes interspersed with short churrs.

2 ORANGE-CRESTED FLYCATCHER *Myiophobus phoenicomitra* 12cm/4.5in

500–1500m. Rare to locally uncommon inside humid foothill and subtropical forest. A dull, yellowish-olive flycatcher lacking in obvious field marks. If seen well, most birds show faint cinnamon wing bars, and may display a narrow yellow eye-ring. Male has an orange crown patch, often concealed. Typically found singly or in pairs in the forest understory; not known to join mixed-species flocks. Orange-crested is hard to detect unless first heard. Typical song is a rising *pit-SIT-sit*, sometimes quickly followed by a series of three to six *pit* notes.

3 BRAN-COLORED FLYCATCHER *Myiophobus fasciatus* 12cm/4.5in

0–2000m. Fairly common in overgrown clearings, secondary growth, and forest edge; not found inside dense forest. No other small flycatcher in our region shares the combination of conspicuously streaked breast, short superciliary that does not extend past eye, and bold, pale brownish-buff wing bars. Male's orange crown patch is usually hidden. Found in singles or pairs, perching low and occasionally sallying out to catch insects. Song is a dry, rapid *weee-wi-wi-wi-wi-wi*; also gives a sharp, inflected *WHIP*.

4 HANDSOME FLYCATCHER *Nephelomyias pulcher* 10cm/4in

1800–2500m. Uncommon in humid subtropical forest and edge; rare in the S part of its mapped W range (e.g., the Mindo-Tandayapa area). Buffy-orange throat and breast, and bold, buff wing bars and tertial edges separate this species from other small flycatchers that share its elevation and habitat. Usually found from mid levels to canopy and frequently joins mixed-species flocks. Vocalizations are varied, often given in quick succession, and include a sharp, rapid *ti-tit*, very fast, buzzy trills, and single *pit* notes.

5 ACADIAN FLYCATCHER *Empidonax virescens* 14cm/5.5in

0–1500m; rarely higher. Boreal migrant, occurring in Ecuador mainly from October to early April. The only "empid" that regularly occurs in W Ecuador; this certainly simplifies ID, but keep in mind that other *Empidonax* species can occur as very rare vagrants, especially in the Quito Botanical Gardens. Acadian Flycatcher is fairly common in forest, edge, and lighter woodland, mostly in the lowlands and foothills but occasionally higher. Look for combination of bold white wing bars, distinct pale eye-ring, yellow base to lower mandible, and grayish breast that contrasts with whitish belly and pale yellowish lower underparts. Solitary; perches fairly low, calling incessantly from a hidden perch. Call given on wintering grounds is a sharp, rather dry *whit*, repeated every few seconds. *Note:* The most likely vagrant empids in our region are **Willow Flycatcher** (*E. traillii*) and **Alder Flycatcher** (*E. alnorum*), not shown; both show a shorter primary projection than Acadian, and usually have fainter eye-ring. They are nearly identical to each other in appearance and best identified by voice (though they are often silent in Ecuador): Willow gives a *fitz-bew!* or *brrrip!*; Alder gives a *brree-wee!* or a sharp *pit!*

6 GRAY-BREASTED FLYCATCHER *Lathrotriccus griseipectus* 13cm/5in

0–1700m. Uncommon in humid and deciduous forest in W and SW from lowlands to subtropics; rare in humid lowland and foothill forest in NW. Gray head and breast contrast sharply with white lower underparts; also note white wing bars and spectacles. Occurs alone or in pairs in lower to mid forest levels, and does not join mixed-species flocks. Typical song is a very buzzy *PEER-PEER-peer* or *PEER-PEER-tdu*.

PYGMY-TYRANTS

Miniscule flycatchers; all but Tawny-crowned Pygmy-Tyrant inhabit humid forest. Black-capped Pygmy-Tyrant is one of the smallest birds on earth.

1 BRONZE-OLIVE PYGMY-TYRANT *Pseudotriccus pelzelni* 11cm/4.5in

800–2000m; lower in SW. An uncommon, nondescript flycatcher of humid foothill and subtropical forest. Note combination of bronzy upperparts and yellowish underparts; otherwise lacks distinctive plumage features. Could be confused with female Golden-winged Manakin (p. 316), which has reddish (not yellow) legs, more uniformly yellow plumage, and often shows a hint of a tuft above the bill. Bronze-olive Pygmy-Tyrant is usually encountered in pairs, flitting actively through the forest understory, frequently giving soft snapping and rattling sounds that are produced with either the bill or the wings. Song is a short, rapid trill.

2 RUFOUS-HEADED PYGMY TYRANT *Pseudotriccus ruficeps* 11cm/4.5in

2000–3500m. Fairly common in subtropical and temperate forest; replaces Bronze-olive Pygmy-Tyrant at higher elevations. Adult is readily identified by rufous head, wings, and tail. Juvenile much duller but usually shows at least some rufous in wings and tail. Behavior and voice very similar to Bronze-olive Pygmy-Tyrant's, but Rufous-headed's trilled song often rises and falls dramatically in pitch.

3 TAWNY-CROWNED PYGMY-TYRANT *Euscarthmus meloryphus* 10cm/4in

0–1500m; locally higher. Fairly common in deciduous forest edge and arid scrub from lowlands to subtropics; also on Isla de la Plata. Buffy-orange face and forecrown contrast with mostly brownish upperparts and yellowish underparts. Usually solitary; skulks in low, dense vegetation, where it can often be hard to spot. Song is a very rapid, sputtering *wi-wi-w-DU-WIT*.

4 BLACK-CAPPED PYGMY-TYRANT *Myiornis atricapillus* 6cm/2.5in

0–900m. Fairly common in humid forest edge and adjacent wooded clearings in the lowlands and foothills. Minute and distinctive with dark gray head, bold white spectacles, and olive back contrasting with pale underparts; male has a black crown and face; female has yellower lower underparts. Usually encountered singly or in pairs, darting from branch to branch from mid levels to canopy. Vocalizations are very insect-like and include a single, inflected *pek* repeated every ½ sec., and a variety of churrs and cricket-like chirps.

5 SCALE-CRESTED PYGMY-TYRANT *Lophotriccus pileatus* 10cm/4in

0–1800m. Widespread in forest and edge from lowlands to subtropics; common in humid zones, but uncommon and local in drier habitats. Rusty crown flecked with black is diagnostic; otherwise note olive upperparts, whitish underparts with dull olivaceous streaking on breast, and pale yellow or buff wing bars. Usually encountered alone, flitting actively at mid heights, favoring vine and twig tangles and bamboo. Calls frequently; gives a variety of loud, insect-like trills and chirps.

Tody-flycatchers are small, colorful birds, with somewhat wide, flat bills, that often forage boldly in the open and are usually easy to see. Spadebills, on the other hand, skulk in rain-forest understory and can be very hard to detect. Ruddy-tailed Flycatcher is a unique humid-forest flycatcher with especially large eyes and long rictal bristles.

1 COMMON TODY-FLYCATCHER *Todirostrum cinereum* 10cm/4in

0–1800m. A common and often conspicuous species found in secondary growth mainly in lowlands and foothills; rare at the upper limit of its elevation range. Gray above, yellow below with white throat; note blackish face and forecrown, contrasting yellow irides, and wing feathers edged yellow. Distinguished from Black-headed Tody-Flycatcher by yellow irides, gray (not yellow) mantle, and lack of discrete wing bars. Common Tody-Flycatcher pairs hop actively through vegetation, tails often cocked up, making short sallies to catch insects. Calls include soft rattles and *tik* notes, given alone, in pairs, or in threes.

2 BLACK-HEADED TODY-FLYCATCHER *Todirostrum nigriceps* 9cm/3.5in

0–1000m. Fairly common in humid lowland and foothill forest, edge, and in clearings with tall trees. Similar to Common Tody-Flycatcher but has yellow mantle, dark iris, and two distinct wing bars. Single birds or pairs forage high in the canopy, where they can be hard to see well from the forest floor; normally do not join mixed-species flocks, but due to canopy habitat are sometimes present as one passes by. Often-heard song is a series of about 20 evenly spaced *tek* notes.

3 RUFOUS-CROWNED TODY-FLYCATCHER *Poecilotriccus ruficeps* 10cm/4in

1500–2600m. Uncommon and local in humid secondary growth, *Chusquea* bamboo patches, and overgrown clearings in the subtropical and temperate zones. The combination of rufous head, mostly yellow underparts, and pale yellow wing bars is diagnostic. Not especially shy, but rather inconspicuous in the dense vegetation it inhabits, until a sudden sally after an insect brings one into view. Frequently gives an explosive, rattled *TCHER* or *P'TCHER*.

4 RUDDY-TAILED FLYCATCHER *Terenotriccus erythrurus* 10cm/4in

0–1000m. Fairly common but very inconspicuous in humid lowland and foothill forest; occasionally comes to forest edge. Rufous underparts, tail, and wings contrast with gray head and mantle and slightly paler throat; note big-eyed appearance. Despite its somber colors, its plumage pattern is shared by no other flycatcher in W. Found in lower to mid levels of the forest; usually solitary but occasionally joins mixed-species flocks. Commonly heard call is a rather distinctive *peer…CHIT*.

5 WHITE-THROATED SPADEBILL *Platyrinchus mystaceus* 10cm/4in

0–1800m. An inconspicuous flycatcher found in humid forest understory from lowlands up to the subtropics. Complex facial pattern and distinctive bill shape is shared in this region only by Golden-crowned Spadebill, with which it can sometimes occur. White-throated Spadebill has a white throat and lacks a golden crown stripe, though it does possess a very small, yellow crown patch that is usually concealed. Found alone or in pairs, darting back and forth between low perches, White-throated is hard to pick out in the dark forest understory. Often-heard call is a low *cup* or *HI-cup*. Infrequently heard song is a rising trill of 20 to 30 notes.

6 GOLDEN-CROWNED SPADEBILL *Platyrinchus coronatus* 9cm/3.5in

0–1000m. Uncommon inside humid lowland and foothill forest; less tolerant of habitat degradation than White-throated Spadebill, it seems to occur only in forest where at least some large trees still remain. Golden-crowned is similar to White-throated Spadebill but slightly smaller, with a pale yellow throat, and always shows a conspicuous golden crown stripe. The female has a brighter, orange, crown stripe than the male. Behavior is similar to that of White-throated Spadebill. Song is an extremely high-pitched and hard to detect descending trill.

Rhynchocyclus flatbills are scarce humid forest species that are rarely observed, though not hard to ID if seen well. The two *Tolmomyias* flycatchers (sometimes also called flatbills) are very similar to each other, but do not usually occur together in our region. Cinnamon Flycatcher and Black Phoebe are extremely distinctive birds unlike any other in W Ecuador.

1 FULVOUS-BREASTED FLATBILL *Rhynchocyclus fulvipectus* 15cm/6in

900–2000m. Rare to locally uncommon in humid foothill and subtropical forest. Note stout, wide bill, fulvous breast, pale eye-ring, and rufous wing-feather edging (not wing bars). Pacific Flatbill lacks the fulvous breast and has more obviously streaked underparts. Fulvous-breasted Flatbill is found singly, in pairs, or occasionally in family groups in lower forest strata, often joining mixed-species flocks. Rather quiet, but occasionally gives a wheezy *weer-pit*, *pur-peer-pit*, or a series of soft whistles.

2 PACIFIC FLATBILL *Rhynchocyclus pacificus* 15cm/6in

0–1200m. Rare to locally uncommon in humid lowland and foothill forest in the NW. Usually occurs below the range of Fulvous-breasted Flatbill, but there is a narrow zone of overlap. Pacific Flatbill is similar to that species but has an olive (not fulvous) breast and more distinct underpart streaking. Habits are similar in the two flatbills. Pacific Flatbill rarely vocalizes, but its song is a very burry *djeeer-djr-djr-djr-djr* that first rises then falls in pitch; also gives a toneless churr, sometimes doubled.

3 YELLOW-OLIVE FLYCATCHER *Tolmomyias sulphurescens* 14cm/5.5in

0–2000m. Common in semi-humid and deciduous forest in W and SW; uncommon and local in the NW, where it occurs mainly near the coast, though it may be spreading due to deforestation. The wide base to the bill separates this species from a number of otherwise similar flycatchers and tyrannulets (pp. 264–266). It can be distinguished from the similar Yellow-margined Flycatcher by the distinct, clear-cut wing bars (not distinct edging to wing-covert feathers). Yellow-olive Flycatcher inhabits mid to upper levels of the forest, and often accompanies mixed-species flocks. Song is a short, sharp *pit!*, repeated every few seconds. Also called **Yellow-olive Flatbill**.

4 YELLOW-MARGINED FLYCATCHER *Tolmomyias assimilis* 13cm/5in

0–900m. Locally fairly common in humid lowland and foothill forest in the NW. The wide base to the bill separates this species from a number of otherwise similar flycatchers and tyrannulets (pp. 264–266). Similar to Yellow-olive Flycatcher, but wing coverts are boldly edged in yellow and lack strong wing bars. Yellow-margined Flycatcher is found from mid-story to canopy and frequently joins mixed-species flocks. Song is a wheezy *chu, CHI-CHI-CHI*. Also called **Yellow-margined Flatbill**.

5 BLACK PHOEBE *Sayornis nigricans* 18cm/7in

100–4000m. Very distinctive and highly tied to fresh water; fairly common along streams and rivers, and occasionally around ponds and lakes in a very wide elevational zone. Mostly black with white wing-feather edging, narrow wing bars, and belly. No really similar species in our region. Usually perches low near water, sometimes on bridges or rooftops; constantly pumps tail. Song is a buzzy *breee, deewit?* repeated constantly.

6 CINNAMON FLYCATCHER *Pyrrhomyias cinnamomeus* 13cm/5in

1000–3400m. A common and often conspicuous bird found in humid forest and edge from the foothills to the temperate zone. Distinctive; no other bird in our region shares the combination of cinnamon underparts and wing bars. Singles, pairs, or family groups perch on open branches in mid to upper forest levels, sallying out to snap up passing insects; frequently join mixed-species flocks. Song is a short, dry, sputtered trill.

Pewees are mostly gray, crested flycatchers that typically sit on exposed perches and sally out after insects, often returning to the same perch afterward. Three of the species in our area are boreal migrants. Tufted Flycatcher is similar to pewees in shape and behavior and has a restricted range in Ecuador.

1 SMOKE-COLORED PEWEE *Contopus fumigatus* 17cm/6.5in

800–3000m; locally lower in coastal hills. Fairly common and often conspicuous in humid forest, edge, and clearings with scattered trees. Occurs over a wide elevation range, from foothills to temperate zone, but avoids flat lowland areas. No other flycatcher in W Ecuador is so uniformly gray with such an obvious crest. Perches on bare branches high in the canopy, on dead snags, and occasionally wires and poles, sallying out to catch insects. Calls frequently, typically a series of three to five *pek* notes; sings a repetitive *wher-di-WIT…whew* at dawn.

2 TUMBES PEWEE *Contopus punensis* 14cm/5.5in

0–1900m. Fairly common in semi-humid and deciduous forest, edge, and adjacent wooded clearings in W and SW; uncommon and local in NW, mainly near the coast. Very similar to wood-pewees (which are present in Ecuador only from mid-August to early May), though only rarely found with them. Typically displays a totally yellow lower mandible, pale lores, and a short primary projection. Behavior is similar to that of other pewees, but Tumbes Pewee is more likely to perch low, and its call is completely different, a strident *peer-pit!* Sometimes lumped with **Tropical Pewee** (*C. cinereus*).

3 WESTERN WOOD-PEWEE *Contopus sordidulus* 15cm/6in

0–2500m; rarely higher. A boreal migrant, present in Ecuador from mid-August to early May. Fairly common in humid forest, edge, and wooded clearings from lowlands to subtropics; occasionally wanders higher. Can be difficult to separate from Eastern Wood-Pewee and Tumbes Pewee; note grayer underparts, darker lores, mostly dark lower mandible (pale only at base), and especially voice. Also keep in mind that Eastern Wood-Pewee is very rare in W Ecuador, and Tumbes Pewee does not occur in most of the NW. Western Wood-Pewee is told from Olive-sided Flycatcher by smaller size, lack of white flank tufts, and lack of distinct pale stripe on underparts. In habits, similar to other pewees. Most common call heard in Ecuador is a flat, mournful *peeer*.

4 EASTERN WOOD-PEWEE *Contopus virens* 15cm/6in

0–1500m; rarely higher. A boreal migrant, present in Ecuador from around September through early May; very rare in W Ecuador (more common in E). Distinguished from Western Wood-Pewee by paler underparts, mostly pale lower mandible, and especially voice. Also extremely similar in appearance to Tumbes Pewee, though the two species are unlikely to occur together; that species has a shorter primary projection, slightly paler lores, brighter yellow lower mandible, and a totally different voice. In habits, Eastern Pewee is similar to other pewees. Call heard in Ecuador is a querulous *Pweee?* that rises in pitch.

5 OLIVE-SIDED FLYCATCHER *Contopus cooperi* 18cm/7in

300–2000m; rarely lower or higher. An uncommon boreal migrant to a variety of wooded habitats, present in Ecuador from September through April. Larger than other pewees; pale stripe down underparts usually gives it a distinctly "vested" appearance; white throat shows more contrast with breast than wood-pewees show. Pale flank tufts that protrude up around rump are diagnostic when visible. Behavior similar to that of Smoke-colored Pewee. Wintering calls include *free…BEER, Quick, beer-me-now*, and *pip-pip-pip*.

6 TUFTED FLYCATCHER *Mitrephanes phaeocercus* 13cm/5in

100–500m. Rare to locally uncommon in humid lowland and foothill forest in far NW. A small flycatcher, similar to the pewees in shape and behavior. Note olive upperparts with rusty breast and yellow belly; pointed crest can sometimes be inconspicuous if held flat. Found alone or in pairs in forest canopy, sometimes lower at edge; sallies out after insects, often returning to the same perch. Voice is typically a rapid, machine-gun-fire *pip-pip-pip-pip-pip-pip…*, sometimes ending in a slurred *wheer!*

MISCELLANEOUS FLYCATCHERS

Various tyrant flycatchers not easily grouped with others, the species on this page range mainly at lower elevations, though Vermilion Flycatcher also occurs in the highlands.

1 LONG-TAILED TYRANT *Colonia colonus* 18–26cm/7–10in

0–1500m. Fairly common at edge of humid forest and in clearings with scattered trees. Unique; unlikely to be confused with any other species unless missing its tail, and even then, combination of black body and mostly white crown should make ID straightforward. Perches on high branches, dead snags, poles, and other conspicuous locations, sallying out frequently to grab insects. Call is a single, rising *sweee?*; typical song (somewhat variable) is *swee?, pee-pee-p'r'r'r*.

2 PACIFIC ROYAL-FLYCATCHER *Onychorhynchus occidentalis* 17cm/6.5in

0–900m. Rare to locally fairly common in forest, including mangroves, in W and SW. Favors deciduous and semi-humid forest, but occurs locally in humid forest as well. Perhaps most easily found in the Manglares-Churute Ecological Reserve. Spectacular fanlike crest is almost never opened, and is usually laid back on the nape, imparting a very distinctive hammerhead shape. Also note white wing spots. Call is a single, repeated note that falls sharply in pitch, giving it an almost two-tone quality, e.g., *keerup*.

3 VERMILLION FLYCATCHER *Pyrocephalus rubinus* 13cm/5in

0–3000m. Fairly common and often conspicuous in open habitats in the lowlands and foothills; avoids humid areas and extensive forest; also locally fairly common at higher elevations in drier inter-Andean valleys. Striking adult male is unlikely to be mistaken; female and immature male (not shown) are much duller but always show at least a little pink on the flanks and crissum, as well as brown streaks on breast and sides. This flycatcher usually perches in the open on a bush, low tree, post, or wire, occasionally sallying out after insects. Typical song is an accelerating *pit......pit...pit-pit'pi'p'p'chu!*

4 BROWNISH TWISTWING *Cnipodectes subbrunneus* 14–18cm/5.5–7in

0–600m. Rare to locally uncommon inside humid lowland and foothill forest; restricted to areas of extensive and relatively undisturbed forest. A fairly large, brown flycatcher with a pale belly, orange irides, wings boldly edged rufous, and a rusty tail. The name "twistwing" refers to the male's twisted outer primaries, used in breeding display flights to produce loud, mechanical rattles. Female (not shown) is similar but smaller and lacks twisted primaries. Might be mistaken for Pacific Royal-Flycatcher, but Brownish Twistwing lacks crest and wing spots. Usually solitary; found only well inside forest (never near edge), where it inhabits lower to mid levels. Calls include a pair of mellow whistles sometimes preceded by bill snaps, e.g., *snap...pew...pew*, and a metallic *tik...few?*

5 MASKED WATER-TYRANT *Fluvicola nengeta* 15cm/6in

0–1500m. Fairly common in open, nonforested areas throughout the humid lowlands, foothills, and subtropics. Handsome, slender, easily identified snow-white bird with black wings, tail, and narrow face mask. White-capped Dipper (p. 324), of very different habitat, is vaguely similar but much chunkier, and the black on its face connects with black wings and back. Masked Water-Tyrant is frequently found in pairs and family groups; sprints along the ground chasing insects, frequently perches on posts, bushes, and other low sites. Call is a single *pek!*; pairs also perform entertaining wing-lifting displays while singing a buzzy, staccato song.

5

CHAT-TYRANTS

Chat-tyrants are small to medium-size flycatchers found only at higher elevations in the Andes. ID is usually straightforward; pay special attention to superciliary and underpart coloration, along with presence or absence of wing bars. Chat-tyrants are generally solitary, usually perch upright, and do not join mixed-species flocks.

1 BROWN-BACKED CHAT-TYRANT Ochthoeca fumicolor 15cm/6in

2700–4200m. Common at edge of humid temperate forest, *Polylepis* woodland, and in páramo with scattered bushes. Mostly brown and rufous plumage, buffy-white superciliary, and rusty wing bars are diagnostic. This large chat-tyrant is less of a forest bird than the other species on this page; it often perches conspicuously in the open, and is quite vocal, giving a variety of strident calls.

2 RUFOUS-BREASTED CHAT-TYRANT Ochthoeca rufipectoralis 13cm/5in

2500–3500m. Fairly common in humid temperate forest and edge. No other species in its range shares combination of rufous breast and wing stripe, white superciliary, and pale lower underparts. Often found in pairs and not very shy, it perches fairly high on exposed branches. Song, sometimes given as a duet, is a rather loud, buzzy *pit-ter-CHU*, repeated rapidly.

3 CROWNED CHAT-TYRANT Ochthoeca frontalis 13cm/5in

2600–4000m. Uncommon in humid temperate forest and edge; regularly seen at Yanacocha Reserve. Large yellow spot above bill merges with white superciliary; otherwise mostly gray with brown mantle, back, and wings; no obvious wing markings. Jelski's Chat-Tyrant (limited, if any, overlap) is similar but has an obvious rufous wing stripe. Crowned Chat-Tyrant is rather inconspicuous and easy to overlook, as it perches low and is not very vocal. Occasionally gives a fairly long, high-pitched, descending trill.

4 YELLOW-BELLIED CHAT-TYRANT Ochthoeca diadema 13cm/5in

2100–3000m. Uncommon to locally fairly common in humid subtropical and temperate forest and edge. Note brownish upperparts and very indistinct wing bars; no other Ecuadorian chat-tyrant has bright yellow superciliary and dull yellow underparts. Usually solitary, perching at low to mid levels. Often seen above Tandayapa along the Paseo del Quinde (Nono-Mindo) Ecoroute. Song is a dry, accelerating trill that rises and falls in pitch.

5 SLATY-BACKED CHAT-TYRANT Ochthoeca cinnamomeiventris 13cm/5in

1700–3000m. Locally fairly common along forested streams in the subtropical and temperate zones. Unique; dark slate and chestnut plumage combined with white "headlights" sets it apart from all other species in its range. Rather solitary, and usually seen perching at mid levels to subcanopy; almost always found in the vicinity of rushing mountain streams or waterfalls. Song is a buzzy *pee-yer*, repeated incessantly, so strident and high pitched that it can often be heard from a moving vehicle.

6 JELSKI'S CHAT-TYRANT Ochthoeca jelskii 13cm/5in

2000–2800m. Uncommon in montane forest, edge, and adjacent scrubby clearings in far SW. Gray and brown plumage with yellow spot over bill is most similar to that of Crowned Chat-Tyrant (little, if any, overlap) but Jelski's is easily recognized by its broad, rufous wing stripe. Usually found alone, perched low inside or at edge of forest. This species has an impressive vocal repertoire of trills, squeaks, and chatters.

White-browed Chat-Tyrant is very rare in Ecuador, known only from a small area in the S highlands. Tumbes Tyrant is a distinctive chat-tyrant-like flycatcher only recently recorded in Ecuador. The *Myiobius* flycatchers, a trio of very similar big-eyed forest birds with yellow rumps and redstart-like behavior, can be hard to tell apart in the field; males all possess a yellow crown patch that is usually concealed.

1 WHITE-BROWED CHAT-TYRANT *Ochthoeca leucophrys* 15cm/6in

2200–2800m. Very rare and local; the only confirmed records come the vicinity of the town of Oña (about halfway between Loja and Cuenca). Found in forest edge, montane scrub, and overgrown clearings. Mostly plain gray below, with a slightly browner back and a white superciliary. Immature (not shown) has brown edging to wing coverts that forms a pair of faint wing bars. Most similar to smaller Jelski's Chat-Tyrant (p. 288); that species always shows conspicuous yellow spot above the bill and has browner upperparts and a single broad rufous wing stripe. In Ecuador, White-browed Chat-Tyrant's calls include a sharp *pek* and softer *puk*; elsewhere gives a variety of loud squeaks, alone or in a series.

2 TUMBES TYRANT *Tumbezia salvini* 14cm/5.5in

200–400m. Known only from deciduous forest and scrub W of the town of Zapotillo in the far SW, where a small population is resident. Striking and unique in its range; plumage pattern suggests a chat-tyrant, but it displays bright yellow underparts, yellow forehead blending into a bold white superciliary, and white wing bars. Usually found alone or in pairs, often staying in dense cover, but may aggressively respond to a Pacific Pygmy-Owl song. Tumbes Tyrant's song is a short, mellow, descending trill, often ending with one or more louder notes. Call is a soft and complaining *few*.

3 TAWNY-BREASTED FLYCATCHER *Myiobius villosus* 14cm/5.5in

600–1600m. Uncommon to fairly common in humid foothill and subtropical forest. Underparts deep tawny except for pale yellow center of belly. Upperparts mostly olive brown, often tinged tawny, with bright yellow rump that is sometimes hidden by folded wings. This species is often hard to separate from Sulphur-rumped Flycatcher, with which it locally overlaps (e.g., Milpe Bird Sanctuary). Tawny-breasted Flycatcher is a bit larger and has rusty-tinged upperparts and deeper tawny on underparts that extends down sides and flanks all the way to the crissum. If seen well, the tawny (not yellow) crissum is diagnostic. Usually found accompanying mixed-species flocks; one or two birds actively flit through the forest, spreading the wings and tail like a whitestart (p. 354) or American Redstart (p. 358), revealing the yellow rump. Song is a *zit-pew-pew-pew-pew-pew-pew*; also often gives a sharp *pit!*

4 SULPHUR-RUMPED FLYCATCHER *Myiobius sulphureipygius* 13cm/5in

0–1300m. Uncommon to fairly common in humid lowland and foothill forest and edge. Similar to Tawny-breasted Flycatcher and best distinguished by grayish (not rusty) upperparts and yellow (not tawny) crissum and lower flanks. Sulphur-rumped is also slightly smaller (hard to judge in the field) and has lighter tawny-buff coloration across breast and onto sides. It is distinguished from Black-tailed Flycatcher by richer tawny-buff (not dull olive-buff) breast and sides. Habitat can also be a clue, since Black-tailed prefers secondary forest and tends to avoid the very humid forest found in much of the NW. Behavior is similar to that of Tawny-breasted. Song of Sulphur-rumped is a *pik!...bew...bew*, slower and with fewer notes than song of Tawny-breasted. Calls include a toneless *chak!* and a loose *chek*.

5 BLACK-TAILED FLYCATCHER *Myiobius atricaudus* 13cm/5in

0–1300m. Uncommon in humid and semi-humid secondary forest and edge in lowlands and foothills. By far the dullest of the *Myiobius*, at best showing just a warm buff coloration across breast that does not extend down the sides and flanks. Black-tailed prefers degraded forest without large trees and is the only *Myiobius* likely to be found in drier habitats. Behavior similar to that of Tawny-breasted Flycatcher. Vocalizations are not well documented in W Ecuador, but elsewhere Black-tailed Flycatcher gives a soft *whi-DIT!* or *zit*.

Ground-tyrants are terrestrial, high-Andean flycatchers of open habitats, especially páramo; they are similar in shape and behavior to the Old World wheatears (*Oenanthe*). Short-tailed Field Tyrant is similar in shape and behavior, but inhabits arid zones at lower to mid elevations.

1 PÁRAMO GROUND-TYRANT *Muscisaxicola alpinus* 19cm/7.5in

3600–4600m. Fairly common in grassy páramo at very high elevations. Mostly gray, with a white superciliary (variable in width and intensity) that reaches just behind eye; also note long legs and upright posture. It can be separated from White-browed Ground-Tyrant by its shorter (and usually wider) white superciliary and lack of rufous in grayish-brown crown. Páramo Ground-Tyrant is found alone, in pairs, or in loose groups, hopping on the ground, occasionally flying to a low perch such as a shrub, rock, or rooftop. Frequently flicks tail. Rather quiet, occasionally giving a series of sharp, curt notes. Also called **Plain-capped Ground-Tyrant**.

2 WHITE-BROWED GROUND-TYRANT *Muscisaxicola albilora* 17cm/6.5in

2500–4000m. A rare to uncommon austral migrant to páramo and temperate forest edge, found in Ecuador only from about June to September. Numbers seem to vary from year to year, and in some years few (if any) are recorded. Similar to Páramo Ground-Tyrant, but smaller, with a longer and crisper superciliary and a rusty tinge on hind-crown. Behavior is also similar to that of Páramo, though White-browed Ground-Tyrant occasionally congregates in large numbers in recently plowed fields. Voice in Ecuador has not been recorded, but elsewhere gives a soft *seet*.

3 SPOT-BILLED GROUND-TYRANT *Muscisaxicola maculirostris* 14cm/5.5in

2500–4000m. Uncommon in highland areas with scattered, low bushes. Prefers drier regions than other ground-tyrants, especially inter-Andean valleys. A rather small, grayish-brown bird lacking in distinctive features, but look for the yellow base (spot) on the lower mandible. Color of underparts varies from pale gray to buff, perhaps relating to plumage wear. More solitary than other ground-tyrants; can be overlooked until it perches on a small bush or performs a display flight. Vocalizations given during aerial displays include a *chu* and an accelerating *tik......tik...tik..tik.tiktitichu!*, reminiscent of the song of Vermilion Flycatcher (p. 286) but drier and lacking the ringing quality.

4 SHORT-TAILED FIELD TYRANT *Muscigralla brevicauda* 11cm/4.5in

0–1200m; locally higher. Uncommon to locally fairly common in open, arid areas with little or no vegetation and in clearings within dense, scrubby desert. A small, chunky bird with long legs and a short tail. Also note grayish upperparts, buffy underparts, pale wing bars and spectacles. Chestnut rump is often hidden by the folded wings. Mostly terrestrial; usually seen running along the ground, occasionally fluttering after insects, and sometimes perching atop a small bush or on a low branch. Song is a rattled *tcheeur*, often preceded by a series of *pik* notes.

Large flycatchers found only at higher elevations in the Andes; they often perch conspicuously atop bushes or trees. Shrike-tyrants are mostly brown, with throat streaking and mostly white tails. Bush-tyrants are colored with shades of brown, gray, and rufous.

1 BLACK-BILLED SHRIKE-TYRANT *Agriornis montanus* 24cm/9.5in

3000–4500m; locally lower. Fairly common in high-elevation páramo, grassy pastures, and recently plowed fields. Mostly grayish brown, with a streaked throat, short white superciliary, and pale irides. Crissum and all but the central pair of tail feathers are white, most obvious when the tail is spread. Adult is similar to White-tailed Shrike-Tyrant but smaller, with less bold throat streaking and all-black bill; pale iris is not always a reliable ID feature. Juvenile Black-billed Shrike-Tyrant is even more similar to White-tailed, with dark irides and pale base to bill, but is browner and lacks strong throat streaking. Black-billed Shrike-Tyrant is typically found in pairs; it runs along the ground and perches on bushes, fences, stone walls, buildings, etc.; flies low over open ground, hunting insects. Often whistles *FewEEEooo*.

2 WHITE-TAILED SHRIKE-TYRANT *Agriornis albicauda* 25–28cm/10–11in

2000–4000m. Rare to locally uncommon in dry, scrubby highland valleys, agricultural areas, and occasionally páramo. Similar to much more common Black-billed Shrike-Tyrant; tail pattern of the two species is nearly identical. White-tailed Shrike-Tyrant adult is larger, shows thicker and darker throat streaking, and pale base to lower mandible; irides are usually brown (not pale), but this is not a reliable ID feature. Juvenile Black-billed also has a pale base to bill and dark iris, but is browner, with less conspicuous throat streaking. Juvenile plumage of White-tailed is unknown. Habitat is also a clue: White-tailed is far more likely to occur in areas of dry montane scrub, and Black-tailed is more likely to occur in wet grassy areas and páramo, though there is some overlap. Behavior is similar, but songs are very different; White-tailed gives a long, leisurely series of whistles of random pitch and intensity, e.g., *few…FOO…fih…few…FEW…*. White-tailed Shrike-Tyrants have been seen with some frequency above the abandoned racetrack near the town of Calacalí, N of Quito.

3 STREAK-THROATED BUSH-TYRANT *Myiotheretes striaticollis* 23cm/9in

2400–4000m; lower in SW. Fairly common in degraded habitats in highlands, including farms, towns, suburban parks, secondary forest, and exotic woodland; on rare occasions also seen in undisturbed temperate forest. Distinctive; no other large highland flycatcher shows combination of brown upperparts, rufous underparts, and bold throat streaking. Usually found alone or in pairs, using an open perch (e.g., a wire, bush, or rooftop) as a base from which to sally out after insect prey. Most common vocalization is a series of well-spaced, languid panpipe-like whistles; occasionally also gives a sharp *ptSEEsit*.

4 SMOKY BUSH-TYRANT *Myiotheretes fumigatus* 20cm/8in

2200–3500m. Uncommon to fairly common in humid temperate forest and edge; occasionally down into the subtropics. Dingy gray-brown overall, lacking distinctive marks; usually shows a whitish superciliary and pale throat, but these marks can be very faint, especially in S Ecuador. Cinnamon wing patches are usually only visible in flight. Typically encountered alone, perching on the very top of a tall tree or dead snag, sallying out after insects. Call is a rather loud whistle that drops sharply in pitch, giving it a two-tone quality: *FWEEooo*. Song is a short series of softer whistles, e.g., *fu-fu-fu-fu*.

5 RED-RUMPED BUSH-TYRANT *Cnemarchus erythropygius* 23cm/9in

2800–4300m. Rare to uncommon in páramo and temperate forest edge. Handsome; mostly gray, with white-frosted foreface, chestnut lower underparts and tail patches, and conspicuous white tertial edging. This striking bird is unlikely to be mistaken, since no other similar species occurs within its range and habitat. Usually encountered perched atop bushes or stunted trees, at times flying to the ground to pounce on prey. Most common call is a loud, whistled *CHEER!*; also gives softer, shorter whistles interspersed with churrs.

Medium to large flycatchers of lower to mid elevations. Some are kiskadee-like, but no kiskadees occur in W Ecuador.

1 RUSTY-MARGINED FLYCATCHER *Myiozetetes cayanensis* 17cm/6.5in

0–1700m. Common in humid secondary forest, edge, and clearings. Extremely similar to Social Flycatcher, and the two species are often found together. Rusty-margined Flycatcher displays rufous edges to the flight feathers, but immature Socials can show this as well. Rusty-margined lacks pale wing-covert edging (but beware of feather wear, which can give the same impression) and has a slightly blacker crown and face, imparting a "cleaner" look. Crown patch (yellow-orange in Rufous-margined, red-orange in Social) is usually concealed. Easiest to tell apart by voice: Rusty-margined's call is a loud, complaining whistle, similar to that of Dusky-capped Flycatcher (p. 298) but higher pitched. Rusty-margined's song is complex and sometimes given by both members of a pair, e.g., *Chwee!-chu-chu-chu*, followed by a rollicking duet.

2 SOCIAL FLYCATCHER *Myiozetetes similis* 17cm/6.5in

0–1500m; higher in SW. Fairly common to common in clearings, secondary forest, and forest edge in both dry and humid regions. Distinguished from Rusty-margined Flycatcher by pale edges to wing coverts, duskier crown and face, and orange to red crown patch (usually hidden). Immature Social (not shown) has some rufous edging to flight feathers, but the pale fringes to the wing coverts can help distinguish it from Rusty-margined. Voice is often the easiest ID clue: Social's call is a two-tone, descending *CHEEoo*. Song, often given in duet, is a series of jumbled churrs.

3 BOAT-BILLED FLYCATCHER *Megarynchus pitangua* 23cm/9in

0–1400m; higher in SW. Fairly common in lowlands and foothills at forest edge and in clearings with taller trees; inhabits both humid and deciduous forest. Distinguished from other similarly plumaged flycatchers by larger size and long, bulbous bill. Typically found alone or in pairs, hawking insects from mid to upper forest levels; also consumes a significant amount of fruit. Vocalizations include a nasal, sneering *ny-ny-ny-nyeah* and a stuttered *djer*.

4 GRAY-CAPPED FLYCATCHER *Myiozetetes granadensis* 17cm/6.5in

0–1400m. Fairly common in humid secondary forest, edge, and clearings with taller trees. Distinguished from other similar flycatchers by lack of a distinct superciliary and plain wings; may also show pale irides. Found from mid levels to canopy, often perched conspicuously, scanning for insects. Most common call is a series of abrupt *pek* notes, with other churrs or *chu* calls occasionally thrown in.

5 WHITE-RINGED FLYCATCHER *Conopias albovittatus* 16cm/6.5in

0–800m. Uncommon in humid forest and edge in lowlands and foothills. Similar to Social and Rusty-margined Flycatchers. If White-ringed Flycatcher is seen from behind, note that superciliaries connect on the nape, whereas they do not meet on Rusty-margined and Social. White-ringed has broad pale edges to tertial feathers (lacking in Rusty-margined and Social); otherwise, wings are rather plain, though immature (not shown) can show rusty wing feather edges. Yellow crown patch is usually not visible. White-ringed prefers less degraded forest than either Social or Rusty-margined, and behavior is different: singles or pairs usually perch very high in canopy and sometimes join mixed-species flocks. Often gives a strident *Whee-d'd'd'd'd'd'd'd'd*; when agitated, pairs sing a rapid, jumbled trill.

6 LEMON-BROWED FLYCATCHER *Conopias cinchoneti* 16cm/6.5in

1000–1500m. Rare and local in humid foothill and subtropical forest and edge (far more common on E slope). No other flycatcher in our region has entirely yellow underparts (including throat) and superciliary. Behavior is similar to that of White-ringed Flycatcher. Calls include *PEEyer-PEEyer-PEEyer* and a longer, faster *Chi't't't't't't'tyer*.

Medium to large flycatchers clad mainly in gray, yellow, and brown. ID can sometimes be difficult, especially of *Myiarchus* species.

1 TROPICAL KINGBIRD *Tyrannus melancholicus* 21–23cm/8.5–9in

0–2600m. Common and widespread over most of its range, found nearly anywhere there are trees; uncommon in areas of extensive forest, and at elevations higher than 2000m. Similar to Snowy-throated Kingbird, but note especially its olive breast separating white throat from yellow underparts, a less conspicuous dark face mask, and larger size. Tropical Kingbird is a conspicuous and often-seen species that perches on trees, wires, snags, and other spots that offer good visibility of passing insects. Common call is a fairly high-pitched twitter, e.g., *pit-pip'p'p-pit*. Pairs give longer and more rapid versions of this call during wing-lifting displays.

2 SNOWY-THROATED KINGBIRD *Tyrannus niveigularis* 19cm/7.5in

0–1600m; rarely to 2800m. A locally common breeder in deciduous forest and desert scrub in W and SW; during the June–November dry season it disperses northward throughout much of the NW, where it inhabits similar areas to Tropical Kingbird; occasionally wanders as high as Quito. Snowy-throated Kingbird is distinguished from Tropical by larger and more prominent dark face mask, smaller size, and perhaps most important, the abrupt transition between white throat and yellow belly (lacking the olive breast). The two species are similar in behavior and voice, but individual notes of Snowy-throated's call are drier, with more of a clicking quality.

3 DUSKY-CAPPED FLYCATCHER *Myiarchus tuberculifer* 16cm/6.5in

0–2500m. Fairly common in humid forest and edge from lowlands to temperate zone; uncommon and local in deciduous forest. Smaller size, darker gray crown (almost appearing black), and voice help separate this species from Sooty-crowned Flycatcher. Dusky-capped Flycatcher is typically found alone or in pairs, often with mixed-species flocks, in mid to upper forest levels. It peers around alertly, with crest occasionally raised; may hover to catch insects. Common call is a mournful whistle that rises and falls, similar to call of Rusty-margined Flycatcher (p. 296), though usually lower pitched. Dusky-capped's song is a rapid, complex series of trills and whistles, which may be given by a pair in duet.

4 SOOTY-CROWNED FLYCATCHER *Myiarchus phaeocephalus* 19cm/7.5in

0–2000m. Fairly common in deciduous and semi-humid forest, edge, lighter woodland, and mangroves; appears to be spreading into degraded forest in more humid areas, probably due to deforestation. Sooty-crowned is larger than Dusky-capped Flycatcher and has a more medium-gray crown that sometimes has a brownish cast. Dusky-capped is much less likely to occur in the dry forest that Sooty-crowned prefers, but there is some overlap. Also see Panama Flycatcher, which is not yet known to overlap in range but potentially could do so. Sooty-crowned's behavior is similar to that of Dusky-capped. Vocalizations include a drawling *pweeeee-wee-wee-wee-wuh-wuh* (with variations), *wiDUP!*, and a rising *pwee!*

5 PANAMA FLYCATCHER *Myiarchus panamensis* 19cm/7.5in

0–100m. Only recently found in Ecuador, where thus far known only from the far NW between San Lorenzo and Las Peñas, where it is uncommon; perhaps occurs elsewhere in the NW lowlands. Found in mangroves, scrub, and secondary forest. Similar to Sooty-crowned Flycatcher (which possibly occurs with it) but has a browner crown and mantle. Note that some Sooty-crowneds show a brownish tinge to the crowns, so ID is best confirmed by voice. Song of Panama Flycatcher is a descending *whee-dee-dee-dee-dee-dee-dee...*, much faster than Sooty-crowned's song. Calls include *weep!* and *wi'duh*; some calls are similar to those of Sooty-crowned.

6 GREAT-CRESTED FLYCATCHER *Myiarchus crinitus* 21cm/8.5in

0–2800m. A very rare boreal migrant to forest and light woodland, with scattered records from lowlands up to as high as Quito; may be more regular in far NW. Sightings to date have all been between November and March. Combination of large size, brownish crown, and conspicuous rufous edging to primaries and tail feathers separates it from all other *Myiarchus* known to occur in W Ecuador. Call is a rising, querulous *wheep?*

A mix of medium to large flycatchers from all over W Ecuador. The first two are migrants, the others are resident species.

1 EASTERN KINGBIRD   *Tyrannus tyrannus*   19–21cm/7.5–8.5in

0–1800m; vagrants can turn up just about anywhere. This boreal migrant is rare in humid forest edge and light woodland in most of W, but fairly common in inter-Andean valleys as well as wooded areas of Quito; it is much more common in E. Recorded from September to April. Slate-gray upperparts contrast with white underparts; also note white tail tip; can appear slightly crested. Molting Fork-tailed Flycatcher might look similar but usually shows at least a slightly notched tail, and has a black crown that contrasts with the paler gray mantle. Wintering birds rarely vocalize, and eat fruit as well as insects; they often associate with other kingbirds.

2 FORK-TAILED FLYCATCHER   *Tyrannus savana*   28–40cm/11–15.5in

0–1000m; rarely as high as Quito. A rare austral migrant to W (much more common in E), recorded from February to November. Usually found in open habitats such as farmland and pastures, but vagrants can turn up almost anywhere. Male (not shown) has an even longer tail than the female; sexes are otherwise similar. Extremely long tail combined with gray and white plumage and dark crown usually makes ID very easy, but immature and molting, short-tailed adult can be confused with Eastern Kingbird. Fork-tailed shows contrast between dark head and lighter gray back, usually shows at least a slight notch in the tail, and lacks the kingbird's pale tail tips. Usually silent in Ecuador.

3 GOLDEN-CROWNED FLYCATCHER   *Myiodynastes chrysocephalus*   21cm/8.5in

800–2400m. Fairly common in humid foothill and subtropical forest, edge, and wooded clearings. A large, chunky, and stout-billed flycatcher, with faintly streaked yellow underparts and a dark mask bordered above and below by buffy stripes. The golden crown is often concealed. No really similar species occurs with it (no overlap with Baird's Flycatcher). Golden-crowned Flycatcher is typically found alone or in pairs, perched high up in a tree, sallying out after insects and sometimes eating berries. Loud, with a large vocal repertoire. Often gives airy "squeeze toy" squeaks, either alone or in a series; dawn song is a *Whee!-di'duh*, uttered over and over.

4 BAIRD'S FLYCATCHER   *Myiodynastes bairdii*   23cm/9in

0–1400m. Uncommon to fairly common in deciduous forest edge, arid scrub, and desert oases in lowlands and foothills of W and SW. A large, bulky flycatcher, with broad black mask, plain brown back, streaked throat, and much rust in wings and tail. No similar species occurs with it. Singles or pairs perch conspicuously, sallying out after insects. Song is series of *purr-wit!* notes, sometimes followed by a chaotic crescendo. Also gives various churrs, twitters, and *pit* calls.

5 STREAKED FLYCATCHER   *Myiodynastes maculatus*   21cm/8.5in

0–1600m. Fairly common in a variety of wooded habitats from lowlands to subtropics. Large, with boldly streaked underparts and rufous tail; underpart color varies from white to pale yellow. Stout bill with pale base separates it from the smaller Piratic Flycatcher. Behavior similar to that of Golden-crowned Flycatcher. Song of Streaked Flycatcher is a repeated *WEE!-ker'ch'wu'it*; calls include a repeated *pek!* or *check!* Note: **Sulphur-bellied Flycatcher** (*M. luteiventris*; not shown) is a very rare vagrant to W. ID can be difficult, but it is usually yellower below than Streaked, and malar streaks are usually darker and may connect on the chin.

6 PIRATIC FLYCATCHER   *Legatus leucophaius*   15cm/6in

0–1500m; occasionally to 2800m. Fairly common in humid forest and edge from lowlands to subtropics. There are also several records from the Quito Botanical Gardens; it is unknown whether these are wanderers from lower elevations or long-distant migrants. Like a small, slender version of Streaked Flycatcher, but note the short, stubby, all-dark bill, finer streaking, and brown tail. Piratic Flycatcher is typically found alone or in pairs perched high in the canopy. The name is derived from its behavior of taking over other species' nests rather than building its own. Song is a squeaky rising and then falling *weyee* followed by a softer *titititit* 1 sec. or so later.

Attilas are medium-size flycatchers with hooked bills. The striking black-and-white-plumaged tityras were formerly treated as flycatchers or cotingas, but are currently classified in a new family, Tityridae, which includes becards, Northern Schiffornis, and various other species. Chocó Sirystes is a scarce, rarely seen flycatcher.

1 OCHRACEOUS ATTILA *Attila torridus* 21cm/8.5in

0–1500m; to 1700m in SW. Uncommon in humid and semi-humid forest and edge; rare in the N part of its mapped range. Mostly bright cinnamon, with yellow lower underparts and rump; wings are dark with cinnamon wing bars; no other species in our region is similar in coloration. Bright-rumped Attila is similar in shape and behavior, but even the rufous morph of that species is nowhere near as bright. Ochraceous Attila is usually found alone or in pairs at mid to upper levels of the forest, sallying out or fluttering up to grab insects; also consumes fruit. Perches vertically and sometimes pumps tail downward. Easily overlooked unless vocalizing. Song is a series of five to eight rising whistles followed by a *whewpit!*; e.g., *fu-fu-Fu-Fu-FU-FU-whewpit!* Calls include a single whistle and a *Fwoo…feeoo-oo*.

2 BRIGHT-RUMPED ATTILA *Attila spadiceus* 19cm/7.5in

0–1400m; very locally to 1900m above Mindo. Uncommon in humid lowland and foothill forest and edge. Plumage is variable but all forms display a yellow rump, yellow belly, brown wing bars, faint throat and breast streaking, and a hooked bill. Head, back, and breast color varies based on morph. Olive morph is the most common in our area; rufous morph is far less common, and gray morph (not shown) is very rare. Behavior similar to that of Ochraceous Attila. Song of Bright-rumped Attila is a *wu-WIHdi-WIHdi-were*. Some calls include a loud, sharp *PIH'D'D!*, often given in pairs, and a fast, rolling *w'du-w'du-w'du-w'du-w'du* that rises and falls in pitch.

3 BLACK-CROWNED TITYRA *Tityra inquisitor* 18cm/7in

0–1300m. Uncommon in humid lowland and foothill forest and edge. Male's striking black-and-white pattern is similar only to that of Masked Tityra, but Black-crowned Tityra is easily distinguished by all-black bill and lack of red facial skin. Female has a rusty-brown facial patch and grayish upperparts; all-dark bill lacking red base and brown face separate her from Masked Tityra. Black-crowned is generally encountered in pairs in forest canopy, feeding on both fruit and insects. Gives a variety of dry, rasping, frog-like calls.

4 MASKED TITYRA *Tityra semifasciata* 21cm/8.5in

0–1600m. Fairly common in humid lowland and foothill forest and edge. Both sexes easily separated from Black-crowned Tityra by mostly red bill and bare red periocular skin. Male Masked Tityra is also distinguished by reduced black on the head, forming a face mask; female has brown face (lacking black). In behavior and voice Masked is similar to Black-crowned, but it is sometimes found in larger groups.

5 CHOCÓ SIRYSTES *Sirystes albogriseus* 19cm/7.5in

0–500m. Rare and local in humid lowland forest where large trees still remain in the NW. Formerly more widespread, but very sensitive to habitat degradation, and numbers have declined propitiously due to deforestation. Pale underparts contrast sharply with slaty crown, gray mantle, black tail, and white-edged dark wings. Found alone or in pairs, high in forest canopy; consumes both fruit and insects. Sometimes joins mixed-species flocks. Common call is a series of fairly rapid *pip!* notes that vary slightly in pitch. Also called **Western Sirystes**.

olive morph 2

rufous morph 2

♂ 3

♀ 3

♂ 4

♀ 4

Becards are small, sexually dimorphic forest-dwelling birds. While most lack bright colors, they are distinctive and quite attractive. Once considered flycatchers or cotingas, they are now included in a new family, Tityridae. The species on this page are found mainly in the Andes, but Black-and-white Becard also occurs in lowland areas.

1 BLACK-AND-WHITE BECARD *Pachyramphus albogriseus* 14cm/5.5in

0–2500m. Uncommon to fairly common in both deciduous and humid forest and edge, from the lowlands to the subtropics. In the NW Andes it must be separated from White-winged Becard: Male Black-and-white Becard has a paler mantle, longer superciliary, and lacks the bright white scapular edging; female has a rufous-tinged crown that contrasts with yellowish mantle. In deciduous forest, see also Slaty Becard (p. 306). Black-and-white Becard is usually found alone or in pairs in upper forest levels, consuming arthropods and fruits; occasionally joins mixed-species flocks. Song is a fast, warbled whistle that can be roughly transcribed as *black-and-white? black-and-white?....*

2 WHITE-WINGED BECARD *Pachyramphus polychopterus* 15cm/6in

600–2300m. Uncommon in humid foothill and subtropical forest. The subspecies occurring in our region, *dorsalis*, is rather similar to Black-and-white Becard, and the two species are often found together. Male White-winged Becard has a much darker (almost black) mantle, bold white edges to the scapular feathers (appearing as a white line between the mantle and the wing), and at best just a very short superciliary. Female White-winged is distinguished from Black-and-white by having brown crown almost concolorous with mantle. White-winged Becard is similar to Black-and-white in behavior, but has a different voice; song is a bit variable but usually something like *chu-chu-chu-chee-chuh-chu*, composed of soft, mellow whistles, and sometimes preceded by a few *chit* notes.

3 BARRED BECARD *Pachyramphus versicolor* 13cm/5in

1300–3500m. Fairly common in humid forest and edge from the foothills to the temperate zone. Small and distinctive; the characteristic barring is not easy to see except at close range, but the male's yellow throat and female's gray crown and rusty wings are useful field marks. Often encountered in pairs at mid to upper forest levels, foraging for insects and fruit. A core member of many mixed-species flocks, and also quite vocal; its often-heard song is a *bzz...pee-pee-pi'pi'pi'p'puh*, rising and falling in both pitch and volume.

Three more becards, these found mainly in lowlands and foothills; ID can sometimes be tricky. Sapayoa is a strange bird related to the Old World broadbills (Eurylaimidae); it is sometimes included in that family, though some ornithologists believe it should be a monotypic family.

1 CINNAMON BECARD *Pachyramphus cinnamomeus* 14cm/5.5in

0–1800m. Fairly common in humid forest, edge, and clearings with scattered trees. Sexes are similar; the pale supraloral line that extends from above bill to just behind eye separates it from female Slaty and One-colored Becards. While female Slaty often shows a pale supraloral mark, it is more of an oblong spot than a line. Singles, pairs, or family groups of Cinnamon Becards forage at all levels, sometimes bob or crane heads, and often join mixed-species flocks. Common call is a thin, piping *peyer-peer-eer-eereereer*, sometimes preceded by a higher *titititi*.

2 SLATY BECARD *Pachyramphus spodiurus* 14cm/5.5in

0–1000m. Uncommon in both deciduous and humid forest and edge in W and SW; rare in NW, where perhaps just a postbreeding wanderer, since most records come from the second half of the year. Both sexes similar to One-colored Becard, which is larger, though this is very hard to judge. Male Slaty differs from One-colored Becard by narrow white margins to most wing feathers and brighter pale spot on lores. Female Slaty is almost identical to One-colored, though may show a pale supraloral spot and a warm, buffy wash on the breast; however, often not safely identified unless heard, or seen together with her mate. Female is also similar to Cinnamon Becard, but lacks that species' long, pale supraloral line, instead showing a faint pale spot. Male Slaty Becard distinguished from male Black-and-white Becard (p. 304) by darker underparts, mantle, and sides of head. Slaty Becard is usually encountered alone or in pairs at any forest level, sometimes with mixed-species flocks. Birds often raise their crests into a bushy "helmet" and bob their heads. Song is a burry, accelerating *fwee-ree-reereereetitititititi-tuh*. Also emits a fast, buzzy 2–3 sec. trill.

3 ONE-COLORED BECARD *Pachyramphus homochrous* 16cm/6.5in

0–1700m. Fairly common in both deciduous and humid forest edge and wooded clearings from lowlands to subtropics. Larger and much more common than the similar Slaty Becard. Male One-colored has plain dark wings that lack white feather edging, and its lores never show an obvious pale spot though sometimes have an indistinct gray smudge. Female One-colored is almost identical to Slaty, though tends to show less of a buffy wash on underparts; best to go by voice; also see Cinnamon Becard. Behavior similar to that of Slaty Becard. One-colored Becard's vocalizations include a thin, descending *FEEyuur* and a rather quick series of sharp *peet* notes that change up and down in tone rather randomly and are sometimes intermixed with sharp chatters.

4 SAPAYOA *Sapayoa aenigma* 15cm/6in

0–600m. Rare to locally uncommon in humid primary forest in the NW. Plumage is mostly dull olive but slightly brighter yellow on breast and belly. Distinguished from Green Manakin and females of various other manakins (pp. 316–318) by larger size, longer tail, and wider bill. Sapayoa is found alone or in pairs in lower to mid forest levels, often near streams, and regularly accompanying mixed-species flocks. Gives a soft 1–2 sec. long melodic trill; a short, dry, nearly toneless rattle; and a longer, more erratic sputtering chatter.

The cotinga family (Cotingidae) contains some of the most colorful and bizarre of all neotropical birds. The species on this page may share the name "cotinga," but they are not particularly similar, other than all being primarily frugivorous. ID is usually straightforward.

1 BLUE COTINGA *Cotinga nattererii* 19cm/7.5in

0–300m. Uncommon in humid lowland forest in far NW. Spectacular male is glittering turquoise, with purple throat and central underparts. Female and immature (not shown) have distinctive buff scaling on dark brown upperparts and breast; belly is buff with brown spotting. No other similar species occurs in W Ecuador; even the drab female is readily identifiable. Singles, pairs, and small groups feed in the canopy of tall, fruiting trees, often with other frugivores, including Black-tipped Cotinga. Single males often perch high in canopy for extended periods of time. Virtually silent but has been occasionally heard to give soft single notes or rattles. This species was once fairly common around San Lorenzo and Yalare, but it is becoming increasingly difficult to find due to continuing deforestation.

2 BLACK-TIPPED COTINGA *Carpodectes hopkei* 22–25cm/8.5–10in

0–900m. Uncommon in humid lowland and foothill forest in NW; range is contracting due to deforestation. Both sexes have black bills and red or orange irides. Male is snow white, with black tips to the primaries and central tail feathers. Female is smaller, mostly light gray with white lower underparts, distinctive white wing markings, and a white to yellowish eye-ring; her overall shape and grayish plumage may suggest a small dove. No similar species occur in range; tityras (p. 302) all have black head markings and/or bright red on bill. Behavior similar to that of Blue Cotinga; the two are sometimes found together in the same fruiting tree. Black-tipped Cotinga is almost silent, though has been heard to make a soft grunting sound. (Female photo digitally modified from another species.)

3 RED-CRESTED COTINGA *Ampelion rubrocristatus* 21cm/8.5in

2300–4000m. Fairly common in humid temperate forest and edge, and in scrubby páramo edge and *Polylepis* woodland near tree line. Sexes alike. Adult is gray with blackish head, wings, and tail; rump and crissum are white with dark streaks; note red irides. Wine-red crest is usually laid back, appearing as a thin line hanging down the nape. This crest can be raised into an impressive fan during nuptial displays or agonistic encounters, though only very lucky observers get to witness this performance. Juvenile (not shown) is quite different; gray plumage is infused with strong rufous scaling, and underparts are pale with dark blotches; various intermediate stages can be seen as immatures gradually attain adult plumage. Red-crested Cotinga is usually found alone or in pairs, perched conspicuously atop a bush or tree; feeds mostly on berries but also catches insects. Common call is a toneless ticking interspersed with soft grunts and rattles, e.g., *tik-tik-tik-t'turr*. Pairs give a weird, nasal *wah-wah-wah…* during crest-lifting displays.

FRUITEATERS

Colorful, plump cotingas of Andean cloud forest. As their names suggest, most species consume fruit almost exclusively, though Scaled Fruiteater has a more varied diet. All of these species regularly join mixed-species flocks and can produce very audible wing whirs in flight.

1 GREEN-AND-BLACK FRUITEATER *Pipreola riefferii* 18cm/7in

1800–3000m. Fairly common in humid subtropical and temperate forest and edge. Both sexes have red legs and dark irides, which help distinguish them from Orange-breasted Fruiteater, especially female. Male Green-and-black lacks orange on breast shown by Orange-breasted male. Green-and-black Fruiteater is usually found alone or in pairs, feeding on berries in mid to upper forest levels; frequently joins mixed-species flocks. Song is a series of very high-pitched *tee* notes that usually decelerates. Call consists of one to three of the same *tee* notes.

2 ORANGE-BREASTED FRUITEATER *Pipreola jucunda* 18cm/7in

600–2000m. Uncommon to fairly common in humid foothill and subtropical forest and edge, mostly at lower elevations than Green-and-black Fruiteater. Male's orange breast makes him easy to ID; female distinguished from female Green-and-black by yellow irides and dark legs. Behavior similar to that of Green-and-black, but voice is quite different. Song of Orange-breasted Fruiteater is a rising, high-pitched whistle, about 3 sec. long. Call is a very short, abrupt, rising whistle about ¼–½ sec. long.

3 BARRED FRUITEATER *Pipreola arcuata* 23cm/9in

2500–3500m. An especially chunky fruiteater; uncommon in humid temperate forest and edge. Both sexes have conspicuously barred underparts, a feature not shared by any other similar-size bird in range; yellow spots on the wings can help separate it from Green-and-black Fruiteater if seen only from behind. Behavior similar to that of other fruiteaters. Song of Barred Fruiteater is a very high-pitched whistle, up to 3–4 sec. long; it may rise and then fall or continuously rise in pitch. Calls include various other shorter whistles of similar or lower pitch.

4 SCALED FRUITEATER *Ampelioides tschudii* 20cm/8in

800–2000m; lower in coastal range. Uncommon in humid foothill and subtropical forest. Unique; both sexes have bold olive and yellow scaled underparts, long, yellow malar, and yellow or orange irides. Male has a mostly black head. Behavior similar to that of other fruiteaters, but Scaled regularly consumes insects, and even snails, along with fruit. Song is a single, loud whistle, much lower pitched than songs of other fruiteaters, that typically rises slightly in pitch before falling; can be imitated.

Large cotingas; some are among the most spectacular birds on the entire continent. All are sexually dimorphic, with males larger, sometimes significantly so. Fruit is their primary food source, but they also consume insects and other animal prey. Apart from Purple-throated Fruitcrow, males of these species gather in communal display areas (leks).

1 ANDEAN COCK-OF-THE-ROCK *Rupicola peruvianus* 30–32cm/12–12.5in

1200–2300m. One of the most iconic species of the Andes; locally fairly common in foothill and subtropical forest and edge, especially along forested river valleys. Male is not likely to be mistaken. Female is brick red with darker wings and a reduced crest. Males gather at leks, where a few birds to as many as 15 or more bow, flap, and squeal in an amazing ritual. Away from leks, birds are quite shy, and most often seen at fruiting trees. Call is a nasal, piglike squeal.

2 PURPLE-THROATED FRUITCROW *Querula purpurata* 25–30cm/10–12in

0–800m. Fairly common in humid lowland and foothill forest and edge. Male recognized by raspberry-colored throat patch. Female can be distinguished from other all-black birds in range by short tail, lack of crest, and rather stout, pale bill. Quite social; not unusual to see flocks of three to eight birds moving noisily through the canopy of the forest, feeding on both fruit and insects. Song is a whistled *FWEE-ooo-AH* (with variations); can be easily imitated, which often causes the whole flock to come flying in, giving scratchy, growling responses.

3 LONG-WATTLED UMBRELLABIRD *Cephalopterus penduliger* 36–41cm/14–16in

200–1200m. Rare to locally uncommon in humid lowland and foothill forest. This unforgettable bird is now encountered infrequently, except at several staked-out leks, such as the one at Buenaventura Reserve, at the southernmost limit of the species' known range. Male's wattle can extend to an almost shocking length during displays; female is smaller and has a smaller crest and inconspicuous wattle (often not evident). Even the dullest female should show a distinct crest that separates it from other all-black birds such as female Purple-throated Fruitcrow. The umbrellabird's flight is distinctively undulating, often giving it the appearance of a large, black woodpecker. Up to 10 males gather at leks, where they lean forward, extend and fluff out their wattles, and give a low, 1 sec. *boooh*, reminiscent of the sound made by blowing over the top of a large soda bottle. Very shy and quiet away from leks, where a very lucky observer might find one visiting a fruiting tree.

4 RED-RUFFED FRUITCROW *Pyroderus scutatus* 36–46cm/14–18in

500–2000m. Rare and local in humid foothill and subtropical forest in far NW; there are recent records from near Maldonado along the Colombian border. This striking scarlet and black bird will not be mistaken with a good view. Female (not shown) resembles male, but is much smaller and has a darker bill. Red-ruffed Fruitcrow is usually solitary, but males gather in leks, where they extend their throat feathers and give very low-pitched hoots; calls are similar to those of Long-wattled Umbrellabird, but usually shorter and repeated a few times in quick succession.

Fairly large birds of forest interior, clad in somber shades of olive or rufous; sexes are similar. They are sensitive to habitat degradation and rarely seen except along quiet forest trails inside mature forest. The family classification has been in a state of flux, but currently pihas are considered cotingas, Rufous Mourner is a flycatcher, and Speckled Mourner has been transferred into the recently erected Tityridae family.

1 OLIVACEOUS PIHA *Snowornis cryptolophus* 24cm/9.5in

1300–2300m. Uncommon inside humid foothill and subtropical forest. Fairly large, stout-billed, and olivaceous; lacks strong plumage features, but faint yellowish underpart streaking and pale yellow eye-ring help to ID it. Male has a black crown patch that is usually concealed. This piha is usually found alone, perching quietly for long periods, but also joins mixed-species flocks; eats both fruit and insects. Mostly silent, but on rare occasions has been heard to give very soft rattles or clucks.

2 RUFOUS PIHA *Lipaugus unirufus* 24cm/9.5in

0–700m. Rare to locally uncommon inside humid lowland and foothill forest. Plumage is extremely similar to that of Rufous Mourner, and the two are often best identified by voice or behavior. Rufous Piha is larger, has a larger bill, sometimes shows a paler throat, and can appear somewhat more uniform in color, lacking the darker crown and wing markings that Rufous Mourner tends to exhibit. None of these features is very reliable for field ID, and silent birds may not always be identifiable. Rufous Piha is usually found from mid levels to subcanopy and does not join mixed-species flocks. Quite vocal, often calls in response to loud noises such as falling branches or exuberant birders. Calls include a variety of very loud, abrupt whistles; whistles are sometimes given in a series, interspersed with clucks.

3 RUFOUS MOURNER *Rhytipterna holerythra* 21cm/8.5in

0–1200m. Uncommon in humid lowland and foothill forest and edge. Very similar to Rufous Piha except in size, voice, and behavior; see that species for physical differences. Rufous Mourner is more apt to be found higher in the canopy and, unlike Rufous Piha, regularly joins mixed-species canopy flocks. It is more likely to come out to forest edge, especially while moving with a flock. Calls are soft and mellow, lacking the abrupt and emphatic qualities of Rufous Piha's calls; examples include a descending *wheeeeeoo*; a high, modulated *weeeeer*; and a repeated *PEEE-ter-PEEE-ter-PEEE-ter...* that can go on for 10 sec. or longer.

4 SPECKLED MOURNER *Laniocera rufescens* 21cm/8.5in

0–500m. Very rare inside humid lowland forest. Mostly rufous (head can be grayish) with faint dark barring on underparts, cinnamon wing bars, and a yellow eye-ring. Male has bright yellow to orange pectoral tufts that are usually completely hidden. If seen well, rufous-spotted wing bars and underpart barring will separate this rare bird from Rufous Mourner and Rufous Piha, and if the pectoral tufts are seen, they are diagnostic. Speckled Mourner forages at all forest levels, consuming fruit and insects and other small animals. Song is a ringing *EEE-yer...EEE-yer...* that can continue for 15–20 sec. or longer.

MANAKINS

Manakins are an enthralling family of diminutive neotropical forest birds. Males of many species are renowned for their bright colors and elaborate courtship displays. Most manakins (and all on this page) are sexually dimorphic; distinctive adult males are usually very easy to ID, but females often possess dull and confusing plumages, and bill and leg color are often essential for ID. Immature males look like females but can show faint hints of adult male plumage. Manakins primarily eat small berries, and often gather at fruiting trees, sallying out to pluck berries from nearby branches. Some insects are also taken.

1 GOLDEN-WINGED MANAKIN *Masius chrysopterus* 11cm/4.5in

400–2000m. Fairly common in humid foothill and subtropical forest and edge. Both sexes have reddish legs. Male is the only black bird in range with a yellow forecrown tuft and yellow throat; the underwing is also bright yellow, but this is mostly or entirely hidden when perched. Female is dull yellowish-olive; she may have a small "bump" of feathers above the bill, not present in any other female manakin in Ecuador; however, this feature is not always evident. Similar female White-bearded Manakin shows orange legs (not reddish); female Red-capped Manakin (p. 318, little overlap) has darker bill (not pinkish). Female is also similar to Bronze-olive Pygmy-Tyrant (p. 278), which has yellowish legs and browner upperparts. Male Golden-winged Manakin's display involves flying onto a fallen log, flashing yellow in wing, and then prancing back and forth while bowing. Call is a flatulent *brrrt*; male display song is a high-pitched descending airy whistle followed by *sip-pi'di'brrt*.

2 WHITE-BEARDED MANAKIN *Manacus manacus* 11cm/4.5in

0–1300m. Common in undergrowth of humid lowland and foothill forest edge and secondary woodland; avoids interior of mature forest. Both sexes have bright orange legs and dark bill. Striking black-and-white male is distinctive. Female is a warm olive color above and dull olive below. Female Golden-winged Manakin shows reddish legs (not orange); female Red-capped Manakin (p. 318) has a pale bill. Several males gather at a lek, where they produce very loud snaps with their wings; vocalizations include an *EEwoo* and a buzzy, descending *pyeer* (this call also sometimes given by females). Males also produce a very audible, mechanical rattle when they fly.

3 CLUB-WINGED MANAKIN *Machaeropterus deliciosus* 10cm/4in

100–1800m. Fairly common in humid foothill forest and edge; uncommon and local at its upper and lower elevation limits, and perhaps only seasonal at the lowest elevations. Rich chestnut male with black-and-white wings is distinctive. Female is mostly olive; best identified by the faint cinnamon wash on lower face and throat, pale underwing that may be visible as white edging on its folded wing, and faint breast striations. Males gather in leks to perform their comical displays, hopping energetically along branches, periodically lifting their wings to "moon" observers, while generating a weird, stridulating *beep!* The sound is produced by the vibrations made when it rapidly rubs its wing feathers together; this is the only bird species currently known to be able to do this. There are several easily accessible leks in Ecuador, including one at Milpe Bird Sanctuary. Male also gives a *pew-pew-pew-pew* at leks. Quiet away from leks; female's calls are apparently unrecorded.

♂ 3

MANAKINS

These birds are found at low to mid levels of humid forest at lower elevations. They avoid secondary forest, and thus tend to be scarce and local due to widespread deforestation. Blue-crowned and Red-capped are "typical" manakins: the colorful males perform courtship displays, and females are dull and confusing. Green Manakin and Northern Schiffornis are not sexually dimorphic. All species on this page eat mostly berries and generally do not join flocks, though several may gather at a fruiting tree. They usually stay inside the forest and are not likely to be seen at forest edge unless there is a plentiful food source to attract them.

1 BLUE-CROWNED MANAKIN *Lepidothrix coronata* 9cm/3.5in

0–1000m. Uncommon inside humid lowland and foothill forest. Male is distinctive; female's mostly bright green coloration and dark bill and legs separate her from all other similar manakins. Green Manakin is larger, not as brightly colored above, and has a larger bill and a longer tail. Male Blue-crowned Manakins sing and do simple, solitary, display flights in well-spaced territories. Song is several *prr-wet!* phrases given about 1 sec. apart. Other calls include a rapid twitter and a rising *fweep?*

2 RED-CAPPED MANAKIN *Ceratopipra mentalis* 10cm/4in

0–1000m. Uncommon inside humid lowland and foothill forest. Striking male should be easy to ID. Dull female is best distinguished by paler bill than any other similar manakins; also note pink or reddish legs and yellow thighs; may have pale or brown irides. Males gather at leks and perform delightful displays on branches that involve wing snapping, tail wagging, and forward and backward "moonwalking" while lifting their tails and exposing their yellow thighs. Vocalizations at lek are extremely varied and include a high, descending *SEEEEeeeerrr*, a rising and falling *fwEEooo*, and various sharp *prrrrt*s, *pit*s, and *chak*s, which are sometimes given in pairs or triplets. Males away from leks and females are very quiet.

3 GREEN MANAKIN *Cryptopipo holochlora* 12cm/4.5in

100–1100m. Uncommon and easily overlooked inside humid lowland and foothill forest. Sexes similar. This dull manakin can be hard to ID not only due to its drab plumage but also since it is usually encountered in dark forest understory. It is mostly olive with yellow lower underparts; can be distinguished from females of the sexually dimorphic manakins by combination of larger, dark bill, dark legs, and longer tail. Differs from Northern Schiffornis by olive, not brown plumage. Sapayoa (p. 306) is larger, slightly darker, and has a more slender, pewee-like shape. Green Manakin is solitary and not known to perform displays. It tends to be very quiet, but sometimes gives a descending *seeeee*.

4 NORTHERN SCHIFFORNIS *Schiffornis veraepacis* 16cm/6.5in

0–1300m. Uncommon inside humid lowland and foothill forest undergrowth. Sexes are similar. Brown plumage and larger size separate this species from all other manakins in our region. Very solitary; does not join mixed-species flocks. Unlike many manakins, it is not known to perform courtship displays. Distinctive song is a deceptively loud, quavering series of ethereal whistles, such as *fweeeEEE-yeee-ee*, *peeeuuuuu-eeee*, or *FEW-ooooo-doo-dee-ee-IT*. Formerly lumped with several other species not found in W Ecuador and called **Thrush-like Schiffornis** (*S. turdinus*).

Small, arboreal birds found in virtually all forest types, though absent from the highest elevations of the Andes. All are primarily insectivorous and often encountered in mixed-species feeding flocks. Peppershrikes are in the same family as the vireos but are slightly larger and have fierce-looking hooked bills.

1 RUFOUS-BROWED PEPPERSHRIKE *Cyclarhis gujanensis* 15cm/6in

0–2500m. Common in semi-humid and deciduous forest edge, light woodland, and clearings with scattered trees. Range has been expanding recently into humid areas of the NW, where it locally overlaps with the similar Black-billed Peppershrike. Rufous-browed can be distinguished from that species by its bright yellow throat and breast, white (not gray) belly, and broader, longer rufous superciliary. Rufous-browed Peppershrike is typically found foraging alone or in pairs at mid to upper heights, often with mixed-species flocks. Song is variable, but typically consists of a series of rapidly changing whistles repeated every few seconds, e.g., *fweeCHUchuWEEchuchu…*; call is a drawling series of whistles such as *peeeu…feee?…peeer…purr.*

2 BLACK-BILLED PEPPERSHRIKE *Cyclarhis nigrirostris* 15cm/6in

600–2000m. Uncommon in humid foothill and subtropical forest and edge; range has contracted northward in recent years, perhaps due to competition with Rufous-browed Peppershrike, which is expanding northward. Black-billed can still be regularly found in some locations such as the Mashpi area and along the Chical road. It can be distinguished from Rufous-browed by mostly gray underparts with olive restricted to sides of breast and neck; its superciliary is also much thinner and shorter, extending only a little past eye. Vocalizations are reminiscent of Rufous-browed Peppershrike's; song tends to be more slurred, and call is shriller and descends in pitch.

3 SLATY-CAPPED SHRIKE-VIREO *Vireolanius leucotis* 14cm/5.5in

200–1300m. Uncommon in humid lowland and foothill forest and edge. Striking head pattern—with steel-gray head, yellow superciliary and subocular spot, and pale irides—is diagnostic in range. This species usually stays in the canopy of tall forest, where it can be rather hard to see. It is nearly always encountered with mixed-species flocks, and its distinctive song can be heard from a great distance: a monotonous, repeated flat whistle that sounds very much like the beeping alarm emitted by a truck backing up.

4 RED-EYED VIREO *Vireo olivaceus* 14cm/5.5in

0–2000m; vagrants higher. Common in a variety of wooded habitats throughout much of W; appears to engage in poorly understood local migrations and may be only a nonbreeding seasonal visitor in more humid parts of the NW. Distinguished from Brown-capped Vireo by nearly all white underparts and gray cap bordered with black. Forages actively from mid levels to canopy, and is a regular member of mixed-species flocks. Sings incessantly in the rainy season in the W and SW, a simple *cheewit* or *chwee* repeated about once every 2 sec. Common call, heard year-round, is a short, buzzy, descending *Zheee.* Boreal migrants also occur as rare vagrants in W (even in Quito), but are very difficult to distinguish from resident birds, and are not known to vocalize in Ecuador. *Note:* **Yellow-green Vireo** (*V. flavoviridis*; not shown) is a very rare vagrant to W; separated from Red-eyed Vireo by obvious yellow sides and flanks as well as lack of black borders to superciliary.

5 BROWN-CAPPED VIREO *Vireo leucophrys* 13cm/5in

400–3000m. Common in humid subtropical and temperate forest edge, light woodland, and adjacent clearings; uncommon and local at the lower limit of its elevation range. Combination of brown cap and pale yellow lower underparts separates this species from other similar vireos. Behavior similar to that of Red-eyed Vireo; also frequently joins mixed-species flocks. Song is a cheerful series of mellow notes that rises and falls in pitch; call is a burry *zhwee-zhwee-zhwee-zhwee.*

6 CHOCÓ VIREO *Vireo masteri* 11cm/4.5in

800–1700m. Rare and local in humid foothill and subtropical forest in NW; recent sightings have come mainly from the Mashpi area. Similar to Brown-capped Vireo, but with two white wing bars and ochraceous wash on sides of breast. Chocó Vireo is usually encountered alone or in pairs, often with mixed-species flocks and very high in the canopy, where angle and foggy conditions can sometimes make it hard to see the diagnostic wing bars. Vocalizations are similar to those of Brown-capped Vireo, but song is somewhat faster, more erratic, and higher pitched.

Greenlets are very small, humid-forest vireos. Gnatcatchers and gnatwrens belong to a family (Polioptilidae) of small, active, insectivorous birds; most are found in forest, though Tropical Gnatcatcher also ranges into arid scrub.

1 LESSER GREENLET *Pachysylvia decurtata* 10cm/4in

0–1500m. Fairly common in humid lowland and foothill forest and edge; locally ranges up into the subtropical zone. This tiny, short-tailed vireo has a plain white face and central underparts that contrast with yellow upperparts and sides. Small groups actively forage for insects in mid to upper forest levels, and frequently join mixed-species flocks. Distinctive and often-heard song is a repeated *witch-ee-witch*; calls include a quick series of soft churrs.

2 TAWNY-CROWNED GREENLET *Tunchiornis ochraceiceps* 11cm/4.5in

0–800m. Uncommon inside humid lowland and foothill forest; does not tolerate much habitat disturbance. Rather dull, but the combination of tawny crown, pale irides, and unmarked brownish-olive wings is diagnostic. Inhabits lower to mid forest levels, and frequently joins mixed flocks of antwrens and other understory species. Hard to see well due to its small size and low light of the forest understory. Tawny-crowned Greenlet is more often recorded by ear than by sight; its song is a ringing *peeer* repeated every few seconds; also gives a sneering *nyeh-nyeh-nyeh....*

3 SLATE-THROATED GNATCATCHER *Polioptila schistaceigula* 11cm/4.5in

0–900m. Uncommon and local in humid lowland and foothill forest in NW. The most distinctive of the world's gnatcatchers, it is slate gray with a white belly and broken white eye-ring. Singles, pairs, or family groups flit about high in forest canopy, often flipping tails seemingly uncontrollably; frequently join mixed-species flocks. Vocalizations include a high, thin, descending trill; a slower, ascending trill, an abrupt *chu*, and a whistled *fweeweeweeweewee*.

4 TROPICAL GNATCATCHER *Polioptila plumbea* 11cm/4.5in

0–1800m. Common in deciduous forest and desert scrub, but also spreading into more humid areas in the NW following deforestation, where it prefers forest edge and clearings. A handsome little bird with gray upperparts and white face and underparts; female lacks male's black crown. Animated pairs conspicuously forage for insects, and are usually the first birds to come in to mob a Pacific Pygmy-Owl (p. 148). Song is a *seep-seep-seep-seep-seep...*; call is a short, buzzy *djee*.

5 TAWNY-FACED GNATWREN *Microbates cinereiventris* 11cm/4.5in

0–1200m. Fairly common inside humid lowland and foothill forest. Best identified by its bright, tawny face, along with shape and behavior. Singles or pairs move quickly through the dark understory, often cocking their tails and lashing them around like angry cats. Sometimes joins mixed understory flocks, though just as often found away from them. Very vocal, emitting a wide variety of calls: a cheerful, descending *peer*, a rapid, burry chatter, and a buzzy *zheer*, given alone or in a series. Sometimes called **Half-collared Gnatwren**.

6 LONG-BILLED GNATWREN *Ramphocaenus melanurus* 12cm/4.5in

0–1200m. Locally fairly common in semi-humid forest and edge; rare or absent in very wet and very dry regions. Exceedingly long, thin bill separates it from all other small passerines in Ecuador, but also note tawny crown and nape, and gray wings amd back. Singles or pairs flit through dense vegetation and vine tangles at low to mid levels, often joining mixed-species flocks. Song is a flat trill about 2 sec. long, often with a distinctive ringing quality.

Mockingbirds and jays, though unrelated, are similar in their size, shape and bold nature. White-capped Dipper is an aquatic passerine unlike any other bird in Ecuador.

1 LONG-TAILED MOCKINGBIRD *Mimus longicaudatus* 27–30cm/10.5–12in

0–2400m. Common and conspicuous in open, nonforest habitats, including cities and towns, in drier areas of W and SW. Gray and white plumage pattern and long tail are unique in its range; no known overlap with Tropical Mockingbird, which lacks the dark malar and cheek patch. Often found in small family groups, perching conspicuously or running along the ground. Song is a long series of churrs intermixed with mellow whistles.

2 TROPICAL MOCKINGBIRD *Mimus gilvus* 25cm/10in

1500–2800m. Locally fairly common; mostly confined to dry inter-Andean valleys between Quito and the Colombian border, but there are scattered records from more humid areas, suggesting that its range may be expanding southward. No known overlap with Long-tailed Mockingbird, which is slightly larger and has a dark malar and cheek patch. Similar behavior to that species, but more likely to be found alone. Song is an erratic series of burry whistles; call is an ugly, metallic rasp.

3 TURQUOISE JAY *Cyanolyca turcosa* 30cm/12in

1700–3500m. Fairly common in humid subtropical and temperate forest and edge. No less beautiful than the similar Beautiful Jay, from which it can be separated by its black collar, brighter blue plumage, and white forecrown (not entire crown). Typically encountered in small flocks that move boldly and noisily through the forest canopy. This species possesses a remarkably varied vocal repertoire; some of the more common calls include a sharp, down-slurred *cheer!*, a weird, metallic *djer!*, and a rather low-pitched whistled *woahr*.

4 BEAUTIFUL JAY *Cyanolyca pulchra* 27cm/10.5in

1500–2400m. Uncommon in humid subtropical forest and edge in the NW, where it often occurs together with larger and brighter Turquoise Jay. Beautiful Jay lacks a black collar and has a more extensive white crown and a black mask that often does not stand out clearly against the dark blue throat. Behavior similar to that of Turquoise Jay, though Beautiful Jay tends to be found in smaller numbers, sometimes even alone. Calls can be strikingly loud and have an electronic-game quality; a few of them include a rapid *CHU-CHU-CHU*, a whipping *WIchee-WIchee-WIchee…*, and *puWIT*.

5 WHITE-TAILED JAY *Cyanocorax mystacalis* 32cm/12.5in

0–1800m. Uncommon to fairly common in deciduous forest, edge, and wooded clearings in W and SW. One of Ecuador's most striking birds, and it will not be mistaken with a good view. Behavior similar to that of other jays, but White-tailed is more likely to come down low, even near the ground. Calls have an almost electronic quality, and include a sharp *MEH-MEH-MEH-MEH…*, often repeated for 10 sec. or longer; *bi-BE*, and softer, frog-like *bih-woo*.

6 WHITE-CAPPED DIPPER *Cinclus leucocephalus* 16cm/6.5in

200–4000m. Locally fairly common along rushing mountain streams and rivers in a wide elevation range. Sooty-black and white plumage along with chunky shape and distinctive habits make it easy to ID, but see much smaller Torrent Tyrannulet (p. 268), which has a vaguely similar plumage pattern and shares the same habitat. The dipper is usually found alone or in pairs, hopping or flying from rock to rock, fearlessly plucking prey from sometimes raging torrents. Unlike some other dipper species, does not totally immerse itself in the water. Its vocalizations are hard to hear over the water noise, but a single, sharp, buzzy note is often given while flying up- or downstream.

Swallows are a familiar group of highly aerial species found nearly worldwide. They often occur in large flocks, circling overhead as they catch insects, and then resting collectively on open perches such as wires, dead snags, and buildings when not feeding. Martins are large swallows and are similar in behavior to the smaller species. Voice is not a particularly useful ID feature so is not described.

1 GRAY-BREASTED MARTIN *Progne chalybea* 18cm/7in

0–1800m; occasionally higher; vagrants can reach the central highlands. Common in a wide variety of habitats, including cities and towns, but avoids areas of extensive forest and is quite scarce in most of the NW away from the coast. Dark blue back, if seen, easily separates this species from Brown-chested Martin. However, in flight, ID can be more difficult due to great individual variation in the amount of gray on the throat. Darker-throated individuals, such as the bird in flight shown here, are distinctive, whereas lighter-throated ones, like the one shown perched on the pole, are more difficult, though they typically show a uniform wash of gray rather than the distinct band of Brown-chested. Also note flight appearance; Gray-breasted holds its wings flat while gliding, whereas Brown-chested glides with down-bowed wings. Gray-breasted Martin is especially common in and around towns, where it can gather in enormous roosts of hundreds or even thousands. *Note:* **Purple Martin** (*P. subis*; not shown) is a very rare boreal migrant in W Ecuador, especially around water in inter-Andean valleys (e.g., Lago San Pablo); any sighting should be carefully documented. Adult male is uniform dark blue. Female and immature can look somewhat like Gray-breasted Martin, though head is not uniform blue but intermixed with scaly brown plumage.

2 BROWN-CHESTED MARTIN *Progne tapera* 17cm/6.5in

0–300m; vagrants can occur much higher. Locally fairly common in open areas, including cities and towns, along the coastal plain; there are also several records from the N highlands of austral migrants. Brown back, faint brown breast band, and (in flight) down-bowed wings separate this species from Gray-breasted Martin; see that species for more details. Can also be confused with Southern Rough-winged Swallow in poor light, or if size cannot be accurately judged. It can be separated from that species by breast band, lack of pink throat, and lack of pale rump, though all of these features can be hard to see under some circumstances. Also see Bank Swallow (p. 330), though that species is much smaller. Note that the birds shown are of the austral migrant subspecies *fusca*, which occurs in our region only as a rare vagrant, especially around highland lakes. The resident subspecies *tapera* is very similar but lacks the vertical line of dark scaling below the breast band.

3 SOUTHERN ROUGH-WINGED SWALLOW *Stelgidopteryx ruficollis* 13cm/5in

0–2000m. Common throughout the lowlands and foothills in virtually any habitat. In some higher-elevation areas (e.g., Tandayapa Valley) it appears to be only a seasonal visitor. If seen well, the pale cinnamon-buff throat is diagnostic. In flight, also look for mostly pale lower underparts, triangle-shaped wings, and whitish rump. At a distance, it can be confused with Brown-chested Martin, which has a more restricted range in W Ecuador; see that species for more details.

SWALLOWS

Small to medium-size swallows. Three are fairly common and relatively widespread, whereas Tumbes Swallow is one of the rarest and most infrequently encountered birds in Ecuador. Behavior typical of that of other swallows (p. 326).

1 BLUE-AND-WHITE SWALLOW *Pygochelidon cyanoleuca* 12cm/4.5in

0–3500m. Common throughout the Andes in virtually all habitats; uncommon and local in lowlands and along the coast. Black crissum contrasts strongly with immaculate white remainder of underparts. Upperparts are glossy blue, face mask black. Brown-bellied Swallow is larger, has smoky gray (not white) on underparts, and occurs mainly at higher elevations, though there is significant overlap.

2 BROWN-BELLIED SWALLOW *Orochelidon murina* 14cm/5.5in

2500–4200m; locally down to 2000m in Pululahua Geobotanical Reserve. Fairly common in virtually any habitat at higher elevations, including cities and towns. Often found near rocky cliffs or roadcuts that serve as roosting and nesting areas. Larger than Blue-and-white Swallow, with smoky-gray (not white) breast and belly, which contrasts less with black crissum.

3 WHITE-THIGHED SWALLOW *Atticora tibialis* 11cm/4.5in

0–1500m. Uncommon to fairly common in humid forest edge and adjacent clearings in lowlands and foothills, locally into subtropics. Small and very dark, can look virtually black in poor light. Uniformly dark gray underparts are diagnostic, along with white thighs, though these are hard to see even while the bird is perched; usually this swallow has to scratch or stretch for them to be revealed. In flight, also note slightly paler rump. Flight call is a rather toneless *chup*, more distinctive than calls of most swallows.

4 TUMBES SWALLOW *Tachycineta stolzmanni* 12cm/4.5in

100–200m. Very rare in lowland desert of far SW near the town of Zapotillo; possibly only a nomadic rainy-season visitor from Peru. Known from mostly barren plains with sparse, low scrub. The only resident swallow in W Ecuador with a bright white rump. Underparts are white with faint gray streaking, and lack the dark crissum of Blue-and-white Swallow.

4 4

Chestnut-collared Swallow is a resident species in drier parts of the country, while the remaining three species on this page are boreal migrants; they occur in greatest numbers during northward and southward passage, during which times they can be seen virtually anywhere in the country

1 BARN SWALLOW *Hirundo rustica* 14–17cm/5.5–6.5in

0–4000m. An uncommon to locally common boreal migrant; seen throughout the year, but numbers are very small from May to August. Widespread in our region, but most common around lakes and wetlands in the lowlands, as well as around some highland lakes. Fresh-plumaged adults are distinctive, but in Ecuador it is not unusual to encounter molting birds or immatures that lack long tail feathers. Look for white spots at the base of the tail, rufous (not white) forehead, and lack of a rump patch to help separate it from similar species (e.g., Cliff Swallow).

2 BANK SWALLOW *Riparia riparia* 12cm/4.5in

0–3500m. An uncommon boreal migrant; occurs in Ecuador from August to April. Most often encountered in lowlands, especially near water, where it is frequently found with other migrant swallows; less frequently seen in the highlands, but small numbers do turn up, mainly during northward and southward passage. A small, sandy-brown swallow with a distinct brown breast band. Superficially similar to Brown-chested Martin (p. 326), but much smaller with a very fluttery flight. Chestnut-collared Swallow has a chestnut (not brown) collar as well as a chestnut rump patch. Sometimes called **Sand Martin**.

3 CLIFF SWALLOW *Petrochelidon pyrrhonota* 13cm/5in

0–3500m. An uncommon boreal migrant found in Ecuador from August to April, and most common during southward passage in August–September. Can turn up almost anywhere, but usually seen along the coast or around lakes and rivers in both the lowlands and highlands. Chestnut throat (not breast band) combined with chestnut rump are diagnostic if seen. At a distance, could be confused with a molting Barn Swallow that lacks its long outer tail feathers, and the two species are often found together; see Barn Swallow for more details.

4 CHESTNUT-COLLARED SWALLOW *Petrochelidon rufocollaris* 12cm/4.5in

0–2000m. Locally fairly common in lightly wooded areas in drier parts of W and SW, especially in towns and around bridges that provide nesting sites. Rather distinctive, with a complete chestnut collar and rump. Bank Swallow has brown (not chestnut) collar, and Cliff Swallow has a chestnut throat (not collar). Chestnut-collared Swallow nests during the rainy season in large colonies of 50 or more birds, which, during the breeding season, do not seem to venture far from these nest sites; nests are most often placed on large buildings such as churches or warehouses, or under bridges. Outside of the breeding season, these swallows often congregate in large numbers near water or at salt pans.

W Ecuador has a high diversity of wrens; at least one species inhabits virtually every part of the region. Wrens are entirely insectivorous and extremely vocal; several are admired for having some of the most beautiful songs in South America; other species have surprisingly "rude" and unpleasant calls that are memorable in their own right.

1   RUFOUS WREN   *Cinnycerthia unirufa*   16cm/6.5in

2500–3600m. Fairly common in humid temperate forest and edge. Mostly uniform rich rufous, with vague dark barring on wings and tail (often indiscernible); note dark lores. Some birds show varying amounts of white on the head and face. Extremely similar in most respects to Sepia-brown Wren, which occurs at lower elevations. In the narrow zone of overlap, ID can be very difficult. Rufous Wren usually shows a richer, rufous plumage, plainer wings and tail, and darker lores, but this can be hard to judge under the often unpredictable viewing conditions of the cloud forest. With experience, call notes can be a reliable way to separate the species; Rufous gives a single, raspy *chup*, whereas Sepia-brown gives a toneless *widit*. Both species sing remarkably elaborate duets, consisting of beautiful series of sweet, rapid whistles and musical trills. Also see Rufous Spinetail (p. 226), which has more extensive black on lores and lacks barring. Rufous Wren is almost always found in flocks numbering from a few to up to 15 or more birds that move together as they forage through lower forest levels.

2   SEPIA-BROWN WREN   *Cinnycerthia olivascens*   16cm/6.5in

1400–2500m. Fairly common in humid subtropical forest. Replaces the very similar Rufous Wren at lower elevations. Sepia-brown Wren is duller rufous brown, with narrow blackish barring on wings and tail; as with Rufous, some individuals show varying amounts of white on the head. See Rufous Wren for more details on separating the two species as well as vocalizations. Sepia-brown may also be mistaken for Rufous Spinetail (p. 226), which is brighter rufous, lacks barring, and has bolder black lores. Behavior of Sepia-brown Wren is much like that of Rufous Wren. Also called **Sharpe's Wren**.

3   GRAY-MANTLED WREN   *Odontorchilus branickii*   12cm/4.5in

100–1000m. Rare in humid lowland and foothill forest. A small, gray and white arboreal wren. Banded tail is often the best ID feature, as it is usually visible even when looking up at this wren, under poor viewing conditions. The even rarer Double-banded Graytail (p. 228) can look similar at a distance, but lacks the banded tail; also note behavior. Gray-mantled Wren forages high in the canopy, where it habitually creeps along branches, peering under them for prey, and is usually observed accompanying mixed-species flocks. Song is a rapid, high-pitched trill, e.g., *see-see-see-see-see-see-see-see*.

4   BAND-BACKED WREN   *Campylorhynchus zonatus*   18cm/7in

0–1300m. Fairly common in humid lowland and foothill forest edge and adjacent wooded clearings in NW. Boldly patterned and distinctive in range. Heavily barred upperparts and flanks, black-spotted throat and breast; note rusty lower underparts. Fasciated Wren (little or no overlap) prefers drier habitats, lacks the rusty ventral color, and is barred (not spotted) below. Usually pairs or small family groups of Band-backed Wren move noisily through the treetops. Vocalizations are harsh, rather toneless rasps and "throat-clearing" churrs, given alone or in a long, rhythmic series.

5   FASCIATED WREN   *Campylorhynchus fasciatus*   19cm/7.5in

0–2500m. Common in deciduous forest edge, lightly wooded areas, desert scrub, gardens, and towns throughout much of the W and SW. Replaces Band-backed Wren in dry country; the two species are rarely or never found together. Fasciated Wren lacks the rusty coloration of the lower underparts as well as the distinct round black breast spots of Band-backed. Fasciated is often found in bands of up to 10 birds that move about noisily, at any level, even on the ground. Vocalizations have a similar quality to those of Band-backed Wren but are even louder and more disagreeable.

6   SEDGE WREN   *Cistothorus platensis*   11cm/4.5in

2800–4500m. Fairly common in grassy páramo at very high elevations; not a forest bird. Mostly brown with bold black and buff dorsal streaks. No other wren shares its range and habitat; House Wren (p. 336) can sometimes be found nearby, but lacks the back streaking. Sedge Wren is usually found alone or in pairs, skulking in tall grass or nearby bushes. Most often detected by its loud buzzy *chu-chu-chu-chu-chu-chu*... call. Song, given from an exposed perch, is a series of sweet, rapid whistles intermixed with buzzes and trills. Sometimes called **Grass Wren**. A paper has been published that proposes splitting Sedge Wren into several species. In this treatment, Ecuadorian birds become **Páramo Wren** (*C. aequatorialis*), and the range of the species extends from W Venezuela S through the Andes to N Peru.

These wrens were formerly included in *Thryothorus*, which has now been split up into several genera. They are boldly marked, and ID is usually straightforward if the birds are seen well. They are usually found in close-knit pairs that sing fantastic songs (often duets) from hidden perches.

1 PLAIN-TAILED WREN *Pheugopedius euophrys* 16cm/6.5in

2000–3300m. Fairly common in *Chusquea* bamboo thickets in humid subtropical and temperate forest. Black spotting on breast and unbarred tail separate this species from Whiskered Wren in their very limited area of overlap (e.g., Tandayapa Valley). Plain-tailed Wren pairs usually stay hidden inside dense bamboo, and can be hard to see unless the observer can enter the bamboo patch or find a gap with good visibility. Their shockingly loud, rapid song duets consist of a rich and rolling series of whistles repeated constantly for 30 sec. or more; can be heard over a great distance. Call is a guttural *cu-wit!*

2 WHISKERED WREN *Pheugopedius mystacalis* 16cm/6.5in

0–2000m. Uncommon and very local in humid and semi-humid forest and edge from lowlands to subtropics. Combination of boldly black-and-white-striped gray head, bright chestnut back, and barred tail is diagnostic. Pairs skulk in dense tangles and dark thickets; tend to be very shy and thus are often frustratingly hard to see. Beautiful song is usually given as a duet and consists of a short, complex series of rich, throaty, and liquid whistles, repeated several times with 3–5 sec. between bouts. Call is a whipping *whit-whit-whit-whit*.

3 SPECKLE-BREASTED WREN *Pheugopedius sclateri* 14cm/5.5in

0–1800m. Fairly common in deciduous and semi-humid forest and edge from lowlands to subtropics. Found mainly in W and SW, but has spread N in recent years (e.g., Río Palenque Science Center). Very distinctive, with boldly black-spotted underparts, strongly marked face, and barred tail. Pairs hide in dense tangles, but frequently come out into the open, even up into the subcanopy. Song is a short series of clear, musical whistles, e.g., *swee-PWEE-eee-piWIT*, repeated every few seconds. Call is a musical rasp, like the sound produced by running a finger along a metal comb.

4 SUPERCILIATED WREN *Cantorchilus superciliaris* 15cm/6in

0–1600m. Uncommon to fairly common in deciduous forest, edge, and desert scrub in W and SW. A dry country bird, not found in humid areas. Plain, unmarked, mostly white underparts and white superciliary separate it from other wrens that occur with it. Pairs skulk in forest understory or dense scrub and can be hard to see in the rainy season when the vegetation leafs out. Songs are quite variable and usually consist of a short, simple series repeated over and over, such as a sweet *witit-TREE-too…* and a loud *tooIT-cheeIT…*. Common call is a crackling rattle.

5 BAY WREN *Cantorchilus nigricapillus* 15cm/6in

0–1600m. Fairly common in humid forest edge and overgrown clearings from lowlands to subtropics. This beautiful wren is not likely to be mistaken if seen well, which is sometimes a challenge, as it often skulks in dense, dark understory tangles. With patience, a viewer may see one emerge into a gap to show off its ornate plumage. Song is variable, but often consists of a short but loud series of repeated notes with a whipping quality, e.g., *fwooEEwidit- fwooEEwidit- fwooEEwidit…*; lacks the more mellow quality of the songs of other wrens that often occur with it. Call is an extended rattle.

6 STRIPE-THROATED WREN
Cantorchilus leucopogon
12cm/4.5in

6

100–900m. Uncommon to locally fairly common inside humid lowland and foothill forest in NW, mainly in less disturbed areas where large trees still remain. A well-named species, as the striped throat is usually the only obvious feature on this small, dark brown bird. Usually found at mid to upper forest levels, frequently in vine tangles near large tree trunks. Sings a series of high, ethereal, ringing notes, e.g., *fweeah-dih-doo-ah…* or *twee-ah-doo*, repeated several times; the series starts softly and gradually becomes louder. Calls include a throaty *ptoo*, *w'dih-wih*, or a single, clear whistle repeated every 1–2 sec.

1 HOUSE WREN *Troglodytes aedon* 12cm/4.5in

0–4000m. A common and familiar species found almost throughout Ecuador (though avoids forest interior); often but not always near buildings. It can be separated from Mountain Wren by lack of a distinct superciliary and brown rather than tawny foreparts. Song is a short musical trill that starts high and abruptly drops in pitch. Most common call is a short *zhwee*.

2 MOUNTAIN WREN *Troglodytes solstitialis* 11cm/4.5in

900–3000m; lower in coastal range. Uncommon to fairly common in humid forest and edge from the foothills to the temperate zone. Similar to the more common House Wren but more richly colored and bears a distinct pale superciliary; the two species have different habitat preferences but occasionally are seen together at forest edge. Mountain Wren is usually found alone or in pairs at all levels of the forest, and frequently joins mixed-species flocks. Song is a quick series of rapidly changing high-pitched notes with a tinkling quality; call is a dry sputter, usually about 1 sec. long and often repeated over and over.

3 GRAY-BREASTED WOOD-WREN *Henicorhina leucophrys* 11cm/4.5in

700–3300m; lower in SW and in coastal range. Common in humid forest and edge in a wide elevation range from the foothills to the temperate zone. A small wren with a stubby tail and strong black-and-white facial pattern. Two subspecies occur in W Ecuador; *hilaris* is found mainly in the foothills and *leucophrys* in the subtropical and temperate zones, though there is a narrow zone of overlap around 1600m elevation. They differ mainly in song, but note that *hilaris* has a whiter throat and breast, with gray restricted to sides, which makes it hard to separate from White-breasted Wood-Wren. See that species for more details. Gray-breasted Wood-Wren is found singly or in pairs, actively foraging in the understory. Very vocal; its songs are among the memorable sounds of the Andean cloud forest. Quite variable, but *leucophrys* usually sings a short series of fast, musical whistles (likened to a car alarm), the same series repeated over and over; *hilaris* sings more slowly and leisurely. Calls of both subspecies include a variety of rattles, and sharp, toneless clicks such as *wih'd* and a rising *p't't'DIH*.

4 WHITE-BREASTED WOOD-WREN *Henicorhina leucosticta* 11cm/4.5in

0–800m. Uncommon to locally fairly common inside humid lowland and foothill forest. W Ecuador birds have extensive gray on the breast and sides, and are very easy to mistake for the *hilaris* subspecies of Gray-breasted Wood-Wren, which can occur with it in the foothills. White-breasted has a narrower white superciliary and darker black markings on sides of neck. Their songs can be hard to tell apart without significant experience, but call notes can be used to separate the two species. White-breasted gives a soft *weeOO* and a metallic-sounding *chup* (alone or in a series), neither of which are given by Gray-breasted.

5 SONG WREN *Cyphorhinus phaeocephalus* 14cm/5.5in

0–1200m. Rare to locally fairly common inside humid lowland and foothill forest. Very sensitive to habitat degradation, Song Wren has declined propitiously due to deforestation but is still fairly numerous in a few protected areas such as the Buenaventura Reserve. It is an oddly shaped wren, with a big head, large bill, and pale periocular patch extending in a teardrop shape behind eye. Usually found in pairs on the forest floor or low in the understory. Song is a bizarre, rhythmic series of low guttural notes, e.g., *whatdititwhat-duh-FWEE-oh...*, repeated for long periods. Call is a low, muffled rattle.

6 SOUTHERN NIGHTINGALE-WREN *Microcerculus marginatus* 11cm/4.5in

0–1500m. Fairly common inside humid lowland and foothill forest; locally up into the subtropics (e.g., the Mashpi area). Brown and white, with a stubby tail; amount of underpart scaling varies regionally. In far NW underparts are mostly white, with scaling restricted to flanks; elsewhere in W Ecuador, entire breast and belly are scaled. Solitary; walks on the forest floor, sometimes coming up to a low perch to sing. Song is one of the most memorable and recognizable in all of Ecuador, a series of short, well-spaced clear whistles; each whistle is lower pitched than the previous, and the whole series can last 2 min. or more. Call is a soft *chup*. Also called **Scaly-breasted Wren**.

hilaris **3**

leucophrys **3**

far NW **6**

Shy thrushes found mainly in humid montane forest; sexes are similar. Solitaires feed on fruit in mid to upper forest levels. Nightingale-thrushes stay near the forest floor. Swainson's Thrush is a long-distance boreal migrant related to the nightingale-thrushes.

1 BLACK SOLITAIRE *Entomodestes coracinus* 23cm/9in

1000–2300m. Rare to locally uncommon in humid foothill and subtropical forest and edge in the NW. Perhaps only a seasonal wanderer in the southernmost part of its range, e.g., the Tandayapa-Mindo area. Black with large white patches on face and in wings; pattern is unique, and Black Solitaire is not likely to be confused with any other Ecuadorian bird. Shy and inconspicuous, usually staying hidden at mid forest levels; often found alone, but small groups may gather at fruiting trees. Most common vocalization is a weird flat, metallic, ringing whistle that lasts about 1 sec. and usually can be heard only if the bird is nearby.

2 ANDEAN SOLITAIRE *Myadestes ralloides* 18cm/7in

600–2600m. Fairly common in humid forest and edge from the foothills to the temperate zone. Gray head and underparts contrast with rich brown back and wings; white wing and tail patches are usually hidden while perched, but can flash conspicuously in flight. Rather shy and solitary, usually staying hidden in the canopy, most easily seen when visiting a fruiting tree. Often-heard song is one of the characteristic sounds of the Andes; the bird gives a short series of metallic, ringing notes, then pauses 1–2 sec., then gives a similar but slightly different burst; the whole series can last 10–15 sec.

3 RUFOUS-BROWN SOLITAIRE *Cichlopsis leucogenys* 20cm/8in

600–1500m. Rare to locally uncommon in humid foothill and subtropical forest in the NW; in recent years not found S of the Mashpi area. Similar in appearance to some female *Turdus* thrushes (pp. 340–342), but it is more richly colored above and has a yellow or orange lower mandible; also tends to perch more upright. Shy and rarely encountered; like other solitaires, most likely to be found at a fruiting tree. Song is a short series of sweet whistles, some of which are warbled, e.g., *fu-fwee-yerr-twidl'dee-dee*. Bouts are separated by a few seconds, and each one is slightly different.

4 SLATY-BACKED NIGHTINGALE-THRUSH *Catharus fuscater* 18cm/7in

900–2600m. Uncommon inside humid forest from the foothills to the temperate zone. Dark gray upperparts, paler gray below, white irides, and orange bill, legs, and eye-ring, separate this species from *Turdus* thrushes (pp. 340–342) that can occur with it. Solitary, shy, and often very hard to see, it skulks on or near the forest floor, often in dense thickets. Song consists of between two and six clear, piping whistles, repeated every few seconds. Call is a rising, rasping *zhwee?*

5 SPOTTED NIGHTINGALE-THRUSH *Catharus dryas* 18cm/7in

200–1800m. Fairly common inside humid foothill forest; locally ranges up into subtropics and on coastal hills. ID is straightforward as long as the peachy-yellow, black-spotted underparts can be seen, which is not always easy in the dark forest. Solitary and extremely shy, it stays very low in the understory, often hopping on the ground. Beautiful song is a long series of soft whistles and metallic trills. Call is a descending *tseee*.

6 SWAINSON'S THRUSH *Catharus ustulatus* 18cm/7in

0–4000m. A fairly common boreal migrant, found in Ecuador from September to April. Can be found in virtually any wooded habitat, though most common in humid forest at mid elevations. Note especially the buffy eye-ring and lores, dark malar, and boldly spotted breast; not similar to any other regularly occurring species, but see note below. Usually found feeding in fruiting trees, often with tanagers and other resident species. The typical call of Swainson's Thrush on its wintering grounds is a soft, abrupt *whip*. Song, a rising, modulated series of whistles, is occasionally heard in March–April. *Note*: **Gray-cheeked Thrush** (*C. minimus*; not shown) is a very rare vagrant to W; it is similar to Swainson's but has gray lores and eye-ring; face lacks the warm buff coloration of Swainson's.

Turdus is a genus of medium to large thrushes found widely in the Americas, Africa, and Eurasia. They consume a wide variety of food, including fruit, insects, and worms. They tend to be solitary, congregating with other birds only at abundant food sources. Immatures (not shown) are heavily mottled and have much duller leg and bill coloration than adults. The species on this page are found mainly at higher elevations.

1 GREAT THRUSH *Turdus fuscater* 30–33cm/12–13in

1800–4200m. A very common species of high elevations in the Andes, found in almost any habitat, including large cities (e.g., Quito) and towns. A large, sooty-brown thrush with orange bill and legs. Male has yellow eye-ring; female and immature male lack this feature and could be confused with Chiguanco Thrush, which is somewhat smaller, more sandy brown, with yellow (not orange) bill and legs. Great Thrush favors more humid areas, but there is some overlap. Bold and conspicuous, it perches in the open and hops around on the ground. While most common in open areas, it is frequently found in forest as well. Song, most often heard predawn, is a leisurely series of mellow whistles intermixed with higher, sharper notes. Calls, numerous and varied, include a squeaky *cheu- cheu- cheu-cheu* and soft clucks.

2 CHIGUANCO THRUSH *Turdus chiguanco* 28cm/11in

1000–3400m. Fairly common in inter-Andean valleys and agricultural areas in central and S Ecuador. Very scarce but possibly spreading at the N limit of its mapped range; it has even been seen in dry valleys near Quito but as yet is not known to occur within the Quito city limits. While Chiguanco Thrush tends to prefer drier areas than Great Thrush, both species locally occur together. Sexes are similar in Chiguanco. Bill and legs are yellow (not orange). Chiguanco is slightly smaller than Great Thrush and not as dark, usually having a distinct sandy cast to its plumage. Voice and behavior are also similar, but Chiguanco does not venture into heavily forested areas.

3 GLOSSY-BLACK THRUSH *Turdus serranus* 24cm/9.5in

1400–3500m. Fairly common in humid subtropical and temperate and edge. Male is smaller and blacker than Great Thrush, but has similar color to bill, legs, and eye-ring; Pale-eyed Thrush lacks eye-ring and displays white irides (dark in Glossy-black). Female more difficult, but look for yellow legs, dark irides, and faint yellow eye-ring, which may be very indistinct in some individuals (immatures?), such as the female shown. Glossy-black Thrush is mostly arboreal, but occasionally forages on the ground as well. Song of male, often given from an exposed perch, is a short, warbling series of ringing notes, repeated somewhat monotonously every 1–2 sec. Most common call is a series of two to five sharp clucks, e.g., *pik-pik-pik*.

4 PALE-EYED THRUSH *Turdus leucops* 21cm/8.5in

1000–2300m; locally lower in coastal range. Rare to locally uncommon in humid foothill and subtropical forest. Both sexes are similar to Glossy-black Thrush. Male, with his staring white eyes, is quite distinctive. Female is much less so, and is quite difficult to tell apart from the female of the more common Glossy-black; note Pale-eyed female's smaller size, paler irides, and lack of eye-ring (though some Glossy-blacks have reduced eye-rings). Some females show faint streaking on the face and neck. Behavior is similar to that of Glossy-black, though voice is quite different. Song of Pale-eyed is highly variable, a seemingly random burst of clear whistles, warbles, and sharp notes with a wide tonal range. Another bout is given every few seconds, totally different from the previous; very unlike the consistent nature of Glossy-black's song. Pale-eyed's most common call is a sharp *chak*, given alone or in a short series; it can also mimic other species. (Female photo digitally modified from another species.)

A set of medium-size *Turdus* thrushes (see also p. 340). With the exception of Andean Slaty-Thrush, the species on this page are not significantly sexually dimorphic.

1 ECUADORIAN THRUSH *Turdus maculirostris* 23cm/9in

0–2400m. Common and widespread in lightly wooded areas and forest edge in both dry and humid regions; not found inside dense forest. Note tan plumage, yellowish bill, and narrow orange eye-ring. Bolder than other thrushes in range, it frequently comes into the open and regularly visits feeders. Beautiful song is a soft, mellow caroling of clear whistles mixed with short trills, lasting 2–10 sec., with a different series given after a short pause. Calls include a rising, catlike *meow!* and a very short, grunting *eh*.

2 PALE-VENTED THRUSH *Turdus obsoletus* 23cm/9in

400–1500m. Uncommon inside humid foothill and subtropical forest. Identified by combination of mostly rich brown plumage, contrasting white belly and crissum, and lack of pale throat patch. Very shy; stays inside mid to upper strata of the forest and only rarely comes to edge; generally found alone, though may congregate with other birds at a fruiting tree. Sings a long and rather random series of short whistles, lacking the "sad" quality of Dagua Thrush's song. Typical call is rising *wheer?*, given alone or in a series.

3 DAGUA THRUSH *Turdus daguae* 21cm/8.5in

100–1300m. Rare to locally fairly common inside humid lowland and foothill forest. Mostly brown, but note especially the white throat patch and bold yellow eye-ring, which often stand out clearly in its dark forest habitat, and help separate it from the locally sympatric Pale-vented Thrush. Dagua Thrush is shy and solitary, inhabiting forest from mid levels to subcanopy. Song is a long and very melancholy series of short whistles, and typical call is a short, complaining *nyeh!* Sometimes lumped with **White-throated Thrush** (*T. assimilis*).

4 PLUMBEOUS-BACKED THRUSH *Turdus reevei* 23cm/9in

0–2500m. Fairly common in deciduous and semi-humid forest and edge in W and SW. A striking thrush; combination of slate-gray upperparts and pale grayish and buff underparts is unique among W Ecuador thrushes; also note staring white irides. Found at mid to upper forest levels and not very shy; usually not hard to see, except in the middle of the rainy season, when the dry forest leafs out. Song is a very variable series of rather husky whistles that change rapidly in pitch. Common call is a querulous, whistled *fooEEEE?*

5 ANDEAN SLATY-THRUSH *Turdus nigriceps* 21cm/8.5in

1200–2500m. A seasonally fairly common breeder in humid subtropical and temperate forest in the far SW, present from at least October to April, though numbers fluctuate from year to year. Slaty male can be distinguished from other gray *Turdus* (p. 340) by white streaks on throat and pale belly and crissum. Female is very similar to female of Glossy-black Thrush (p. 340) but has distinct throat streaking and paler lower underparts; she is separated from female Ecuadorian Thrush by dark bill and darker brown plumage. Singing male Andean Slaty-Thrush can sometimes perch conspicuously and be easy to find; otherwise this species is shy, secretive, and seldom seen. Typical song is a 4–5 sec. series of harsh, metallic notes and chatters; this is repeated every few seconds with minor variations. Calls include various metallic rasps. Sometimes called **Slaty Thrush**. (Female photo digitally modified from another species.)

♂ 5

EUPHONIAS

Euphonias are small, short-tailed, arboreal finches (Fringillidae) related to the siskins (p. 348). All are sexually dimorphic. Males are strongly patterned, but plainer females are sometimes difficult to ID. Euphonias are almost never found alone. They move through the canopy in pairs or small groups, and often join mixed-species flocks. They eat mainly fruit (mistletoe berries are a favorite), but also some insects and other arthropods. Some species regularly visit feeders. Voices of the species on this page are not very distinctive without significant field experience and, except for that of Thick-billed Euphonia, are not described here.

1 ORANGE-BELLIED EUPHONIA *Euphonia xanthogaster* 11cm/4.5in

0–2400m. Common in virtually all wooded habitats in humid areas from lowlands to subtropics; avoids very dry regions. Male has warm yellow crown and underparts, glossy blue-black upperparts and throat; note white undertail. Similar Orange-crowned Euphonia shows rich orange (not yellow) crown and underparts and lacks white undertail. Female Orange-bellied is similar to females of other euphonias, but note especially gray-tinged nape and breast and orange-washed forecrown.

2 ORANGE-CROWNED EUPHONIA *Euphonia saturata* 10cm/4in

0–1800m. Uncommon and local in lightly wooded areas in both dry and humid regions from lowlands to subtropics. Male is similar to more widespread Orange-bellied Euphonia but has rich orange crown and underparts (not yellow), and lacks white in the undertail. Female is extremely similar to female of Thick-billed Euphonia (lacking that species' whitish foreface) and not always safely identifiable in the field unless the corresponding male is seen. The two species sometimes occur together, and Thick-billed usually outnumbers Orange-crowned.

3 WHITE-VENTED EUPHONIA *Euphonia minuta* 10cm/4in

0–900m. Uncommon in humid lowland and foothill forest and edge. Very small; both sexes are rather distinctive. Male has a white lower belly, vent, and undertail; yellow on head is restricted to a small spot above the bill. Female has white throat and central lower underparts separated by a distinctive yellow-olive breast band that extends along sides and flanks.

4 THICK-BILLED EUPHONIA *Euphonia laniirostris* 11cm/4.5in

0–2000m. Common and widespread from lowlands to subtropics in almost any wooded habitat. Male differs from all other male euphonias in range by yellow underparts extending all the way up to the bill (lacking dark throat). Female's uniformly bright yellow underparts separate it from most other female euphonias; difficult to separate in the field from female Orange-crowned Euphonia, but Thick-billed female may show a whitish patch between bill and eye. Immature male Thick-billed Euphonia, frequently encountered, displays a dark mask on otherwise plain female-type plumage. Thick-billed Euphonia is a surprisingly good mimic, and male sometimes sings a squeaky song consisting of copies of vocalizations of other birds; some imitations are quite good and others rather imperfect.

Chlorophonias are closely related to euphonias. Males have exceptionally colorful plumages, and even the females are quite distinctive. As with euphonias, they are strongly sexually dimorphic and behavior is similar. Apart from Fulvous-vented Euphonia, the species on this page only occasionally join mixed-species flocks.

1 FULVOUS-VENTED EUPHONIA *Euphonia fulvicrissa* 10cm/4in

0–500m. Uncommon in humid lowland forest and edge in the NW. Both sexes can be distinguished from other similar euphonias (p. 344), especially Orange-bellied, by bright tawny crissum and belly. Fulvous-vented Euphonia typically stays fairly high in the canopy, but will come down lower to feed on fruiting shrubs at forest edge, and regularly joins mixed-species flocks. It has a more distinctive voice than other euphonias in range; call is a short, rapid-fire series, e.g., *t't't't't* or *t't't'di'di'di*. Song is a very long and even faster series with a gravelly quality, interspersed with some high-pitched squealing notes.

2 GOLDEN-RUMPED EUPHONIA *Euphonia cyanocephala* 11cm/4.5in

1200–3000m. Fairly common in dry scrub and light woodland in inter-Andean valleys; uncommon and perhaps seasonal in humid forest edge and wooded clearings on the outer slopes of the Andes. Both sexes are colorful, with a light blue crown, but only the male has a golden rump. ID should be straightforward; female Chestnut-breasted Chlorophonia also has a blue crown, but her upperparts, throat, and neck are bright green rather than yellow. Commonly heard call of Golden-rumped Euphonia is a short, descending whistled *peer*. Song is a long series of fast, scratchy twitters and rapidly changing notes interspersed with the *peer* call.

3 YELLOW-COLLARED CHLOROPHONIA *Chlorophonia flavirostris* 10cm/4in

300–2000m. Seasonally fairly common in humid forest and edge in the NW. Most common in the foothills, but small numbers also range lower and higher. It is thought to undertake local migrations (which are not understood), since it is usually present only between November and April. Tiny with bright orange bill and legs and pale irides; the vibrant green and yellow male is one of the most uniquely colored birds of the entire Chocó region. Female is slightly duller, more uniform green, and lacks yellow nuchal collar of male. Behavior is similar to that of euphonias, but sometimes encountered in large flocks of 20 or more individuals. Most common call is a clear, high-pitched descending *peee*; other, harsher notes are also given.

4 CHESTNUT-BREASTED CHLOROPHONIA *Chlorophonia pyrrhophrys* 11cm/4.5in

1400–3000m. Rare to locally uncommon in humid subtropical and temperate forest and edge. Ornate male is one of the most colorful birds in Ecuador and should not be mistaken. Female is duller but still quite pretty; combination of blue crown and bold red superciliary is distinctive; green upperparts also help separate her from female Golden-rumped Euphonia. Chestnut-breasted Chlorophonia is rather infrequently encountered, and may even be somewhat nomadic, since it can go unrecorded from some sites for months at a time. Vocalizations are varied, and some have an odd, almost electronic quality to them. One call is a ringing *peee*, louder and flatter than the one described for Yellow-collared.

Siskins are small finches (Fringillidae) related to the euphonias (pp. 344–346). With the exception of Andean Siskin, they are strongly sexually dimorphic: males have a black hood or cap, which females lack; all display bright yellow wing patches. Siskins are quite social, often occurring in large flocks. They eat mainly seeds, thistle, and other plant material, but also some insects. Voices of all species are quite similar, typically thin, metallic whistles or twitters, and are not described in detail.

1 HOODED SISKIN *Spinus magellanicus* 10cm/4in

1200–4000m; down to at least 600m in SW. Fairly common in open and lightly wooded habitats, including páramo, montane scrub, farms, gardens, and towns, mostly at higher elevations. Plumage is quite variable in both male and female, sometimes leading to ID difficulties; several variations are shown. Adult male is fairly distinctive, with full black hood; immature male in intermediate plumage can show a partial hood, even just a black cap, causing confusion with Andean Siskin (see that species for more details). Female is duller and can be mostly gray, brown, or dull yellow, though not as yellow as Saffron Siskin female.

2 ANDEAN SISKIN *Spinus spinescens* 10cm/4in

3000–3600m. Locally fairly common in temperate forest and edge of páramo near the Colombian border (e.g., Páramo El Angel and Cerro Mongus). Status farther S is unclear due to confusion with Hooded Siskin, but it is at best a very rare wanderer there. Adults of both sexes have a well-defined black cap that extends only to bill, eye, and rear crown. Immature male Hooded Siskin gradually obtains black hood and during this period can appear very similar to Andean Siskin. True Andeans should never have any black markings below the chin or eye, whereas immature male Hooded often shows black blotches or flecks in these areas. Lone birds seen associating with flocks of Hooded Siskins need to be identified with care. Away from the border region, this species should be carefully observed and documented.

3 SAFFRON SISKIN *Spinus siemiradzkii* 10cm/4in

0–2000m. Rare to uncommon and nomadic in dry habitats of W and SW. Occurs mainly at lower elevations than Hooded Siskin, but there is some overlap in the mountains of the far SW. Male is almost identical to male Hooded Siskin but averages somewhat brighter, especially on the mantle; lone males in the area of overlap with Hooded Siskin are difficult to ID with certainty. Female Saffron Siskin is much brighter yellow than almost all female Hooded Siskins. As siskins are usually seen in monospecific flocks, it is often best to look at the mix of individuals; flocks of Saffron Siskins will be more uniformly bright yellow than flocks of Hooded Siskins.

4 YELLOW-BELLIED SISKIN *Spinus xanthogastrus* 11cm/4.5in

300–2000m. Uncommon to fairly common in fields, clearings, and forest edge in humid areas, mainly in the foothills. Male is the most distinctive siskin in Ecuador—mostly black with yellow restricted to wing patch and lower underparts. Female is more olive-toned than any other siskin in our region, with yellow lower underparts, usually showing some contrast between olive breast and yellow belly.

Miscellaneous small passerines of open, often grassy habitats. Lesser Goldfinch is in the same genus as the siskins (p. 348). Yellowthroats are in the New World Warbler family (Parulidae); see p. 352 for general information on the family.

1 LESSER GOLDFINCH   *Spinus psaltria*   11cm/4.5in

800–2800m. Uncommon and local in lightly wooded areas and montane scrub from the foothills to the temperate zone; locally fairly common in inter-Andean valleys. Similar to the siskins (p. 348), but with white instead of yellow in the wing. Male has completely yellow underparts, and might be mistaken for Thick-billed Euphonia (p. 344) in poor light. Female can be confusing unless seen with male; distinguished from similar species by strong contrast between dark olive wings and back and yellowish underparts and by pale wing bars and speculum. Similar in voice and behavior to siskins.

2 PÁRAMO PIPIT   *Anthus bogotensis*   15cm/6in

3000–4200m. Uncommon in páramo grassland and pastures at high elevations. Ecuador's only resident pipit, and that fact is one of its key ID features. Look for the thin bill, overall tan and brown plumage with dark necklace, and white outer tail feathers, most easily seen in flight. Usually found alone or in pairs walking through the grass, easy to overlook until one flushes off the ground, flashing its white outer tail feathers. Song is a short, spritely mixture of buzzes and warbles, often given as it flutters high in the air during a display flight before gliding back to the ground.

3 BLACK-LORED YELLOWTHROAT   *Geothlypis auricularis*   13cm/5in

0–1800m. Uncommon in dense, secondary growth in overgrown clearings and at forest edge. Gray crown and smaller, arrowhead-shaped black mask distinguish male from Olive-crowned Yellowthroat male. Female is similar to Olive-crowned female, but has a faint gray crown and usually shows a more prominent eye-ring; the photo of the female is of **Masked Yellowthroat** (*G. aequinoctialis*), with which Black-lored is sometimes lumped. Black-lored pairs tend to stay hidden in dense vegetation, but male sometimes sings from more open perches, and may react strongly to pishing. Male sings a series of musical whistles that usually descends in pitch, e.g., *fwee-fwee-wee-tu-tu-ti-ti-ti-ti-tu*. Calls include various churrs as well as an accelerating *pu-pu-ti-t't't't*.

4 OLIVE-CROWNED YELLOWTHROAT   *Geothlypis semiflava*   13cm/5in

0–2300m. Common in grassy clearings, pastures, and adjacent secondary growth in humid areas from lowlands to subtropics. Male has an ample black mask covering most of face, much larger than the face patch of Black-lored Yellowthroat. Female distinguished from female Black-lored by darker lores, lack of gray on the crown, fainter and broken eye-ring, and usually shows a vague yellowish superciliary. Female Yellow Warbler (p. 354) is also similar, but is brighter and less olive above, and lacks the superciliary. Behavior of Olive-crowned Yellowthroat is similar to that of Black-lored. Song is a fairly long series of rollicking musical notes that gradually decreases in pitch and gets faster, e.g., *wee-dewee, wee-dewee, wer-di-d'dittle-er-it*; calls include a descending, buzzy *djer*, and a long, harsh rattle.

The New World Warblers (Parulidae) form a large family of small, active, insectivorous birds found nearly throughout the Americas. While some of the colorful species well known to North American birders reach W Ecuador as migrants, a number of other species are full-time residents in the region. The species on this page are nonmigratory, and sexes have identical plumage. They are usually found in pairs or small family groups that forage boldly in forest understory or at edge, often joining mixed-species flocks.

1 BLACK-CRESTED WARBLER *Myiothlypis nigrocristata* 13cm/5in

2000–3500m. Common in subtropical and temperate forest edge and overgrown clearings. Yellow plumage with black-and-yellow-striped head is distinctive in range; no overlap with the similar Chocó Warbler, which occurs at much lower elevations. Prefers rather dense vegetation such as *Chusquea* bamboo and dense fern clusters, and is less likely to join mixed-species flocks than other similar species. Song is variable. In the NW it gives a "bouncing-ball" series of *tik* notes that starts slow and toneless and then accelerates rapidly, with the individual notes becoming progressively sweeter in tone. In SW, song is much shorter and slows down at the end. Calls are similar to the *tik* notes that begin the song.

2 RUSSET-CROWNED WARBLER *Myiothlypis coronata* 14cm/5.5in

1500–3500m. Fairly common in subtropical and temperate forest and edge. Well named and attractively patterned; no similar species occur with it. Frequently bobs tail up and down as it hops along branches. Its beautiful song, usually given as an antiphonal duet, is one of the most characteristic sounds of the cloud forest. It begins with one bird giving a series of descending *tik*s that quickly explodes into a complex series of burry notes and clear whistles. Its mate gives a similar series at the same time that blends in so well it can be hard to tell two different birds are singing. Typical call is a buzzy *widit*.

3 CHOCÓ WARBLER *Myiothlypis chlorophrys* 13cm/5in

300–1400m. Fairly common in humid foothill forest and edge. A small, olive-yellow warbler with faint dusky and yellow face and head stripes, and inconspicuous orange central crown patch (not always visible in the field). Can be found together with Three-striped Warbler, but that species is buffy olive rather than olive yellow, and has a much bolder head pattern with dark cheek patch. Song of Chocó Warbler is usually given in duet. One bird sings a metallic, accelerating rasp, and its mate answers with a higher, sweeter, *seeeip?* Calls include a series of inflected churrs as well as *chak* notes. Sometimes lumped with **Golden-bellied Warbler** (*M. chrysogaster*).

4 GRAY-AND-GOLD WARBLER *Myiothlypis fraseri* 14cm/5.5in

0–2000m. Fairly common in deciduous and semi-humid forest and edge in W and SW; locally also occurs in more humid forest. Bluish-slate upperparts and tail contrast strongly with bright yellow underparts. Crown streak, which is usually concealed, varies from orange in N part of range to yellow in SW. Three-banded Warbler lacks the bluish tones and has a bold postocular line and a yellow tail. Song of Gray-and-gold Warbler is a short series of whistles with a burry quality, e.g., *witi-witi-witi'd'DEEDEEduh*. Common call is a harsh *chak*.

5 THREE-BANDED WARBLER *Basileuterus trifasciatus* 13cm/5in

800–3000m. Fairly common in both humid and deciduous forest and edge as well as in montane scrub in the SW Andes. Not likely to be mistaken within its small range; note pale grayish head, with dusky postocular line and crown stripes, and yellow tail. Gray-and-gold Warbler has slaty-blue upperparts and tail and lacks the dark postocular line. Song of Three-banded Warbler is a rapid series of tinkling notes that starts clear and then becomes burry. Its mate often answers with a rather random series of rattles and churrs. Call is a loose *check*.

6 THREE-STRIPED WARBLER *Basileuterus tristriatus* 13cm/5in

800–2400m. Common in humid foothill and subtropical forest and edge. Olive back, dingy yellowish-buff underparts, and dark cheek patch separate it from other stripe-headed warblers, which are mostly bright yellow and/or gray. Song is similar to that of Three-banded Warbler, but longer and even faster. Calls include various ticks, rasps, and churrs.

Whitestarts, sometimes rather inaccurately called "redstarts," are distinctive warblers that are most common in Andean cloud forest. All species on this page are resident except for Yellow Warbler, included here due to its similarity to Mangrove Warbler (and with which it is sometimes lumped).

1 SLATE-THROATED WHITESTART *Myioborus miniatus* 13cm/5in

600–2600m; lower in coastal range. Common in humid foothill and subtropical forest and edge; ranges up into temperate forest in SW. Occurs mainly at lower elevations than Spectacled Whitestart, but there is some overlap in the subtropical zone. Slate-throated Whitestart is distinctive, and confusion is most likely only with immature Spectacled Whitestart (see that species). Slate-throated is often encountered in pairs that flit actively through the branches, flaring out their white tail feathers, and regularly join mixed-species flocks. Song is a short series of thin, sweet notes that often alternate rapidly in pitch, e.g., *tsip-itsee-itsee-itsee-tsip-ip*. Call is a single, high-pitched *tsip*.

2 SPECTACLED WHITESTART *Myioborus melanocephalus* 13cm/5in

2100–4000m. Common in humid subtropical and temperate forest; also occurs in stands of *Polylepis*. Adult—with yellow lores and spectacles—is easy to ID, but immature (not shown) can have a very indistinct facial pattern and show some gray on the throat and breast, but still usually shows faint yellow facial markings and lacks Slate-throated Whitestart's well-defined hood. Behavior is like that of Slate-throated. Song of Spectacled Whitestart is a long series (10 sec. or longer) of sweet, rapidly changing notes that starts softly and becomes much louder by the end. Calls include soft twitters and high-pitched notes.

3 TROPICAL PARULA *Setophaga pitiayumi* 11cm/4.5in

0–2300m. Fairly common in humid and deciduous forest, edge, and light woodland from the lowlands to the subtropics. Combination of slate-blue upperparts, yellow underparts, orange breast, and white wing bars is distinctive; no really similar species occurs in range. Usually found in pairs foraging high in canopy; frequently joins mixed-species flocks. Song is a fast, chippered *si'si'si'si'si'si'si'si'ee'ee'ee'ee't't 't't't't't't't't't't't't.t*. Call is a sharp, somewhat toneless *tik*.

4 BUFF-RUMPED WARBLER *Myiothlypis fulvicauda* 13cm/5in

0–1300m. Fairly common near forested streams, rivers, and ponds in the humid lowlands and foothills. A well-named species; the bright buff on rump and base of tail is always conspicuous, contrasting with the somber hues of the rest of its plumage. Found in singles or pairs on or close to the ground, and always near water; tail is often pumped or wagged. Frequently emerges onto trails, roads, or clearings after heavy rains to forage around puddles. Song is very distinctive, starting with a few slow, sweet notes but quickly accelerating into a rapid series of loud chips, and slowing slightly at the end, *see-see-fwee-fwi-fi-t't't't't't't't't't't't't'di-di-dih*. Common call is a sharp, metallic *tik*.

5 MANGROVE WARBLER *Setophaga petechia* 12cm/4.5in

0–100m. Locally fairly common in mangroves; occasionally ventures to other nearby patches of trees, but not found any distance inland. Adult male's chestnut crown separates it from the migratory Yellow Warbler (with which it is lumped by some authorities). Female is very similar to Yellow Warbler, and the two may not be separable in the field; Mangrove is slightly duller and more olive, especially on the back. Immature male (not shown) has reduced chestnut on the crown, which makes the chestnut difficult to see, especially when viewed from below. Mangrove Warbler is typically found in pairs, foraging at all levels, even dropping to the ground during low tide. Song is a short and very sweet series, such as *sip-sip-see-twee-ee-ee-oo*, but quite variable. Call is a repeated *chak*.

6 YELLOW WARBLER *Setophaga aestiva* 12cm/4.5in

0–2800m. An uncommon boreal migrant; found in Ecuador from September to April. Most common in lightly wooded areas near the coast; rare in most of the rest of W Ecuador but a surprisingly regular visitor to the Quito Botanical Gardens. Male is bright yellow with chestnut underpart streaks, lacking Mangrove Warbler's chestnut crown. Female is rather plain and lacks streaking, but is brighter yellow than female of both Mangrove Warbler and Olive-crowned Yellowthroat (p. 350). Yellow Warbler is usually found alone and is not known to sing in Ecuador. Calls include a snappy *chip* and a loose *pek*.

Boreal winter visitors from North America, found in Ecuador mainly from October to April, with rare individuals arriving as early as September or lingering into May. Only Blackburnian Warbler is common in our region; others are uncommon to very rare. Several other species have reached our region as extremely rare vagrants and are not treated here (see Appendix I, p. 425); if encountered, they should be carefully documented. The range maps and the stated elevations indicate where each species is most often recorded, but as with all long-distance migrants, these birds can sometimes turn up in very unexpected places. All species on this page are arboreal and tend to be found singly, sometimes in small groups during migration. They frequently join mixed-species flocks. Basic plumage is usually retained until February, when birds begin molting into alternate plumage, completing molt by April. They are rather quiet in Ecuador; usually only chip notes are heard, which are not described here.

1 BLACKPOLL WARBLER *Setophaga striata* 13cm/5in

0–2800m. Rare (much more common in E); most often encountered in humid forest edge and light woodland in lowlands and foothills, with a few records from the Quito Botanical Gardens. Basic plumage is similar in male and female, and resembles that of Bay-breasted Warbler; Blackpoll lacks chestnut coloration on sides and flanks, and has yellowish feet and legs—the amount of yellow varies but should always be somewhat evident. Male in alternate plumage has a distinct black cap; alternate female (not shown) is similar but lacks the black cap and upperparts are tinged with olive; she can resemble Black-and-white Warbler (p. 358), but note Blackpoll's yellow leg color, lack of bold head stripes, and very different behavior.

2 BAY-BREASTED WARBLER *Setophaga castanea* 13cm/5in

0–1400m. Very rare; most records are from light woodland and humid forest edge in the lowlands and foothills. In basic plumage (similar in both sexes), distinguished from Blackpoll Warbler by entirely black feet and legs, and chestnut coloration on sides and flanks that contrasts with paler belly; the amount of chestnut varies and may be very faint or absent on some individuals. Alternate plumage is very unlikely to be seen in Ecuador, and female (not shown) is slightly duller than the male.

3 CERULEAN WARBLER *Setophaga cerulea* 12cm/4.5in

300–2000m. Rare; most records from W Ecuador come from humid forest and edge in the foothills. Alternate and basic plumages are similar. Adult male is distinctive if seen well; look especially for bluish upperparts and thin pectoral collar. Immature (not shown) and female are more difficult and somewhat variable, but note combination of bold white wing bars, yellowish superciliary, grayish to greenish upperparts, and yellowish or buff underparts showing indistinct (or no) streaking.

4 BLACKBURNIAN WARBLER *Setophaga fusca* 13cm/5in

300–3000m. Common in humid foothill and subtropical forest and edge; uncommon at the lower and upper elevation extremes. Alternate plumage male is striking and not likely to be mistaken. Female (not shown) is similar to basic plumage male, and though these plumages are duller than the alternate male, no other warbler in our range shares the combination of yellow throat and superciliary, gray cheek patch, and streaked sides and flanks.

bas. ♂ 4

alt. ♂ 4

bas. 1

alt. ♂ 1

bas. 2

alt. ♂ 2

♀ 3

♂ 3

MIGRATORY WARBLERS

Four more boreal migrants, gracing Ecuadorian forests from September to April. The species on this page are uncommon or rare, and while they often join mixed-species flocks, only one individual of a given species is normally encountered. ID of these species is usually straightforward. As with other warblers, they are arboreal and insectivorous. They are rather quiet in Ecuador; usually only chip notes are heard, which are not described here.

1 BLACK-AND-WHITE WARBLER *Mniotilta varia* 13cm/5in

200–2800m. Uncommon in humid foothill and subtropical forest and edge; rare at higher and lower elevations. Strongly patterned black-and-white plumage is almost unmistakable. Alternate and basic plumages are similar, though alternate plumage tends to be slightly glossier. Male Pacific Antwren (p. 248) is chunkier, has a different facial pattern, and very different behavior. Alternate female Blackpoll Warbler (p. 356) may appear similar to female but has yellow feet and legs and lacks the bold white superciliary. Black-and-white Warbler hitches along trunks and branches in a rather woodcreeper-like fashion.

2 TENNESSEE WARBLER *Oreothlypis peregrina* 12cm/4.5in

1000–2800m. Rare in humid foothill and subtropical forest, edge, and light woodland; there are also numerous records from the Quito Botanical Gardens. Small, with thin, pointed bill, plain wings, and faint, pale superciliary. Only alternate plumage male and female are shown. Basic plumage (both male and female) and immature resemble alternate female but show variable amounts of yellow on underparts, head, and nape.

3 CANADA WARBLER *Cardellina canadensis* 13cm/5in

800–2800m. Uncommon in humid foothill and subtropical forest and edge; rare at higher elevations. Alternate and basic plumage are similar. Combination of gray upperparts, yellow underparts, and streaked necklace is unique in W Ecuador. Female's necklace is often very indistinct, and it can be helpful to note her white eye-ring, yellow supraloral, and white crissum. Canada Warbler often forages at rather low levels in trees and shrubs.

4 AMERICAN REDSTART *Setophaga ruticilla* 13cm/5in

200–2800m. Uncommon in humid forest edge and light woodland from lowlands to subtropics; rarely higher. Alternate and basic plumage are similar. Black, orange, and white male should be easy to ID. Female is much plainer, but yellow tail, wing, and pectoral patches along with plain face separate her from other mostly gray passerines. A hyperactive little bird, constantly flaring tail and wings, exposing their bright colors, as it dashes after insects.

Large to very large tropical orioles well known for their large, hanging, woven nests. Plumage is similar in both sexes, but male is much bigger. All adults display bright-colored irides; immatures' irides are dark. All species are gregarious, often occurring in large, noisy flocks. With the notable exception of Yellow-billed Cacique, they are conspicuous and easy to see. Oropendolas and Yellow-rumped Cacique always nest communally in large, exposed trees; other caciques place their nests in more hidden, dispersed locations. All are omnivorous, eating a variety of fruit, insects, and just about any other animal that is small enough for them to catch and swallow.

1 CHESTNUT-HEADED OROPENDOLA *Psarocolius wagleri* 28–35cm/11–14in

0–800m. Rare in humid lowland and foothill forest, edge, and wooded clearings; now seldom encountered in Ecuador due to widespread deforestation. Large size and bulbous, ivory-colored bill set this species apart from all others in our region. Male display song is a splattering rasp, vaguely resembling the sound of a bucket of thick mud being dumped onto the ground. Calls include various soft clucks and low, liquid notes.

2 RUSSET-BACKED OROPENDOLA *Psarocolius angustifrons* 35–48cm/14–19in

1000–2400m. Uncommon in humid foothill and subtropical forest and edge. Peach-colored bill and yellow forehead differentiate it from Chestnut-headed Oropendola, which inhabits lower elevations. Male display song rather variable, usually a rising series of liquid notes, often mixed with metallic churrs. Most common call is a rising *chuk*.

3 YELLOW-RUMPED CACIQUE *Cacicus cela* 23–28cm/9–11in

0–800m. Fairly common in all types of wooded habitats, even in areas with just scattered trees in the lowlands; uncommon in the foothills. Yellow rump, crissum, and wings contrast with otherwise black plumage; bill dusky and iris pale blue. ID is usually easy, but see Lemon-rumped Tanager (p. 372). Yellow-rumped Cacique has an immense vocal repertoire, impossible to adequately describe here, but its calls frequently have a screeching, metallic quality; it also mimics other birds.

4 NORTHERN MOUNTAIN-CACIQUE *Cacicus leucoramphus* 24–28cm/9.5–11in

2000–3000m. Very limited distribution W of the continental divide in Ecuador; known only from subtropical and temperate forest in the Río Jubones valley SW of Cuenca; much more widespread in E. No overlap with the similar Yellow-rumped Cacique, which has yellow crissum and tail base and blue irides. Most common call is a series of whiny, nasal notes, e.g., *nyeah!-meh-meh-meh*. Sometimes lumped with Southern Mountain-Cacique (*C. chrysonotus*, not found in Ecuador), and simply called **Mountain Cacique**.

5 SCARLET-RUMPED CACIQUE *Cacicus microrhynchus* 20–24cm/8–9.5in

0–1300m. Fairly common in humid lowland and foothill forest. Note yellow bill and pale blue irides; scarlet rump is usually hidden by the wings and often not visible except in flight. If rump is not seen, this cacique can look quite similar to Yellow-billed Cacique, but that species has a paler bill, yellow irides, and has very different behavior, skulking in dense lower growth. Scarlet-rumped Cacique tends to travel in groups of several birds that move through mid to upper forest levels and often join mixed-species flocks. Vocalizations are varied and far-carrying, including a series of down-slurred screeches (e.g., *cheer!, cheer!, cheer!*), a fast, ringing *tu-tu-tu-tu-tu-tu-tu-tu*, and various single, clear whistles.

6 YELLOW-BILLED CACIQUE *Amblycercus holosericeus* 22–24cm/8.5–9.5in

0–3500m. Uncommon in dense undergrowth of deciduous and semi-humid forest in lowlands and foothills; also rare and local in *Chusquea* bamboo patches in subtropical and temperate forest. Plumage entirely glossy black, with no rump patch; pale yellowish-white bill and bright yellow irides are diagnostic. Otherwise, superficially similar to Scarlet-rumped Cacique (whose rump is often hidden) but with totally different behavior. Yellow-billed Cacique skulks in dense vegetation and is usually very hard to see; clear views can usually be obtained only by patiently peering through openings in the vegetation. Mostly located by voice; often gives a series of mellow, down-slurred whistles, e.g., *WEyou-WEyou-WEyou...*, or a nasal, whinnied *nyeh'd'd'd'd'd'd*.

Cowbirds are brood parasites; they lay eggs in the nests of other birds and take no part in the rearing of their young. Cowbirds fly in an undulating pattern, reminiscent of woodpecker flight. Scrub Blackbird is cowbird-like in appearance, but is not a brood parasite; the impressively large Great-tailed Grackle is restricted to coastal areas.

1 GIANT COWBIRD *Molothrus oryzivorus* 29–34cm/11.5–13.5in

0–2000m. Widespread but uncommon in clearings, lightly wooded areas, and forest edge from lowlands to subtropics. A large, bulky blackbird best identified by its large size and iris color (red in male, yellow or orange in female). Female is vaguely similar to male Great-tailed Grackle but is much smaller, shorter-tailed, and less iridescent. Flying birds have a hunchback shape that facilitates ID at a considerable distance. More solitary than other cowbirds, typically found alone or sometimes in small groups. Giant is an obligate brood parasite specializing in caciques and oropendolas, though occasionally also parasitizes other larger birds such as jays. Vocalizations include various jarring, screechy notes as well as soft grunts.

2 SHINY COWBIRD *Molothrus bonariensis* 19–21cm/7.5–8.5in

0–2800m. Common to abundant in open habitats in the lowlands and foothills; uncommon to rare at higher elevations; most often found near farms and livestock. Adult male is black with a glossy, iridescent blue sheen. Immature male (not shown) may lack iridescence, and can look much like Scrub Blackbird, but has a shorter, more wedge-shaped bill. Female is dull, but with her uniformly brown plumage and wedge-shaped bill is not particularly similar to any other bird in this region. Shiny Cowbird is rather gregarious, usually occurring in flocks, sometimes very large ones where food is abundant; forages on the ground, eating both seeds and insects. It is an obligate brood parasite, laying eggs in the nests of a wide variety of smaller birds, mainly passerines. Male has a surprisingly beautiful, liquid song consisting of rapid twitters mixed with soft, musical notes.

3 SCRUB BLACKBIRD *Dives warszewiczi* 22cm/8.5in

0–2400m. Common and widespread in open habitats, and spreading due to deforestation. Sexes are similar. Easily mistaken for male Shiny Cowbird, Scrub Blackbird has a longer, less wedge-shaped bill and never shows iridescence in its plumage. Voice is also very different: song is variable but always a very loud series of sharp and often inflected notes, e.g., *ker-CHEEder, ker-CHEEder, ker-CHEEder*, usually given from a conspicuous perch such as a wire or a post, and while pumping its body up and down; call is a descending *tseee*. Usually found in pairs or small flocks, not associating with cowbirds, and forages both on the ground and in trees.

4 GREAT-TAILED GRACKLE *Quiscalus mexicanus* 33–44cm/13–17.5in

0–100m. Locally common in and near mangroves and estuaries near the coast, including cities and towns; not found any distance inland. Large and lanky, with long, thin bill; male, with its long tail, iridescent plumage, and yellow irides, is quite impressive and hard to mistake, but see Giant Cowbird. Smaller female is brown, but large size and yellow irides also preclude confusion. Great-tailed forages mainly on or near the ground, marching around fearlessly. During the day found in pairs or small groups, but often roosts in large, noisy aggregations. Voice consists of various loud, tortured squeals along with soft rattles.

♂ 4

♀ 4

Ecuador's orioles are similarly plumaged but easily identified if the relevant field marks can be seen; sexes are alike. Meadowlarks are sexually dimorphic and occur in open areas away from forest; they forage on the ground, and often perch on fence posts or other exposed spots, especially singing males.

1 WHITE-EDGED ORIOLE   *Icterus graceannae*   21cm/8.5in

0–1500m. Fairly common in deciduous forest, edge, and desert scrub in W and SW. Distinguished from Yellow-tailed Oriole by black-and-white (not yellow) undertail and solid white wing patch (not just white feather edging). Immature (not shown) is duller, with reduced black on throat, but still possesses white wedge on wing. White-edged Oriole is usually found in pairs or small groups, conspicuously foraging at any level in the forest. Song is a varied series of low, nasal notes and rasps.

2 YELLOW-TAILED ORIOLE   *Icterus mesomelas*   22cm/8.5in

0–1700m. Fairly common in a wide variety of wooded habitats in both humid and dry areas, but avoids areas of extensive humid forest. Similar to White-edged Oriole, but note yellow undertail and white on wing restricted to feather edges. Immature (not shown) is dull, with reduced black on throat, but still has yellow undertail. Behavior similar to that of White-edged, but Yellow-tailed Oriole is much more tolerant of human-modified habitats, even living in oil palm and banana plantations. Song is a sweet, repetitive series of up-and-down whistles, starting out quietly and then gradually increasing in volume. *Note:* **Yellow-backed Oriole** (*I. chrysater*; not shown) has been recorded on one occasion in mangroves in extreme NW Ecuador near the Colombian border. Its yellow mantle and unmarked black wings separate it from Yellow-tailed Oriole.

3 RED-BREASTED MEADOWLARK   *Sturnella militaris*   19cm/7.5in

0–800m. A newcomer to our region, first found in W Ecuador in the mid-2000s. Occurs locally in grassy pastures in the lowlands and foothills of the NW, but likely to spread. Its zone of overlap with Peruvian Meadowlark (currently only near the coast in the far NW), is also likely to expand. Male Red-breasted lacks the bold white superciliary of Peruvian, though in fresh plumage it can show a hint of one. Female Red-breasted Meadowlark can be distinguished from female Peruvian by dark line (bordering the superciliary) that extends from eye toward nape. Song of Red-breasted Meadowlark consists of a few short, sharp notes followed by a drawn-out, buzzy rasp. Call is a fast series of sharp, tinkly notes. Formerly called **Red-breasted Blackbird**.

4 PERUVIAN MEADOWLARK   *Sturnella bellicosa*   21cm/8.5in

0–3400m. Fairly common in a wide variety of open habitats, including farms and deserts, from the lowlands to the central highlands. While widespread in our region, it does not occur in the Andes around Quito and in the heavily birded areas W of the city. Male is distinctive; bold white superciliary separates it from male Red-breasted Blackbird. Female and immature male (not shown) have varying amounts of red staining on the underparts, and can be separated from Red-breasted Blackbird by dark cheek and lack of a discrete dark postocular line. Song is similar to that of Red-breasted Blackbird, but introductory notes of Peruvian Meadowlark song are more varied and musical. Most common call is a single *chuck*.

BUSH-TANAGERS (CHLOROSPINGUSES)

Bush-tanagers inhabit Andean cloud forest, and at least one species can be found at virtually any elevation. All share similar behavior and are not sexually dimorphic. They inhabit mid to upper levels of the forest, feed on small fruits, insects, and other arthropods, are usually found in pairs or small groups, and often join mixed-species flocks. Despite their being clad in rather dull colors, ID is usually straightforward; pay special attention to eye color, throat color, and the presence or absence of a breast band. The genus *Chlorospingus* recently was transferred from the tanager family (Thraupidae) to the emberizid finches (Emberizidae); these birds (all on this page except for Gray-hooded Bush Tanager) are now sometimes given the English name "chlorospingus." We feel that name is awkward and the change unnecessary, so prefer to retain the traditional "bush-tanager."

1 COMMON BUSH-TANAGER *Chlorospingus flavopectus* 14cm/5.5in

600–1500m. In W Ecuador, range is restricted to a small area of humid foothill forest in the SW Andes, locally fairly common and most easily seen at the Buenaventura Reserve. Ashy-throated Bush-Tanager, which often occurs with this species, is similar but lacks white irides and has a "cleaner" gray head, a white throat, and a well-defined white patch on lower underparts. Song is a long series of chips that accelerates into a fast chatter at the end.

2 DUSKY BUSH-TANAGER *Chlorospingus semifuscus* 14cm/5.5in

900–2400m. Found in humid foothill and subtropical forest and edge in the NW; at its upper elevation limit it can be one of the most common birds, though it is uncommon at the lower limit. Note rather dull plumage and ruby irides. Lacks the yellow breast band of Ashy-throated and the yellow throat of Yellow-throated Bush-Tanager. Song is a long series of *tsip* notes that sometimes ends in a series of pulsating chatters.

3 YELLOW-THROATED BUSH-TANAGER *Chlorospingus flavigularis* 15cm/6in

300–1800m. Common in humid foothill and subtropical forest along most of the W slope; uncommon and local at lower elevations in the coastal range. Yellow throat that contrasts strongly with gray breast distinguishes it from all other bush-tanagers in W Ecuador. Song is a long series of wheezy *dzip* notes; other vocalizations include a fast chatter, *chak* notes, and soft grunts.

4 YELLOW-GREEN BUSH-TANAGER *Chlorospingus flavovirens* 14cm/5.5in

500–1200m. Rare and local in humid foothill forest in NW. Uniform olive plumage, including entire underparts, separates it from other bush-tanagers. Similar to Ochre-breasted Tanager (p. 370) but much smaller and with a much smaller bill. Song (rarely heard) is *zit-zit-twi'ti't'dit*, or similar variations. Calls include *chip-tsip* and a series of high *seep* notes.

5 ASHY-THROATED BUSH-TANAGER *Chlorospingus canigularis* 14cm/5.5in

400–1500m. Uncommon to fairly common in humid foothill forest; rare and local at the N limit of its W Ecuador range (e.g., Milpe Bird Sanctuary and the Mindo area). Combination of dark irides and yellowish breast band is distinctive; compare especially with duskier Common Bush-Tanager, which is similar but has obvious white irides, dusky-gray head, dirty-white throat, and less well-defined white patch on lower underparts. Vocalizations of Ashy-throated are not especially memorable, often a series of tinkly notes interspersed with sharp *chaks*; also gives soft twitters.

6 GRAY-HOODED BUSH-TANAGER *Cnemoscopus rubrirostris* 16cm/6.5in

2400–3200m. Very rare (much more common in E) in humid temperate forest in the NW. Not closely related to the other bush-tanagers on this page. Distinctive, with a pink bill, gray hood, and yellow lower underparts. Constantly pumps tail. Song is a lazy *swee?, dju, swee?, dju…*, repeated for long periods. Calls include an assortment of *chip, tsit, zit*, and other similar notes.

Despite their English names, tanagers of the genus *Piranga* are now classified as cardinals (Cardinalidae). All are sexually dimorphic. They inhabit forest canopy, consume both fruit and insects, and sometimes join mixed-species flocks. These species are not known to visit feeders in W Ecuador. Except for the migratory species, they are almost always found in pairs or small family groups.

1 HEPATIC TANAGER *Piranga flava* 17cm/6.5in

0–2500m. Fairly common in deciduous and semi-humid forest and edge in W and SW; does not inhabit the more humid forests of the NW. Both sexes similar to the migratory Summer Tanager. Hepatic Tanager has a mostly gray bill that may appear paler at the base, but never shows the horn color seen on most Summer Tanagers. Hepatic has a distinct "tooth" midway along its upper mandible, a feature lacking in Summer, though this can be seen only at close range. Hepatic Tanager may also show dark lores, though this is not a very reliable feature. Song is a leisurely series of chirpy whistles that randomly rise and fall in pitch. Call is a descending *wi-di-dit*. Birds in W Ecuador, along with the rest of South America and S Central America are sometimes split as **Tooth-billed Tanager** (*P. lutea*).

2 SUMMER TANAGER *Piranga rubra* 17cm/6.5in

0–2800m. A fairly common boreal migrant to humid and semi-humid forest edge and wooded clearings from lowlands to subtropics; regularly reaches as high as Quito; occurs in Ecuador from September to April. Very similar to Hepatic Tanager, which can occur with it in semi-humid areas; see that species for ID details, and keep in mind that basic Summer Tanagers can have bills nearly as dark as Hepatics. Immature male Summer Tanager is mottled red and yellow (can look orange) and might be mistaken for Red-hooded Tanager, however that species is much more clean-cut, with red restricted to head and breast. Common call given on wintering grounds is a descending, rattled *wididididit*, usually longer than the corresponding call of Hepatic Tanager.

3 SCARLET TANAGER *Piranga olivacea* 17cm/6.5in

0–1500m; rarely higher. A rare boreal migrant (more common in E) to humid forest edge and lightly wooded clearings from the lowlands to the subtropics, occasionally as high as Quito; recorded from September to April. Female (not shown) resembles basic plumage male but shows yellowish-green margins to the dark wings. Males usually obtain alternate plumage by around January. Dark wings in all plumages immediately distinguish Scarlet from both Summer and Hepatic Tanagers, which are otherwise similar. Call given on wintering grounds is *pit-djeer*.

4 WHITE-WINGED TANAGER *Piranga leucoptera* 14cm/5.5in

600–2300m. Fairly common resident of humid foothill and subtropical forest. White wing bars in both sexes immediately separate it from other similar species, especially Scarlet Tanager. Pairs are usually seen while accompanying mixed-species canopy flocks, and often perch in the open on treetops. Typical song is a very sweet, descending *see-see-see-see*, sometimes followed by a higher-pitched note.

5 RED-HOODED TANAGER *Piranga rubriceps* 18cm/7in

2200–3000m. Very rare in humid subtropical and temperate forest in NW; few recent records in our region (more common on E slope). Male has a slightly larger red hood than female. Striking red and yellow plumage unlike any other Ecuadorian bird (but see immature male Summer Tanager). Usually found in small groups that feed in the forest canopy and often perches conspicuously on treetops. Song is a high, sweet *seeseeseeseesee*, sometimes followed by a *sooee*?

A set of mainly lower-elevation passerines that are generally lacking in bright colors. All eat mostly insects but also consume some fruit, and spend much of the day amid mixed-species flocks. Only White-lined Tanager regularly visits feeders. *Chlorothraupis* has recently been reclassified and placed with the cardinals (Cardinalidae).

1 WHITE-SHOULDERED TANAGER *Tachyphonus luctuosus* 14cm/5.5in

0–1500m. Fairly common in humid lowland and foothill forest and edge. Distinctive male is all black with a bold white shoulder patch—the white is always visible, unlike the mostly hidden white underwing of White-lined Tanager. Female is very different, with yellow underparts and gray head; no other bird in range is really similar, but compare with bush-tanagers (p. 366). Usually encountered in pairs and almost always with mixed-species flocks in mid to upper levels of the forest. Rather quiet; occasionally a soft *tsip-tsip* or a buzzy rattle is given.

2 TAWNY-CRESTED TANAGER *Tachyphonus delatrii* 14cm/5.5in

0–1100m. Fairly common in humid lowland and foothill forest and edge. Male is unique with its striking tawny "mohawk" crest; female is plain chocolate brown, not bright cinnamon-rufous like female White-lined Tanager. Tawny-crested Tanager is usually found in groups, of sometimes 10 or more birds that move noisily through lower growth, tending to hug the edge of the forest; also joins mixed-species flocks. Foraging birds give a variety of sharp *chek* and chip notes, and sometimes a rapid twitter.

3 WHITE-LINED TANAGER *Tachyphonus rufus* 17cm/6.5in

0–2000m. Fairly common at edge of humid secondary forest, lighter woodland, and clearings with scattered trees; avoids dense forest. Male is pure black with white wing linings that are often completely invisible at rest, but sometimes show as a narrow white edge bordering wing. Female is uniform cinnamon-rufous, not dark chocolate like female Tawny-crested Tanager. Almost always found in close-knit pairs, and the combination of a black bird and rufous bird moving together can be a useful ID feature; silvery color and shape of bill also help distinguish male from other all-black birds of similar size. Rarely heard to vocalize; song (usually given at dawn) is a long, leisurely series of chirps that varies slightly in pitch; call is a sharp *pek* repeated every few seconds. A regular visitor to feeders at Mirador Río Blanco in the town of San Miguel de Los Bancos near the Milpe Bird Sanctuary.

4 OCHRE-BREASTED TANAGER *Chlorothraupis stolzmanni* 18cm/7in

300–1500m. Fairly common in humid foothill forest edge and adjacent wooded clearings. Note bulky shape, mostly uniform ochre coloration, and stout bill, which the bird often opens very wide while singing, exposing its yellow mouth lining. Somewhat similar to the rare Yellow-green Bush-Tanager (p. 366), but much larger, with a notably bulkier bill. During much of the year, birds sing loudly and incessantly at dawn from fairly exposed perches. An hour or so afterward, they stop singing and spend most of the rest of the day with mixed-species flocks at mid to upper forest levels. Song is a very loud, long series of whistles interspersed with high-pitched buzzy churrs (sounding like a jumbled chorus of several different species). Common call is a short, twangy rattle.

5 LEMON-SPECTACLED TANAGER *Chlorothraupis olivacea* 17cm/6.5in

0–500m. Uncommon and local inside humid primary forest in lowlands of far NW. Does not tolerate any significant habitat degradation, therefore it now survives only in remote forested areas such as Playa de Oro. Very distinctive, with bold yellow spectacles and throat. Most often encountered accompanying understory mixed-species flocks. Its song, delivered only early in the morning, is a mellow series of whistles that often accelerates and rises in pitch partway through. Typical call, given frequently throughout the day, is a short, fast series of low, squeaky notes that usually rises and then falls in pitch.

The first three species on this page are some of the most common and conspicuous lower-elevation species in W Ecuador; voices are no particularly help for ID so are not described. The remaining two, while somewhat less common, are still regularly encountered at higher elevations.

1 LEMON-RUMPED TANAGER *Ramphocelus icteronotus* 18cm/7in

0–2000m. Common to locally abundant in humid and semi-humid forest edge, light woodland, and clearings with scattered trees from the lowlands to the subtropics; rarely or never enters dense forest. Velvet-black male has a huge yellow rump patch that extends to flanks, sometimes giving the illusion that there is yellow in the wing. Inexperienced observers may confuse it with Yellow-rumped Cacique (p. 360), though bill shape and color are different. The brown and yellow female is so different from male that she is often confusing to first-time visitors, even though no other bird is particularly similar; note yellow rump and stout bluish-gray bill. Usually seen in small groups that conspicuously forage in the open, often with Blue-gray and Palm Tanagers, and frequently visits feeders. Sometimes lumped with **Flame-rumped Tanager** (*R. flammigerus*).

2 BLUE-GRAY TANAGER *Thraupis episcopus* 16cm/6.5in

0–2800m. Common and widespread in virtually any wooded habitat from the lowlands to the subtropics, though tends to avoid forest interior; uncommon and local at its upper elevation limit. No similar species occurs together with it. Sexes are identical; immature (not shown) is similar but duller. A very adaptable species, feeds on fruit, insects, and other arthropods, foraging at all levels, from canopy to low level in shrubs at edge, and common at feeders; often joins mixed-species flocks.

3 PALM TANAGER *Thraupis palmarum* 17cm/6.5in

0–1900m. Common in all types of wooded habitats in humid areas from lowlands to subtropics; not found in extremely dry areas, and a rare wanderer above about 1600m. Sexes are similar. Olive-washed gray plumage with contrasting dark flight feathers is diagnostic, though keep in mind that under poor lighting conditions, the greenish tones are not distinguishable and the bird appears mostly gray. Behavior is similar to that of Blue-gray Tanager, with which it often occurs. As its name suggests, Palm Tanager is often found in palm trees, though it is by no means restricted to them. It only occasionally visits feeders.

4 BLUE-CAPPED TANAGER *Thraupis cyanocephala* 17cm/6.5in

1500–3000m. Fairly common in humid subtropical and temperate forest and edge. Sexes are alike. Readily identifiable if seen well, though under poor viewing conditions the blue crown and nape may not be discernible; note contrst between mostly dark gray underparts and brighter olive-yellow upperparts; yellow thighs are often concealed. Often found in pairs and regularly joins mixed-species flocks, feeding on fruit in the canopy but also preying on insects. Song is rapid, high-pitched series of squeaky notes, sometimes with a warbling quality; at other times the pitch stays mostly level. Does not visit feeders.

5 BLUE-AND-YELLOW TANAGER *Pipraeidea bonariensis* 17cm/6.5in

1800–3200m. Locally fairly common in lightly wooded areas in the central highlands, including towns and cities such as Quito. Colorful adult male is not likely to be mistaken, but female and immature male (not shown) can be very dull and confusing, even appearing uniformly drab brown in poor light. However, the typical tanager bill and body shape should be evident, and the very few other tanagers that might occur with this species all have much brighter plumage. Often inconspicuous, tends to favor shaded, leafy cover, but may perch in the open in early mornings or late afternoons. Song is quite variable but usually consists of a series of sweet whistles that alternate up and down in pitch, e.g., *see-su-swee-su-swee-su-swee-su-swee*. Does not visit feeders.

Spectacular humid forest tanagers; the first two are lowland to foothill species, while the others occur at higher elevations; none show significant sexual dimorphism. All of these species are primarily frugivorous, though some insects and arthropods are taken; none visit feeders. They sometimes join mixed-species flocks but, except for Grass-green Tanager, are more often seen away from them.

1 GOLDEN-CHESTED TANAGER *Bangsia rothschildi* 16cm/6.5in

100–700m. Rare in humid lowland and foothill forest and edge in far NW. Striking yellow breast and throat are distinctive and no similar species occurs in its limited range. Tends to be encountered alone, often perched for long periods on an exposed branch in mid-story or subcanopy. Typical vocalization is an odd, buzzy *zhwee?*, often repeated several times in fairly rapid succession.

2 MOSS-BACKED TANAGER *Bangsia edwardsi* 16cm/6.5in

400–1800m. Locally fairly common (e.g., the Mashpi area) in humid foothill and subtropical forest in NW. Its range appears to be contracting to the N, and it is no longer seen in areas such as Milpe Bird Sanctuary, where it was once fairly common. Blue and olive-yellow plumage is quite distinctive; in poor light or fog, the yellow breast spot often stands out as the most obvious feature. Usually found alone or in well-spaced pairs, often perching conspicuously on an open branch. Most common vocalization is a rapid rattle that often rises and falls; also gives a down-slurred *tseee*.

3 GRASS-GREEN TANAGER *Chlorornis riefferii* 20cm/8in

2000–3500m. Fairly common in humid subtropical and temperate forest and edge. Green with red face, crissum, bill and legs. This gem is one of the most uniquely colored birds in all of the Andes, and will not be mistaken if seen clearly. Usually encountered in groups of four or five birds that are almost always amid mixed-species flocks. Vocalizations have a very nasal quality and include metallic trills and single *tink* notes.

4 PURPLISH-MANTLED TANAGER *Iridosornis porphyrocephalus* 16cm/6.5in

1700–2400m. Locally fairly common in humid subtropical forest and edge in a very small area near the Colombian border; in recent years most often seen near the pass along the Chical road. A few old records from farther S may only pertain to wandering birds. Mostly blue with a bright yellow throat and chestnut crissum. This is another striking tanager that cannot be mistaken in range with a good view. Most often found in pairs at lower to mid levels in stunted, melastome-dominated cloud forest, often hopping around conspicuously in the open. Song is a high-pitched, wavery, sibilant whistle that falls and then rises, e.g., *tseeeeeeyou?*

5 GOLDEN-CROWNED TANAGER *Iridosornis rufivertex* 16cm/6.5in

2500–3500m. Uncommon in humid temperate forest edge and adjacent scrubby clearings; in our region, most easily found at Yanacocha Reserve. This spectacular tanager is unique in our range and will not be mistaken if seen well; the golden-yellow crown stands out like a beacon even under foggy conditions. Typically ranges in pairs or small family groups that forage unobtrusively in lower growth. Rarely heard song is a chattery series of high-pitched chips. Calls include various high-pitched *tsip*, *seet*, or buzzy *zeet* notes.

6 BUFF-BREASTED MOUNTAIN-TANAGER *Dubusia taeniata* 19cm/7.5in

2500–3600m. Uncommon in humid temperate forest and edge. Pale blue superciliary (composed of tiny streaks) and buffy breast band separate this species from the much larger Hooded Mountain-Tanager (p. 376). Often found alone; quite shy and inconspicuous compared to other mountain-tanagers, typically staying well hidden inside vegetation. Its presence is often first revealed by its song, a descending *FEEE-beee*, or a more complicated series such as *FEEE-FEEE-bee*. with the last note lower pitched.

MOUNTAIN-TANAGERS

Seeing these large and colorful Andean cloud-forest tanagers is often a highlight of a trip to Ecuador. Sexes are alike, and behavior of all species is fairly similar. They are usually encountered in small groups, which often join mixed-species flocks, feeding on both fruit and insects in the forest canopy, occasionally descending lower if there is an abundant food source. Most species are relatively conspicuous and easy to observe, but only Blue-winged and Black-chinned Mountain-Tanagers visit feeders. Since voice is rarely necessary to ID these species, it is not described here.

1 BLUE-WINGED MOUNTAIN-TANAGER *Anisognathus somptuosus* 18cm/7in

1100–2500m. Common in humid subtropical forest and edge; rare in the foothills at its lower elevation limit. Striking bright yellow crown and underparts, black mask and upperparts, and dual blue wing patches distinguish this species. The more range-restricted Black-chinned Mountain-Tanager differs by orange-tinged underparts, narrow yellow crown stripe, and yellow-olive mantle; note also, black on face extends to chin. Blue-winged Mountain-Tanager visits feeders in the Tandayapa Valley.

2 BLACK-CHINNED MOUNTAIN-TANAGER *Anisognathus notabilis* 18cm/7in

1400–2200m; lower in SW. Uncommon to locally fairly common in humid subtropical forest and edge. Frequently occurs with Blue-winged Mountain-Tanager, which usually outnumbers it. Black-chinned Mountain-Tanager differs by having a bright yellow-olive mantle, orange-tinged yellow underparts, a single blue patch on each wing, smaller crown stripe, and black chin. Visits feeders at a few locations in the Mindo area, e.g., Paz de las Aves Refuge.

3 SCARLET-BELLIED MOUNTAIN-TANAGER *Anisognathus igniventris* 18cm/7in

2300–3800m. Common in humid temperate forest and edge at high elevations; rare at its lower elevation limit, where perhaps present only as a seasonal wanderer. This beautiful and uniquely colored tanager, with its dashing scarlet, black, and blue plumage, is not likely to be mistaken. While usually found in small groups, occasionally (seasonally?) gathers in flocks of 20 or more birds.

4 LACRIMOSE MOUNTAIN-TANAGER *Anisognathus lacrymosus* 18cm/7in

2500–3600m. On the W slope, this species is restricted to a small area of temperate forest SW of Cuenca. There are also a few sight records from the NW (e.g., Yanacocha Reserve); these may pertain to wandering birds from the E slope, where the species is common. Mostly blue and yellow with a black face; best identified by the yellow facial spots ("tears") below eye and on sides of nape.

5 HOODED MOUNTAIN-TANAGER *Buthraupis montana* 23cm/9in

2300–3600m. Fairly common in humid temperate forest; rare and perhaps seasonal down into the subtropics. A notably large and bulky tanager with a ruby-red eye. Distinguished from Black-chested Mountain-Tanager by blue (not olive) back and entirely black head lacking blue crown. Buff-breasted Mountain-Tanager (p. 374) displays a distinct superciliary, buffy breast band, and dark irides.

6 BLACK-CHESTED MOUNTAIN-TANAGER *Cnemathraupis eximia* 20cm/8in

2700–3800m. Uncommon and local in humid temperate forest and edge; regularly encountered at the Yanacocha Reserve. Green mantle, dark irides, and black bib separate this gorgeous bird from other mountain-tanagers. Blue crown is often inconspicuous.

No species scream "Andean avifauna" more than *Tangara* tanagers. These small colorful birds are found virtually anywhere there is humid forest, including forest edge and even rather disturbed areas with scattered trees, as long as fruit is available. They are usually seen in mixed-species flocks with other *Tangara*s, along with other tanagers, warblers, flycatchers, barbets, etc. While mainly sticking to the canopy, they readily come down lower if there is an abundant food source, such as a fruiting bush or a feeder. All are mainly frugivorous but also take insects and other arthropods. Voices are not distinctive without significant field experience, and are rarely needed for ID, so they are not described here. The species on this page are not sexually dimorphic.

1 GOLDEN TANAGER *Tangara arthus* 14cm/5.5in

500–2400m. Common in humid foothill and subtropical forest and edge; ranges at lower elevations in the SW. Rich, deep yellow-orange, with round black auricular spot and black-striped mantle and wings. Emerald Tanager (p. 382) has a similar pattern, but is bright green, and auricular patch is crescent-shaped. Silver-throated Tanager is yellower, lacks the auricular patch, and has narrow black malar and pale throat. Golden Tanager regularly visits feeders.

2 SILVER-THROATED TANAGER *Tangara icterocephala* 13cm/5in

200–1700m. Fairly common in humid foothill and subtropical forest and edge; uncommon and local at its upper elevation limit (e.g., Tandayapa Valley), and perhaps only a sporadic wanderer to the lowlands. Mostly yellow with a contrasting white throat; not likely to be misidentified with a good view, but compare Golden Tanager, which lacks the white throat and has a black auricular patch. A regular visitor to feeders at Mirador Río Blanco in the town of San Miguel de Los Bancos.

3 GOLDEN-NAPED TANAGER *Tangara ruficervix* 13cm/5in

700–2400m. Fairly common in humid subtropical forest; ranges down into the foothills in SW (e.g., Buenaventura Reserve). Mostly bright bluish turquoise with black mask and buffy lower underparts; golden "nape" is actually a small, and often rather inconspicuous patch on hind-crown. Occasionally visits feeders in the Tandayapa Valley.

4 METALLIC-GREEN TANAGER *Tangara labradorides* 13cm/5in

1300–2400m. Uncommon to fairly common in humid subtropical forest. This bird's English name is very misleading, as it is mainly pale turquoise and neither metallic nor green. The black wings, mask, and crown are the best ID features, though also note the peach-colored crissum. Pale forehead area separating the mask and the crown often gives the impression of a white superciliary. Metallic-green Tanager does not visit feeders.

5 BERYL-SPANGLED TANAGER *Tangara nigroviridis* 13cm/5in

700–2500m. Common in humid subtropical forest; occurs down into the foothills in SW (e.g., Buenaventura Reserve). This beautiful tanager has a unique plumage, and no other species is really similar. The black spots and scales that dominate its turquoise plumage can stand out even under foggy conditions; also note black mask and pale crown. Visits feeders only occasionally.

6 BLUE-AND-BLACK TANAGER *Tangara vassorii* 13cm/5in

2000–3600m. Fairly common in humid subtropical and temperate forest. Bright ultramarine blue with black flight feathers, tail, and narrow black mask. No really similar species, but blue plumage and masked look could suggest certain flowerpiercers (p. 398) if seen under poor viewing conditions; flowerpiercers have hooked bills, and none shows black flight feathers and tail. Does not visit feeders.

Five more Andean *Tangara* tanagers. See p. 378 for general genus characteristics. Scrub Tanager is exceptional in that, at least in Ecuador, it is rarely found in humid forest. Black-capped and Silver-backed Tanagers are sexually dimorphic; the other species on this page are not.

1 SAFFRON-CROWNED TANAGER   *Tangara xanthocephala*   13cm/5in

1500–2300m. Fairly common in humid subtropical forest and edge near the Colombian border; uncommon farther S and very rare in the Tandayapa-Mindo area; this species is much more common on E slopes. Mostly turquoise, with black mask bordered by yellow crown and neck. In very foggy conditions or poor light it might be confused with Flame-faced Tanager, but that species has a black mantle and dark wings with distinct pale markings. Saffron-crowned Tanager is not known to visit feeders in W Ecuador.

2 FLAME-FACED TANAGER   *Tangara parzudakii*   13cm/5in

700–2400m. Fairly common in humid foothill and subtropical forest and edge. Strikingly patterned with orange, yellow, and black head and black mantle. Immature (not shown) is similar but orange on head is replaced with yellow. Saffron-crowned Tanager lacks the black mantle and wings. Flame-faced Tanager is a regular visitor at feeders.

3 BLACK-CAPPED TANAGER   *Tangara heinei*   13cm/5in

1100–2400m. Fairly common in humid foothill and subtropical forest edge and lightly wooded areas; less tied to forest than other *Tangara* that share its range. Handsome male is distinctive with his blue and turquoise plumage and black cap. Female is much duller, but no other bird in range has the combination of green body, turquoise hood, and dark streaking on throat and breast. No overlap with Silver-backed Tanager. Occasionally visits feeders in the Tandayapa Valley.

4 SILVER-BACKED TANAGER   *Tangara viridicollis*   13cm/5in

1300–2800m. Fairly common in humid subtropical and temperate forest in far S Ecuador. Unique male displays black head, neck, and underparts, rufous throat, and silvery mantle. Female is very different; note combination of mostly green upperparts, rufous throat, and pale gray belly. No overlap with Black-capped Tanager. Silver-backed Tanager does not visit feeders in Ecuador. Also called **Silvery Tanager**.

5 SCRUB TANAGER   *Tangara vitriolina*   14cm/5.5in

800–2800m. Fairly common in scrub, light woodland, parks, and gardens in inter-Andean valleys from the Colombian border S to the Quito area. There are few scattered records from humid subtropical forest in NW, though it is unknown whether these are simply wandering birds or its range is actually expanding. The only *Tangara* over most of its range; no other similar bird displays combination of mostly blue-gray plumage with rufous cap and black mask. Occasionally visits feeders.

Six more fabulous *Tangara* tanagers found in humid forest at lower to mid elevations. The species on this page are not sexually dimorphic, and ID is usually straightforward. See p. 378 for general information on the genus.

1 GRAY-AND-GOLD TANAGER   *Tangara palmeri* 15cm/6in

100–1200m. Uncommon to locally fairly common in humid lowland and foothill forest and edge in the NW. Black, gray, and white plumage, with gold tinge to black-speckled breast, is completely unlike that of any other tanager. The black mask and breast spotting stand out even under poor lighting conditions. Gray-and-gold Tanager does not visit feeders.

2 BLUE-WHISKERED TANAGER   *Tangara johannae* 13cm/5in

0–600m. Rare and local in humid lowland and lower foothill forest and edge, mostly in the far NW, though still occasionally seen as far S as Río Silanche Bird Sanctuary. This species is very sensitive to habitat disturbance, and its range is contracting to the N due to rampant deforestation. Green with a mostly black face and throat; blue whisker distinguishes it from Emerald Tanager, with which it frequently travels in the same mixed-species flocks. Blue-whiskered Tanager does not visit feeders.

3 EMERALD TANAGER   *Tangara florida* 13cm/5in

100–1200m. Uncommon to locally fairly common in humid lowland and foothill forest and edge in the NW. Emerald green with largely black wings and black auricular patch; overall pattern similar to that of Golden Tanager (p. 378), but green replaces rich yellow-orange, and auricular patch is crescent-shaped. Blue-whiskered Tanager shows a black face and throat and has a blue whisker. Emerald Tanager is a rare visitor to feeders at Mirador Río Blanco in the town of San Miguel de Los Bancos.

4 BLUE-NECKED TANAGER   *Tangara cyanicollis* 13cm/5in

0–1500m. Fairly common in humid lowland and foothill forest, edge, and adjacent wooded clearings. Turquoise hood contrasts strongly with darker rest of body; yellow patch on wing coverts and dark lower underparts help separate it from Golden-hooded Tanager. Blue-necked is also somewhat similar to Scarlet-thighed Dacnis (p. 390), but that species' blue hood is broken by a black throat, and it lacks yellow wing patches. Blue-necked Tanager occasionally visits feeders, e.g., Milpe Bird Sanctuary and Mirador Río Blanco.

5 GOLDEN-HOODED TANAGER   *Tangara larvata* 13cm/5in

0–1000m. Fairly common in humid lowland and foothill forest, edge, and lightly wooded areas in NW; the most common *Tangara* in flat, lowland areas, and rather tolerant of habitat degradation, found even in areas with just scattered trees. Black breast forms a distinct band between the golden hood and white belly, a good feature to note under poor viewing conditions. Blue-necked Tanager has a blue hood, yellow wing coverts, and almost uniformly black lower underparts. Golden-hooded Tanager is not known to visit feeders in W Ecuador.

6 RUFOUS-THROATED TANAGER   *Tangara rufigula* 12cm/4.5in

500–1500m. Fairly common in humid foothill forest and edge in NW. Combination of mostly black upperparts, rufous throat, and scaled breast is completely different from plumage of any other tanager; in poor light, the rufous throat might not be evident, but the black head stands out against the paler black-spotted breast and flanks. Occasionally visits feeders at Mirador Río Blanco.

Three final *Tangara* (see p. 378 for more details on this genus), as well as two other very distinctive tanagers from the NW. Only Glistening-green Tanager is known to visit feeders in W Ecuador.

1 BAY-HEADED TANAGER *Tangara gyrola* 13cm/5in

0–1500m. Common in humid and semi-humid forest and edge from lowlands to subtropics. Exceptionally colorful, even for a tanager. Sexes alike; rufous head, turquoise underparts and rump, and green mantle, wings, and tail are unique in our range. Immature (not shown) is similar but duller and head may appear brown. Male Rufous-winged Tanager differs by rufous flight feathers, bright golden nape and mantle, and reduced turquoise below.

2 SPECKLED TANAGER *Tangara guttata* 13cm/5in

500–800m. Known in our region from a handful of sightings in the lower parts of the Buenaventura Reserve in SW; this population is still poorly known, and more research could show that it is an undescribed subspecies or possibly even a new species. At time of writing, only two photos exist for this population, and neither was suitable for publication. The photo here is from Venezuela; Buenaventura birds appear to be similar but may show more black in the wings and thinner lores. Sexes are likely very similar.

3 RUFOUS-WINGED TANAGER *Tangara lavinia* 13cm/5in

0–900m. Uncommon in humid lowland and foothill forest and edge in NW. Male is similar to Bay-headed Tanager but has rufous wing patches, bright golden nape and mantle, and underparts green with little turquoise. Female has much-reduced rufous, almost lacking in some individuals (immatures?), leading to possible confusion with other all-green birds, such as female Glistening-green Tanager (which occurs mainly at higher elevations) and female Green Honeycreeper (p. 392), which has a very different bill shape.

4 GLISTENING-GREEN TANAGER *Chlorochrysa phoenicotis* 13cm/5in

600–1900m. Uncommon in humid foothill and subtropical forest and edge in NW; there is also an isolated population in the SW at Buenaventura Reserve. Brilliant emerald-green male has small red and white patches behind the eye. Female (not shown) is similar but somewhat duller, and some (immatures?) may lack facial markings; however green plumage is brighter than that of any other similar tanager in range; even the dullest female Rufous-winged Tanager (little overlap) shows at least a hint of rufous in wings; female Green Honeycreeper has a very different bill shape. Glistening-green Tanager is similar in behavior to *Tangara* tanagers, though it consumes more insects than fruit, actively gleaning and even leaping to grab prey from the underside of foliage. Visits feeders in the Mashpi area. Voice, more distinctive than in most tanagers, is a series of high-pitched, airy, buzzy whistles, e.g., *tsit-seeseeseesee*.

5 SCARLET-BROWED TANAGER *Heterospingus xanthopygius* 17cm/6.5in

0–900m. Uncommon in humid lowland and foothill forest and edge in NW. Black male's scarlet and white superciliary and white pectoral tufts are unique. Female lacks supercilary and is more gray than black. Both sexes have a yellow rump that can be hard to see unless the bird takes flight. Female might be confused with male White-lined Tanager (p. 370) if yellow rump is not seen, but is not as dark and is very unlikely to occur in the cutover habitats White-lined prefers. Scarlet-browed Tanager is usually found in pairs high in the forest canopy, consuming both fruit and insects; joins mixed-species flocks.

Dissimilar tanagers from all over the region (none visit feeders), along with Bananaquit, a bird of uncertain taxonomic affinities, which most authorities currently include with the tanagers. Voices are usually not critical for ID and are described only when especially distinctive.

1 RUFOUS-CRESTED TANAGER *Creurgops verticalis* 15cm/6in

1500–2500m. Uncommon in a very small area of humid subtropical forest near the Colombian border (e.g., the Chical road); much more widespread on the E slope; a few records from the Mindo area may represent wandering birds. Note gray upperparts, rufous underparts, and a small black mask. Male has narrow rufous crown patch, lacking in female (not shown). Frequently joins mixed-species flocks from mid-story to canopy, and eats mostly insects.

2 DUSKY-FACED TANAGER *Mitrospingus cassinii* 18cm/7in

0–1200m. Fairly common in humid lowland and foothill forest and edge. Sexes are similar; combination of gray and olive plumage pattern and white irides is unique. Usually found in large, chattering groups that move through forest undergrowth, not associating with other species except by chance. Along with fruit, it consumes a variety of insects, spiders, etc.

3 FAWN-BREASTED TANAGER *Pipraeidea melanonota* 14cm/5.5in

400–3000m. Fairly common and widespread over a broad elevation range, preferring humid forest edge and lightly wooded areas. Striking, with black mask, red irides, blue hood, and buff underparts; female and immature male (not shown) are slightly duller than male but still show a dark mask. Typically found alone or in pairs, only occasionally with mixed-species flocks, foraging for both fruit and insects at mid to upper heights. Song is a sweet, high-pitched *see-see-see-see-see*.

4 SCARLET-AND-WHITE TANAGER *Chrysothlypis salmoni* 12cm/4.5in

0–1000m. Rare to locally uncommon in humid lowland and foothill forest and edge in the NW. This fabulous tanager is very sensitive to forest fragmentation, and is now rare or absent from some areas where it was formerly seen regularly, such as Río Silanche Bird Sanctuary. Male should not be mistaken. Female, however, is quite dull and can be confusing; the best field marks are her whitish flanks and lower underparts that contrast with the buffy throat and breast; this contrast can be seen even in rather poor lighting conditions if the observer knows to look for it.

5 BANANAQUIT *Coereba flaveola* 10cm/4in

0–2000m. Common and widespread in secondary forest, edge, and clearings with scattered trees from lowlands to subtropics. Small, with short decurved bill, white eyebrow, and white speculum in wing. Immature is duller but still has the same basic pattern. Primarily a nectar feeder, but also takes small berries and insects. It frequently congregates with other small birds at fruiting or flowering bushes or hummingbird feeders, but does not usually accompany mixed-species flocks. Song is a very gravelly warble lasting about 2 sec. and repeated regularly.

5

imm. (top), ad. (bottom) 5

MISCELLANEOUS TANAGERS

Four final tanagers; these have little in common with one another. Only Guira Tanager visits feeders.

1 GUIRA TANAGER *Hemithraupis guira* 13cm/5in

0–1400m. Fairly common in humid and semi-humid lowland and foothill forest and edge. Male has blackish face-to-throat mask, orange breast and rump, and pale orange bill; these markings are fainter on immature (not shown). Female is plain pale yellow below, with grayish flanks; note yellow bill and pale yellow superciliary and eye-ring; overall coloration and shape often suggest a warbler. Usually found in pairs or small groups in the forest canopy, foraging along outer branches and often joining mixed-species flocks; consumes insects and arthropods along with fruit.

2 SWALLOW TANAGER *Tersina viridis* 15cm/6in

0–1700m. Fairly common in humid lowland and foothill forest and edge; at its upper elevation limit, it is only a rare wanderer; it may undertake seasonal movements, which are not understood. Its name comes from its wide, swallow-like bill; otherwise there is little similarity with the swallows. Male is easy to ID, with bright turquoise plumage, distinctive black mask, and contrasting white triangular ventral area. Female is very different, but is the only stubby-billed, bright green bird with obvious underpart barring and scaling; note yellow ventral area. Swallow Tanager frequently occurs in large groups, though not normally with mixed-species flocks; perches upright. Feeds mainly on fruit in forest canopy, but takes some arthropods as well. Its most common vocalization is a squeaky *squee?*, almost like a kiss.

3 BLACK-AND-WHITE TANAGER *Conothraupis speculigera* 16cm/6.5in

0–2000m. Seasonally fairly common during the rainy months (ca. January–May, but varies yearly) in deciduous forest and desert scrub in W and SW. During the remainder of the year, it is either very rare or entirely absent, and there is strong evidence to suggest that it migrates to E Peru. Handsome male is surprisingly similar to Black-and-white Seedeater (p. 414) in pattern, but is larger, lacks the stubby seedeater bill, and occurs in different habitats. Female and immature male (no suitable photos could be obtained for either) are totally different: upperparts are yellow-olive; underparts are whitish with yellowish wash and faint streaking on breast. Black-and-white Tanager is very shy and hard to get a glimpse of, typically remaining hidden in dense vegetation, though male occasionally sings from an exposed perch. It primarily eats insects. Male's song, sometimes given incessantly during the height of the rainy season, is a very strange, ringing *tchKER*.

4 RUFOUS-CHESTED TANAGER *Thlypopsis ornata* 13cm/5in

1700–3300m. Uncommon in humid subtropical and temperate forest edge, montane scrub, and lightly wooded areas. Small and slender, with a thin bill, which may lead an observer to think it is not a tanager, but no other small bird in range has mostly orange plumage, with gray back and white center of underparts. Sexes alike. Usually found alone or in pairs at all forest levels, sometimes with mixed-species flocks; eats primarily insects.

DACNISES

Small birds related to the tanagers, dacnises inhabit humid forest at lower elevations. Males are brightly colored; females are much duller, but ID is not usually too difficult if they are seen well. Dacnises usually stay in the forest canopy, feeding on berries, nectar, and insects, but will come down lower if there is an ample food source; they frequently join mixed-species flocks. They are not known to visit feeders in W Ecuador. With the exception of Scarlet-breasted Dacnis, their voices are unremarkable and are not described here.

1 SCARLET-BREASTED DACNIS *Dacnis berlepschi* 12cm/4.5in

0–700m. Rare to locally uncommon in humid lowland and foothill forest and edge in the NW. Colorful male is one of the most striking birds of the region, with its blue hood, scarlet breast and belly, and bright yellow irides. Female is mostly brown and yellow, but can still be identified by scarlet breast and yellow irides. Male has a surprisingly distinctive song (for a dacnis): *b'zit-tik'tik'tik'tik'tik'tik'tik....*

2 YELLOW-TUFTED DACNIS *Dacnis egregia* 11cm/4.5in

0–1600m. Fairly common in humid lowland and foothill forest; rare at its upper elevation limit. Male is the only turquoise and yellow bird in range with black mask and yellow irides. Female is drab; look for combination of grayish-olive plumage with contrasting yellowish belly and yellow-orange irides. Sometimes lumped with **Black-faced Dacnis** (*D. lineata*).

3 SCARLET-THIGHED DACNIS *Dacnis venusta* 12cm/4.5in

0–900m. Uncommon in humid lowland and foothill forest and edge in NW. Both sexes have turquoise hood and red irides; scarlet thighs are usually hidden from view. All-black underparts of male are diagnostic. Female is mostly gray, but if seen well the pale blue hood is still distinctive. Male most closely resembles Blue-necked Tanager (p. 382), but that species has a full turquoise hood (lacking black throat) as well as yellow wing patches.

4 BLUE DACNIS *Dacnis cayana* 12cm/4.5in

0–1200m. Fairly common in humid lowland and foothill forest and edge. Male is deep blue, with a black throat, mantle, and wide line through face. Female is totally different, with mostly green plumage, light blue head, and white throat. Male is vaguely similar to some male honeycreepers (p. 392), but has a thicker bill and pinkish legs. Female is the only mostly green bird with a blue crown in range. The birds shown here belong to a subspecies from outside our region; the photos were artificially darkened to make them appear similar to W Ecuador birds.

Honeycreepers are small tanagers with slender, decurved bills suitable for feeding on nectar, but they also eat small fruits, insects, and other arthropods. They are often found in close-knit pairs and frequently join mixed-species flocks, spending most of their time at mid to upper levels of the forest, occasionally coming down lower where food is available. Males are brightly colored; females are duller, but except for Golden-collared Honeycreeper female they are usually not hard to ID if seen clearly. Voices are rather unremarkable and are not described here.

1 PURPLE HONEYCREEPER *Cyanerpes caeruleus* 11cm/4.5in

0–1300m. Fairly common in humid lowland and foothill forest and edge. Bright yellow legs and black throat distinguish male from male Red-legged Honeycreeper; male Blue Dacnis (p. 390) is somewhat similar but has pink legs and a thicker bill. Female Purple Honeycreeper has slightly duller legs than male, but rufous-orange face, blue malar, and brighter overall plumage help separate her from female Red-legged.

2 RED-LEGGED HONEYCREEPER *Cyanerpes cyaneus* 12cm/4.5in

0–500m. Locally fairly common in semi-humid forest and edge near the coast in NW; rare in the more inland parts of its mapped NW range. Along with red legs, the light blue crown and the lack of a black throat patch separate male from both Purple Honeycreeper and Blue Dacnis (p. 390). Female Red-legged Honeycreeper is quite dull but still shows reddish legs; also note the dark line through the eye bordered above by a white superciliary; she lacks the rufous face and blue malar of female Purple Honeycreeper. Eclipse plumage male is like female but has black wings and varying amounts of purple flecking.

3 GREEN HONEYCREEPER *Chlorophanes spiza* 13cm/5in

0–1300m. Fairly common in humid lowland and foothill forest, edge, and wooded clearings. Turquoise male with black hood and bicolor black and yellow bill is distinctive. Female is uniform green, though usually shows some yellow in the bill (the female shown may be an immature, since bill shows little yellow); the fairly long, slender bill can help distinguish her from other all-green tanagers, such as female Rufous-winged and female Glistening-green (both p. 384).

4 GOLDEN-COLLARED HONEYCREEPER *Iridophanes pulcherrimus* 12cm/4.5in

600–2000m. Uncommon in humid foothill and subtropical forest from the Mashpi area N to the Colombian border; perhaps formerly ranged farther S. Distinctive male has black hood, golden nuchal collar, pale back, rump, and underparts, and blue in wings. Female is quite dull and unremarkable, often best identified by the presence of the male, which is usually close by, but features to look for include the faint golden nuchal collar, buffy-tinged underparts, gray head, and pale crissum.

Hemispinguses are warbler-like tanagers of subtropical and temperate Andean forest. Sexes are similar. They primarily eat insects and other arthropods, but occasionally consume berries as well. Pairs or small groups are almost always found accompanying mixed-species flocks. Both Western and Piura Hemispinguses are sometimes lumped with **Black-eared Hemispingus** (*Hemispingus melanotis*). Tit-like Dacnis (not closely related to other dacnises) is an enigmatic species restricted to very high elevations.

1 SUPERCILIARIED HEMISPINGUS   *Hemispingus superciliaris*   14cm/5.5in

2400–3700m. Fairly common in humid temperate forest and edge. Dark olive above, yellow below, with contrasting white superciliary. General color pattern and superciliary might suggest a warbler, but no warblers in W Ecuador share that pattern. Black-capped Hemispingus is more ochraceous below, entire crown and face are black, and superciliary is longer. Superciliaried Hemispingus usually stays high in the canopy, and is almost always encountered with mixed-species flocks. Song is a short, toneless rattle.

2 WESTERN HEMISPINGUS   *Hemispingus ochraceus*   14cm/5.5in

1600–2400m. Uncommon in humid subtropical forest, especially in areas with extensive *Chusquea* bamboo. Mostly brown with dull tawny underparts and a gray head; often appears uniformly dingy in the field, especially under poor viewing conditions; however, it is essentially the only dull brownish warbler-like bird within its range and habitat. Usually found foraging acrobatically in tangles at lower to mid forest levels, occasionally higher, especially in large bamboo patches. Song is a fast, explosive chattering, often given as a duet.

3 PIURA HEMISPINGUS   *Hemispingus piurae*   14cm/5.5in

1700–2600m. Rare to locally uncommon in *Chusquea* bamboo patches within humid subtropical and temperate forest in the highlands of SW; nearly all sightings in our region come from in and around the Utuana Reserve, and near the town of Sozoranga to the W. Unique in range, and the combination of rufous underparts, black head, and long white superciliary is diagnostic. Behavior and song are similar to those of Western Hemispingus (no overlap).

4 BLACK-CAPPED HEMISPINGUS   *Hemispingus atropileus*   15cm/6in

2300–3400m. Rare to locally uncommon (more common in E) in humid subtropical and temperate forest and edge; seems to prefer areas with extensive *Chusquea* bamboo. Mostly ochraceous, but black head divided by long white superciliary is very distinctive. Superciliaried Hemispingus has less black on the head, yellow rather than ochre underparts, and mainly forages in the canopy. Black-capped Hemispingus is typically found in pairs at lower forest levels. Song, usually given only at dawn, is a leisurely series, such as *tsee-see-chu-chu-chu-see-tsee-tsee*.... Calls include various wheezy whistles, *tik* notes, and chatters.

5 TIT-LIKE DACNIS   *Xenodacnis parina*   14cm/5.5in

3600–4200m. Found in only a few high-elevation sites in the S Andes, where there is *Polylepis* woodland interspersed with *Gynoxys* (a shrub related to the sunflower). Occurs mainly in E, but small numbers are found W of the continental divide near El Cajas National Park, where it is quite common. Male is deep blue with azure striations. Female is brown with a blue forehead; no similar bird occurs with it. Tit-like Dacnis is usually found in groups of several birds, often very tame and approachable. Calls have a squeaky, almost electronic quality, e.g., *zhwee-zhwee-zhwee* or *wi-wi-squi-squee-squee-squee*.

♂ 5   ♀ 5

Conebills are small Andean tanagers named for their conical, sharply pointed bills. They are mostly insectivorous and are often seen with mixed-species flocks. Rusty Flowerpiercer's plumage is unlike that of any other flowerpiercer in our region; see p. 398 for more details on this group.

1 GIANT CONEBILL *Oreomanes fraseri* 15cm/6in

3500–4200m. Restricted to *Polylepis* at very high elevations, where it can be fairly common in larger, undisturbed forest patches. Sexes are alike. No other bird looks remotely similar in its very specific habitat. Usually found in pairs or small groups that creep along branches, probing bark for insects and other arthropods; often with mixed-species flocks. Song is a series of short bursts of random notes lasting 20 sec. or longer.

2 CINEREOUS CONEBILL *Conirostrum cinereum* 12cm/4.5in

2300–4000m. Fairly common in temperate forest edge, montane scrub, parks, and gardens. Small and warbler-like; combination of dingy gray and buff plumage, pale superciliary, and conspicuous white speculum in wing are diagnostic. Sexes are alike. Usually found alone or in pairs, sometimes with mixed-species flocks. Song is a pulsating, gravelly twitter lasting several seconds.

3 BLUE-BACKED CONEBILL *Conirostrum sitticolor* 13cm/5in

2500–3800m. Fairly common in humid temperate forest and edge. Colorful and distinctive, with black hood, mainly blue upperparts, and rufous underparts; no similar species occurs with it. Sexes are alike. Typically found alone or in pairs, and almost always encountered with large mixed-species flocks. Most common call is a rather random series of jumbled notes.

4 CAPPED CONEBILL *Conirostrum albifrons* 13cm/5in

1900–2800m. Fairly common in humid subtropical and temperate forest. Male is very dark blue (nearly black) with lighter blue patches on the head, wings, and rump. Unless seen in very good light, male usually looks completely dark and monochromatic; bill shape, tail pumping, accompanying female, and voice can all help clinch the ID. Female is totally different, mostly yellow, with a blue crown and gray face and throat. Both sexes pump their tails up and down almost constantly, a very useful ID feature. Capped Conebill is nearly always seen in pairs that join mixed-species flocks. Song is a series of high-pitched whistles, sometimes alternating up and down slightly in pitch (e.g., *sweeseesweeseesweesee...*), at other times seeming to be more random.

5 RUSTY FLOWERPIERCER *Diglossa sittoides* 12cm/4.5in

1600–3400m. Fairly common in montane scrub, parks, and gardens in inter-Andean valleys and in drier parts of the SW highlands; uncommon and local at edge of more humid forest on the W slope. Bicolor male is handsome and distinctive. Female is mostly dull brown, with blurry streaking on the breast and faint wing bars; her hooked flowerpiercer bill is her best ID feature, but see female White-sided Flowerpiercer (p. 398), which shows white sides and lacks the breast and wing markings. Male Rusty Flowerpiercer often sings from an exposed perch, giving a short trill or rattle.

♂ 5

♀ 5

FLOWERPIERCERS

Flowerpiercers are small Andean tanagers that specialize in feeding on nectar. They use their hooked bills to pierce flowers at the base, rather than taking the nectar through the opening, in essence stealing, since they are not aiding in pollination. They also consume small insects. While they may congregate with other flowerpiercers and hummingbirds at large flower patches or feeders, most species do not join mixed-species flocks. Except for White-sided Flowerpiercer, the species on this page are not significantly sexually dimorphic.

1 MASKED FLOWERPIERCER *Diglossa cyanea* 14cm/5.5in

1700–3800m. Common in humid subtropical and temperate forest and edge. Combination of blue plumage, red irides, and ample black mask is diagnostic for adults. Immature often lacks a distinct black mask and has brown irides, and can easily be mistaken for Bluish Flowerpiercer; however, Masked immature lacks the whitish belly and well-defined black lores that Bluish typically shows. Juvenile Masked (not shown) is similar to immature, but has grayish underparts. Masked Flowerpiercer's song is a rapid high-pitched chatter.

2 BLUISH FLOWERPIERCER *Diglossa caerulescens* 13cm/5in

1700–3000m. Inexplicably very rare on the W slope (much more common in E) in humid subtropical and temperate forest and edge. Slightly duller blue than Masked Flowerpiercer, with black on face reduced to lores; also note whitish tinge to belly. Could be confused with immature Masked (see that species for details). Indigo Flowerpiercer is much brighter blue and lacks the whitish belly. Song of Bluish Flowerpiercer is a descending series of slurred, high-pitched whistles.

3 INDIGO FLOWERPIERCER *Diglossa indigotica* 11cm/4.5in

1100–2100m. Uncommon to locally fairly common in humid foothill and subtropical forest in the NW; very rare S of the Mashpi area. Beautiful shining deep-blue plumage separates it from the much duller Bluish Flowerpiercer, which has whitish wash on belly that Indigo lacks. Immature Indigo (not shown) not well known but may be somewhat darker. Song is a long, 10 sec. series of very high-pitched notes (*ti-ti-ti-ti-ti…*) that descends steadily in pitch.

4 GLOSSY FLOWERPIERCER *Diglossa lafresnayii* 14cm/5.5in

2600–3800m. Fairly common at edge of humid temperate forest and in tall bushes at the edge of páramo. Silvery patches on shoulders separate it from Black Flowerpiercer, which often occurs with it. Song is a very long series of chirps and chips that changes pitch seemingly randomly.

5 BLACK FLOWERPIERCER *Diglossa humeralis* 13cm/5in

2400–4000m. Fairly common in lightly wooded habitats in the highlands, including scrub, forest edge, gardens, and city parks. Uniform black, lacking the silvery shoulders of Glossy Flowerpiercer and white sides of male White-sided Flowerpiercer. Immature (not shown) is dark brown, somewhat similar to female Rusty Flowerpiercer (p. 396) but darker and more heavily streaked. Song is a short burst of rattling notes with a pulsating quality.

6 WHITE-SIDED FLOWERPIERCER *Diglossa albilatera* 12cm/4.5in

1700–3100m. Fairly common in humid subtropical and temperate forest and edge. Dark gray male and brown female both have white flank tufts that are partially hidden by their wings; these patches are not always conspicuous, especially on female, but are usually visible if the observer knows to look for them. Female could be mistaken for Female Rusty Flowerpiercer (p. 396), which lacks flank tufts and always shows streaking on the breast. Vocalizations include a variety of dry rattles and churrs or sometimes a more musical trill.

A diverse set of sparrows and the finch-like Chestnut Munia; two species are introduced. These birds are found all over W Ecuador; none joins mixed-species flocks.

1 RUFOUS-COLLARED SPARROW *Zonotrichia capensis* 14cm/5.5in

800–4000m. One of the most common and familiar birds of the Andes, found in most habitats except forest interior, and prevalent even in large cities. Often among the first birds a visitor sees, if the trip begins in Quito. Striped head, small crest, and rufous collar make ID straightforward; however, if it is seen briefly or in flight, some visitors might mistake it for House Sparrow, due to their familiarity with that species. Rufous-collared Sparrow is usually found in pairs or small family groups, hopping on the ground or sitting on a low perch such as a bush, wall, or wire. Song usually consists of two or three sweet whistles followed by a trill.

2 TUMBES SPARROW *Rhynchospiza stolzmanni* 15cm/6in

100–1800m. Uncommon to locally fairly common in desert scrub in the far SW. Boldly chestnut-striped head, pale underparts, and rusty color in wings are distinctive in range. Usually found singly or in pairs hiding in dense scrub or feeding on the ground. Pishing will often bring it out to perch briefly on the top of a bush. Has a large vocal repertoire, including various trills and churrs, but high-pitched, ticking contact calls are usually heard most often.

3 BLACK-STRIPED SPARROW *Arremonops conirostris* 16cm/6.5in

0–1500m. Fairly common in humid secondary growth, such as overgrown clearings and wooded borders of fields and roads, from lowlands to subtropics. Note striped head and olive back and wings; no other bird in range is very similar. Normally found alone or in pairs, often hidden in dense vegetation or even on the ground, but sometimes sings from an exposed branch high in a tree. Typical vocalization in W Ecuador is a very simple *fip!, gurt…*, repeated over and over for 30 sec. or longer, with about 2 sec. between notes; only rarely gives the fast, musical trill that is often heard elsewhere in its range.

4 CHESTNUT MUNIA *Lonchura atricapilla* 12cm/4.5in

0–300m. Native to Asia, but recently introduced in the W lowlands. At time of publication it was still rather uncommon, but has been increasing rapidly. Most sightings have been from wet, grassy areas such as rice paddies, marshes, and pastures. Though increasing in numbers, it may not spread much beyond its mapped range due to its habitat preference. ID is easy, as no remotely similar bird occurs with it. In Ecuador, it is usually encountered in small groups of two to five birds that feed on the ground or while clinging to grass stems.

5 HOUSE SPARROW *Passer domesticus* 15cm/6in

0–2500m. Introduced; native to Eurasia. Common only in towns and cities in the W lowlands; very localized elsewhere. House Sparrows do not yet occur in the city of Quito, but they have reached some of the N and E suburbs located in drier valleys. Most visitors are familiar with this species, but sometimes jump to wrong conclusions if a Rufous-collared Sparrow flies in their line of vision.

♂ 5

♀ 5

Arremon comprises a number of non–sexually dimorphic sparrows and brush-finches that inhabit forest understory. They typically range in pairs or small family groups, often feeding on the ground, and eating mainly insects; some species consume seeds and even fruit. They don't generally join mixed-species flocks.

1 ORANGE-BILLED SPARROW *Arremon aurantiirostris* 14cm/5.5in

0–1400m. Fairly common inside humid lowland and foothill forest. A striking species with black face, striped head, olive back, and black breast band to go along with its shocking-orange bill. Immature's bill is mostly black. Very local overlap with Gray-browed Brush-Finch in SW, but that species lacks a black breast band. Orange-billed Sparrow is usually found alone or in pairs in the forest understory, and sometimes on the ground; it does not join mixed-species flocks. Often hard to spot in the dark rain-forest understory, but not especially shy and even visits feeders in a few places, such as Milpe Bird Sanctuary. Song is a short, rapid burst of high notes that changes rapidly in pitch. Call is a sharp *tik*.

2 BLACK-CAPPED SPARROW *Arremon abeillei* 15cm/6in

0–1600m. Fairly common in deciduous and semi-humid forest in W and SW. This gray, black, and white sparrow is distinctive, although confusion can arise with the smaller male Collared Warbling-Finch (p. 412); Black-capped Sparrow has a blacker crown, somewhat narrower breast band, and shorter superciliary that starts above the eye, and lacks white in tail; also note habitat differences. Black-capped Sparrow is usually found in pairs, skulking in dense forest understory vegetation, where it can be easily overlooked. Not especially shy, it often ventures into the open in response to pishing or squeaking. Song is a few high-pitched raspy notes followed by a chippered trill. Call is a sharp, high-pitched *peet*.

3 CHESTNUT-CAPPED BRUSH-FINCH *Arremon brunneinucha* 19cm/7.5in

400–2800m. Fairly common in humid forest in a very wide elevation range; though very local at the lower limit. Quite handsome, with a black face, chestnut cap, and white throat that is often fluffed out like a beard. Gray-browed Brush-Finch lacks the chestnut cap and underparts are mostly white. Chestnut-capped pairs hop boldly about on or near the forest floor, peering curiously about and often flaring out their throat feathers, which can be their most conspicuous feature in low light. High-pitched, burry song is quite variable, and is often given as a duet, with male giving a 2 sec. series, followed quickly by female giving a slightly different set of notes, e.g., *SWEE-swee-suh-swee-SWEE* (male), *swit-sit-swisisisit* (female).

4 GRAY-BROWED BRUSH-FINCH *Arremon assimilis* 19cm/7.5in

2500–3600m; down to 700m in SW. Uncommon to locally common in humid temperate forest and edge; uncommon and local in humid foothill forest in the SW (e.g., Buenaventura Reserve). Note combination of gray, black-striped crown, black mask, olive back, and mostly white underparts. It differs from Chestnut-capped Brush-Finch by lack of chestnut cap and whiter underparts, and from immature Orange-billed Sparrow by lack of black breast band and narrower head stripes. Gray-browed Brush-Finch usually skulks inside very dense thickets in the understory, making it often quite hard to catch a glimpse until it pops into a gap between bushes; occasionally hops on trails or roadsides just before dawn. Song is variable, but typically a very slow series of high-pitched whistles, e.g., *SEEwit, fuhSEET, SEE, fuhSEET...*, with about 2 sec. between phrases. This species, along with several others that do not occur in Ecuador, were formerly lumped as **Stripe-headed Brush-Finch** (*A. torquatus*).

5 OLIVE FINCH

Arremon castaneiceps 16cm/6.5in

700–2000m. Rare and local in humid foothill and subtropical forest; usually seen around streams or in steep-sided wet valleys. No other bird in range shares the pattern of olive body, gray face and throat, and chestnut cap. Found alone or in pairs, low in the understory, and often hard to see well in the gloom of the forest. Song is extremely high pitched (so as to be heard over the sound of rushing water), typically a repeated melody of around 10 sibilant notes, e.g., *seeseeSWEESWEE-ee-eeSEE-sihswihswihswih...*, repeated over and over for several minutes without pause. Call is a high-pitched trill.

Atlapetes is a large genus of non-sexually dimorphic montane emberizid finches (family Emberizidae); in Ecuador. They are restricted to the Andes but occupy a wide range of habitats, including dry scrub and humid forest. They are usually found in pairs or small groups in low to mid forest levels, feeding on arthropods, seeds, and berries. Early in the morning, they may sing from an elevated perch. A few species join mixed-species flocks.

1 YELLOW-BREASTED BRUSH-FINCH *Atlapetes latinuchus* 17cm/6.5in

2300–3700m; lower in SW. Fairly common in montane scrub and at edge of humid subtropical and temperate forest, ranging up to tree line in some areas, such as Yanacocha Reserve. Note rufous crown, black mask, gray upperparts, and mostly yellow underparts bordered by gray sides and flanks. Two subspecies occur in our region: *spodionotus*, which occupies most of the species' W Ecuador range, and *comptus* in far SW. They are fairly similar, but *comptus* has a yellow loral spot, more prominent malar, and slightly paler upperparts. Rufous crown, gray sides and flanks, and paler overall appearance distinguish the species from Chocó Brush-Finch. Pairs or small groups forage at lower to mid heights but regularly sing from high, exposed perches early in the morning. Song is variable, but often consists of a few loud whistles that are sometimes followed by a short trill, e.g., *cheu-cheu-chu-chu* or *Cheeu-chu-t't't't*; duet given by agitated birds is a very complex series of whistles and trills. Also called **Rufous-naped Brush-Finch**.

2 CHOCÓ BRUSH-FINCH *Atlapetes crassus* 18cm/7in

600–2300m. Fairly common in humid foothill and subtropical forest and edge. Similar to Yellow-breasted Brush-Finch, but tawny (not rufous) crown, almost uniformly yellow underparts (lacking gray sides and flanks), and darker overall coloration separate it; the two species overlap very locally (e.g., in the upper parts of the Tandayapa Valley). Pairs or small groups forage at lower to mid forest levels, and sometimes join mixed-species flocks. Song is a series of notes that accelerates into a fast rattle, e.g., *chu-chu-chi-chi-chi-t't't't't't't*. Agitated birds give a long series of rattles intermixed with wheezy notes. Formerly lumped with **Tricolored Brush-Finch** (*A. tricolor*).

3 WHITE-HEADED BRUSH-FINCH *Atlapetes albiceps* 16cm/6.5in

400–1200m. Uncommon and local in desert scrub in the foothills of the SW. Plumage is unique; note especially the white face and forecrown contrasting with black hind-crown and nape, and the gray on back and wings; white speculum is usually prominent. No overlap with Pale-headed Brush-Finch. White-headed Brush-Finch is found in pairs and small groups that stay low in dense scrub and do not join mixed-species flocks. May perch atop a bush in response to pishing. Typical song is a short series of buzzy notes and sweet whistles, e.g., *PITPITdjitdjitdjitSWEEsweesit't't't*. Agitated birds also give a rapid, chattery trill.

4 WHITE-RIMMED BRUSH-FINCH *Atlapetes leucopis* 18cm/7in

2200–2800m. Very rare in W Ecuador, known from only a few records on hard-to-access forested mountain slopes W of Otavalo. Plumage is distinctive, with olive underparts, rufous crown, and bold white eye-ring that continues behind the eye in a short, wide line. Typically found in pairs in the forest understory, usually not with mixed-species flocks. Song is a series of loud, sweet whistles, e.g., *swee-WEET-weet-chu-chu-PEER-PEER-PEER*, but with many variations. Pairs also give beautiful and very complex extended duets of rapidly changing whistles, trills, and churrs that can go on for 20 sec. or longer.

5 PALE-HEADED BRUSH-FINCH

Atlapetes pallidiceps 16cm/6.5in
1600–2000m. Endemic to Ecuador, and one of the most critically endangered birds on earth. Nearly the entire known population is restricted to the Yunguilla Reserve. Washed-out brown and cream-colored plumage with white speculum is unique, and no similar bird occurs in its tiny range; no overlap with White-headed Brush-Finch. Behavior and voice similar to those of White-headed, but song is sweeter and lacks the buzzy quality.

spodionotus 1

comptus 1

2

2

3

4

Two more *Atlapetes* brush-finches (see p. 404 for more information on this genus), along with two odd Andean cloud-forest species, Tanager Finch and Plushcap. Both of these were formerly classified as emberizid finches (Emberizidae), but have been transferred to the tanagers (Thraupidae).

1 BAY-CROWNED BRUSH-FINCH *Atlapetes seebohmi* 16cm/6.5in

1300–2600m. Uncommon in humid montane scrub, overgrown clearings, and forest edge in the SW Andes. Mostly gray and white, with broad black mask and ample chestnut crown; note weak black malar. Similar to *dresseri* White-winged Brush-Finch, but lacks white speculum in wing and extensive whitish mottling on head. Bay-crowned Brush-Finch usually occurs in small groups that move surreptitiously through dense scrub, independent of other birds. Song is quite variable, but typically consists of a short series of sweet notes that usually descends in pitch, e.g., *seet-sweet-seet-fweeweeweewee*.

2 WHITE-WINGED BRUSH-FINCH *Atlapetes leucopterus* 16cm/6.5in

1600–2600m; down to 600m in SW. Locally fairly common in subtropical and temperate forest, edge, and adjacent overgrown clearings; ranges down into the foothills in drier parts of SW. Two subspecies occur in W Ecuador; both display a white speculum in wing, pale underparts, and pale cinnamon-rufous crown. NW birds (*leucopterus*) are unique in their range, with a solid black face and white spot above the lores. SW birds (*dresseri*) are more washed out and show variable whitish mottling on head; confusion is possible with Bay-crowned Brush-Finch, but that species lacks the white wing speculum and face mottling. White-winged is quiet for a brush-finch, especially *leucopterus*, which occasionally gives a short raspy series of notes. Song of *dresseri* is fairly similar to that of Bay-crowned.

3 TANAGER FINCH *Oreothraupis arremonops* 20cm/8in

2000–2600m. Rare to locally uncommon at edge of humid subtropical and temperate forest in NW. All recent records come from near the pass above the Tandayapa Valley along the Paseo del Quinde (Nono-Mindo) Ecoroute, but it presumably also occurs locally at similar elevations N toward the Colombian border. Note mostly chestnut plumage and black head with gray crown stripe and superciliary; no similar species is found with it. Most often seen alone or in pairs in dense roadside vegetation, though does occasionally join mixed-species flocks; can be extremely confiding. Song is a high-pitched, wavering series of buzzy rasps, e.g., *zhweezeeseet't't't'd'zihzihzeezeezeezeezeezee*, which can go unnoticed due to its similarity with one of Speckled Hummingbird's (p. 164) calls.

4 PLUSHCAP *Catamblyrhynchus diadema* 14cm/5.5in

1600–3300m. Uncommon in humid subtropical and temperate forest and edge; restricted to areas with extensive *Chusquea* bamboo. Adult, with chestnut head and underparts and slaty upperparts, is unique and readily identifiable; its bright golden-yellow forecrown stands out even in the fog. Juvenile is dull brown with only a wash of rufous on the breast, and best identified by its thick, stubby bill, bamboo habitat, and (with luck) the presence of a parent. Pairs or small family groups are always found in or near *Chusquea* bamboo, often with mixed-species flocks that usually have at least one species of hemispingus (p. 394). Plushcaps feed on insects, but also have been observed "biting" bamboo stalks, though what they obtain by doing so is not yet known. Song is a long series of chirps that changes pitch slightly and seemingly randomly. Also called **Plush-capped Finch**.

ad. **4**

juv. **4**

leucopterus 2

dresseri 2

SIERRA-FINCHES AND SLATY FINCH

Sierra-finches are small to medium-size nonforest birds with narrow, conical bills found primarily in the Andes; two species also inhabit desert and dry scrub in lowlands and foothills. They feed mainly on the ground, taking both seeds and arthropods. Despite their English names, sierra-finches are currently classified with the tanagers (Thraupidae). Slaty Finch is superficially similar to a sierra-finch but inhabits forest and is strongly tied to *Chusquea* bamboo.

1 PLUMBEOUS SIERRA-FINCH *Phrygilus unicolor* 14cm/5.5in

3000–4800m. Fairly common in páramo at very high elevations. Male is uniform gray, sometimes appearing bluish-tinged, and has a black bill; he lacks the white superciliary and throat of the smaller male Ash-breasted Sierra-Finch. Female Plumbeous is darker and much more boldly streaked below than female Ash-breasted. Plumbeous Sierra-Finch is often found in conspicuous pairs or small groups feeding on the ground or sitting on a low perch. Song is a flat, buzzy rasp.

2 ASH-BREASTED SIERRA-FINCH *Phrygilus plebejus* 12cm/4.5in

600–3600m; locally down to sea level. Fairly common in drier montane scrub throughout much of the highlands; uncommon and local in lowland deserts in far SW. Thin, conical bill helps separate both sexes from Plain-colored Seedeater (p. 418). Male is paler gray than Plumbeous Sierra-Finch, and has a white throat and faint superciliary. Female and immature male (not shown) can be identified by the pale superciliary and streaking on underparts restricted to breast. Ash-breasted Sierra-Finch is typically encountered in pairs, sometimes in small flocks that join other seed-eating species at abundant food sources. Song resembles that of Plumbeous Sierra-Finch but is shorter and drier.

3 BAND-TAILED SIERRA-FINCH *Phrygilus alaudinus* 14cm/5.5in

1200–3400m; locally to sea level. Uncommon to locally fairly common in open, arid areas with scattered small bushes; found mainly in inter-Andean valleys, but also locally in coastal deserts in W and SW. Both sexes possess a white tail band (most obvious in flight). Male's dark hood, butter-yellow bill, and legs are diagnostic. Female and immature male (not shown) differ from Ash-breasted Sierra-Finch by larger size, lack of pale superciliary, larger bill, and the tail band (if seen). Band-tailed Sierra-Finch is usually found alone or in pairs, often conspicuous in its favored barren habitat. Typical song is a sharp *cheedlee-chidilit*.

4 SLATY FINCH *Haplospiza rustica* 12cm/4.5in

1500–3700m. Usually rare in humid subtropical and temperate forest, but can become locally abundant when a patch of *Chusquea* bamboo begins to seed. Male is dark gray; female is brown, with indistinct breast streaking and olive-washed upperparts. Bill shape might suggest a sierra-finch, but Slaty Finch is a forest bird and not normally found in open country. Encountered only infrequently away from bamboo, where it is sometimes seen feeding alone on a roadside or trail. When a large patch of bamboo is seeding, hundreds of males can burst onto the scene, each one singing almost incessantly. Song includes various mostly toneless rattles, buzzes, and trills with a harsh, gravelly quality.

Sicalis is a widespread neotropical genus; the three Ecuadorian species are quite different in range, habitat, and behavior, though all are primarily seedeaters. Crimson-breasted Finch is a unique bird of uncertain taxonomic affinities. All species on this page are currently classified with the tanager family (Thraupidae).

1 SAFFRON FINCH *Sicalis flaveola* 13cm/5in

0–2800m. Fairly common to common in more open habitats such as farmland, clearings, deserts, and towns. Its range has been expanding N and E in recent years. Also locally fairly common in and around Quito, but it is unknown whether this population came from natural expansion or from escaped cage birds. Adult is distinctive, with bright yellow plumage and orange forecrown. Immature is gray, with variable amounts of yellow; some individuals have much less yellow than the bird shown, and can be mostly gray with a streaked back. Saffron Finch is typically found in pairs or flocks, feeding on the ground, eating mostly seeds but also insects and other arthropods. Song is a slow series of sometimes doubled chirps.

2 GRASSLAND YELLOW-FINCH *Sicalis luteola* 12cm/4.5in

1200–3500m. Uncommon to locally fairly common in inter-Andean valleys, inhabiting montane scrub, grassy fields, and marshy lake edges. Look for combination of brown, boldly streaked upperparts, bright yellow underparts, white eye-ring, and faint yellow superciliary; some birds also show a faint malar. Female is slightly duller than male, with yellow restricted to belly, but may show a more conspicuous eye-ring. Saffron Finch, which could spread into similar habitats in the near future, never shows such brown upperparts or the facial pattern. While large flocks can congregate around an abundant food source such as a recently plowed field, Grassland Yellow-Finch is also frequently encountered alone, feeding on the ground, sitting on an open perch such as a wire, or hovering in the air in a display flight. Male's song, usually given during display flights, is a long, fast series of notes or short churrs that almost always has a buzzy or gravelly quality.

3 SULPHUR-THROATED FINCH *Sicalis taczanowskii* 12cm/4.5in

0–100m. Rare in sparsely vegetated desert in W and SW; most records come from the Santa Elena Peninsula. Occurrence appears to be erratic, and in some years it goes entirely unreported. A very pale finch with varying amounts of yellow on the face and throat, and an oversize bill. Adults that show large amounts of yellow are fairly distinctive, but immature (not shown) can show almost no yellow, in which case it can look much like female Parrot-billed Seedeater (p. 416), with which Sulphur-throated Finch often occurs. Parrot-billed Seedeater has a much more deeply curved culmen, though this may be hard to judge at a distance. As both species are rarely seen without others of their kind, it can help to look at multiple members of the flock before making an ID. Sulphur-throated Finch is sometimes encountered in large flocks of hundreds of birds feeding on the ground or perching by the dozen in small bushes. Rarely heard vocalizing, but occasionally gives soft buzzes and churrs.

4 CRIMSON-BREASTED FINCH *Rhodospingus cruentus* 11cm/4.5in

0–600m. A seasonally common rainy-season breeder in deserts of W and SW. During the dry season, it disperses widely throughout lowland areas of W Ecuador, even into more humid areas, where it prefers scrubby areas such as overgrown fields and secondary forest edge. The male's fiery-red underparts and crown are diagnostic. Female is much duller and is best recognized by the slight buffy tinge on her breast; size, shape, and horizontal posture are also good clues. Usually found alone or in pairs, sometimes in small flocks outside the breeding season; feeds on the ground, in bushes, or in tall grass, and often perches conspicuously in the open. Song is a short, harsh rasp, sometimes preceded by a clearer note, e.g., *p'zheeee*.

♂ (right), ♀ (left) 4

Grassquits are small seed-eating birds that are found widely in secondary habitats; they do not venture inside dense forest. They can be found alone, in pairs, or in small groups, sometimes gathering with seedeaters at a bountiful food source. They feed mainly on seeds, but some insects are also taken. Males sing from conspicuous perches such as a wire, fence post, or the top of a small bush. Collared Warbling-Finch is a desert specialist and the only member of its genus that occurs in Ecuador. All species on this page are currently classified as tanagers (Thraupidae).

1   YELLOW-FACED GRASSQUIT   *Tiaris olivaceus*   10cm/4in

200–2500m. Locally fairly common and spreading in overgrown clearings, roadsides, edges of farmland and pastures, and other open habitats. Ornate, black-and-yellow-faced male is distinctive; female can be distinguished from Dull-colored Grassquit by the olive tinge to her upperparts and breast and lack of two-tone appearance to bill. Male Yellow-faced Grassquit's song is a flat, high-pitched trill usually lasting about 1 sec.

2   BLUE-BLACK GRASSQUIT   *Volatinia jacarina*   10cm/4in

0–2600m. Fairly common and widespread in open, nonforested habitats, especially where there is tall grass. Adult male is uniformly glossy blue-black; much smaller and thinner-billed than other similarly colored small birds. Obvious streaking on breast is the female's best ID feature; she lacks the pale superciliary of female Collared Warbling-Finch and Ash-breasted Sierra-Finch (p. 408), which can look similar. Immature male Blue-black Grassquit transitions gradually from female-type plumage to adult plumage, and various blotchy intermediate stages are frequently seen in the field. Male sings a buzzy *bihZEEjoo* from an exposed perch, often jumping up and down in the process.

3   DULL-COLORED GRASSQUIT   *Tiaris obscurus*   11cm/4.5in

0–2400m. Uncommon in secondary habitats, including overgrown clearings, scrubby forest edge, and isolated stands of tangled vegetation. A well-named species; sexes are alike, mostly uniform brown, slightly paler on belly. The best ID feature is the bicolor bill, with a pale lower mandible that contrasts slightly with the dark upper mandible. Female Yellow-faced Grassquit lacks the bicolor bill and is never as brown as Dull-colored, showing an olive wash on upperparts and breast. Dull-colored Grassquit's song is very similar to that of Blue-black Grassquit, but it does not jump up and down.

4   COLLARED WARBLING-FINCH   *Poospiza hispaniolensis*   13cm/5in

0–1500m. Fairly common in lowland deserts, including Isla de la Plata; also rare and local in arid montane scrub in SW. Both sexes have mostly white outer tail feathers, which are conspicuous in flight. Striking male can be confused only with larger Black-capped Sparrow (p. 402), which has a much narrower black breast band, a superciliary that does not extend in front of the eye, and lacks white in the tail. Female Collared Warbling-Finch is much duller but still relatively easy to ID based on the long, broad superciliary and whitish throat. Collared Warbling-Finch is usually found in pairs or small groups, not associating with other species, and feeds mainly on insects rather than seeds or fruits. Typical song is a sharp, ringing *wik, wikwititchu*.

Seed-eating birds found widely throughout the neotropics. Males are usually easy to ID, but females are often impossible to reliably separate in the field. *Oryzoborus* seed-finches have massive bills that help separate them from the smaller *Sporophila* seedeaters. All species on this page are currently classified as tanagers (Thraupidae).

1 THICK-BILLED SEED-FINCH *Oryzoborus funereus* 13cm/5in

0–1400m. Uncommon in overgrown clearings and forest edge in more humid areas of the lowlands and foothills. Male's almost uniform black plumage and large, black bill separates it from other similar species; white speculum in wing is not always visible. Female could be confused with the rare Large-billed Seed-Finch, which is slightly larger and has a more massive bill. Thick-billed Seed-Finch is usually found alone or in pairs, not often associating with other birds, foraging low in grasses, bushes, or even on the ground. Male often sings, from an elevated perch, a series of rapidly changing whistles that usually has a drawling or nasal quality. Formerly lumped with **Chestnut-bellied Seed-Finch** (*O. angolensis*) from E of Andes and called **Lesser Seed-Finch**.

2 LARGE-BILLED SEED-FINCH *Oryzoborus crassirostris* 15cm/6in

0–900m. Rare in wet, grassy areas and in dense vegetation near water in lowlands and foothills. Massive pale bill of male makes it easily recognizable; also sometimes shows a white speculum in wing. Except for larger size and bill proportions, female is nearly identical to female Thick-billed Seed-Finch, and positive field ID can be difficult; in Large-billed, upper mandible appears to merge with head in a smooth arc, whereas forehead appears to protrude slightly on Thick-billed female. Also similar to Thick-billed in behavior and song, but song has an even stronger nasal quality.

3 YELLOW-BELLIED SEEDEATER *Sporophila nigricollis* 11cm/4.5in

0–2500m. Common and widespread in open habitats, especially where there is tall grass. Male is best distinguished from Black-and-white Seedeater by plain olivaceous upperparts (not black) that contrast with black hood; intensity of yellow on underparts is quite variable, and some birds are almost white below, though rarely, if ever, as white as in Black-and-white. Females of the two species are virtually identical and can't be reliably separated in the field. Yellow-bellied Seedeater is usually found in small flocks, often clinging to tall grass stems while plucking seeds, and frequently associates with other seedeaters. Song is rather variable but usually consists of a series of very sweet whistles intermixed with buzzy notes.

4 VARIABLE SEEDEATER *Sporophila corvina* 11cm/4.5in

0–1700m. Common in open habitats, including farms, towns, overgrown clearings, and forest edge at lower elevations; uncommon in very dry areas and at its upper elevation limit. Strikingly black-and-white-patterned male, with black hood and pectoral collar, is easily recognized. Female is similar to other seedeater females, though typically shows a warm ochraceous or yellowish cast, especially on the head, that is lacking in other species. Behavior is similar to that of Yellow-bellied Seedeater, but Variable Seedeater also forages in fruiting trees. Song is quite variable, but often a fast series of rapidly changing notes intermixed with short buzzes.

5 BLACK-AND-WHITE SEEDEATER
Sporophila luctuosa 11cm/4.5in

0–2800m. Uncommon to fairly common in open areas, especially where there is tall grass, in a wide elevation range; most often encountered in foothills and subtropics. Sharp black-and-white plumage (lacking gray or olive on the back), and small white speculum in wing separate male from Yellow-bellied Seedeater male; speculum may be partly or completely obscured. Male could also be mistaken for male Black-and-white Tanager (p. 388), but is smaller and has a stubbier bill and different habitat preference. Brownish female Black-and-white Seedeater (not shown) cannot be safely separated from female Yellow-bellied in the field, and the two species' behavior is also similar. Typical song of Black-and-white Seedeater consists of two or three buzzes or whistles followed by a trill, e.g., *bzzz-purWEERit't't't't't't't't'ti'ti'ti'ti'ti'ti'ti*.

1 RUDDY-BREASTED SEEDEATER *Sporophila minuta* 10cm/4in

600–1800m. Fairly common in a small area of far NW, where it inhabits cleared areas such as farmland and pastures in the foothills and subtropics. Gray and chestnut male is distinctive; female is mostly uniform brown but variable in color; many individuals probably cannot be reliably identified in the field. Females do tend to show more discernible pale edging to their wing feathers than other similar species, and some birds (immature males?) can show a faint speculum in the wing. In Ecuador this seedeater is usually found in small numbers, feeding while clinging to grass stems or sitting on fences. Song is a short, squeaky series of notes that rapidly changes up and down in pitch.

2 CHESTNUT-THROATED SEEDEATER *Sporophila telasco* 10cm/4in

0–1500m. Fairly common in open habitats in W lowlands; very local at its upper elevation limit (e.g., Catamayo). After heavy rains, Chestnut-throated Seedeater can become briefly abundant in desert areas, where males seem to sing from every bush. Both sexes have a speculum in the wing, which is occasionally concealed. Male is usually easy to ID, but chestnut throat may not be obvious at a distance, in which case note contrast between immaculate white underparts and gray upperparts; female is duller but can be distinguished by her pinkish bill and pale underparts. While sometimes encountered alone, this seedeater is often encountered in large flocks with other seedeaters, feeding on the ground or clinging to grass stems. Song is a slow, hesitant series of sharp notes.

3 PARROT-BILLED SEEDEATER *Sporophila peruviana* 12cm/4.5in

0–1400m. Fairly common in lowland desert scrub; uncommon and local at its upper elevation limit (e.g., Catamayo). Both sexes are identified by the large bulbous bill with sharply curved culmen. Male has black bib and lateral white neck patches; female might be confused with immature Sulphur-throated Finch (p. 410) or female Chestnut-throated Seedeater, though neither species ever shows such a strongly curved culmen. Found alone or in pairs while breeding, Parrot-billed Seedeater can form large flocks with other seed-eating birds during the dry season. Its large bill presumably allows it to eat larger, harder seeds than other competing species, though this has not been studied. Most common vocalization is a buzzy *djwee?*; also sings a more complex series of churrs, buzzes, and rasps, which can be given in flight.

4 DRAB SEEDEATER *Sporophila simplex* 11cm/4.5in

600–2000m; lower at Cerro Blanco. Uncommon and local in dry scrub, secondary forest, and overgrown clearings in the SW Andes; also recorded from Cerro Blanco Protected Forest. Well named; sexes are similar, though male tends to be slightly grayer than female. Bill color varies from pink while breeding to black outside the breeding season. Bold wing bars set it apart from all seedeaters except female Parrot-billed, whose bulbous bill should preclude confusion. Drab Seedeater is usually encountered alone, but occasionally joins flocks of other foraging seedeaters. Song is a fast, short series of squeaky or buzzy notes, e.g., *weeweeDJEEdjihdjihdjihDJAH*.

5 SLATE-COLORED SEEDEATER *Sporophila schistacea* 11cm/4.5in

0–1900m. Rare; poorly known in our region, where it has been seen mainly at humid forest edge and in clearings with scattered tall trees. Elsewhere in its range it shows a strong predilection for bamboo. Male is fairly distinctive, with dark gray plumage and bright yellow bill; amount of white on side of neck and extent of speculum on wing are variable. Female (not shown) is uniform brown, similar to female Ruddy-breasted Seedeater, and like that species occasionally shows a faint speculum on wing. Female probably cannot be safely identified in the field. Song of male Slate-colored Seedeater, sometimes given from the top of a tall tree, typically consists of several high, ringing notes followed by a dry trill.

alt. **4**   bas. **4**   ♂ **5**

MISCELLANEOUS SEEDEATERS

Catamenia seedeaters are found primarily at higher elevations of the Andes; behavior is fairly similar to that of *Sporophila* (pp. 414–416), and *Catamenia* is likewise now classified with tanagers (Thraupidae). Blue Seedeater is an unrelated species (currently in the Cardinalidae); it is a *Chusquea* bamboo specialist found in humid forest at mid elevations.

1 BAND-TAILED SEEDEATER *Catamenia analis* 12cm/4.5in

2000–3500m. Fairly common in montane scrub and agricultural areas at higher elevations, especially in inter-Andean valleys. Both sexes have a white band on the underside of the tail and a faint white wing patch; these features are most obvious in flight. Male Páramo Seedeater is sooty gray, has a white bill, and lacks white in tail. Female Plain-colored Seedeater is rather similar to female Band-tailed (especially if tail band cannot be seen) but usually shows some pink in bill, unlike Band-tailed's yellowish or dark bill. Band-tailed Seedeater is found alone or in small flocks, foraging on the ground or low in vegetation. Song is a short "machine-gun" burst of about 10 buzzy notes.

2 PLAIN-COLORED SEEDEATER *Catamenia inornata* 13cm/5in

2400–4200m. Fairly common at high elevations in open, grassy areas with scattered bushes, including páramo and scrubby farmland borders. The only highland seedeater with a pink bill; male is also much lighter gray than other high-elevation seedeaters and lacks a tail band. Female is paler and less streaky than other sympatric seedeaters, and lacks the wing and tail markings of Band-tailed. Plain-colored Seedeater is usually found alone or in pairs, occasionally in flocks with other seedeaters, feeding on the ground or clinging to low stalks. Typical song is a drawn-out, rising buzz that may or may not be followed by one or more very long, clear, and high-pitched whistles.

3 PÁRAMO SEEDEATER *Catamenia homochroa* 13cm/5in

2500–4000m. Uncommon at edge of temperate forest, especially in stunted tree-line scrub near páramo, though not usually in the páramo itself. Male's dark sooty-gray plumage and chalky-white bill is distinctive. Female and immature male (not shown) are somewhat variable, but usually much darker than other high-elevation seedeaters, with grayish tones to the head, chestnut crissum, and dull pinkish bill; some are much paler than the female bird shown, and some have almost all-dark bill. Infrequently encountered, but when Páramo Seedeater is found it can often be in quite large groups, sometimes even with mixed-species flocks. It forages on the ground or low in dense vegetation. Song consists of cicada-like buzzes mixed with very clear, drawn-out whistles at various pitches.

4 BLUE SEEDEATER *Amaurospiza concolor* 12cm/4.5in

1100–2400m; down to at least 800m in coastal range. Usually rare to uncommon in humid foothill and subtropical forest; strongly associated with patches of *Chusquea* bamboo, and may briefly become locally common when the bamboo begins to seed. Male is uniformly dark blue; female is uniformly chocolate brown and similar to females of several *Sporophila* seedeaters and seed-finches (pp. 414–416); she is best identified by habitat. Blue Seedeater is usually encountered alone or in pairs, and may gather in larger concentrations around seeding bamboo. Song is a short, sweet series of somewhat staccato whistles.

♂ 4

♀ 4

Medium-size to large passerines with huge bills. They eat a wide variety of fruit, insects, and other arthropods along with seeds. They are typically found singly or in pairs and do not normally join mixed-species flocks.

1 BLUE-BLACK GROSBEAK *Cyanocompsa cyanoides* 17cm/6.5in

0–1400m. Uncommon in humid and semi-humid lowland and foothill forest; not found in very dry areas and very local at its upper elevation limit (e.g., Mindo). Both sexes can be identified by their relatively large size and huge bills. Very deep blue male can look nearly black in poor light. Female is somewhat similar to female seed-finches (p. 414), but is larger and has a pointier bill and different habitat (forest interior rather than open areas). Blue-black Grosbeak is encountered singly or in pairs in lower growth of forest, often in dense tangles where hard to see well; quite wary and rarely comes out to edge. Song is a soft series of slurred notes with a nasal quality; call is a soft, metallic *chk*, given either alone or in a short series. *Note*: **Blue Grosbeak** (*Passerina caerulea*; not shown) is a very rare vagrant to W; both sexes are somewhat similar in appearance to Blue-black, but have bold brown wing bars and prefer open habitats.

2 GOLDEN GROSBEAK *Pheucticus chrysogaster* 21cm/8.5in

0–3600m. Fairly common in a wide range of habitats and elevations; found in desert scrub in the lowlands and foothills, humid forest edge at mid elevations, and montane scrub and agricultural areas in the highlands. Pure golden head of male is distinctive; female can be separated from female Black-backed Grosbeak by plainer, mostly yellow head lacking in strong markings. Song of Golden Grosbeak is variable but always consists of a slow series of sweet, usually inflected notes. Most common call is a sharp, metallic *tink!* Also called **Golden-bellied Grosbeak** or **Southern Yellow-Grosbeak**.

3 BLACK-BACKED GROSBEAK *Pheucticus aureoventris* 21cm/8.5in

1500–3500m. Uncommon and local in agricultural areas, scrub, parks, and gardens in inter-Andean valleys; often occurs with Golden Grosbeak. Male Black-backed Grosbeak can be separated by its black head; female has large brown blotches on head but is otherwise similar to female Golden. Vocalizations are much like those of Golden, but song of Black-backed tends to be lower pitched and have fewer notes.

4 ROSE-BREASTED GROSBEAK *Pheucticus ludovicianus* 20cm/8in

0–2800m. An uncommon boreal migrant, present in Ecuador from October to April. It is most frequently encountered in light woodland and humid forest edge in the foothills and subtropics, but occasionally turns up elsewhere (e.g., parks in Quito). Male is usually easy to ID; female is very different, but no other Ecuadorian passerine shows the combination of large bill, broad white superciliary, and streaked underparts. The species is nearly silent in Ecuador, though presumably, at least occasionally, gives a metallic *tink!* similar to that of other *Pheucticus*.

♂ 4

♀ 4

SALTATORS

Saltator is a genus of fairly large, mainly arboreal passerines. They are usually conspicuous and easy to see, and pairs often join mixed-species flocks in forest canopy. Fruit makes up a large part of their diet, but they also consume seeds, insects, and other arthropods. Slate-colored Grosbeak (a saltator despite its name) is the only sexually dimorphic species on this page.

1 SLATE-COLORED GROSBEAK *Saltator grossus* 20cm/8in

0–1200m. Uncommon in humid lowland and foothill forest and edge. Large, bright orange bill and white throat are diagnostic in both sexes. Male is darker gray than female, and has black head and breast. This saltator is more sluggish than other members of the genus, often perching in one place for long periods, especially when singing, and less likely to join mixed-species flocks. Song is a series of three to six rich, sometimes slurred whistles, repeated every few seconds; the bird sometimes repeats the same set, other times alternates between two different sets. Call is a short, nasal whine.

2 BUFF-THROATED SALTATOR *Saltator maximus* 21cm/8.5in

0–1800m. Common in humid lowland and foothill forest edge and adjacent wooded clearings; occasionally (seasonally?) ranges up into the subtropics. Note olive back, white superciliary, and faint buff throat bordered by black malar stripes; no really similar species occurs in our region. A common member of mixed-species flocks and sometimes visits feeders. Song is a rather thrush-like series of soft, warbling whistles. Calls include a short series of sharp whistles that mostly descend in pitch, and a sharp, high-pitched *seep*.

3 BLACK-WINGED SALTATOR *Saltator atripennis* 21cm/8.5in

100–2000m. Fairly common in humid foothill and subtropical forest, edge, and wooded clearings; uncommon and local in the lowlands. Olive back, black wings, and mostly black head with unique facial pattern should make ID straightforward. Regularly joins mixed-species flocks and even comes to feeders in the Tandayapa Valley. Vocal repertoire is impressive; some of the more common songs and calls include a series of loud, clear whistles, e.g., *woo?-whoo?-FWEEFWEEooo*; a rollicking chatter followed by a dry trill; and a long, decelerating metallic trill that descends in pitch.

4 STREAKED SALTATOR *Saltator striatipectus* 20cm/8in

0–2500m. Two subspecies are found in W Ecuador; both are fairly common in suitable habitat. The highland subspecies *striatipectus* inhabits scrub, woodland, and gardens in inter-Andean valleys in N. The W subspecies *flavidicollis* ranges in deciduous and semi-humid forest and lighter woodland in W and SW. Highland birds are much more strongly marked, and can be identified by their heavily streaked underparts, dark malar stripe, and yellow patches on the gape and tip of the bill. The W subspecies may or may not show faint underpart streaking, but can be identified by the combination of olive upperparts, pale underparts, and bold, white superciliary. Songs of both subspecies are similar; at dawn, listen for a very long series of short, quavering notes that alternate up and down in pitch; later in the day, a much shorter series of four to six notes is given.

5 BLACK COWLED SALTATOR *Saltator nigriceps* 22cm/8.5in

1500–2900m. Locally fairly common in humid forest and scrub in highlands of far SW; regularly seen in roadside forest patches near the Utuana Reserve and the town of Sozoranga to the W. A very handsome species, with black hood and large, bright orange bill; no really similar species occurs with it. It forms a core member of mixed-species flocks in its limited range. Song is variable but usually consists of one to a few loud, often ringing whistles that may be slurred, e.g., *wip, DJEEyeeyeer*.

■ ACKNOWLEDGMENTS

While we have relied on our own field experience for much of the information in this book, field guides such as this one incorporate vast amounts of information gathered through the years and made available by dedicated ornithologists and birders. We have drawn deeply from a number of sources, most notable among them *The Birds of Ecuador* by Robert S. Ridgely and Paul J. Greenfield, published in 2001. Paul of course was the artist of that monumental work, and it also hugely influenced everyone else involved in this guide, which is due in no small part to the enormous effect it had on boosting interest in birding in Ecuador. Other sources we used extensively include: *Birds of Peru* by Thomas S. Schulenberg, Douglas Stotz, Daniel F. Lane, John P. O'Neill, and Theodore A. Parker III; and *Handbook of the Birds of the World*, edited by Josep del Hoyo et al., the online version of which, *HBW Alive* (www.hbw.com), made accessing its wealth of information much faster and easier.

We would like to thank our collaborators, Iain Campbell, Pablo Cervantes, Sam Woods, and Andrew Spencer, who provided nearly 400 of the photos used in this guide. Iain Campbell, with help from his daughter, Amy Campbell, did many of the complex digital manipulations that we used for some species, especially nightjars in flight.

More than 60 other talented photographers contributed additional images, without which this book would have been impossible. All photographers are credited in Appendix II, but we would like to acknowledge particularly those who provided the greatest number of images: Roger Ahlman, Dušan M. Brinkhuizen, Ian Davies, Tom Friedel, Glenn Bartley, Mike Danzenbaker, Ken Behrens, and Félix Uribe.

Roger Ahlman and Mitch Lysinger provided valuable feedback on the range maps and the manuscript.

eBird (www.ebird.org) was also an excellent source of sighting data, and each of the many hundreds of birders who have shared their Ecuador sight records with eBird can take some small credit for the range maps included in this volume.

We referred to many audio recordings while describing the bird vocalizations in the species accounts. Some of these were our own personal recordings, but many were also sourced from the indispensable DVD collection *Bird Sounds of Ecuador: A Comprehensive Collection*, by John V. Moore, Niels Krabbe, Olaf Jahn, and 153 other recordists. We supplemented these recordings with others that are available on the superb website www.xeno-canto.org.

While we have mentioned only a few of you by name, we are also indebted to the many birders and ornithologists who published or otherwise shared their knowledge over the years.

We are grateful to Robert Kirk for giving us the opportunity to produce this book and to the other hardworking folks at Princeton University Press, including Kathleen Cioffi, Samantha Nader, and David Campbell, who all helped make it a reality. We thank as well our copyeditor, Amy K. Hughes, and David and Namrita Price-Goodfellow and their design team at D & N Publishing.

Last but (not at all) least, we would like to express our heartfelt appreciation to our families for their continued support as we dedicate our lives to the wonderful challenge of understanding and protecting Ecuador's avifauna.

◼ APPENDIX I: SPECIES NOT INCLUDED

In the interest of keeping this field guide to a reasonable size, we have not included a number of species that have been recorded in W Ecuador. Some of these species are mentioned in notes within the species accounts, especially when very similar to the species being described. We divide the excluded species up into several categories.

VAGRANTS

Long-distance migrants and other wanderers that have been reported from W Ecuador on very few occasions. It was difficult to decide which species to exclude; in general, we left out birds that were not reported from W Ecuador in most years.

American Wigeon *Anas americana*
Northern Shoveler *Anas clypeata*
Green-winged Teal *Anas crecca*
Ring-necked Duck *Aythya collaris*
Humboldt Penguin *Spheniscus humboldti*
Black-browed Albatross *Thalassarche melanophris*
Southern Giant-Petrel *Macronectes giganteus*
Southern Fulmar *Fulmarus glacialoides*
Buller's Shearwater *Puffinus bulleri*
Wilson's Storm-Petrel *Oceanites oceanicus*
White-faced Storm-Petrel *Pelagodroma marina*
Puna Ibis *Plegadis ridgwayi*
Reddish Egret *Egretta rufescens*
Great Frigatebird *Fregata minor*
Masked Booby *Sula dactylatra*
Brown Booby *Sula leucogaster*
Swainson's Hawk *Buteo swainsoni*
Blackish Oystercatcher *Haematopus ater*
American Avocet *Recurvirostra americana*
Piping Plover *Charadrius melodus*
Long-billed Dowitcher *Limnodromus scolopaceus*
Curlew Sandpiper *Calidris ferruginea*
Dunlin *Calidris alpina*
Buff-breasted Sandpiper *Calidris subruficollis*
Bonaparte's Gull *Chroicocephalus philadelphia*
Belcher's Gull *Larus belcheri*
Ring-billed Gull *Larus delawarensis*
California Gull *Larus californicus*
(American) Herring Gull *Larus smithsonianus*

Lesser Black-backed Gull *Larus fuscus*
Caspian Tern *Hydroprogne caspia*
Large-billed Tern *Phaetusa simplex*
Chilean Skua *Stercorarius chilensis*
South Polar Skua *Stercorarius maccormicki*
Long-tailed Jaeger *Stercorarius longicaudus*
Yellow-billed Cuckoo *Coccyzus americanus*
Belted Kingfisher *Megaceryle alcyon*
Large Elaenia *Elaenia spectabilis*
Willow Flycatcher *Empidonax traillii*
Alder Flycatcher *Empidonax alnorum*
Dark-faced Ground-Tyrant *Muscisaxicola maclovianus*
Sulphur-bellied Flycatcher *Myiodynastes luteiventris*
Crowned Slaty Flycatcher *Empidonomus aurantioatrocristatus*
Gray Kingbird *Tyrannus dominicensis*
Yellow-green Vireo *Vireo flavoviridis*
Tree Swallow *Tachycineta bicolor*
Purple Martin *Progne subis*
Gray-cheeked Thrush *Catharus minimus*
Red-throated Pipit *Anthus cervinus*
Ovenbird *Seiurus aurocapilla*
Northern Waterthrush *Parkesia noveboracensis*
Golden-winged Warbler *Vermivora chrysoptera*
Prothonotary Warbler *Protonotaria citrea*
Connecticut Warbler *Oporornis agilis*
Mourning Warbler *Geothlypis philadelphia*
Chestnut-sided Warbler *Setophaga pensylvanica*
Black-throated Green Warbler *Setophaga virens*

Wilson's Warbler *Cardellina pusilla*
Bobolink *Dolichonyx oryzivorus*

Gray Seedeater *Sporophila intermedia*
Blue Grosbeak *Passerina caerulea*

PELAGIC SPECIES

These birds may be regular in Ecuadorian waters, but are normally found well offshore, and they are extremely unlikely to be seen from shore, especially by a casual observer. A dedicated and experienced sea watcher could well find many of these, especially from La Chocolatera at the tip of the Santa Elena Peninsula.

Cape Petrel *Daption capense*
Galapagos Petrel *Pterodroma phaeopygia*
White-chinned Petrel *Procellaria aequinoctialis*
Galapagos Shearwater *Puffinus subalaris*
Least Storm-Petrel *Oceanodroma microsoma*
Band-rumped Storm-Petrel *Oceanodroma castro*

Black Storm-Petrel *Oceanodroma melania*
Hornby's (Ringed) Storm-Petrel *Oceanodroma hornbyi*
Bridled Tern *Onychoprion anaethetus*
Pomarine Jaeger *Stercorarius pomarinus*
Parasitic Jaeger *Stercorarius parasiticus*

EAST SLOPE "SPILLOVERS"

These are species found mainly on the E slope of the Andes but occur very locally W of the continental divide in locations such as Cerro Mongus, the Cajanuma sector of Podocarpus National Park, Cerro Toledo, the W side of the Antisana Ecological Reserve, and the W side of Papallacta Pass.

Andean (Black-faced) Ibis *Theristicus (melanopis) branickii*
Black-winged Ground Dove *Metriopelia melanoptera*
Andean Hillstar *Oreotrochilus estella*
Flame-throated (Little) Sunangel *Heliangelus micraster*
Neblina Metaltail *Metallura odomae*
Rufous-capped Thornbill *Chalcostigma ruficeps*
Mountain Avocetbill *Opisthoprora euryptera*
Emerald Toucanet *Aulacorhynchus atrogularis*
Jocotoco Antpitta *Grallaria ridgelyi*
Slate-crowned Antpitta *Grallaricula nana*
Crescent-faced Antpitta *Grallaricula lineifrons*

Chusquea Tapaculo *Scytalopus parkeri*
Orange-banded Flycatcher *Nephelomyias lintoni*
Chestnut-bellied Cotinga *Doliornis remseni*
Pale-footed Swallow *Orochelidon flavipes*
Citrine Warbler *Myiothlypis luteoviridis*
Pale-naped Brush-Finch *Atlapetes pallidinucha*
Slaty Brush-Finch *Atlapetes schistaceus*
Black-headed Hemispingus *Hemispingus verticalis*
Masked Mountain-Tanager *Buthraupis wetmorei*
Black-backed Bush Tanager *Urothraupis stolzmanni*
Masked Saltator *Saltator cinctus*

EXTIRPATED AND POSSIBLY EXTIRPATED SPECIES

These birds were resident in W Ecuador in the past, but there are no recent records. Some may still persist in remote areas.

Grasshopper Sparrow *Ammodramus savannarum*
American Coot *Fulica americana*
Yellow-eared Parrot *Ognorhynchus icterotis*
Agami Heron *Agamia agami*

Boat-billed Heron *Cochlearius cochlearius*
Harpy Eagle *Harpia harpyja*
Turquoise-throated Puffleg *Eriocnemis godini*
White-crowned Manakin *Dixiphia pipra*

HYPOTHETICAL SPECIES

The species listed here are known from W Ecuador from one to several sight records, but they have not been substantiated with photos, sound recordings, or specimens.

Highland Tinamou *Nothocercus bonapartei*
Crested Eagle *Morphnus guianensis*
Yellow-breasted Crake *Porzana flaviventer*
White-backed Stilt *Himantopus melanurus*
Ruff *Calidris pugnax*
Peruvian Sheartail *Thaumastura cora*

Highland Elaenia *Elaenia obscura*
Black-throated Tody-Tyrant *Hemitriccus granadensis*
Blue-naped Chlorophonia *Chlorophonia cyanea*
Cinereous Finch *Piezorina cinerea*

OTHER SPECIES

These birds do not fit into the other categories.

Andean Flicker *Colaptes rupicola*—This species is found along the continental divide near the Peruvian border in extreme S Ecuador. We chose not to include it because the area is remote and very rarely visited by birders.

Sulphur-bellied Tyrannulet *Mecocerculus minor*—Known to be resident on the W slope in the extreme N near the Colombian border, e.g., the Chical road and near Maldonado. Mentioned in a note under White-tailed Tyrannulet (p. 266).

Golden-faced Tyrannulet *Zimmerius chrysops*—Now known to be fairly common in subtropical forest in extreme NW Ecuador, e.g., the Chical road. Mentioned in a note under Chocó Tyrannulet (p. 268).

Rufous-tailed Tyrant *Knipolegus poecilurus*—This E slope species has turned up in the Quito Botanical Gardens on at least two occasions. Since it is not known to be migratory, we did not include it as a vagrant.

Bicolored Antvireo *Dysithamnus occidentalis*—There is one documented W slope record from subtropical forest on Cerro Golondrinas in the far N.

Yellow-backed Oriole *Icterus chrysater*—Known in Ecuador from a 2011 sighting of a flock in mangroves in the extreme NW near the Colombian border. The species is possibly resident in this area. Mentioned in a note under Yellow-tailed Oriole (p. 364).

Tawny-throated Dotterel *Oreopholus ruficollis*—After it was thought to be possibly extirpated in Ecuador, this species was seen and photographed on the Santa Elena Peninsula in June 2015.

◾ APPENDIX II: PHOTOGRAPHER CREDITS

Abbreviations: B=bottom, L=left, LL=lower left, LR=lower right, R=right, U=upper, UL=upper left, UR=upper right. The number of photos supplied by each photographer is given in parentheses after their name.

Nick Athanas (764) – Tropical Birding Tours – www.tropicalbirding.com – www.antpitta. com. Any photo not otherwise credited below.

Sam Woods (110) – Tropical Birding Tours – www.tropicalbirding.com. 25-1, 29-3, 31-2, 33-3L, 37-6L, 47-6, 53-1LL, 55-1B, 59-2LL&LR, 64-4, 65-1R, 66-4L, 74-3L, 75-2UR, 84-3, 85-3R, 89-3L, 93-3, 93-4, 94-4L, 99-3, 103-1, 105-5L, 107-4R, 108-5R, 109-2R, 111-4L&R, 111-5R, 119-1R, 122-4U, 123-1B, 137-3, 139-2L, 141-5, 147-4, 149-4L, 151-1L&R, 151-4, 152-4L, 153-3L, 157-3L, 163-2, 169-2L, 173-1L, 173-2L, 178-3U, 182-4R, 185-3R, 187-1L, 191-3R, 196-4R, 205-4, 207-4, 209-3L, 213-3L, 217-1L, 219-1L, 223-1L, 223-2L, 223-3L, 225-1L, 239-1, 243-1L, 249-1R, 253-2R, 285-4, 286-5, 289-4, 295-4, 295-5, 303-4L, 307-2R, 309-2L&R, 311-2L&R, 315-1L, 330-4LL, 333-1L, 337-2, 347-1R, 349-1UR, 350-4L, 355-5L, 356-4R, 357-2R, 357-3L&R, 359-1R, 359-2L, 365-1L, 365-3L&R, 377-5, 379-3, 381-2, 383-2, 393-1L, 394-5L&R, 397-1, 399-1L, 402-5L, 405-4, 407-3, 415-1R, 421-2L

Andrew Spencer (107) – Tropical Birding Tours – gwwarbler@gmail.com. 27-2, 27-5, 47-4, 58-3, 59-1R, 60-3U, 66-4R, 77-2U, 81-2UL, 86-4L, 89-1L, 89-3R, 91-3, 95-1L, 97-4R, 99-5R, 100-5, 103-4, 105-1R, 105-2R, 105-4, 106-5, 109-3R, 109-4L&R, 112-5, 118-3B, 119-1B, 127-6, 133-4, 134-5R, 139-1R, 139-2R, 143-4, 145-3, 147-5, 148-4, 157-1L, 159-5R, 165-4, 168-4R, 169-3L, 171-2, 174-5R, 175-4R, 181-1R, 183-3L, 189-2L, 195-3R, 198-3R, 202-4L, 207-1, 213-2, 215-3R, 216-5L, 217-3L&R, 217-4, 221-1R, 227-4, 241-2, 249-3L, 253-2L, 261-3, 263-1B, 265-2, 265-4, 265-5, 269-1, 269-6, 271-5, 281-2, 291-3L&R, 292-4L, 293-1L, 295-2, 307-1R, 313-3L, 314-4L&R, 319-1R, 321-3, 323-4L, 325-4, 330-4LR, 333-1R, 339-3, 340-4L, 348-4L&R, 355-2, 357-2L, 359-2R, 361-1, 369-2R, 375-1, 375-2, 383-6, 385-1, 389-2L, 393-1R, 401-2L, 405-3, 411-4R, 415-4R, 423-1L

Pablo Cervantes Daza (105) – Tropical Birding Tours – www.flickr.com/photos/ pablocervantesdaza. 3UL, 7, 35-4, 37-4, 39-1U&LL, 41-1, 43-2R, 51-1C, 58-3L, 63-1L, 65-3R, 73-1UR, 87-2U&LL, 91-5, 99-1R, 107-3L, 108-5L, 127-4, 129-3, 135-1L&R, 143-2, 149-1R, 155-4L, 156-4R, 163-5, 165-6, 167-2, 169-1R, 170-5L, 175-4L, 177-2L, 180-5L, 181-2L, 181-3, 183-2L&R, 184-4L&R, 185-1B, 185-3L, 191-2L&R, 193-1LL, 196-4L, 198-3L, 199-1R, 200-3L, 203-2L, 205-2, 205-3, 211-1R, 211-3L, 215-2, 215-3L, 219-2L??, 221-2R, 229-1L, 231-3, 237-5, 241-1L, 248-5, 254-5, 257-3, 257-5, 261-1L, 267-1, 267-3, 294-1L, 297-3, 313-1L&R, 315-1R, 317-3L, 325-6, 337-3R, 341-1L&R, 356-4L, 361-2, 361-4, 363-3L, 367-2, 367-6, 371-3L&R, 377-2, 377-3, 377-4, 379-2, 379-5, 381-2, 381-3L, 389-1L&R, 391-2L, 399-1R, 399-6L, 405-2L, 409-1L, 415-4L, 417-2L, 419-2R

Roger Ahlman (76) – www.pbase.com/ahlman. 35-1R, 39-3, 39-4, 39-6, 41-4R, 45-3R, 48-B, 53-1LR, 71-1LR, 71-2R, 70-3LR, 72-2UL, 74-3C, 75-2LL, 76-3B, 78-3L, 80-3L&R, 83-1LR, 89-1R, 91-1, 95-1R, 103-3, 116-5, 119-2R, 121-1, 121-4U, 121-5R, 123-2, 133-2, 159-2, 161-1, 161-3, 161-5, 163-6, 171-3R, 188-5R, 189-3R, 192-3L&R, 193-2L, 194-4R, 197-1R, 200-3R, 203-1R, 237-3, 247-2R, 257-6, 271-4R, 273-3, 273-4, 295-1R, 299-6, 301-2, 317-2R, 321-2, 329-2R, 329-3L, 335-4, 337-4, 341-2, 345-3R, 349-1UL, 351-1L&R, 359-3R, 361-3, 367-1, 379-6, 387-1, 409-3R, 415-2L, 416-4L&C, 419-1R, 420-4R

Iain Campbell (74) – Tropical Birding Tours & Capturing Nature Photo Tours. 8, 12R, 33-2L&R, 43-3, 47-5, 51-1LR, 52-2, 53-2L, 59-1L, 59-2UL, 76-3UR, 85-2L, 87-1L&R, 97-3L, 99-5L, 99-6L, 101-1L, 105-3, 107-1, 111-3, 113-1L, 117-3U, 121-4LR, 125-4, 129-1, 131-3L, 133-1, 133-5, 136-5L, 141-3, 143-5, 145-4, 153-3R, 163-3, 165-2, 165-5, 174-5L, 193-2R, 199-2L, 201-1L, 203-3L, 215-1, 215-4R, 219-2R, 227-5, 231-6, 246-5L, 252-1R, 267-5, 269-4, 287-3L, 293-3, 297-2, 299-2, 303-4R, 310-4R, 321-1, 323-3, 323-4R, 325-5, 339-1, 343-4, 364-4L, 365-1R, 365-2R, 369-2L, 369-3L, 375-5, 392-4L, 395-2, 423-4L&R

Dušan M. Brinkhuizen (48) – www.sapayoa.com. 25-4, 27-4, 33-4L&R, 37-5, 41-2, 60-3U, 69-3L&R, 70-3U, 78-3R, 83-1U, 88-4, 90-4, 97-4L, 103-5, 111-2, 116-4, 129-5, 149-2, 156-2L, 171-4R, 186-5, 187-3L&R, 187-4R, 190-4R, 195-1LR, 209-3R, 214-5, 241-3, 245-3L, 259-2, 277-2, 277-3, 299-5, 303-2L, 305-1R, 311-3L, 312-4, 313-3R, 359-3L, 384-5R, 391-1L&R, 399-3, 404-5, 408-4L

Ian Davies (27) – www.flickr.com/uropsalis. 31-4, 35-1L, 35-2, 85-2R, 85-3L, 99-6R, 101-4, 105-1L, 105-2L, 107-4L, 109-1R, 109-3L, 121-4LL, 161-6, 189-4L, 229-4, 233-4, 311-3R, 331-1L, 331-2L&R, 331-3R, 355-6R, 357-1L, 369-3R, 406-4R, 419-1L

Tom Friedel (23) – www.birdphotos.com. 25-2, 29-1, 33-1, 145-2, 155-5, 171-4L, 179-2L&R, 186-6, 251-1R, 277-4, 303-3R, 311-1L&R, 329-2L, 363-1L, 372-5R, 385-3R, 391-3L, 392-4R, 397-4R, 417-1L&R

Glenn Bartley (18) – www.glennbartley.com. 33-3R, 37-2R, 43-4, 50-2R, 83-2R, 113-3L, 138-5R, 152-4R, 191-3L, 197-2R, 202-4R, 265-6, 285-5, 301-1, 317-2L, 317-3R, 333-3, 391-3R

Mike Danzenbaker (15) – www.avesphoto.com. 77-1R, 77-2LL, 83-2L, 93-5L, 113-4R, 118-3U, 155-2L, 161-4, 275-3, 275-6, 323-2, 327-2R, 328-4L&R, 331-3L

Ken Behrens (11) – Tropical Birding Tours – www.flickr.com/kbehrens. 40-5L, 41-3R, 47-3L, 55-2UL, 93-1, 113-2R, 117-1L, 117-2L, 121-3, 123-UR, 359-1L

Fèlix Uribe (10) 65-2C, 71-2L, 133-6, 139-3, 303-3L, 305-2R, 349-2, 384-5L, 391-2R, 421-1R

Andrés Vásquez N. (6) – Tropical Birding Tours – andres0208@hotmail.com. 57-1LL, 147-1R, 195-2L, 225-2L, 237-2, 259-6

José Illanes (5) – Tropical Birding Tours – jillanesh@hotmail.com. 77-1L, 169-1L, 176-4R, 194-4L, 343-2

Luke Seitz (5) – www.lukeseitzart.com. 61-2LL, 77-1C, 159-3, 345-2R, 421-1L

Anselmo d'Affonseca (4) 63-1R, 69-2L, 129-4, 345-3L

Marc Fasol (4) – ibc.lynxeds.com/users/marc–fasol. 61-2UR, 68-3, 163-1, 291-1

Alex Vargas (4) – www.pbase.com/alex_vargas. 93-2, 149-3, 313-2L, 323-6

Juan José Arango (3) – www.flickr.com/jjarango/. 138-5L, 335-2, 345-2L

Diego Calderón-F. (3) – Colombia Birding – www.colombiabirding.com. 31-3, 187-4L, 347-3L

Derek Kverno (3) – birdingecuador.blogspot.com. 57-1U, 260-5L, 422-5

Scott Olmstead (3) 65-2R, 87-1C, 153-2

Yamil Saenz (3) – www.flickr.com/ysaenz. 31-1, 139-4, 188-5L

Francesco Veronesi (3) – www.flickr.com/francesco_veronesi. 243-2R, 385-4, 419-3R

Rudimar Narciso Cipriani (2) 81-2B, 89-2L

Jacob C. Cooper (2) – www.flickr.com/blackhawkbirder. 117-1C, 119-2L

Lee Dingain (2) – www.almostbirding.com. 81-1C, 141-4

Brian Krohnke (2) – Mindo Cloudforest Foundation – www.mindocloudforest.org. 13, 15LR

Ian Maton (2) – www.albertanaturephotography.com. 129-2, 379-4

János Oláh (2) 151-5, 349-3
Xavier Amigo (1) – Ecuador Experience. 103-6
John Anderson (1) – www.pbase.com/crail_birder. 267-4
Nancy Bell (1) – www.bellbird.us. 415-2R
Demis Bucci (1) – www.demisbuccifotografia.com.br. 153-1R
Jim Burns (1) – www.jimburnsphotos.com. 79-1L
John Cahill (1) – johnpaulcahill@gmail.com. 418-4R
Dick Daniels (1) 35-6L
Wim de Groot (1) – www.pbase.com/wimdegroot. 309-1L
Trevor Ellery (1) – Rockjumper Birding Tours – www.rockjumperbirding.com. 79-2UL
Alonso Quevedo Gil (1) – Fundación Proaves – www.proaves.org . 347-3R
Harold F. Greeney (1) –Yanayacu Biological Station – www.yanayacu.org. 307-2C
Trevor Hardaker (1) – www.hardaker.co.za. 35-6R
Mark Harper (1) 67-2L
Antonio Hidalgo (1) – www.flickr.com/antoniohidalgo. 369-4R
Jeff Higgott (1) – sequella.co.uk. 161-2
Martin Hoogerwaard (1) 134-5L
Doug Janson (1) – www.pbase.com/dougj. 131-3R
Phil Jeffrey (1) – www.catharus.com. 77-2LR
Sean Kite (1) – seankite927@yahoo.com. 81-1R
James Lowen (1) – www.jameslowen.com. 351-3R
Mike Nelson (1) – Birdtour Asia. 61-2LR
Pat O'Donnell (1) – BirdingFieldGuides – http://birdingfieldguides.com. 130-4L
Lars Petersson (1) – www.larsfoto.se. 79-2UR
Marco Vinicio Salazar Romero (1) – Universidad Técnica Particular de Loja – mvsalazar75@gmail.com. 155-3L
Paul Salaman (1) – Rainforest Trust. 321-6
Octavio Campos Salles (1) – www.octaviosalles.com.br. 81-2UR
Robert Scanlon (1) – www.pbase.com/rsscanlon. 76-3UL
Fabrice Schmitt (1) –WINGS Birding Tours Worldwide. 154-5
Donna L. Schulman (1) – www.flickr.com/queensgirl. 130-4R
Tuomas Seimola (1) – seimola@tarsiger.com – www.tarsiger.com. 231-2
Dubi Shapiro (1) – www.pbase.com/dubisha. 151-3
José Julián Silva Photography (1) – jjsilvaleon@gmail.com. 139-1L
Frederico Acaz Sonntag (1) 271-4L
Tadeusz Stawarczyk (1) 307-2L
Mark Sutton (1) 65-1C
Joe Tobias (1) – Imperial College London. 159-4
Scott Watson (1) –Tropical Birding Tours. 135-4
Dave Wendelken (1) – www.flickr.com/wendeldh . 309-1R
Peter Wendelken (1) 351-3L
Kevin J. Zimmer (1) –Victor Emanuel Nature Tours Inc.. 229-5
Julian Zuleta (1) – www.apiatierradeaves.com. 416-5R

■ GLOSSARY

Alternate plumage Sometimes called "breeding plumage." Some birds—especially shorebirds, gulls, terns, and warblers—molt into a different plumage before the breeding season. This alternate plumage is retained until the end of the breeding season, sometimes somewhat longer. Alternate plumage is usually more colorful than *basic*, or nonbreeding plumage.

Antiphonal Refers to a type of song duet given by some birds, such as certain warblers and wrens, in which the male sings one phrase, and the female usually responds with a different, often complementary phrase.

Arthropod A general term for invertebrates such as insects, spiders, scorpions, crustaceans, centipedes, and millipedes.

Austral migrant A species that migrates between its breeding grounds in S South America and wintering grounds farther northward.

Basic plumage Nonbreeding plumage; see *alternate plumage*.

Boreal migrant A species that migrates between its breeding grounds in North America and wintering grounds farther southward.

Carpal In bird topography, the area near the bend of the wing along the wing's leading edge; e.g., carpal bar, carpal spot.

Chusquea A native genus of bamboo with a narrow, solid stem. It is common in humid subtropical and temperate forest in the Andes.

Covert A type of feather that covers the base of another, larger feather; wing coverts cover the bases of wing feathers, and tail coverts cover bases of tail feathers.

Culmen The upper ridge of a bird's bill.

Decurved Downcurved; refers to the bill shape of some birds.

Diagnostic In bird identification, refers to features (one or more) that are enough to identify the species correctly.

Dihedral In references to a flying bird, a dihedral is the angle formed by the wings when they are held above the plane of the bird's body, making a shallow V shape. Only a few species characteristically do this, such as the Turkey Vulture (p. 56).

Diurnal Active during the day; opposite of *nocturnal*.

Eclipse plumage A dull, female-like plumage briefly attained by males after the breeding season. In W Ecuador, only some species of ducks and Red-legged Honeycreeper have an eclipse plumage.

Endemic Restricted to a certain native region.

Extirpated Extinct in a region (but not globally).

Flight feathers The primaries, secondaries, and tertials (see figures, pp. 20–21) are sometimes collectively referred to as "flight feathers."

Frugivore An animal that eats fruit.

Fulvous A reddish-yellow color, slightly darker than tawny.

Genus (pl., *genera*; adj, *generic*) A taxonomic rank used in the classification of organisms. The species of many bird genera share some plumage or behavioral characteristics.

Gorget A patch of colored feathers found on the throat of some birds, especially hummingbirds.

Heliconia	A genus of flowering plant common in humid lowland, foothill, and subtropical forest in Ecuador. Many species have bright orange and yellow flowers with a characteristic "lobster-claw" shape. Heliconia is a favorite food of hermit hummingbirds (p. 162).
Immature	A young bird; when used in this guide, it indicates that the bird posesses a different plumage than an adult.
Iris (pl., *irides*)	Used to refer to the eye color of a bird in order to distinguish it from other features of the ocular area, such the eye-ring.
Juvenile	The first plumage held by a bird after it leaves the nest; juvenile plumage is held for only a few weeks in some species but up to a year in larger species such as raptors.
Lek	A chosen area or site where males of certain species gather to perform nuptial displays.
Lump	In taxonomy, to no longer recognize an organism as a distinct species but rather as a subspecies of another species. See also *split*.
Mesial stripe	A short, vertical line located on the the throat of some birds of prey.
Mixed-species flock	A group of birds made up of two or more species (in rare instances up to 30 or more) that forage together.
Montane	Pertaining to the mountains.
Morph	Some birds show variations in their plumage that are not related to age or sex; these are often referred to as "morphs."
Nomadic	Refers to a species whose local occurrence is primarily based on the temporary abundance of a needed resource, such as a specialized type of food or water. These species tend to wander widely and may be absent from a site for an extended period of time and then become briefly common or abundant.
Ochraceous	Having an ochre coloration (intermediate between yellow and orange).
Passerine	A bird belonging to the order Passeriformes, which encompasses all species on pp. 222–423; sometimes also called "songbirds" or "perching birds."
Pectoral	Relating to the chest area; e.g., pectoral collar.
Pelagic	Describes a species that spends most of the year far out at sea, normally coming to land only to breed.
Periocular	The region around the eye; the term is often used in descriptions of birds that have a patch of bare skin around the eye.
Pied	Black and white.
Pishing	An onomatopoeic term describing a harsh, airy sound that birders produce with their mouths in order to provoke a reaction in birds. It is most effective with small birds such as warblers, brush-finches, and seedeaters.
Playback	The act of using an electronic or other device to play recorded bird vocalizations with the purpose of encouraging the bird to respond or approach. Overuse of playback is considered to be detrimental to a bird's well-being.
Primary projection	The distance that the primaries (see figures, pp. 20–21) extend past the other flight feathers on a perched bird. It can be a useful

	ID feature for some flycatchers, such as pewees (p. 284) and *Empidonax* (p. 276).
Rictal bristles	Stiff, hair-like feathers located at the base of a bird's bill.
Río	"River" in Spanish.
Rufous	Reddish brown; a color frequently used in plumage descriptions.
Sexually dimorphic	Used in reference to species in which males and females differ in plumage, size, and/or other features.
Speculum	A patch of color on the secondary feathers of the wing. In ducks, the speculum is usually visible only in flight, while in smaller birds such as seedeaters, the speculum is often visible as a small patch on the folded wing as well.
Split	In taxonomy, to reclassify a subspecies as a separate, distinct species. See also *lump*.
Subcanopy	Below the forest canopy; often used in reference to birds that stay high in the forest but do not normally perch on the treetops.
Sympatric	Inhabiting the same range and habitat as another species.
Tarsus (pl., *tarsi*)	The segment of a bird's leg between the foot and the backward-bending joint (see figures, pp. 20–21). The term is often used with raptors, some of which have feathered tarsi.
Ventriloquial	A bird vocalization that has a sound quality that makes is difficult to locate its source.

■ SPECIES INDEX
(ENGLISH AND SCIENTIFIC NAMES)